Get the eBook FREE!

(PDF, ePub, Kindle, and liveBook all included)

We believe that once you buy a book from us, you should be able to read it in any format we have available. To get electronic versions of this book at no additional cost to you, purchase and then register this book at the Manning website.

Go to https://www.manning.com/freebook and follow the instructions to complete your pBook registration.

That's it!
Thanks from Manning!

The Joy of JavaScript

The Joy of JavaScript

LUIS ATENCIO

MANNING

SHELTER ISLAND

Manning Publications Co.
20 Baldwin Road
PO Box 761
Shelter Island, NY 1196

Development editor:	Frances Lefkowitz
Technical development editor:	Peter Perlepes
Review editor:	Aleks Dragosavljević
Production editor:	Deirdre S. Hiam
Proofreader:	Melody Dolab
Technical proofreader:	Jahred Love
Typesetter:	Dennis Dalinnik
Cover designer:	Marija Tudor

ISBN: 9781617295867
Printed in the United States of America

To my children, Luke and Matthew, and my wife, Ana, for being my support pillars in life and helping me at every step of this journey. To all of my family for their love and support. Thank you.

brief contents

contents

ix

preface

I learned to program computers in a traditional, academic way. The universities I attended based their curricula primarily on class-oriented languages such as Java, C++, and C#. When I came out of those programs, my brain was trained to think that classes were the best (maybe even only) way to design programs and that anything else would be an abomination.

Years later, like any other developer in the world, I stumbled onto JavaScript—I should say jQuery, because at the time, jQuery was JavaScript. JavaScript was diametrically opposite to most of what I had learned. I struggled with every fundamental aspect of programming, including representing domain models, encapsulating behavior and data into logical modules, and dealing with events and asynchronous functions. I said to myself, Fine, let's use jQuery and a slew of third-party libraries to "fix the language" and forget all about this.

But JavaScript didn't need fixing: I needed to get fixed. I knew I couldn't get away from it. Because JavaScript was pretty much everywhere, it was only a matter of time before I'd stumble onto it again, so I decided to explore it more deeply. Learning about its prototype mechanism and closures showed me the true meaning of object-oriented programming. When Alan Kay invented this term in the early 2000s, he wanted to bring together concepts such as message-passing (objects passing or sending messages to other objects), encapsulation (exposing only what's necessary), and dynamic linking (resolving properties of an object by name at runtime). Unlike all the other languages I'd learned, JavaScript had these principles deeply rooted in its design; more important, the concepts were easily accessible to developers. Then it dawned on me that I finally understood programming.

Armed with newfound motivation, I continued learning about JavaScript and found higher-order functions, which opened my eyes to functional programming and composable software. Suddenly, programming wasn't frustrating; it was a joy. This realization propelled my career as an author of books such as *Functional Programming in JavaScript* (Manning, 2016), *RxJS in Action* (Manning, 2017), and now *The Joy of JavaScript* (Manning, 2021).

This book is for developers who, like me, have had the good fortune to learn about amazing features such as closures, prototypes, and higher-order functions, and want to take them to the next level so that they can enjoy working with JavaScript every single day. *The Joy of JavaScript* shows what the language has to offer on its own, without any third-party libraries and frameworks. Due to the sheer number of topics surrounding JavaScript, this book doesn't spend much time digging into basic concepts (but offers good resources for them); neither is it a guide to writing ECMAScript 2019, 2020, and so on. Rather, it gives you a close-up view of exciting topics, trends, and techniques that will allow you to master areas of the language that you probably didn't know existed. As a bonus, the book introduces you to some additions to the language that may land in the years to come. It's valuable to learn about these proposals so that you'll understand where the language is headed and how it's evolving.

Writing this book helped me get through these uncertain and anxious times, and I sincerely hope that you find the same joy in reading it that I did writing it. While working on this manuscript, I gained a fresh perspective on programming as a whole, and I hope that it does the same for you.

acknowledgments

This book was a lot of work. But I believe that all that work resulted in a fine book that nicely complements what's already out there, and I hope that you will think so as well.

I'd like to thank quite a few people for helping me along the way.

First and foremost, I want to thank my wife, Ana. You've always supported me, always patiently taking care of things (including our two amazing boys, Luke and Matthew) while I struggled to get this book done. You always made me believe I could finish it. I love you.

Next, I'd like to acknowledge my longtime, flawless editor at Manning, Frances Lefkowitz. Thank you for working with me, guiding me every step of the way, and making the writing process delightful (not to mention bearable). Your commitment to the quality of this book made it better for everyone who will read it. Thanks as well to all the other folks at Manning who worked with me on the production and promotion of the book: Deirdre Hiam, and Melody Dolab. It was truly a team effort.

I'd also like to thank the reviewers who took the time to read my manuscript at various stages during its development and who provided invaluable feedback: Al Pezewski, Alberto Ciarlanti, Amit Lamba, Birnou Sébarte, Daniel Posey, Daniel Bretoi, Dary Merckens, Dennis Reil, Didier Garcia, Edwin Kwok, Foster Haines, Francesco Strazzullo, Gabriel Wu, Jacob Romero, Joe Justesen, Jon Guenther, Julien Pohie, Kevin Norman D. Kapchan, Kimberly Winston-Jackson, Konstantinos Leimonis, Jahred Love, Lora Vardarova, Matteo Gildone, Miranda Whurr, Nate Clark, Pietro Maffi, Rance Shields, Ray Booysen, Richard Michaels, Sachin Singhi, Satej Kumar Sahu, Srihari Sridharan, Ubaldo Pescatore, and Víctor M. Pérez.

Special thanks to Gleb Bahmutov (https://twitter.com/bahmutov), vice president of engineering at Cypress.io (https://www.cypress.io), and James Sinclair (https://twitter.com/jrsinclair) for their insightful review of the book and code. Gleb and James are amazing JavaScript advocates, and I highly recommend that you follow their work. Thanks also to my brother, Carlos, who took the time to read the book and offered lots of important, constructive feedback.

Finally, I'm standing on the shoulders of giants. Thank you, Kyle Simpson, for teaching us JavaScript the right way in your book series *You Don't Know JS* (https://github.com/getify/You-Dont-Know-JS), and to Eric Elliot for his unique views on composable software (https://leanpub.com/composingsoftware). Also, thanks to Brendan Eich, without whom JavaScript would not exist. You make work a joy!

about this book

JavaScript fatigue is real—not only because programmers have more than a million NPM packages to choose from, but also because they have an equal amount of online resources to turn to for information and guidance. *The Joy of JavaScript* was written to synthesize some of the most cutting-edge and exciting developments in the JavaScript language, to help you go beyond the basics and reach the next level. The book begins by comparing and contrasting object-oriented modeling techniques that highlight JavaScript's prototype chains and dynamic linking. Then it puts the spotlight on higher-order functions and on using JavaScript's functional programming capabilities to arrive at truly composable software—a theme that in one way or another permeates the entire book. Next, the books tackles static and dynamic separation of concerns with modules and metaprogramming, respectively. The book ends with a discussion of ways to handle asynchronous flows of data streams effectively. My hope is that this four-part journey will help turn fatigue into joy.

Who should read this book

The Joy of JavaScript is for professional developers who already possess a solid foundation and are looking to expand their breadth of knowledge into other parts of the language–including aspects they may have seen or heard about but never had the opportunity or time to learn. Although the book targets intermediate to advanced developers, it gently introduces some of the most difficult topics, so it's also suitable for a beginner enthusiast who is passionate and willing to catch up on the side.

How this book is organized

Each chapter contributes to the book's goal of showing how to build up software from simple, composable pieces. The chapters are grouped in four parts, with each part looking at JavaScript from a different angle: objects, functions, code, and data. The book's four parts cover nine chapters and should be read in order, as each chapter and part builds on the previous one. To give you a fuller idea of what's in store, here's a summary of each part.

Part 1: Objects

The first part sheds light on JavaScript's object system. Syntactical support for class declarations gives you a clean, simple way to establish inheritance relationships in your domain model so that you can take advantage of proper data encapsulation and create highly cohesive, well-structured domains. Despite many advances that added class-oriented artifacts (such as classes, private properties, and inheritance), JavaScript is far from being a class-oriented language; in reality, it's quite the opposite. The underlying prototype mechanism makes JavaScript's object system incredibly malleable, versatile, and far more dynamic than that of other languages.

This part exposes you to techniques that help you build and instantiate your domain model entities, understanding the pros and cons of each approach. In this part, you'll learn that although classes have a place in JavaScript, they are not the only ways to model your objects and certainly don't reflect the way JavaScript works. To be proficient in the language, you must understand how the object system works.

Part 2: Functions

After defining the shape of our objects in the first part, in part 2 we connect them by using pure functions and composition. Functions bring the fun to *The Joy of JavaScript*. JavaScript has powerful functional programming capabilities that make functions the main units of computation. Believe it or not, functions have always been the strongest parts of JavaScript. The language's support for higher-order functions is the key to writing modular, composable, and maintainable software.

In this part, you will learn how to use functional programming (FP) principles centered on immutability, purity, and algebraic data types (ADT) to drive the business logic of your application forward. You place functions front and center in your design to take advantage of JavaScript's strongest feature: higher-order functions. By this point, you'll be well versed in modern JavaScript idioms, and you'll have taken a peek at slick new language features such as the pipeline and bind operators.

Part 3: Code

An area in which JavaScript was lacking was a standardized, official module system. Many attempts were made over the years to solve this problem, but nothing worked well across client/server platforms. By borrowing the best from all these attempts, JavaScript introduced the ECMAScript Modules (ESM) system—aka ES6 modules.

This static module system allows the JavaScript runtime to perform lots of optimizations and makes build tools smarter, enabling them to introspect and analyze the structure of your code to create the most optimal distributions.

Modules are not the only ways to separate reusable pieces of code. In addition, you'll learn about JavaScript's standard APIs that hook into your data dynamically, known as Proxy and Reflect. These APIs allow you to separate concerns like a pro and dynamically introduce cross-cutting policies such as tracing, logging, and performance counters without modifying or polluting your main application's logic.

Part 4: Data

The web evolves rapidly. The reality of modern software architecture is that everything is distributed and API-driven nowadays. As the language of the web, JavaScript comes with powerful constructs, APIs, and syntax to meet your asynchronous and stream-based programming needs. In this part, you'll learn about promises, async/await, async iterators, async generators, observable streams, and much more.

About the code

This book contains many examples of source code, both in numbered listings and inline with normal text. In both cases, source code is formatted in a fixed-width font like this to clearly separate it from ordinary text.

When it comes to parsing out the code, here are are some things to keep in mind.

To examine the contents of a variable or object property, this book often places that variable or property reference followed by an inline comment (//) to show its value. In these cases, (//) means *equals* or *returns*. Here's an example:

```
proxy.foo; // 'bar'
```

When referring to a property accessible from a constructor function's prototype, as in Function.prototype.call, the # symbol is used in place of prototype references, like this: Function#call.

All code samples assume that JavaScript is in strict mode ("use strict";). If you don't know what this term means, visit http://mng.bz/goaE.

Occasionally, arrow functions are used to improve legibility, especially for functions that are meant to be anonymous or that fit in a single line.

To keep code samples short, this book often omits unnecessary details such as code that has been shown before or code that the reader is assumed to understand without much effort. In these cases, an inline comment is followed by an ellipsis, (//...).

In many cases, the original source code has been reformatted; I've added line breaks and reworked indentation to accommodate the available page space in the book.

The code that accompanies this book is in line with real-world coding but is meant to be simple, contrived to avoid additional complexity. Its only purpose is teaching, so it's not meant to be used as is in any production system.

Any time a nonofficial future part of the language is used, Babel is used to transpile that code to standard JavaScript. This book doesn't cover Babel, but appendix A provides a brief introduction.

Source code for the examples in this book is hosted in a public GitHub repository and is available for download from the publisher's website at https://www.manning .com/books/the-joy-of-javascript. To run each chapter's listings, you have two options: download and install Node.js v14 or later to run the code locally, or use a minimal Docker configuration (provided) that configures a virtual environment with Node.js 14 and contains all the required project configurations. Docker is convenient if you don't want to or can't upgrade your environment. The Docker sandbox ensures that all the code works regardless of your system configuration or even which operating system you use. You can sign up for and download a Docker engine for your specific OS at https://www.docker.com/products/docker-desktop.

Other online resources

- *You Don't Know JS*, by Kyle Simpson (https://github.com/getify/You-Dont-Know-JS)
- *Composable Software*, by Eric Elliot (https://leanpub.com/composingsoftware)
- Mozilla Developer Network (https://developer.mozilla.org/en-US)

about the author

Luis Atencio (@luijar) is a principal cloud engineer for Citrix Systems in Fort Lauderdale, Florida. He has a B.S. and an M.S. in Computer Science and now works full-time developing and architecting cloud web applications with JavaScript and Java. Luis is involved in the community and has presented on several occasions at global conferences and local meetups. When he is not coding, he writes a developer blog (https://medium.com/@luijar) that focuses on software engineering. He has written several articles for PHPArch and DZone. Luis is also the author of *Functional Programming in JavaScript* (Manning, 2016) and co-author of *RxJS in Action* (Manning, 2017).

about the cover illustration

The figure on the cover of *The Joy of JavaScript* is captioned "Groenlandais," or Greenlander. The illustration is taken from a collection of dress costumes from various countries by Jacques Grasset de Saint-Sauveur (1757-1810), titled *Costumes de Différents Pays*, published in France in 1797. Each illustration is finely drawn and colored by hand. The rich variety of Grasset de Saint-Sauveur's collection reminds us vividly of how culturally apart the world's towns and regions were just 200 years ago. Isolated from each other, people spoke different dialects and languages. In the streets or in the countryside, it was easy to identify where they lived and what their trade or station in life was just by their dress.

The way we dress has changed since then and the diversity by region, so rich at the time, has faded away. It is now hard to tell apart the inhabitants of different continents, let alone different towns, regions, or countries. Perhaps we have traded cultural diversity for a more varied personal life—certainly for a more varied and fast-paced technological life.

At a time when it is hard to tell one computer book from another, Manning celebrates the inventiveness and initiative of the computer business with book covers based on the rich diversity of regional life of two centuries ago, brought back to life by Grasset de Saint-Sauveur's pictures.

JavaScript reloaded

1

This chapter covers

- Evaluating the key aspects of day-to-day coding: objects, functions, code, and data
- Comparing prototype- and delegation-based object models
- Understanding the composability of functions and types
- Achieving clear separation of concerns through modularity and metaprogramming
- Using promises and streams programming to create unidirectional data pipelines
- Introducing the sample blockchain application

Any application that can be written in JavaScript, will eventually be written in JavaScript.

—Jeff Atwood

It's an amazing time to be a JavaScript developer. Today, JavaScript developers can write code that runs virtually anywhere from tablets, smartphones, desktops, bots, and cloud platforms to the Internet of Things, such as toasters, refrigerators, thermostats,

1

and even spacesuits! Also, we can program all tiers of an application stack, from the client and server, all the way down to the database. The world is at our fingertips.

Despite JavaScript's resounding popularity, most developers—even those who use it every day—still struggle to decide how to approach writing a new application. Most of the time, you or your organization will have a prearranged framework of choice, which gives you a good starting point. But even in these situations, frameworks only get you so far; business-domain logic (done in plain JavaScript coding) will always be the most difficult and uncertain part of the equation—one that you can't throw a library at to do. For these cases, it's important to have a good grasp of the language's syntax, the features it has to offer, and the paradigms it supports.

Most general-purpose programming languages typically have a recommended way of solving a certain type of problem. Java and similar languages are hard-set on classes to represent your business model, for example. With JavaScript, however, there are many more options to consider: functions, object literals, creational APIs, and even classes. Because JavaScript glues the web together, not only in browsers and mobile devices, but also increasingly in the server, it's continuously evolving to meet the demands of diverse developer communities and rise to the new challenges imposed by these (sometimes opposite) environments. Examples of these challenges include managing asynchronous data originating from a user clicking buttons to performing lower-level file I/O and breaking complex parts of your business logic into simple, maintainable modules that can be shared and used across clients and servers. These problems are unique.

In addition, when we use JavaScript at scale, we also need to concern ourselves with how to instantiate objects from proper abstractions that match our way of reasoning, decomposing complex algorithms into simpler, reusable functions and handling potentially infinite streams of data. All these tasks require good design skills so that the code is simple to reason about and easy to maintain.

That is where *The Joy of JavaScript* comes in. The goal of this book is to help you identify and work with the different features of the language so that you become a well-rounded JavaScript professional who understands how expert developers are using JavaScript. The topics covered will give you enough information to allow you to focus on and master what you need to tackle today's and tomorrow's challenges. The book will also prepare you to use some of the new features that might be coming into the language in the coming years, including pipeline and bind operators, throw expressions, and observables. My aim is to make you a better, more productive programmer so that you can do more with less. After a few chapters—and certainly by the end of the book—you should be writing even leaner and more elegant code than you are already writing. In short, you'll emerge from this book with a batch of new tools and techniques at your disposal for more effective and efficient programming, whether you are writing code for the frontend or the backend.

Many years ago, JavaScript development wasn't particularly associated with "joy." It was cumbersome to manage deep object hierarchies, for example, or to package your application into modules that would work across environments. The problem of implementing cross-platform, cross-vendor compatible code, plus the lack of tool support, made lots of developers cringe at the idea of having to write or maintain JavaScript code for a living. But that's changed; in fact, it's quite the opposite.

Fortunately, we're now in the modern days of JavaScript development, which means several things:

- First, we can closely monitor JavaScript's steady evolution with a well-defined, fast-paced, task group called TC39 that pushes new language features every year, all in the open and transparently. This creates both excitement and angst, because it inevitably forces you to rethink or throw away old habits and get ready for what's coming. Not all developers embrace change well or keep an open mind, but I hope that you do.
- Second, the days of copy-paste programming are long behind us, and gone with them is the stigma of having *Script* in the name as somehow describing an inferior language. This sentiment was a global one many years ago, but that's no longer the case. The JavaScript ecosystem is among the most vibrant and cutting-edge ecosystems, and today, JavaScript developers rank among the highest-paid professionals in the industry.
- Finally, the misconception that a JavaScript developer is a jQuery, React, Angular, Vue, Svelte, or <name-your-framework> developer is fading. You're a JavaScript developer—period. The decision to use any of these frameworks or libraries is yours to make. By using good practices and learning how to properly use the wide spectrum of tools that JavaScript gives you, plain-vanilla JavaScript is powerful enough to let your creativity run wild and contribute to any kind of project.

To bring you into the present and future of JavaScript programming, this book explores the language in the context of the most popular paradigms—functional, reflective, and reactive—and describes how to work with key coding elements within each paradigm. The book is organized around the four themes used in addressing most programming problems: objects, functions, code, and data. Within these themes, you'll learn which proper object models to use to design your business domain, how to combine functions and transform these objects into the desired output, how to modularize your applications effectively, and how to manage the data that flows through your application, whether that data is synchronous or asynchronous.

As you can see from the spectrum of topics covered, this book is not for a JavaScript newcomer or beginner. This book assumes that you already have some professional experience and a strong grasp of the basics (such as variables, loops, objects, functions, scopes, and closures), and that you have gone through the exercise of implementing and configuring JavaScript programs and setting up a transpiler such as Babel or TypeScript.

Modern JavaScript development is possible only when the language has a consistent, steady evolution of features and syntax that tackle these problems.

1.1   *Evolving JavaScript*

For many years, the evolution of JavaScript was stagnant. To put matters in perspective, ECMAScript, the specification language for JavaScript, had been stuck at version 3.1 across major JavaScript engines since December 2009. This version was later renamed as the better-known ECMAScript 5, or ES5. We waited for nearly six agonizing years—since June 2015, to be exact—to see any progress made in the language. In tech years, six years is a long time; even ATM machines get updated sooner.

During this time, a standards committee known as TC39 (https://github.com/tc39), with the help of institutions such as the OpenJS Foundation (https://openjsf.org), gave birth to ECMAScript 2015, also known as ES6. This change was the biggest leap that JavaScript had made since its inception. Among the most important features in this release (http://es6-features.org) were classes, arrow functions, promises, template literals, blocked-scoped variables, default arguments, metaprogramming support, destructuring assignment, and modules. Aside from all these most-needed language features, the most important change was that JavaScript's evolution shifted to a yearly release cadence, allowing the language to iterate quickly and address problems and shortcomings sooner. To help you keep track of where we are, ES6 refers to ECMAScript 2015, ES7 to ECMAScript 2016, and so on. These incremental releases are much easier to adopt and manage by platform vendors than large, monolithic releases.

TC39 is composed of members of leading web companies that will also continue evolving ECMAScript, the specification language set to standardize JavaScript, known internationally as ISO/IEC 16262 or ECMA262 for short. (That's a lot of acronyms, I know, but I hope that you got the gist.) TC39 is also a platform that gives the whole community some input into where the language is headed through participation in IRC channels and mailing lists, as well as through finding and helping to document issues in existing proposals. If you take a quick look at the language proposals on TC39's GitHub site, you can see that each one goes through a set of stages. These stages are well documented on GitHub, so I'll summarize them for you here:

- *Stage 0 (strawman)*—This stage is informal, and the proposal can have any form, so anyone can contribute to the further development of the language. To add your input, you must be a member of TC39 or registered with ECMA International. If you're interested, feel free to register at https://tc39.github.io/agreements/contributor. When you're registered, you can propose your ideas via the es-discuss mailing list. You can also follow the discussions at https://esdiscuss.org.
- *Stage 1 (proposal)*—After a strawman has been made, a member of TC39 must champion your addition to advance it to the next stage. The TC39 member must explain why the addition is useful and describe how it will behave and look when it's implemented.
- *Stage 2 (draft)*—The proposal gets fully spec'd out and is considered to be experimental. If it reaches this stage, the committee expects the feature to make it into the language eventually.

- *Stage 3 (candidate)*—At this stage, the solution is considered to be complete and is signed off. Changes after this stage are rare and generally are made only for critical discoveries after implementation and significant use. You can feel comfortable using features in this stage. After a suitable period of deployment, the addition is safely bumped to stage 4.
- *Stage 4 (finished)*—Stage 4 is the final stage. If a proposal reaches this stage, it is ready to be included in the formal ECMAScript standard specification.

This healthy stream of new proposals is important so that JavaScript keeps up with the demands of today's application development practices. Aside from discussing the cool techniques and paradigms that come alive only with JavaScript, this book introduces you to a few proposals that will forever change how we write JavaScript in the near future, some of which I'll mention briefly in this chapter. Here they are, in the order in which they'll appear in the rest of the book:

- *Private class fields* (https://github.com/tc39/proposal-class-fields) allow you to define access modifiers (private, static) to a class's properties.
- *The pipeline operator* (https://github.com/tc39/proposal-pipeline-operator) brings the UNIX-like pipe feature of functional languages to JavaScript functions.
- *The bind operator* (https://github.com/tc39/proposal-bind-operator) is a new language syntax that abstracts the use of `Function.prototype.bind`.
- *Throw expressions* (https://github.com/tc39/proposal-throw-expressions) allow you to treat a `throw` statement as though it were a function or a variable.
- *Observables* (https://github.com/tc39/proposal-observable) enable the stream-based, reactive paradigm.

For most of the remainder of this chapter, I'll introduce you to the book's four major themes so that you understand the big picture and see how the themes relate to one another. I'll start with objects.

1.2 Objects

An *object* is nothing more than a memory reference that points (links) to other memory locations. At its core, JavaScript is an object-oriented language, and there are many ways to define objects and the association among them in JavaScript. In this book, we'll look at many ways to define objects.

For one-time use, for example, a simple object literal is probably the best and quickest approach. An object literal comes in handy when you need to group multiple pieces of data that need to be passed to, or returned from, a function. When you need to create multiple objects with the same shape, however, it's best to use a creational API like `Object.create` to act as a factory of objects. You can also use your own functions as object factories when combined with the `new` keyword. In the same vein, classes have become popular in recent years and behave in much the same way. But if objects are nothing more than references (links) to other objects, JavaScript also lets you mash multiple small objects into one big one by using the spread operator or even an API like `Object.assign`.

Regardless of the approach you take, you often need to share data and a set of methods to avoid duplicating code. JavaScript uses two central mechanisms: the property resolution mechanism and prototypes. These mechanisms are intertwined. JavaScript uses the object's internal prototype reference as a path to navigate an object hierarchy during property resolution, which can happen when you query properties of an object or invoke a method. Suppose that you have the inheritance configuration shown in figure 1.1.

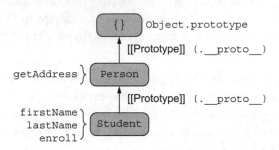

Figure 1.1   A simple prototype hierarchy in which objects of Student inherit from objects of Person

Here, objects constructed from `Student` inherit from objects constructed from `Person`, which means that all `Student` instances have at their disposal the data and methods defined in `Person`. This relationship goes by the name *differential inheritance*, because as the object graph becomes longer, every object borrows the shape of the one above it and differentiates itself (becomes more specialized) with new behavior.

From figure 1.1, calling `enroll` on a `Student` invokes the desired property right away because it's local to the object, but calling `getAddress` uses JavaScript's property lookup mechanism to traverse up the prototype hierarchy. The downside of this approach is that when your object graphs become a lot more complex, a change to a base-level object will cause a ripple effect in all derived objects, even at runtime. This situation is known as *prototype pollution*, and it's a serious issue that plagues large Java-Script applications.

Because the prototype is an internal implementation detail of objects in JavaScript, from the point of view of the caller the `Student` API is a façade with four properties: `firstName`, `lastName`, `getAddress`, and `enroll`. Similarly, we can obtain the same shape by composing object literals describing a `Person` and `Student`. This approach is a slight twist on the configuration in figure 1.1, but an important one. Take a look at figure 1.2.

With figure 1.2, the main difference is that we replaced prototype references with a copy operation to symbolize that we're essentially taking all the properties of `Student` and `Person` and copying them (actually, assigning them) to an empty object. So instead of linking objects, we created separate objects with the same shape. From the

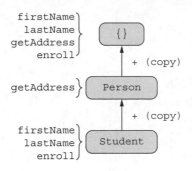

Figure 1.2 **Two concrete objects (`Student` and `Person`) mesh into a brand new object with all properties assigned from the combined objects. Although no prototypal inheritance is at play here, the directions of the arrow is kept the same as in figure 1.1 to convey the similar mental model of both approaches.**

caller's point of view, these objects are exactly the same, and you still benefit from code reuse. In this scenario, `Student` and `Person` are not constructors or factories; they are simple mixins (pieces of an object). Although this approach saves you from unintended downstream changes and prototype pollution to some degree, the downside is that every new object you create adds a new copy of the assigned properties in memory, making the memory footprint a bit larger.

As you know, most things in computer science are trade-offs. Here, you trade the memory-efficient approach of prototypes, which JavaScript engines highly optimize, for ease of maintainability and reusability. In chapters 2 and 3, we'll talk in detail about these and other patterns, as well as the code that implements them.

If objects are the fabric of JavaScript, functions represent the needles used to thread the pieces together. JavaScript functions are by far the strongest parts of the language, as we'll discuss in section 1.3.

1.3 Functions

Functions implement the business logic of your application and drive its state (such as the data inside all the objects in memory) to its desired outcome. At a fundamental level, you can think about functions in two ways:

- In the procedural or imperative mindset, a function is nothing more than a group of statements that execute together, used to organize and avoid duplicating similar patterns of code. The object-oriented paradigm inherits from procedural programming, so it's also a sequence of statements or commands that modify objects. The reader is expected to be familiar with this approach.
- On the other hand, you can think about functions as expressions through the lens of functional programming (FP). In this view of the world, functions represent immutable computations that are assembled like Lego bricks.

Figure 1.3 shows a flowchart of a hypothetical program of minor complexity that uses a procedural style. We've been trained to think like computers and map out data flows in this way. But as you'll see over the next couple of figures (figure 1.4 and 1.5), when you use the right techniques, you can simplify even the most complex program as a streamlined sequence of expressions.

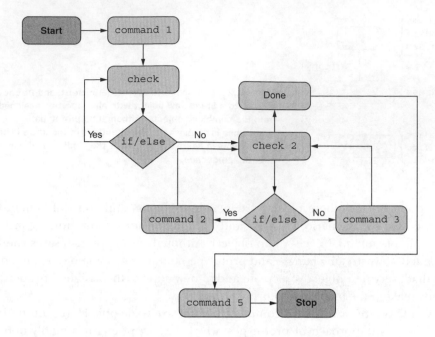

**Figure 1.3   A hypothetical description of a program illustrating `if/else`
conditions and looping**

You should be writing maintainable, declarative code that your users and teammates
can understand, and letting the computer parse and optimize code for its own understanding. FP can help a lot in this regard. You've probably heard or read that React
allows you to build UIs "the functional way" or that Redux promotes immutable state
management. Have you ever wondered where all these concepts come from? You can
code functionally by taking advantage of higher-order functions. In JavaScript, a function is an object capable of carrying or linking to variables in its lexical scope (also
known as its closure or *backpack*) and one that you can pass as an argument and return
as a callback. This fundamental part of the language, which has existed since the birth
of JavaScript, has infinite potential for designing code.

FP expresses computations and data as a combination of pure functions. Instead of
changing the state of the system on every call, these functions yield a new state; they
are immutable. Coding with FP will prevent a lot of bugs—ones you don't have to
bother to code around—and yield code that you can look at years later and reason
about more easily. This feature isn't part of JavaScript per se, but it complements coding with JavaScript's higher-order functions.

Chapter 4 teaches you enough FP to significantly affect the way that you do your
day-to-day coding. It goes through an exercise of decomposition (breaking complex
problems into small, manageable chunks) and composition (pulling the pieces back
together). Abstractly, the coding mindset is shown in figure 1.4.

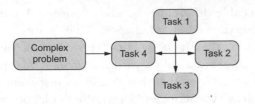

Figure 1.4 **FP programs tend to decompose big problems and solve them as the composition of smaller tasks.**

Inevitably, you'll tend to create much simpler functions that work on some input and produce an output based solely on this input. When you've been able to disassemble a complex problem and represent it as multiple functions, you'll use techniques such as currying and composition to string all these functions back together. You can use functions to abstract any kind of logic—such as conditional execution, loops, and even error handling—to create a pipeline of information that looks like figure 1.5.

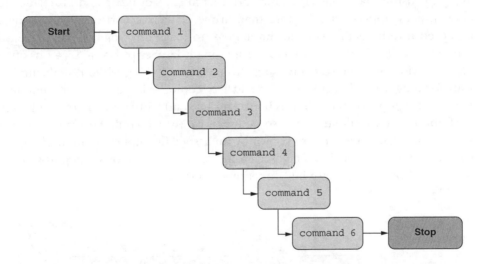

Figure 1.5 **Composition allows you to build function pipelines in which the output of one function becomes the input to the next.**

We're fortunate to use a language that can give us this kind of support. In future releases of the language, figure 1.5 could be encoded directly in JavaScript with the new pipeline operator (|>) syntax, which you'll learn about in chapter 4:

```
const output = [input data] |> command1 |> command2 |> ... |> command6;
```

Like a UNIX shell, this operator allows you to "pipe" the output of one function as the input to the next. Let's assume that you created a split function to break apart a string by spaces into an array and a count function to return the length of the array. The following line is valid JavaScript code:

```
'1 2 3' |> split |> count;  // 3
```

Furthermore, one of the most noticeable differences between figures 1.3 and 1.5 is the removal of the conditional logic (the diamond shapes). How is this possible? Chapter 5 introduces a concept known as the Algebraic Data Type (ADT). In our case, *type* means an object with a certain shape, not a static type, which is what it commonly refers to in other language communities. Given that there's a lot of discussion about static type systems for JavaScript (such as TypeScript and Flow), this book does spend a little bit of time talking about static types in JavaScript in appendix B.

ADTs are commonplace nowadays in many programming languages and libraries as an elegant solution to common problems such as data validation, error handling, null checks, and I/O. In fact, JavaScript's own optional chaining, pipeline, promises, and nullish coalesce operators, as well as `Array.prototype{map, flatMap}` APIs (all discussed in this book), are inspired in these algebraic types.

Earlier, we discussed composition in terms of functions. How can composition apply to custom data objects? You'll learn that `Array`'s own `map` and `flatMap` methods conceptually apply to much more than arrays. They are part of a set of universally accepted interfaces that you can implement to make any object behave like a function; we'll call this object a functor or a monad. JavaScript's own `Array` has functor-like behavior, and you've been using this pattern all along without realizing it when transforming arrays by using `map`. This style of coding is important as a foundation for many of the topics covered in this book, so I'll spend a little time here going over it.

Suppose that you've declared some functor F (which could be `Array`) and given it some input data. Functors are known by their specific implementation of `map` so that you can transform the data enclosed inside F. Figure 1.6 shows a step-by-step view of sequentially applying (mapping) functions to a string.

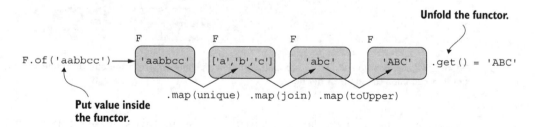

Figure 1.6 A functor object (`F`) uses `map` to transform the data contained inside it. Functors are side-effect-free, as every application of `map` yields a new instance of `F` while the original stays intact.

`map` is a contract that can apply to any F that meets the functor requirements. When dealing with functions that you want to apply consistently across different independent objects, you may be inclined to use `Function.prototype.bind` to set the target object receiving the function call. With JavaScript's new bind operator (`::`) syntax, this process got easier. Here's a contrived example:

```
const { map } = Functor;

(new F('aabbcc'))
    :: map(unique)
    :: map(join)
    :: map(toUpper); // 'ABC'
```

There are many use cases in which functors are useful, so let's hone in on the issue of conditional logic for validation. In chapter 5, we will implement our own ADT from scratch to abstract over if/else logic with an expression such as "If data is valid, do *X*; else, do *Y*." The flow of data, although following the declarative recipe-like paradigm of figure 1.5, will execute proper branching logic internally, depending on the result of the validation check. In other words, if the result of a validation check is successful, the callback function is executed with the wrapped input; otherwise, it's ignored. These two code flows are shown in figure 1.7.

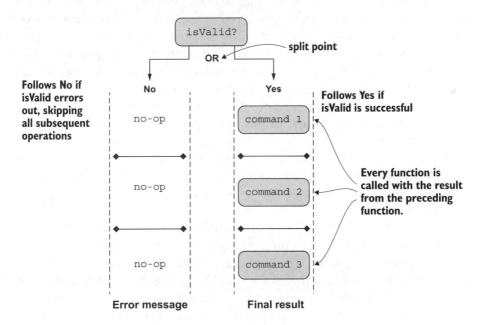

Figure 1.7   An ADT to implement conditional logic models mutually exclusive (OR) branching. On the Yes (success) side of the branch, all mapped operations are executed against the data contained inside the ADT. Otherwise, on the No (failure) side, all operations are skipped. In both cases, the data flows sequentially from beginning to end.

Learning about ADTs now will prepare you for where the language is headed. Early proposals include features such as pattern matching, which is proper for more functional alt-JS programming languages such as Elm. I don't cover pattern matching in this book, as this proposal was in early draft form at the time of this writing.

Now that you've learned object-oriented and functional techniques to model your business domain, section 1.4 introduces you to JavaScript's official module system, known as ECMAScript Modules (ESM), to help you organize and deliver your code in an optimal manner.

1.4   Code

Chapter 6 focuses on how to import and export code across your application by using ESM. The main goal of this feature is to standardize how code is shared and used in a platform-agnostic fashion. ESM supersedes earlier attempts at a standard module system for JavaScript, such as AMD, UMD, and even CommonJS (eventually). ESM uses a static module format that build/bundler tools can use to apply a lot of code optimizations simply by analyzing the static layout of your project and its interdependencies. This format is especially useful for reducing the size of bundled code that is sent over the wire to remote servers or directly to a browser.

JavaScript can use its module system to load modules as small as a single function to as big as monolithic classes. When you use well-established, tried-and-tested keywords such as `export` and `import`, creating modular, reusable code is straightforward.

Being able to change one area of your code without affecting others is the cornerstone of modularity. Separation of concerns doesn't apply only to the global project structure, but also to running code—the topic of chapter 7.

Chapter 7 talks about separation of concerns by taking advantage of JavaScript's metaprogramming capabilities. Using JavaScript symbols and APIs such as `Proxy` and `Reflect` to enable reflection and introspection, you can keep your code clean and focused on the problem at hand. We'll use these APIs to create our own method decorators to dynamically inject cross-cutting behavior (such as logging, tracing, and performance counters) that would otherwise clutter your business logic, doing so only when you need it.

As a simple example, suppose that during debugging and troubleshooting you want to turn on logging of any property access (reading the contents of a property or calling a method) on some critical objects of your application. You'd like to do this without modifying a single line of code and be able to turn it off when you're done. With the right instrumentation in place, you can create dynamic proxies that decorate objects of your choice and intercept or trap any calls to that object to weave new functionality. This simple example is depicted in figure 1.8.

Now imagine replacing this simple trap with performance counters before and after areas of code that you want to optimize, or using global security policies that can mangle or obfuscate sensitive strings inside objects before printing them to the screen or a log file. These method decorators become useful in a large number of use cases. We'll look at how to do these things in chapter 7.

Now that you have objects, functions, and your code properly organized, all that's left to do is manage the data that flows through it.

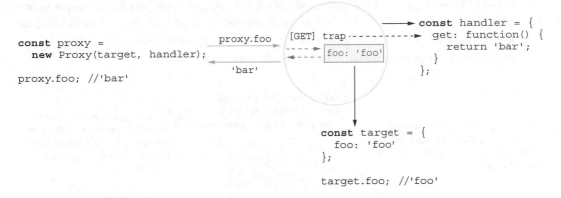

```
const proxy =                    proxy.foo    [GET] trap            const handler = {
  new Proxy(target, handler);                                         get: function() {
                                                                        return 'bar';
                                  'bar'          foo: 'foo'            }
proxy.foo; //'bar'                                                  };


                                              const target = {
                                                foo: 'foo'
                                              };

                                              target.foo; //'foo'
```

Figure 1.8   Creating a proxy object dynamically around some target object. Any property access (`foo`) is trapped by the proxy object, so you can inject any code you want. In this simple case, the proxy object traps the access to `foo` and dynamically changes its return value to `'bar'`.

1.5   Data

Because JavaScript is critically positioned as the language of the web (both server and client), it needs to handle data of many shapes and sizes. Data can arrive synchronously (from local memory) or asynchronously (from anywhere else in the world). It may come in all at once (single object), in an ordered sequence (array), or in chunks (stream). JavaScript engines, at a high level, rely on an architecture featuring a callback queue with an event loop that can execute code continuously in a concurrent fashion and without halting the main thread.

Without a doubt, using promises as a pattern for abstracting time and data locality has made it simpler to reason about asynchronous code. A `Promise` is an object that behaves like a function representing an eventual value, with an API that bears a lot of resemblance to ADTs. In your mind, you can replace `then` with `map`/`flatMap`. A `Promise` can be in one of several states, as shown in figure 1.9, of which the most noticeable are `'fulfilled'` and `'rejected'`.

As you can see, promises also models two branches of code. These two branches move your logic forward to execute your business logic to the desired outcome

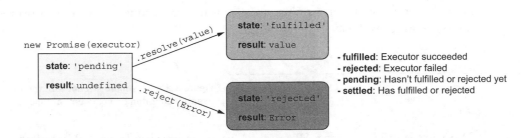

```
new Promise(executor)          state: 'fulfilled'
                  .resolve(value)
  state: 'pending'             result: value              - fulfilled: Executor succeeded
                                                          - rejected: Executor failed
  result: undefined                                       - pending: Hasn't fulfilled or rejected yet
                  .reject(Error) state: 'rejected'        - settled: Has fulfilled or rejected

                               result: Error
```

Figure 1.9   A new `Promise` object and all its possible states

('fulfilled') or produce some sort of error message ('rejected'). Promises are composable types, much like ADTs and functions, and you can create chains of sequential logic to attack complex problems involving asynchronous data sources and profit from proper error handling along the way (figure 1.10).

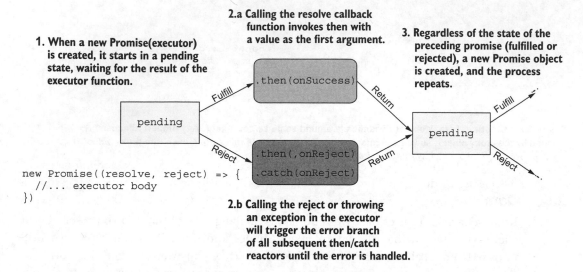

2.a Calling the resolve callback function invokes then with a value as the first argument.

1. When a new Promise(executor) is created, it starts in a pending state, waiting for the result of the executor function.

3. Regardless of the state of the preceding promise (fulfilled or rejected), a new Promise object is created, and the process repeats.

```
.then(onSuccess)
```

```
pending
```

```
.then(,onReject)
.catch(onReject)
```

```
pending
```

```
new Promise((resolve, reject) => {
  //... executor body
})
```

2.b Calling the reject or throwing an exception in the executor will trigger the error branch of all subsequent then/catch reactors until the error is handled.

Figure 1.10   How `Promise` objects chain to form new `Promise` objects. Along the way, the same pattern repeats. Both success and rejection cases lead to a new `Promise` object returned.

In chapter 8, we discuss promises and the `async`/`await` syntax that appeals to developers from a more imperative or procedural background, yet shares the behavioral semantics of promises. With `async`/`await`, you have the visual advantage of writing code that looks as though it's pausing and waiting for a command to execute (as in fetching data with an HTTP request), but behind the scenes, it's all promises interacting with the underlying event loop architecture. In chapter 8, we also explore topics implemented on top of promises such as async iterators and async generators.

Promises model single, asynchronous values, but async generators allow you to deliver potentially infinite sequences of data over time. Async generators are a good mental model for understanding streams, which are sequences of events over some period of time, as depicted in figure 1.11.

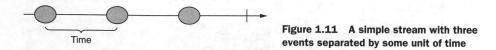

Time

Figure 1.11   A simple stream with three events separated by some unit of time

There are standard `Stream` APIs to read/write streams implemented in both browsers and Node.js. Examples are file I/O streams in Node.js and the Fetch API in browsers.

Nevertheless, given the diversity of the data types we deal with on a daily basis, instead of using `Promise` for a single-value event and `Stream` for sequences of events, ideally we'd use a single API to abstract over all these data types with the same computing model. This approach is attractive to framework and library authors alike because it allows them to provide a consistent interface. Fortunately, JavaScript proposes the `Observable` API as the solution.

Any time you see an `Observable` object, you should be thinking in terms of figure 1.11. JavaScript's inclusion of `Observable` built into the language seeks to standardize the amazing things you can do with libraries like RxJS. With observables, you can subscribe to events coming from any source: a simple function, an array, an event emitter (such as DOM), an HTTP request, promises, generators, or even WebSockets. The idea is that you can treat each piece of data as some event in time and use a consistent set of operators (observable functions) to process it. Like functions, promises, and ADTs, observables are composable. Do you see a pattern? This pattern isn't a coincidence; it's the coding pattern of modern software and one that most languages are increasingly adopting. Hence, you can also create chains or pipelines by calling a sequence of composable operators that work on or transform the data flowing through an observable object to process data synchronously or asynchronously as it propagates forward in time. Figure 1.12 shows how a source observable is transformed by some operator (maybe `map`?) to yield a new observable.

In chapter 9, we'll create our own little library of operators. These pipeable operators are themselves higher-order functions, and the functions you provide to them

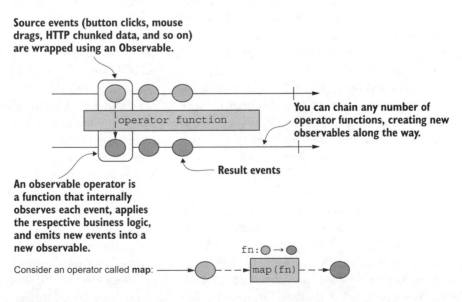

Figure 1.12 A source `Observable` object (first long arrow) with all its events piped into an operator function and transformed. All new values are emitted by means of a new `Observable`.

encode your domain-specific business logic. As I said at the beginning of this chapter, and as you'll see time and time again throughout the book, higher-order functions are by far the strongest feature of JavaScript.

I hope that this overview sounds exciting. I've kept the discussion at a high level for now, but each chapter after this one will dive into lots of detail and code. In this book, you'll not only be exposed to new cutting-edge techniques, but also see them implemented in the context of a more contemporary type of application. Before we dive into all those nifty topics, let me introduce you to the sample application we'll be building throughout this book. Section 1.6 helps set the context for all the code you'll see.

1.6   *Sample application: Blockchain*

It's been my experience that most programming books use trivial examples, often numeric or foo/bar, to demonstrate a particular feature of a technology. Although these examples are effective because they assume zero domain knowledge, the downside is that you're left wondering how they fit into a more complex, realistic application.

If you haven't been living under a rock for the past few years, you've seen a lot of hype about blockchain and cryptocurrencies, which have taken the world by storm. Many analysts consider blockchain to be one of the most important technologies to learn in the years to come. Blockchains are so ubiquitous and prevalent nowadays that getting familiar with them will add an invaluable skill to your tool belt—not to mention the fact that blockchains are cool. Certainly, teaching this technology is not simple, but this application is deliberately kept small and simple to fit in this book. No ramp-up is needed, and no background is required. Your own passion and drive, with some JavaScript background, are the only prerequisites.

In this book, we'll build some parts of a simple, naive blockchain protocol from scratch to illustrate how we can apply modern JavaScript techniques to a real-world problem. Because the focus is on teaching JavaScript, teaching blockchain is purely pedagogical and far from a production-ready implementation. Nevertheless, you'll be exposed to some interesting techniques from the blockchain world, such as immutability, hashing, mining, and proof of work. For the sake of exploring the wide breadth of JavaScript features, we'll find creative ways to plug in as many features and techniques as possible into this small, contrived sample application.

To give you some background, a blockchain is a type of database made up of a list of records (called blocks) that may store any type of data in some chronological order. Unlike traditional databases, blocks are immutable records; you can never alter the contents of a block, only add new ones.

Blocks are linked cryptographically. No pointer or reference connects one block to the next, as in a linked list. Rather, each block contains a cryptographically secure hash (such as SHA-256), and the hash of a new block depends on the hash of the block that preceded it, thereby forming a chain. Because every block is hashed from the previous block's hash, this chain is inherently tamperproof. Manipulating even a single property of any transaction in the history of all blocks will result in a different hash value that will invalidate the entire chain. This fact is one of the main reasons why blockchain data structures are desired not only in financial software, but also in secure document-storage solutions, online voting, and other industry segments.

The process of computing block hashes daisy-chains all the way back to the first block in the chain, which is known as the genesis, or block of height 0. In real life, a blockchain is much more complex. For purposes of this book, though, it's enough to picture it as a sequential data structure in which each block stores the most recent transactions that occurred. This simplified structure is shown in figure 1.13.

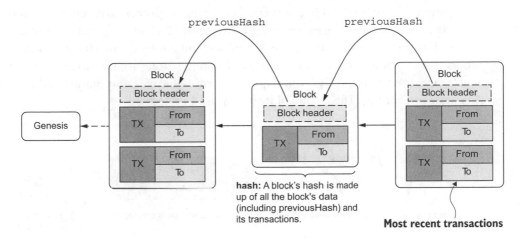

Figure 1.13 A simple representation of a blockchain, in which each block stores the previous block's hash. This hash is used to compute the current block's own hash, effectively connecting all these blocks in a chain.

As you can see in the figure, each block is made up of a block header, which is the metadata associated with each block. Part of this header is a field, previousHash, that stores the previous block's hash. Aside from metadata, each block may contain a payload, which more commonly is a set of transactions. The latest block contains the most recent transactions that were pending in the chain at the moment it was created.

A transaction looks like a typical bank transaction and has the form "A transferred X amount of funds to B," where A and B are cryptographic public keys that identify the parties involved in the transaction. Because the blockchain contains all the transactions that occurred in history, in the world of digital currencies like Bitcoin, it is known as a public ledger. Unlike your bank account, which is private, a blockchain like Bitcoin is public. You might be thinking, "My bank is in charge of validating every transaction, so who validates these transactions?" Through a process called mining, which you'll learn about in chapter 8, you can validate all the transactions stored in a block, as well as all those stored in history. Mining is a resource-intensive process. While mining is happening, the transactions are said to be pending. All these pending transactions combine to form the next block's data payload. When the block gets added to the blockchain, the transaction is complete.

A cryptocurrency acquires monetary value when the backing resource is scarce and expensive to find, extract, or "mine," such as gold, diamonds, or oil. Computers can use their powerful processors or arithmetic logic units to perform high-speed math that solves a mathematical problem, which is known as proof of work. We'll look at the implementation details of our proofOfWork function in chapter 7.

Consider an example of how a transaction is added and then secured by the blockchain protocol. Suppose that Luke buys coffee from Ana's Café for 10 Bitcoin. Users are identified by their digital wallets. The payment process triggers logic to transfer funds in the form of a new pending transaction. The set of pending transactions is stored inside a block; then the block is mined and added to the chain for validation to occur. If all validation checks are good, the transactions are said to be complete. The incentive for a miner to run this expensive proof-of-work computation is that there's a reward for mining. This protocol is summarized in figure 1.14.

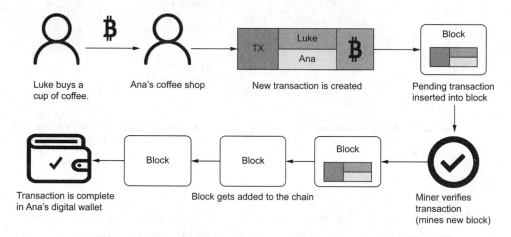

Figure 1.14   Luke buys coffee from Ana's coffee shop, paying with his digital wallet. The payment process creates a new transaction, set to pending. After a certain period, miners compete to validate this transaction. Then all the transactions that happened, including Luke's payment, are added as a block in the chain, and the payment is complete.

Taking these concepts into account, figure 1.15 shows a simple diagram of all the objects involved in this sequence.

As we progress through the chapters, we'll flesh out all these objects as well as the business logic that ties them together. Concretely, we'll implement code to validate the entire chain, calculate the Bitcoin balance of a specific user (wallet account), execute a simple proof-of-work algorithm, and mine a block into a blockchain.

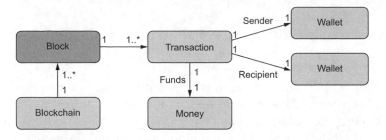

Figure 1.15   The main objects of the domain layer at play in our simple blockchain application

Where to find the code

The code for this book is freely available on GitHub (https://github.com/JoyOfJava Script/joj). The repository contains the worked-out blockchain application as well as all code listings in the form of unit tests. It's important to mention that all code samples in this book assume strict mode (`"use strict";`), which is the recommended way of writing JavaScript.

Strict mode is beneficial because it disallows some bad parts of the language, such as employing the infamous `with` statement, calling `delete` on a variable (it would be nice if JavaScript also forbade calling `delete` on an object property), and using some of the newly reserved keywords (such as `interface`). Strict mode also turns some passive errors into full-blown exceptions.

The repository also includes Babel configuration files to transpile some nonstandard proposals that will change your JavaScript coding in the future. Babel is not covered in the chapters, but you can read a bit more about it in appendix A.

To run each chapter's listings, you have two options: download and install Node.js v14 or later to run the code locally, or use a minimal Docker configuration that configures a virtual environment with Node.js 14 and contains all the required project configurations. Docker is convenient if you don't want to or can't upgrade your environment. The Docker sandbox ensures that all the code works regardless of your system configuration or even which operating system you use. It's straightforward to sign up and download a Docker engine for your specific OS from https://www.docker.com/products/docker-desktop.

Visit the GitHub project's README.md file for instructions about how to get started.

This 10,000-foot introduction to some of the ideas and new concepts covered in this book scratches the surface. By the end, you'll see that JavaScript possesses all the expressive power you need to let your limitless creativity and imagination run wild while writing lean and clean code.

So welcome aboard. I trust that you will find this book fun and engaging as you embark on the journey that is the joy of JavaScript!

Summary

- JavaScript has two important features that differentiate it from other languages: a prototype-based object model and higher-order functions. You can combine these features in systematic ways to craft powerful, elegant code.
- TC39, ECMAScript's standards body, has committed to releasing new features to JavaScript every year. Now we have a community-driven process to evolve JavaScript following the ECMA standard as well as to fix any shortcomings quickly. In this book. you'll learn how to use the bind and pipeline operators, code with observables, and use many other new features, all originating from this process.
- JavaScript's dynamic object model makes it easy to use mixin composition over prototype inheritance by taking advantage of dynamic object extension.
- Abstractions should make code more specific or refined by stripping ideas down to their fundamental concepts. ADTs refine code branching, error handling, null checking, and other programming tasks.
- FP uses techniques such as function composition to make your code leaner and more declarative.
- JavaScript is one of the few languages that has had first-class support for asynchronous programming since the beginning. It was revamped with the advent of `async`/`await`, which completely abstracts the asynchronous nature of the code.
- Observables use the streams programming model to provide a consistent pane of glass over any type of data source—synchronous, asynchronous, single-value, or infinite.

Part 1

Objects

The journey to discovering what makes JavaScript a joy to code with starts with its object system. Objects are the foundation for everything you do and everything you will be able to do with the language. Object design is used to make sense of your domain and how all its pieces relate and pass messages to one another. As powerful as the object system is, however, it can be quite stressful to figure out which patterns to use—a task that everyone seems to do slightly differently. We can catalog patterns based on two groups: prototypal and delegation. This part gives you an overview of each pattern and its strengths.

In chapter 2, we start by reviewing JavaScript's prototype mechanism. Anything meaningful you do with JavaScript requires you to understand how prototype hierarchies work and how properties are resolved by the JavaScript runtime. Prototypal inheritance enables some nice object-oriented techniques to construct objects by using `Object` APIs, constructor functions, and classes.

Prototypal inheritance may lead to a tight coupling among objects that belong to the same hierarchy, which tends to become brittle over time. Chapter 3 teaches you some techniques to combat this situation. These techniques are compositional in nature, clearly demarcating object links to make your object models a bit more maintainable. In this chapter, you'll learn about techniques such as OLOO (Objects Linked to Other Objects) and mixins.

For teaching purposes, in this part we'll use a combination of these techniques to build the skeleton of our blockchain domain model.

Inheritance-based object modeling

This chapter covers

- Prototypal inheritance, constructor functions, and classes
- JavaScript's property resolution mechanism
- The "prototypal inheritance" oxymoron
- Advantages and drawbacks of classes in JavaScript

Merely adding "prototypal" in front to distinguish the actually nearly opposite behavior in JavaScript has left in its wake nearly two decades of miry confusion.

—Kyle Simpson

Aside from a few primitives, everything in JavaScript is an object. Yet for something that we deal with routinely, objects continue to be the most intimidating, hard-to-get-right parts of the language. The most common question that I hear is "How should I write the prototype chain to relate X, Y, and Z?" Every article or book you read does it in slightly different ways, and for some reason, even experienced developers need to turn to a search engine to relearn the process once in a while. The reason is twofold: on one side, a lot of boilerplate code is required, and on the other, we're confusing the terms *inheritance* and *prototype*.

Inheritance is a powerful pattern of code reuse and is something we'll take advantage of in this book, but we should not limit our understanding of prototypes to creating parent-child relationships. Inheritance is only one of the many applications of prototypes (and an important one indeed), but prototypes can do much more. Because one of the largest segments of JavaScript developers comes from class-oriented languages, to ensure their seamless transition, it was decided to make classes a first-class citizen of the language in ECMAScript 2015. Support for classes snowballed into a bunch of new features to support private and static properties. Once again, JavaScript's history is tainted with attempts to make it look like Java. All this syntax is not welcomed with open arms by many JavaScript purists because it masks the underlying mechanics of JavaScript's great object system.

For better or for worse, a lot of the domain modeling has been moving to use the streamlined setup of classes instead of the unnecessary boilerplate code of direct prototype configuration. It's important to have a firm understanding of how JavaScript's object system works, however. In this chapter, we'll discuss two patterns that use the prototype feature to model inheritance relationships: constructor functions and ECMAScript 2015 classes. Both these patterns give you the benefit of sharing data and behavior through JavaScript's internal prototype references and property resolution mechanism.

Let's begin by reviewing the basic prototype inheritance configuration that you've probably seen many times.

2.1 *Reviewing prototypal inheritance*

JavaScript borrowed prototypes from a language called Self. The prototype mechanism is a big part of what allows JavaScript to be object-oriented; without it, you would not be able to send messages to objects higher up in the hierarchy of a complex network of interconnected objects (aka inheritance).

In this section, we'll review the code needed to set up a basic prototype chain and lay the groundwork for learning about JavaScript's property resolution mechanism, which is JavaScript's central mechanism for object access.

Given your experience, you've probably dabbled with objects and their prototypes, so I'll jump straight into some code. The first API we'll look at to establish what looks like a parent-to-child relationship is

```
Object.create(proto[,propertiesObject]);
```

This API creates a new object linked to a prototype and optionally accompanied by a collection of new property definitions. For now, we'll focus only on the first argument (`proto`), as shown in the following listing.

> **Listing 2.1 Using `Object.create` to create an object from a prototype**

```
const proto = {
    sender: 'luis@tjoj.com',
};
```

```
const child = Object.create(proto);      ◁─┐   Using Object.create to configure a new child object
child.recipient = 'luke@tjoj.com';             based on a parent object (proto). Internally, the
                                               child object has a reference to the parent to access
child.sender;      // 'luis@tjoj.com'          any of its properties. Another way to do this is to
child.recipient;   // 'luke@tjoj.com'          call the Object.setPrototypeOf(child, proto) API.
```

With this code, any properties of the parent (proto) object, hereafter called the
prototype, are accessible from the child object. Nothing interesting is going on
here, let's do something more meaningful and model our first blockchain concept,
a transaction.

A transaction represents an exchange of certain goods, such as money, from a
sender to a receiver. For the most part, a transaction in the blockchain world looks
exactly like that of a traditional banking system. To start, we'll make sender and
recipient simple email addresses and funds a number of fake Bitcoin amount as our
form of currency. In our example, Luke uses Bitcoin from his digital wallet to buy coffee from Ana's Café, as shown in figure 2.1.

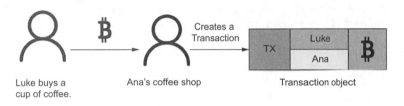

**Figure 2.1   A transaction object captures the details of a sender (Luke)
sending Bitcoin to a receiver (Ana) to purchase coffee.**

Let's begin constructing this example. Listing 2.2 uses Object.create to establish a
prototype configuration between two objects, moneyTransaction and transaction,
and adds support for funds. In the wild, you'll find some slight variations of this setup,
but the general idea is always the same.

Listing 2.2   Transaction objects linked by a basic prototype setup

```
const transaction = {              ◁─┐   Prototype object from which
   sender: 'luis@tjoj.com',              to derive other objects—a
   recipient: 'luke@tjoj.com'            regular object, not some
};                                       abstract blueprint
                                                                    Creates a derived
                                                                    object from the
const moneyTransaction = Object.create(transaction);      ◁─       prototype
moneyTransaction.funds = 0.0;
moneyTransaction.addFunds = function addFunds(funds = 0) {   ◁─┐
   this.funds += Number(funds);
}                                           Adds new methods to the child
                                            object. Repeating the function name
                                            in the declaration helps build more-
moneyTransaction.addFunds(10.0);            informative stack traces.
moneyTransaction.funds; // 10.0
```

Let's check whether our assumptions continue to be valid in the next listing.

Listing 2.3   Inspecting the new transaction objects

```
Object.getPrototypeOf(moneyTransaction) === transaction; // true
moneyTransaction.sender;  // 'luis@tjoj.com'
moneyTransaction.funds;   // 10
```

Verifies that inherited properties are accessible from the child object

Checks whether the prototype link has been established

Let's unpack listing 2.2 a bit further. The prototype object (`transaction`) is in fact an arbitrary object literal that we'll use to group common properties. As you can see, prototypes are objects that can be manipulated at any time, even at runtime, not created from thin air at the point of forming an inheritance association. This fact is important to understand; we'll come back to why it matters when we talk about classes in section 2.3.

Here's another take on this code, using `Object.create`'s second parameter, which receives an object of data descriptors:

```
const moneyTransaction = Object.create(transaction, {
  funds: {
    value: 0.0,
    enumerable: true,
    writable: true,
    configurable: false
  }
});
```

This second argument gives us fine control over how this newly created object's properties behave:

- *Enumerable*—Controls whether the property can be enumerated or viewed (as when you pass the object to `console.log`, enumerating the keys with `Object.keys`), or whether it's seen by `Object.assign` (a topic that we'll circle back to in chapter 3).
- *Configurable*—Controls whether you're allowed to delete an object's property with the `delete` keyword or whether you can reconfigure the field's property descriptor. Deleting a property alters the shape of an object and makes your code more unpredictable, which is why I prefer to use this attribute's default value (`false`) or omit it from the data descriptor.
- *Writable*—Controls whether you can reassign the value of this field, effectively making its assignment immutable.

When you create a property by using the dot notation directly on the object, as in listing 2.2, that act is equivalent to defining a property with a descriptor with all settings set to `true`. Typically, most developers don't bother with data descriptors, but they can come in handy when you're writing your own libraries and frameworks for others to use and want to do things such as hide a certain field from view or make some fields immutable. Data descriptors help enforce certain design principles and communicate clear intentions about how your APIs work. We'll come back to this issue of immutability and why it's important in chapter 4.

As you can see, `Object.create` offers a simple, elegant way to create objects from a shared prototype and establishes the proper inheritance linkage to resolve property lookups.

2.1.1 Property resolution process

A discussion of JavaScript's prototype mechanism is moot without a discussion of its property lookup mechanism, which is the most important concept behind implementing object-oriented patterns in JavaScript. According to the ECMAScript specification, an internal reference known as [[Prototype]] (accessible via the __proto__ property in objects) is configured by `Object.create` and effectively links `moneyTransaction` to `transaction`, as shown in figure 2.2. This is the sole reason why we can properly resolve `moneyTransaction.sender` to the value `'luis@tjoj.com'`, as shown in figure 2.2.

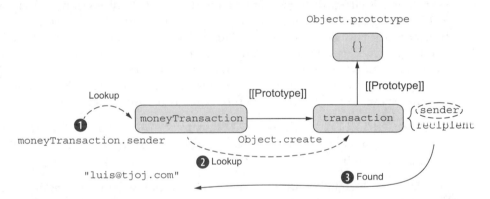

Figure 2.2 The internal reference [[Prototype]] is used to link an object (`moneyTransaction`) to another (`transaction`) in a unidirectional fashion, eventually ending in `Object.prototype`.

This figure points out the relationship among the objects through the prototype chain, which guides the JavaScript engine to find a property by a certain key. I'll explain this process in more detail. When requesting a member field, the JavaScript engine first looks for the property in the calling object. If JavaScript can't find the property there, it looks in [[Prototype]]. The property `sender` is not declared in `money-Transaction`, yet it still resolves successfully. Why? Any property access or method invocation in `moneyTransaction` will travel up the prototype chain, continuing to `transaction` until it finds the property there and returns it. But what if it doesn't? The lookup process would continue further, finally terminating at the empty object literal `{}` (aka `Object.prototype`). If resolution fails, the result of the operation is `undefined` for a value property or a `TypeError` for a function-valued property.

Behind the scenes, you can think of the hidden __proto__ property as being the bridge that allows you to traverse the chain. When we use prototypes to implement inheritance, which is the most common scenario, we say that property resolution "moves up" the inheritance chain.

You should never use __proto__ directly in your applications, as it's meant to be used internally by the JavaScript engine. Hypothetically, if surfaced in userland code, it would look something like this:

```
const moneyTransaction = {
  __proto__: transaction,
  funds: 0.0,
  addFunds: function addFunds(funds = 0) {
    this.funds += Number(funds);
    return this;
  }
}
```

> **NOTE** The use of __proto__ has been the subject of a heated debate over the years, and it's currently being deprecated. It was standardized in ECMAScript 2015 as a legacy feature only so that web browsers and other JavaScript runtimes could maintain compatibility. Please don't use it directly (even though you might see it used in the book for teaching purposes), as it might cease to work after some time. If you need to manipulate this field, the recommended APIs are Object.getPrototypeOf and Object.setPrototypeOf. You can also call the Object#isPrototypeOf method directly on the object.
>
> With regard to notation, when referring to a property accessible from a constructor function's prototype, as in Object.prototype.isPrototypeOf, throughout this book the # symbol is used instead: Object#isPrototypeOf.

Figure 2.2 looks straightforward but can get tricky with long, intertwined object graphs. I won't delve into those specific use cases to keep the discussion centered on object construction techniques, but you can find out more by exploring the great resources in the following sidebar.

Understanding the idiosyncrasies of JavaScript objects

In this book, we'll be using well-formed, simple object hierarchies, so we won't go into detail about what things can go wrong when prototype chains are broken or when properties in an object are shadowed. The ins and out of JavaScript objects could easily take up an entire book. In fact, an amazing book series by Kyle Simpson, *You Don't Know JS* (https://github.com/getify/You-Dont-Know-JS/tree/1st-ed), describes this example in great detail. The series dives deeply into the nuances of manipulating object chains, offers lots of good tips and best practices for behavior delegation (which we'll study in chapter 3), and debunks the myths behind object creation and the prototype mechanism. This series has been a great inspiration and has highly influenced the way I code JavaScript today. It should be on every JavaScript developer's bookshelf.

Now that we've reviewed the basic prototype setup in JavaScript, let's discuss why it's fundamentally inaccurate to use the overloaded term *inheritance* to describe JavaScript's object-oriented model.

2.1.2 Differential inheritance

Differential inheritance, in which derived objects maintain references to the objects from which they are derived, is common in prototypal languages. In JavaScript, differential inheritance is called [[Prototype]]. By contrast, in class-based inheritance, a derived object copies all the state and behavior from its own class, as well as all its derived classes. The key distinction is copy versus link.

Although this term sounds a bit intimidating, *differential inheritance* is a simple concept referring to how extended behavior separates a derived object from its linked generic parent. If you think about a JavaScript object as being a dynamic bag of properties, differentiation means adding properties to another bag and linking the two bags. As you saw in figure 2.2, because the prototype resolution mechanism flows unidirectionally from a calling object to its linked object (and so on), any newly derived object is meant to differentiate itself from its parent with new behavior. New behavior includes adding new properties or even overriding an existing property from a linked object (known as shadowing). I don't cover shadowing in this book, but you can visit http://mng.bz/OEmR for more information.

Consider another scenario in which we extend the generic `transaction` object to define `hashTransaction`. This object differentiates itself from its parent by adding a function (`calculateHash`) to compute its own hash value. At a high level, hashing is using an object's state to generate a unique string value, much as `JSON.stringify` does, but we need to target only the values, not the entire shape of the object. This hash value has many uses in industry, such as fast insert/retrieval from hash tables or dictionaries, as well as data integrity checks.

In the world of blockchains, a hash is typically used as a `transactionId` that uniquely identifies a certain transaction that took place. For simplicity, we'll start with a simple (insecure) hashing function in the next listing.

Listing 2.4 Creating `hashTransaction` with basic hashing calculation

```
const hashTransaction = Object.create(transaction);        Adds a method
                                                           to calculate its
hashTransaction.calculateHash = function calculateHash() {  own hash
   const data = [this.sender, this.recipient].join('');     Properties that
   let hash = 0, i = 0;                                      become input
   while (i < data.length) {                                 to the hashing
     hash = ((hash << 5) - hash + data.charCodeAt(i++)) << 0; algorithm
   }
   return hash**2;        Uses the exponentiation operator
}                         to square the hash value

hashTransaction.calculateHash(); // 237572532174000400
```

To take another approach, you can also use `Object.setPrototypeOf` to differentiate a child object. Suppose that you want to extend `moneyTransaction` from `hashTransaction`. All the same mechanisms apply:

```
const moneyTransaction = Object.setPrototypeOf({}, hashTransaction);
moneyTransaction.funds = 0.0;
moneyTransaction.addFunds = function addFunds(funds = 0) {
   this.funds += Number(funds);
};
moneyTransaction.addFunds(10);
moneyTransaction.calculateHash(); // 237572532174000400
moneyTransaction.funds;      // 10
moneyTransaction.sender;     // 'luis@tjoj.com'
moneyTransaction.recipient; // 'luke@tjoj.com'
```

Now that we've reviewed a couple of examples involving simple object literals, it's much more useful to create new transactions with different data in them. Section 2.2 jumps into using constructor functions.

2.2 Constructor functions

The constructor functions (aka object constructors pattern) have been the modus operandi for building objects in JavaScript for many years. Although object literals offer a terse way to define a single object, this method doesn't scale when you need to create hundreds of objects of the same shape. In this case, the constructor function acts as a template to initialize objects populated with different data. You're probably familiar with this pattern, but this section discusses some advanced techniques that you may not have encountered before.

2.2.1 Functions as templates

Using functions instead of straight object literals to build objects allows your model to better evolve because you have much more control of how the objects are built. Functions allow you to export a facade to the caller under which changes don't necessarily need to propagate to the calling code. The details of how an object gets initialized, such as enforcing any preconditions, are properly tucked away inside the constructor.

The following code snippet, for example, never reveals unnecessary details about the shape of `HashTransaction` or any operations that might take place during instantiation. Encapsulation is always a good choice:

```
const tx = new HashTransaction('luis@tjoj.com', 'luke@tjoj.com');
```

This fundamental design decision makes your code less fragile and more maintainable, so in most cases, using functions to build objects is the preferred approach.

By convention, a constructor function name is capitalized to denote a kind of poor man's class, if you will. Let's take the use case from listing 2.4 and refactor it using constructors (listing 2.5). We have several options here. The simplest way to have an object inherit properties from another is to add all its properties to this new object;

there's no need to rely on the prototype chain. Because your objects are created dynamically (when the function is invoked), you need to pack these properties (fill the bag) into a single object context (this) within each constructor invocation.

Listing 2.5   Building and linking objects using the constructor functions pattern

Base constructor →

```
function Transaction(sender, recipient) {
    this.sender = sender;
    this.recipient = recipient;
}

function HashTransaction(sender, recipient) {
    if (!new.target) {
        return new HashTransaction(sender, recipient);
    }
    Transaction.call(this, sender, recipient);

    this.calculateHash = function calculateHash() {
        //...
    }
}

const tx = new HashTransaction('luis@tjoj.com', 'luke@tjoj.com');
tx.calculateHash();   // 237572532174000400
tx.sender;            // 'luis@tjoj.com'
```

> **Detects whether the instantiation of the child object omits the new keyword and fixes the call. This line helps developers who forget to write new. I'll come back to this topic in section 2.2.2.**

> **Calls the parent's constructor to initialize any parent member properties into this object's context**

> **Adds a new calculateHash method to every instance created**

> **Uses the new keyword to instantiate new objects. The new keyword is required to pass the newly created object as the this context.**

By using functions, you can easily instantiate as many HashTransaction objects as you like, all of them containing the properties defined in Transaction as well. One caveat is that you need to call the function with the new keyword to ensure the context (this) is initialized properly.

These objects do not share references to any properties, however. You defined calculateHash directly on HashTransaction's context (this variable), for example, adding a new calculateHash property to each instance of HashTransaction. In other words, if you create two instances, you'll see two copies of the same method:

```
const tx1 = new HashTransaction('luis@tjoj.com', 'luke@tjoj.com');
const tx2 = new HashTransaction('luis@tjoj.com', 'luke@tjoj.com');

tx1.calculateHash === tx2.calculateHash; // false
```

To fix this problem, you need to configure how prototypes links are set up as new objects are created.

2.2.2   *Sharing properties by using constructors and prototypes*

One interesting aspect of using constructors is that for every constructor F, JavaScript automatically creates the object F.prototype:

```
HashTransaction.prototype; // HashTransaction {}
```

This object is added to facilitate code sharing and reuse, especially with methods, where it's unnecessary to define more than one copy. Hence, a more optimal approach is to add `calculateHash` to `HashTransaction`'s `prototype` so that it's shared among all `HashTransaction` instances, for example:

```
HashTransaction.prototype.calculateHash = function calculateHash() {
    //...
}
```

With this slight twist, these two properties refer to the same memory location:

```
tx1.calculateHash === tx2.calculateHash; // true
```

The same applies to any methods added to `Transaction.prototype`. Suppose that you add a new method called `displayTransaction` that you want all objects to share:

```
Transaction.prototype.displayTransaction = function displayTransaction() {
    return `Transaction from ${this.sender} to ${this.recipient}`;
}
```

As the code is set up, calling it would yield a `TypeError`, indicating that the JavaScript engine tried to resolve that property but couldn't:

```
TypeError: tx.displayTransaction is not a function
```

This error is expected because you had not configured the prototype chain:

```
Transaction.prototype.isPrototypeOf(tx); // false
```

You can fix this problem easily. As before, you can use `Object.create`. The following listing shows the complete prototype configuration.

Listing 2.6   Configuring the prototype chain using the constructor functions pattern

```
function Transaction(sender, recipient) {
    this.sender = sender;
    this.recipient = recipient;
}
Transaction.prototype.displayTransaction = function displayTransaction() {
    return `Transaction from ${this.sender} to ${this.recipient}`;
}


function HashTransaction(sender, recipient) {
    if (!new.target) {
        return new HashTransaction(sender, recipient);
    }
    Transaction.call(this, sender, recipient);
}


HashTransaction.prototype.calculateHash = function calculateHash() {
    const data = [this.sender, this.recipient].join('');
```

```
      let hash = 0, i = 0;
      while (i < data.length) {
        hash = ((hash << 5) - hash + data.charCodeAt(i++)) << 0;
      }
      return hash**2;
}
```

> Links prototypes for the lookup mechanism to work in case you need to resolve properties from Transaction.prototype

```
HashTransaction.prototype = Object.create(Transaction.prototype);
HashTransaction.prototype.constructor = HashTransaction;
```

> Fixes or sets the constructor value. Without this line, tx would be a Transaction object or constructed from Transaction.

```
const tx = new HashTransaction('luis@tjoj.com', 'luke@tjoj.com');
const tx2 = new HashTransaction('luis@tjoj.com', 'luke@tjoj.com');

Transaction.prototype.isPrototypeOf(tx); // true

tx.calculateHash === tx2.calculateHash;  // true
tx.displayTransaction === tx2.displayTransaction; // true

tx.__proto__.__proto__;
// Transaction { displayTransaction: [Function: displayTransaction] }
```

From the caller's point of view, whether you pack all the properties into a single object or use prototype resolution, both pieces of code behave and are called in exactly the same way. Internally, the object layout in memory is different, but it's abstracted away by the powerful and efficient JavaScript engine. Figure 2.3 illustrates the inner workings of listing 2.6.

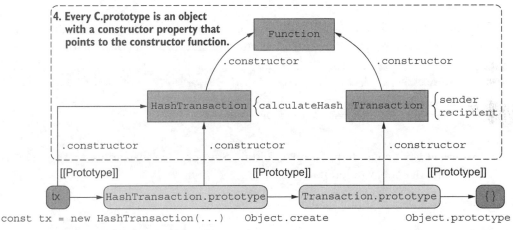

Figure 2.3 The instantiation of `tx` per listing 2.6, together with a complete picture of all prototype links and constructor references. In JavaScript, constructor functions automatically obtain a reference to the `prototype` property upon instantiation with the `new` keyword. The navigation annotated with [[Prototype]] represents the internal `__proto__` link between objects.

Although constructor functions are a bit more sophisticated and powerful than traditional object literals, the drawback of using this pattern is that it leaks a lot of the internal plumbing of JavaScript's prototype mechanism, as you need to deal with the nittygritty details of the prototype configuration. If you don't write everything perfectly, you run the risk of strange and unexpected behavior.

> ### Difference between __proto__ and prototype
>
> Reading the sample code, you have encountered references to two properties: __proto__ and prototype. As I said earlier, __proto__ is discouraged, but prototype isn't. In case you're wondering what the difference is, __proto__ is the object used in the lookup chain to resolve methods, whereas prototype is the object used to build __proto__ when you create an object with new.

As mentioned earlier, always remember to call the constructor with new. Many developers forget. Again, using the new keyword with a function implicitly sets what this points to in newly created objects. This task has been a nuisance because forgetting to write it changes the resulting object's context, so we needed to include the defensive bit of code I highlighted earlier:

```
if (!new.target) {
    return new HashTransaction(sender, recipient);
}
```

Old-timers probably remember that the workaround (pre-ECMAScript 2015) was to insert the control in the following listing into the body of each constructor.

Listing 2.7   Pre-ECMAScript 2015 way to check for proper constructor call

```
if (!(this instanceof HashTransaction)) {
    return new HashTransaction(sender, recipient);
}
```

Let's look at what could happen if you didn't. Suppose that instead of writing the preceding control code, you left it as

```
function HashTransaction(sender, recipient) {
    Transaction.call(this, sender, recipient);
}
```

Then you tried to create a new instance:

```
const instance = HashTransaction('luis@tjoj.com', 'luke@tjoj.com');
```

Oops! This code throws a TypeError because the implicit this context is undefined. The error message is alluding to setting a member property of undefined, but not to the actual user error:

```
TypeError: Cannot set property 'sender' of undefined
```

Here, the developer forgot to write new in front of the function call:

```
const instance = new HashTransaction('luis@tjoj.com', 'luke@tjoj.com');
```

Now let's look at a different, more subtle trap. Suppose that we want transactions to have a descriptive name too:

```
function HashTransaction(name, sender, recipient) {
    Transaction.call(this, sender, recipient);
    this.name = name;
}

HashTransaction.prototype = Object.create(Transaction);
```

Now create a new instance:

```
  const instance = new HashTransaction(
    'Coffee purchase',
    'luis@tjoj.com',
    'luke@tjoj.com'
  );
```

Boom! Another type error occurs. This time, the error is even more cryptic and doesn't happen in all JavaScript engines:

```
  TypeError: Cannot assign to read only property 'name' of object
  '[object Object]'
```

Can you find the issue? Don't worry; I'll spare you from wasting your time. The issue is forgetting to link prototypes correctly. The code should have read

```
HashTransaction.prototype = Object.create(Transaction.prototype);
```

Again, writing this code manually every time is painful, leading to different behavior that easily escapes you or any linting tool you use.

Reducing boilerplate

Using the Node.js util library, you can cut down a bit on boilerplate code so that you can avoid making some mistakes. Instead of explicitly writing the prototype augmentation statement

```
HashTransaction.prototype = Object.create(Transaction.prototype);
```

you can use util.inherits to accomplish the same task, saving you from making the same mistake again:

```
require('util').inherits(HashTransaction, Transaction);
```

> **(continued)**
>
> If you read the documentation, however, you'll find that the Node.js community dis-courages this practice in favor of using `class` and `extends`, indicating that calling `inherits` with prototypes is "semantically incompatible." You don't say! Earlier, I briefly alluded to the fact that prototypes and classes are incompatible. Section 2.3 evaluates this topic in detail.

This idea of using a constructor function with `new` to create new instances is what we know today as the pseudoclassical model. With the advent of ECMAScript 2015, this model has been largely replaced by a more familiar, streamlined class-oriented model that also addresses the amount of boilerplate needed. In fact, with classes, forgetting to write `new` when invoking a constructor now generates a clear error, as in this example for a `Transaction` class:

```
const tx = Transaction(...);

TypeError: Class constructor Transaction cannot be invoked without 'new'
```

Section 2.3 explores the advantages of classes, as well as some of the newer proposals that accompany them.

2.3   *Class-based inheritance*

In this section, we'll pick up the discussion of the classes and prototypes dichotomy. Next, we'll look at how the mental model of classes makes it simpler to represent inheritance hierarchies, as well as provide the syntactical advantage of cleaning up and smoothing the rough edges over the complex boilerplate code of constructor functions.

We've been trained to think that the only form of object orientation is through classes, and that's not the case. Class-oriented does not equate to object-oriented, and JavaScript was an object-oriented language long before classes.

Classes were introduced to solve a specific problem, which is to make domain modeling in terms of inheritance easier, especially for developers coming from class-oriented languages such as Java, C#, and TypeScript. All the cruft and boilerplate code of prototype references had to be removed. Ideally, TC39 should have done this in a way that remained compatible with JavaScript's origins, but the community clamored for the familiar class-like design.

In a language such as Java, a class is the basic unit of computation. Every object derives from some class, which provides the template that gets filled with data and allocated in memory during the process of instantiation. During this time, all of a class's member properties, together with any inherited properties, get copied into a new object and populated at construction time.

As you learned in section 2.2. however, prototypes in JavaScript work differently. Prototypes are well-formed, concrete objects that get created at the same time they are declared (object literal) or as a byproduct of calling a function (constructor function), not through a separate instantiation process involving some inanimate blueprint or template. In fact, you can use a prototype object as you would any other before it's even added to any inheritance chain.

Remember that the key factor that separates JavaScript from a language such as Java is that JavaScript links to instead of copies from objects higher up in the chain. In chapter 3, we'll discuss patterns that rely heavily on linking and delegation.

In terms of classes, inheritance is configured with keywords `class` and extends. Although inheritance looks dramatically different from direct prototype references, it's syntactic sugar over constructor functions (pseudoclassical model) that accomplishes the same thing. As an example, de-sugaring a class like

```
class Transaction {
  constructor(sender, recipient, funds = 0.0) {
    this.sender = sender;
    this.recipient = recipient;
    this.funds = Number(funds);
  }
  displayTransaction() {
    return `Transaction from ${this.sender} to ${this.recipient}
        for ${this.funds}`;
  }
}
```

is analogous to

```
function Transaction(sender, recipient, funds = 0.0) {
    this.sender = sender;
    this.recipient = recipient;
    this.funds = Number(funds);
}

Transaction.prototype.displayTransaction = function displayTransaction() {
    return `Transaction from ${this.sender} to ${this.recipient}
        for ${this.funds}`;
}
```

Another enormous difference from class-based languages is that JavaScript objects can access parent properties declared even after the child object was instantiated. Inherited properties from some base object are shared across all instances of child objects, so any changes to it dynamically ripple to all instances as well, which might lead to undesired, hard-to-trace behavior. This powerful, yet dangerous, mechanism leads to a well-known issue called prototype pollution. Encapsulation certainly helps, which is why exporting functions to build your objects as discussed in section 2.2.1 is much better than exporting the actual objects literals themselves. By the same token, exporting classes has the same benefits.

Let's look at the pros and cons of classes more concretely. To do so, we'll refactor Transaction yet again, this time using classes, and add a bit more code toward the real-life implementation that we'll need for the rest of the book. As listing 2.8 shows, funds is now a property of Transaction, and we've added support for computing transaction fees, which is a common banking task.

To illustrate the ease with which classes allow you to set up the prototype chain, let's refactor Transaction and HashTransaction. I'll also take the opportunity to showcase new syntax proposals related to private class fields (http://mng.bz/YqVB) and static fields (http://mng.bz/5jgB) that you may not be familiar with.

Listing 2.8   Transaction and HashTransaction objects defined using classes

```
class Transaction {
    sender = '';
    recipient = '';
    funds = 0.0;
    #feePercent = 0.6;

    constructor(sender, recipient, funds = 0.0) {
        this.sender = sender;
        this.recipient = recipient;
        this.funds = Number(funds);
    }

    displayTransaction() {
        return `Transaction from ${this.sender} to ${this.recipient}
          for ${this.funds}`;
    }

    get netTotal() {
        return  Transaction.#precisionRound(this.funds * this.#feePercent, 2);
    }

    static #precisionRound(number, precision) {
        const factor = Math.pow(10, precision);
        return Math.round(number * factor) / factor;
    }
}

class HashTransaction extends Transaction {
    transactionId;
    constructor(sender, recipient, funds = 0.0) {
        super(sender, recipient, funds);
        this.transactionId = this.calculateHash();
    }
    calculateHash() {
        const data = [
            this.sender,
            this.recipient,
            this.funds
          ].join('');
        let hash = 0, i = 0;
        while (i < data.length) {
            hash = ((hash << 5) - hash + data.charCodeAt(i++)) << 0;
```

Declares public fields for this class with default values. I recommend using default values, because they help code editors perform rudimentary type hinting for you.

Uses the static private field and method declarations

The prototype setup is cleanly tucked away behind the use of class and extends.

Uses the keyword super to invoke the parent constructor. When you override a constructor, you must remember to invoke the super constructor with the required arguments as the first line.

```
        }
        return hash**2;
    }

    displayTransaction() {
        return `${this.transactionId}: ${super.displayTransaction()}`;
    }
  }

const tx = new HashTransaction('luis@tjoj.com', 'luke@tjoj.com', 10);
tx.displayTransaction();

// Prints:
// 64284210552842720: Transaction from luis@tjoj.com to luke@tjoj.com for 10
```

At a glance, the refactoring done in listing 2.8 looks clean, terse, and elegant. I took the liberty of embellishing the code a little by adding private access to variables that need to be encapsulated, as well as a couple of private static functions for validation. As you know, these functions are shared by all instances, giving us true private access control. So querying for a private field from outside the class throws a `SyntaxError`:

```
tx.#feePercent; // SyntaxError
```

It's worth pointing out the use of private fields and the private methods feature, prefixed with the hash (#) modifier. This feature was much needed to get proper encapsulation with classes, something you could have done by using modules and closures with the Module pattern, shown in listing 2.9 for comparison. (I'll revisit this pattern in chapter 6.) By the same token, private fields and privileged methods are emulated by taking advantage of the closure or lexical scope that exists within the class—a function behind the scenes.

Listing 2.9   Transaction object implemented using the Module pattern

```
const Transaction = (function() {
                                          Private variables and/or
    const feePercent = 0.6;          ◁──┤ privileged functions

    function precisionRound(number, precision) {
        const factor = Math.pow(10, precision);
        return Math.round(number * factor) / factor;
    }
                                        Public variables
    return {                        ◁──┤ and/or functions
        construct: function(sender, recipient, funds = 0.0) {
            this.sender = sender;
            this.recipient = recipient;
            this.funds = Number(funds);
            return this;
        },
```

```
        netTotal: function() {
            return precisionRound(this.funds * feePercent, 2);
        }
    }
})();
```

```
const coffee = Transaction.construct('luke@tjoj.com', 'ana@tjoj.com', 2.5);
coffee.netTotal(); // 1.5
```

With classes, the private state is visible only to methods in the scope of the class itself—also known as privileged. Also, static methods such as `static #precisionRound` won't unnecessarily leak out to outside users—something that is cumbersome to achieve with regular constructor functions or even the Module pattern.

Taking a look back at listing 2.8, do you see a reference to the `prototype` property anywhere in this snippet of code? Nope! Classes have a well-defined structure, which makes them great at abstracting the mundane prototype details away from you and, hence, are less error-prone. Also, they offer a syntactical advantage for grouping data and behavior in a cohesive manner. Furthermore, `class` and `extends` literally put the icing on the cake for us and make third-party libraries such as Prototype's extend, Lodash's `_.extend`, or even Node's `util.inherits` obsolete. Figure 2.4 illustrates this new, simplified mental model.

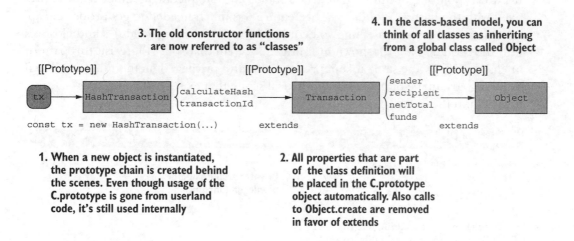

Figure 2.4   Building the `HashTransaction` class and its ancestor `Transaction`. Instances of `HashTransaction` will inherit all the public fields present in the parent. Using `class` and `extends` properly sets up the prototype chain so that property lookup is done effectively and constructor references line up perfectly.

This figure is somewhat similar to figure 2.3 but severely cuts the number of artifacts to achieve the same prototype configuration. The basic resemblance is deliberate because classes work like functions in JavaScript behind the scenes. The most obvious difference from figure 2.3, however, is that all of a class's properties (fields and methods) are automatically part of the object's prototype, accessible via the internal __proto__ object. You don't have the option that you did with constructor functions. You lost that flexibility in favor of more structure.

Creating a new instance looks like the previous pseudoclassical approach (hence its name), with no changes:

```
const tx = new HashTransaction(
    'luis@tjoj.com',
    'luke@tjoj.com',
    10
);
tx.transactionId; // 197994095955825630
```

On the surface, this code looks clean and compact. Classes are simpler to work with than constructor functions, without a doubt. But it's important to realize that you're adding a familiar façade over prototypes only to be able to think of inheritance as done in a class-oriented language.

This chapter covered two object construction patterns: constructor functions and classes. Both are inheritance-centric in that one way or another, you need to explicitly configure how child objects (or classes) relate to parent objects (or classes). Chapter 3 takes a different approach, presenting patterns that shift the mental model from inheritance to behavior delegation and linking.

Summary

- JavaScript offers many choices for building objects, including prototypal inheritance, constructor functions, and classes.

- The phrase *prototype inheritance* is an oxymoron because the idea of a shared linked prototype object is contradictory to the class inheritance model, in which instances gain copies of the inherited data.

- Constructor functions have been the standard mechanisms used to mimic the idea of classes in JavaScript.

- Classes smooth over the details of the prototype configuration for newcomers or developers coming from other class-based languages and have become the preferred choice of JavaScript developers.

- The class syntax can blur your understanding of JavaScript's prototype inheritance mechanism. Classes are useful, but remember that JavaScript is different from other class-based languages you may have seen or used.

Linked, compositional object models

3

This chapter covers

- Understanding the Objects Linked to Other Objects (OLOO) pattern of behavior delegation with linked objects
- Combining classes with mixins for concatenative dynamic extension
- Using `Object.assign` and the spread operator to build new objects

Class inheritance is very rarely (perhaps never) the best approach in JavaScript.

—Eric Elliot

In chapter 2, we looked at some of the scaffolding needed to create prototype chains to model inheritance and how classes streamline this process. Remember that the goal of using inheritance is to improve reusability. Now we'll continue the topic of assembling your objects to achieve the same level of code reuse, but in a way that doesn't require you to think in terms of inheritance.

The first technique, discovered by Kyle Simpson, is called Objects Linked to Other Objects (OLOO) and relies on `Object.create` to create associations among the objects that constitute your domain model. This technique has the simplicity of classes of stripping away the complicated prototype jargon while setting up the

42

prototype chain properly. This pattern is interesting because it allows you to look at your domain model as a collection of peer objects that delegate to one another to carry out their work.

The second approach is based on composing objects that capture a small set of behavior known as *mixins* to create a much richer model, as you can see on full display in the works of Eric Elliot, Douglas Crockford, and other JavaScript experts. In this case, instead of acquiring properties from a long prototype chain, mixins allow you to integrate various independent pieces of behavior and/or data into a single object. A good example of this technique outside JavaScript is a CSS preprocessor such as Sass. You can use @mixins to group repetitive stylesheet information and apply it to many rule sets. In many cases, this technique is preferred to @extends.

In this chapter, we'll be talking about links between objects as being explicit (set directly in code) or implicit (wired via JavaScript's runtime). These types of links are important to understand before jumping into the patterns mentioned in this section.

3.1 Types of object links

In JavaScript, you can associate objects in two ways: implicitly and explicitly. Both types of association allow one object to send messages to another (aka delegation), but they behave a bit differently. Figure 3.1 illustrates the difference.

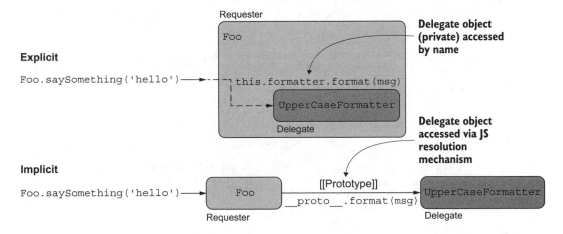

Figure 3.1 Explicit delegation occurs through a property known directly by name. Implicit delegation occurs through JavaScript's prototype lookup process, chained by the internal __proto__ property.

Let's start with implicit (implied) links.

3.1.1 Implicit

An *implicit* link is known only internally—in other words, is not visible in the code. In JavaScript, links to objects that delegate behavior by using the [[Prototype]] internal reference can be considered implicit because the runtime uses it to send messages to other objects (up the chain, in the case of inheritance) on your behalf as part of property resolution, as shown in the next listing.

> **Listing 3.1   Implicit reference between `Foo` and `UpperCaseFormatter`**

```
const Foo = Object.create(UpperCaseFormatter);
Foo.saySomething = function saySomething(msg) {          format is resolved through
  console.log(this.format(msg));                          the prototype chain.
}
Foo.saySomething('hello'); // Prints HELLO
```

The association formed is one in which object A delegates to B by an "is a" relationship, and the same object context (`this`) is used to access the full set of behavior. In this example, we say that `Foo` "is a" `UpperCaseFormatter`.

Implicit linking or delegation is the fundamental method of accessing properties and behavior in prototype-based languages. This method is used by all the object construction patterns we've discussed so far (classes and constructor functions) and is also used by OLOO and mixins, which we'll discuss in sections 3.2 and 3.5, respectively.

3.1.2   *Explicit*

On the other hand, objects are linked explicitly when the link is well-known and visibly set in code, perhaps through a public or private property. I don't cover this technique in the book, but it's important to look at a simple example for comparison, shown in the next listing.

> **Listing 3.2   Explicit link between `Foo` and `UpperCaseFormatter`**

```
const UpperCaseFormatter = {
  format: function(msg) {
    return msg.toUpperCase();
  }
};

const Foo = {                              Explicitly passes an
  formatter: UpperCaseFormatter,           object to another
  saySomething: function print(msg) {
    console.log(this.formatter !== null
        ? this.formatter.format(msg)
        : msg
    );
  }
};

Foo.saySomething('hello'); // Prints HELLO
```

Again, if we were to label these relationships, when the relation is explicit, we say that some object A delegates to B with a "uses" label, also known as object composition. In this case, `Foo` uses `UpperCaseFormatter` to carry out its work, and both objects have different life cycles. In this configuration, it's sensible to check whether this.formatter !== null. Visually, you can see the explicit relationship because UpperCaseFormatter's properties are accessed by delegating through a known reference (formatter), explicitly typed in the code.

In the case of an implicit link, the life cycles of both objects are intertwined, in that UpperCaseFormatter's properties would be accessed via this; it's understood that the runtime is resolving these properties via __proto__.

Now that you understand this fundamental difference, let's begin with a pattern that uses implicit links to achieve behavior delegation.

3.2 OLOO

The OLOO pattern was presented by Kyle Simpson in his book series *You Don't Know JS* (mentioned in chapter 2) as well as his entertaining and thorough video series "Deep JavaScript Foundations" (https://frontendmasters.com/courses/javascript-foundations). This pattern is interesting to study because it changes our mindset when it comes to visualizing parent-child relationships among objects. OLOO's view of differential inheritance is different from the mental model of classes in that it doesn't consider child objects to derive from a base object. Rather, it considers objects peers that link together and delegate functionality by passing messages to each other. All that inheritance-related terminology disappears, and we no longer say that an object *inherits* from another; we say that it *links* to another, which is a much simpler model to understand.

Furthermore, OLOO keeps the good parts of the language while throwing away the deceiving class-based design and the complex prototype configuration of the constructor function pattern. OLOO still uses the [[Prototype]], but that mechanism is cleverly hidden behind Object.create and provides a much simpler userland model for designing objects. If you were to look under the hood of Object.create (http://mng.bz/zxnB), you'll see the minimal implementation of the constructor functions pattern, shown in the next listing.

Listing 3.3 Under the hood of Object.create

```
Object.create = function(proto, propertiesObject) {
    if (typeof proto !== 'object' && typeof proto !== 'function') {
        throw new TypeError('Object prototype may only be an Object: ' +
            proto);
    }

    function F() {}              ← Creates a new superfluous
    F.prototype = proto;            constructor function, F
    return new F();             ← Sets the prototype of the
};                                  constructor function
                             ← Returns the new object
                               invoking the new keyword
```

Now that we know that Object.create takes care of the boilerplate code for us, let's take proper advantage of it and use it to wire up the chain connecting all our objects. I'll start showing you this pattern with a simple example that introduces some of the components of this pattern. In this snippet of code, we'll begin to play with the concept of the blockchain data structure. A `Blockchain` is an object that stores consecutive elements, called *blocks*:

```
const MyStore = {
    init(element) {
        this.length = 0;
        this.push(element);
    },
    push(b) {
        this[this.length] = b;
        return ++this.length;
    }
}

const Blockchain = Object.create(MyStore);

const chain = Object.create(Blockchain);
chain.init(createGenesisBlock);
chain.push(new Block(...));
chain.length; // 2
```

In this example, we first link the objects `MyStore` and `Blockchain`; then we link the object `chain` (which we consider to be the actual instance object with all the functionality) with `Blockchain`. In the definition of `MyStore`, the `init` initializer method is in charge of typical object constructor logic that sets the properties of the new instance. As you can see from the preceding code snippet, `chain` properly delegates to properties of its peers: `init`, `push`, and `length`.

Another interesting aspect of OLOO is that after `Object.create(Blockchain)` is called, all the links get created in memory. `Blockchain` knows about `init` and `push` because of the prototype chain, but the objects have not been initialized because `init` has not been called. At this point, the shape of the object is in memory and instantiated, but actual initialization of the data happens when `init` is called, which sets everything in motion, populates the first block in the chain, and returns a ready-to-use object to its caller. As you can see, the objects are linked properly:

```
MyStore.isPrototypeOf(Blockchain); // true
chain.__proto__.init // [Function: init]
```

You can think of `init` as having some of the responsibilities of a class constructor. But unlike a class constructor, which performs construction and initialization at the same time, OLOO separates the two actions as different steps. Separating declaration from use allows you to define and lazily pass around the actual object representation (a template, perhaps) as a first-class object, similar to passing a class definition around. Then you can initialize this lazily built, minimal object with its full set of data only when needed.

This pattern resembles the Builder pattern (https://en.wikipedia.org/wiki/Builder _pattern), which is used a lot in object-oriented design.

But if you'd like to call both steps fluently inline, you can do so easily by returning this from the init method:

```
const MyStore = {
    init(element) {
        this.length = 0;
        this.push(element);
        return this;
    },
    //...
}

const Blockchain = Object.create(MyStore);

const chain = Object.create(Blockchain).init(createGenesisBlock);
chain.push(new Block(...));
chain.length; // 2
```

A noticeable difference with OLOO compared with constructor functions and classes is that the reliance in the prototypal inheritance is much more controlled and less exposed. When `MyStore.isPrototypeOf(Blockchain)` is true, you can't inadvertently change the shape of all initialized objects, protecting you from prototype pollution. In fact, `MyStore` and `Blockchain` are not constructor functions at all, so they do not have a `prototype` property to do this:

```
MyStore.prototype;    // undefined
Blockchain.prototype; // undefined
```

Now that you've seen the pattern in a simple scenario, let's use this same idea to refactor `Transaction`. The next listing shows a simple OLOO implementation; listing 3.5 shows the full implementation.

Listing 3.4 `HashTransaction` with simple object linking

```
const Transaction = {
  init(sender, recipient, funds = 0.0) {          ◁── The init method is the exact
    this.sender = sender;                             equivalent of a class constructor
    this.recipient = recipient;                       (merely a convention; you can use
    this.funds = Number(funds);                       any method name you like).
    return this;                                   ◁── Because the object is returned directly, results
  },                                                  in the properties of this object contained
  displayTransaction() {                              inside the specialized object
    return `Transaction from ${this.sender} to ${this.recipient} for
      ${this.funds}`;
  }
}

const HashTransaction = Object.create(Transaction);

HashTransaction.calculateHash = function calculateHash() {
    const data = [this.sender, this.recipient, this.funds].join('');
```

```
      let hash = 0, i = 0;
      while (i < data.length) {
        hash = ((hash << 5) - hash + data.charCodeAt(i++)) << 0;
      }
      return hash**2;
  }

  const tx = Object.create(HashTransaction)
      .init('luis@tjoj.com', 'luke@tjoj.com', 10);

  tx.sender;        // 'luis@tjoj.com'
  tx.recipient;     // 'luke@tjoj.com'
  tx.calculateHash(); // 64284210552842720
  tx.displayTransaction();
```

> Uses Object.create to build new objects and nicely separate prototype linkage from object initialization

> This method is invoked through the prototype chain.

Everything should look straightforward so far. The only thing we've added compared to the `MyStore` example is a bit more functionality to each object. Figure 3.2 shows the structure of the objects and the links among them.

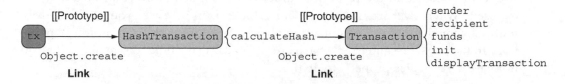

Figure 3.2   Surface view of how the three object peers are linked

Figure 3.2 shows that you can establish implicit links among objects and at the same time remove the prototypal boilerplate code that you would have otherwise needed to write with classes and (to greater extent) constructor functions. The following listing builds out the full-fledged `Transaction` object in all its glory.

Listing 3.5   Modeling `Transaction` with behavior delegation (OLOO)

```
const Transaction = {
  init(sender, recipient, funds = 0.0) {
    const _feePercent = 0.6;

    this.sender = sender;
    this.recipient = recipient;
    this.funds = Number(funds);

    this.netTotal = function() {
      return _precisionRound(this.funds * _feePercent, 2);
    }

    function _precisionRound(number, precision) {
      const factor = Math.pow(10, precision);
      return Math.round(number * factor) / factor;
    }
```

> The entire chain is based on simple objects, with Transaction at the base of the hierarchy.

> The init functions are analogous to a class's constructor. Also, the use of the function keyword is deliberate to establish the proper behavior of this.

> Private properties are nicely encapsulated in the object's closure, allowing only privileged methods to access them.

```
      return this;
    },
    displayTransaction() {
      return `Transaction from ${this.sender} to ${this.recipient}
        for ${this.funds}`;
    }
}

const HashTransaction = Object.create(Transaction)

HashTransaction.init = function HashTransaction(
    sender, recipient, funds
  ) {
    Transaction.init.call(this, sender, recipient, funds);
    this.transactionId = this.calculateHash();
    return this;
}

HashTransaction.calculateHash = function calculateHash() {
    // same as before...
}
```

> **Because I'm using a plain function as constructor, there is no implied this, so we need to return it ourselves.**

> **Using JavaScript's Object.create properly creates the implicit delegation linkage using [[Prototype]].**

> **The init functions are analogous to a class's constructor. Also, the use of the function keyword is deliberate to establish the proper behavior of this.**

> **Equivalent to the use of super within a child class's constructor**

This code is the same as in listing 3.4 but adds more initialization logic to Hash-Transaction to clearly separate initialization from instantiation. Figure 3.3 shows a more complete diagram.

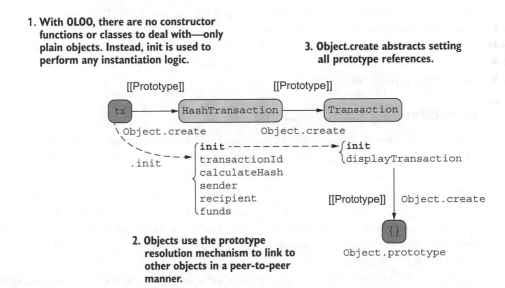

1. With OLOO, there are no constructor functions or classes to deal with—only plain objects. Instead, init is used to perform any instantiation logic.

3. Object.create abstracts setting all prototype references.

2. Objects use the prototype resolution mechanism to link to other objects in a peer-to-peer manner.

Figure 3.3   A full-fledged implementation of the OLOO pattern to implement HashTransaction, linking to Transaction to delegate basic functionality

As figure 3.3 shows, the `init` function nicely encapsulates any private state inside its lexical scope (à la the Module pattern) and exposes only what's needed through `this`. You could take the opportunity to define any private functions that are needed as part of object construction, and nothing would leak out to the caller. Also, you see a very visible management of the object context (`this`) being passed from one `init` block to the next upstream until reaching the parent object. This is not done to create the prototype linkage (as `Object.create` does that for you), but to initialize the entire chain up to the base object.

Up to now, you've learned about object modeling techniques that share the idea of using the prototype resolution mechanism with implicit links to delegate to other objects, whether that delegation is up the chain or along the chain. But all these techniques lack the ability to share behavior from more than one object, because prototypes establish a single, unidirectional path in which properties are dynamically resolved. These situations do not occur frequently in software, but when they do, the prototype chain is insufficient to model them correctly. Take a simple example extracted from nature. Amphibians are animals with both aquatic and terrestrial characteristics. If you were to map out the objects `Amphibian`, `Aquatic`, and `Terrestrial`, how could you model this relationship in a prototypal manner so that `Amphibian` links to both `AquaticAnimal` and `TerrestrialAnimal`? Multiple inheritance, perhaps?

You don't need to use inheritance at all. Let's explore another software construction pattern that relies on object composition. It's important to add that when I mention composition of objects, I'm not referring to the well-known object-oriented pattern that goes by that name. This pattern is much simpler. Here, I'm referring to the ability to assemble a rich object by gluing together small individual pieces or traits—composition in the structural sense. JavaScript's object model is one of a kind that lets us perform this task, and the API to use is `Object.assign`. Section 3.3 discusses this API first and then shows you how it's used to compose objects. You'll use the API to implement mixins in section 3.4.

3.3   Understanding Object.assign

Software evolves quickly, and requirements change drastically. The problem with prototypal object models is that they tend to become too rigid and brittle over time, making it difficult to introduce big changes to your model with the guarantee that those changes won't break something else up or along the chain of delegation. Mishandling base objects higher up in the hierarchy may cause rippling downstream effects throughout your model—an issue known as the fragile base class problem. You can use patterns to minimize this problem by physically copying properties down to derived objects.

State copying over state sharing isn't a new concept. Instead of assembling rigid hierarchies of objects, why don't you build objects by handing them copies of all the properties they need? With JavaScript, in which objects are dynamic bags of properties, this process is simple. JavaScript allows you to glue together various pieces (bags) of properties (call them partial objects, if you will) to create a whole, feature-rich object, like pouring the contents of several bags into a larger one. This process is done not by linking to a prototype, but by integrating or merging copies of simpler, individual objects.

Aside from instantiation, from the perspective of the user, using objects built this way feels no different from the approaches listed earlier; the shape of the object on the surface is the same. From a code-reasoning point of view, however, the process is radically different. In the following sections, we explore the JavaScript APIs that support this process and some behind-the-scenes features that make it possible.

3.3.1 *Object.assign uncovered*

You can use `Object.assign` to merge the properties of various objects. In this section, we'll discuss in depth how to use this API. `Object.assign` is a nice little Swiss army knife to have in your tool belt. It comes in handy in several use cases. Suppose that you're developing a mashup of several API responses and would like to deliver the response body as a single JSON. Another common task is to perform a shallow clone by assigning the properties of an object to a new, empty object `{}`. Many libraries that accept configuration objects as arguments use `Object.assign` to provide defaults. In the next listing, the function `doSomething` takes a `config` object that allows the user to specify settings for the hypothetical logic carried out by this function.

> **Listing 3.6 Using `Object.assign` to implement options with defaults**

```
function doSomething(config = {}) {
  config = Object.assign(
    {
      foo: 'foo',                 Configuration
      bar: 'bar',             ◁┘  defaults
      baz: 'baz'
    }, config);

  console.log(`Using config ${config.foo}, ${config.bar}, ${config.bar}`);
}

doSomething();                  // Prints Using config foo, bar, bar
doSomething({foo: 'hello'}); // Prints Using config hello, bar, bar
```

By merging the user-provided object with defaults, it's easy to obtain the desired `config`. `Object.assign` copies the enumerable properties that one or more objects owns (as defined by `Object#hasOwnProperty`) into a target object, returning the target object. The following listing shows a simple example.

> **Listing 3.7 Using `Object.assign` to merge two objects into a new object**

```
const a = {                These properties are enumerable and
  a: 'a'              ◁┤   owned by the object, so they get copied.
};
```

```
const b = {
  b: 'b'
};
```
These properties are enumerable and
owned by the object, so they get copied.

```
Object.assign({}, a, b);  //{ a: 'a', b: 'b' }
```

In this case, all the objects in question have their properties as `enumerable: true`, which means that `Object.assign` will scan and copy them.

Now consider a non-enumerable property, which will be skipped:

```
const a = {
  a: 'a'
};
```

```
const b = {};
Object.defineProperty(b, 'b', {
  value: 'b',
  enumerable: false
});
```

```
Object.assign({}, a, b);  //{ a: 'a' }
```

You can find enumerable properties by iterating over an object, using a construct such as `for...in` for properties that have `enumerable: true`. You can control this meta-attribute as well as three others (`writable`, `configurable`, and `value`) at the point of definition. Recall from chapter 2 that the meta-object containing these four attributes is known as a property or data descriptor.

Following `Object#hasOwnProperty`, owned properties refer to properties found directly in the source objects, not properties accessible via their prototype. In the following code snippet, the inherited property `parent` is never assigned to the target object:

```
const parent = {
  parent: 'parent'
};
```

```
const c = Object.create(parent);
c.c = 'c';
```

```
Object.assign({}, c);  // { c: 'c' }
```

Now consider a property with the same name, with the objects being merged. In this case, the rule is that the object to the right overrides the set of properties of the object to the left in the list. Here's a simple use case:

```
const a = {                           const c = {
  a: 'a'                                  a: 'ca',
};                                        c: 'c'
                                      };
const b = {
  b: 'b'                              Object.assign({}, a, b, c);
};

Object.assign({}, a, b);

//{ a: 'a', b: 'b' }                  //{ a: 'ca', b: 'b', c: 'c' }
```

This rule is important, and I'll circle back to it in section 3.4.2.

At this point, you may be thinking that `Object.assign` simply copies properties right to left. Well, not always. There's a subtle difference between definition and assignment.

3.3.2 Assignment vs definition

Assigning a value to an existing property doesn't define how a property behaves, the way that `Object.defineProperty` does. Assignment falls back to defining a property only if an assignment is made for a property that doesn't exist. Hence, for new properties, JavaScript uses the [[DefineOwnProperty]] internal process as outlined in the specification, and for existing properties, it uses [[Set]], which won't alter the property's meta-attributes, as happened in our first example with doSomething (see the following listing).

> **Listing 3.8 Using `Object.assign` to assign values to new and existing properties**

```
function doSomething(config = {}) {
  config = Object.assign(
    {
      foo: 'foo',           │ foo gets set to 'hello', and bar
      bar: 'bar',       ◁───┤ and baz are newly defined
      baz: 'baz'            │ during Object.assign.
    }, config);

  console.log(`Using config ${config.foo}, ${config.bar}, ${config.bar}`);
}

doSomething({foo: 'hello'});
```

Most of the time, this distinction makes no difference, but sometimes it does. Let's explore the difference with another example:

```
const Transaction = {
  sender: 'luis@tjoj.com'
};
Object.assign(Transaction, { sender: 'luke@tjoj.com' });
```

The preceding call works as expected, and `sender` is set to `'luke@tjoj.com'`. But what if `sender` wasn't a string property, but a setter method? According to the specification, `Object.assign` invokes the [[Set]] meta-operation for an existing property key. Consider the scenario in the next listing.

Listing 3.9   `Object.assign` invokes [[Set]] when encountering the same property name

```
const Transaction = {
  _sender: 'luis@tjoj.com',

  get sender() {
    return this._sender;
  },
  set sender(newEmail) {
    this._sender = Transaction.validateEmail(newEmail);
  }
};
```

A regular
expression that
matches valid
email addresses

```
const EMAIL_REGEX = /^((([^<>()\[\]\\.,;:\s@"]+(\.[^<>()\[\]\\.,;:\s@"]+)*)|
(".+"))@((\[[0-9]{1,3}\.[0-9]{1,3}\.[0-9]{1,3}\.[0-9]{1,3}\])|(([a-zA-Z\-0-9]
+\.)+[a-zA-Z]{2,}))$/;

Transaction.validateEmail = function validateEmail(email) {
  if (EMAIL_REGEX.test(email.toLowerCase())) {
    return email;
  }
  throw new Error(`Invalid email ${email}`);
};

Object.assign(Transaction, { sender: 'invalid@email' }); // Error!    ◄──  Sending input with
                                                                          invalid email address
```

Here, `sender` is considered to be an existing property and gets processed through JavaScript's internal [[Set]] property, causing the setter logic to execute and fail when the email address is badly formatted.

Now that you understand the basic workings of this built-in API, let's use it to support our last object construction pattern: mixins.

3.4   *Assembling objects using mixin composition*

The idea behind composing or assembling objects is a bit different from the approaches you've seen so far. With prototypes, you link to a single object to share its state and behavior, but with mixins, you copy fine-grained pieces of multiple independent slices of objects that together represent the entirety of the object's API. This section teaches you how to use `Object.assign` to achieve a technique called *concatenative object extension* with mixins.

Think of mixins as adding flavors to your ice cream or toppings to your sandwich; every new addition adds a twist to the overall flavor but doesn't overpower it. Before we dive into our final version of `Transaction`, let's study a simple use case. Consider these trivial object literals:

```
const HasBread = {
  bread: 'Wheat',
  toasted: true
};

const HasToppings = {
  sauce: 'Ranch'
};

const HasTomatoes = {
  tomatoe: 'Cherry',
  cut: 'diced'
};

const HasMeat = {
  meat: 'Chicken',
  term: 'Grilled'
};
```

Our `Sandwich` object can be created by joining any or all of these parts:

```
const Sandwich = (size = '6', unit = 'in') =>
  Object.assign({
    size, unit
  },
  HasBread,
  HasToppings,
  HasTomatoes,
  HasMeat
);

const footLong = Sandwich(1, 'ft');
footLong.tomatoe; // 'Cherry'
```

More succinctly, you can take advantage of the spread operator:

```
const Sandwich = (size = '6', unit = 'in') => ({
  size, unit,
  ...HasBread,
  ...HasToppings,
  ...HasTomatoes,
  ...HasMeat
});
```

A mixin object like `HasBread` doesn't provide much value on its own, but it can be used to enhance some target object—`Sandwich`, in this case. Going back briefly to the OLOO pattern, you may have caught a glimpse of it as the properties (methods and data) of a parent object were added during the execution of the derived object's constructor. This process repeats at every level of the linked object graph. In fact, to ease the transition of using `Object.assign` as a means to define object relationships, consider a slight twist on the OLOO example that combines the object-linking step (const HashTransaction = Object.create(Transaction)) and defines new properties on this new object, as shown next.

Listing 3.10   OLOO implemented with `Object.assign`

```
const Transaction = {
  init(sender, recipient, funds = 0.0) {
    this.sender = sender;
    this.recipient = recipient;
    this.funds = Number(funds);
    return this;
  },
  displayTransaction() {
    return `Transaction from ${this.sender} to ${this.recipient} for
      ${this.funds}`;
  }
}

const HashTransaction = Object.assign(                ⟵⎯┐ Defines the properties
  Object.create(Transaction),                              of HashTransaction
  {                                                        through assignment
    calculateHash() {                                      using Object.assign
      const data = [this.sender, this.recipient, this.funds].join('');
      let hash = 0, i = 0;
      while (i < data.length) {
        hash = ((hash << 5) - hash + data.charCodeAt(i++)) << 0;
      }
      return hash**2;
    }
  }
);
```

A mixin is an object with simple behavior, typically made from one or two methods. In this case, there's one method, `calculateHash`, which we'll refactor into its own object in section 3.5.1. The simpler mixins are, the easier they are to compose and reuse in many parts of your code. Mixins should have a narrow focus, much smaller than a class. They could capture a single responsibility or perhaps even a slice of a responsibility. It's acceptable for a mixin to look incomplete as long as it's self-sustaining and has everything needed to carry out its task.

> **NOTE**   This book discusses mixins only superficially. For more information on the mixin pattern, check out Composing Software, by Eric Elliot (https://leanpub.com/composingsoftware).

Object composition promotes creating HAS-A or USES-A rather than IS-A relationships among objects. So instead of implicitly delegating to an object's parent, you circumvent inheritance and copy all the properties you need directly to the target object. You can imagine this process as being analogous to squashing an inheritance hierarchy two or three levels deep into a single object literal. Because you're adding new properties to an object after it's been defined, this process is called dynamic or concatenative object extension.

Mixins might sound a little complicated, but the pattern has been widely used for some time. I mentioned its use in CSS preprocessors, but there are others uses in JavaScript itself. In browsers, the behavior instilled by the global `window` object is in part implemented by the `WindowOrWorkerGlobalScope` mixin. Similarly, browser events are handled by the `WindowEventHandlers` mixin. These mixins are used to group a common set of properties between the global objects used in browsers (`window`) as well as the Web Worker API (`self`). The browsers premix this code for you, of course, so that you don't have to, but consider a more obvious example. If you've ever used the popular Mocha and Chai unit testing libraries, you probably know that you can extend their functionality by injecting new behavior dynamically, using

```
chai.use(function (_chai, utils) {
  // ...
});
```

The method name (`use`) is appropriate. Many other third-party libraries already take advantage of this feature. To streamline testing with promises, for example, you can extend Chai with the chai-as-promised (https://www.npmjs.com/package/chai-as-promised) library:

```
chai.use(chaiAsPromised);
```

Dynamic concatenation embodies the principle of composition well: combine simple objects to build a complex one, which we're achieving here.

Circling back to `Transaction`, we'll use the class definition we started in chapter 2 as its core structure, with mixins to borrow shared modules of code. The first thing you'll notice is that the definition of `calculateHash` is not part of the class declaration anymore; it was moved to an object called `HasHash`. Separating `calculateHash` into own module will make it easier to add hashing behavior to other classes of our domain, such as `Block` and `Blockchain`. As listing 3.11 shows, instead of a simple object, a function allows us to configure the hashing behavior as needed with arguments, such as specifying the fields of the object used as part of the hashing process.

NOTE   For these mixins, because we're returning a new object, we're going to use arrow functions to save some typing. A regular function declaration would work equally well.

> **Listing 3.11   Defining the `HasHash` mixin**

```
const HasHash = keys => ({
  calculateHash() {
    const data = keys.map(f => this[f]).join('');      ◁──  Creates a string from the
    let hash = 0, i = 0;                                      values of the specified
    while (i < data.length) {                                 property keys
```

```
    hash = ((hash << 5) - hash + data.charCodeAt(i++)) << 0;
  }
  return hash**2;
  }
});
```

HasHash is a mixin wrapped by a function expression, so the mixin part is this object literal:

```
{
  calculateHash() {
    const data = keys.map(f => this[f]).join('');
    let hash = 0, i = 0;
    while (i < data.length) {
      hash = ((hash << 5) - hash + data.charCodeAt(i++)) << 0;
    }
    return hash**2;
  }
});
```

For completeness, if we replace this body of code in the OLOO example (listing 3.10), we obtain the result in the next listing.

Listing 3.12   OLOO pattern for `Transaction` using the `HasHash` mixin

```
const Transaction = {
  init(sender, recipient, funds = 0.0) {
    this.sender = sender;
    this.recipient = recipient;
    this.funds = Number(funds);
    return this;
  },
  displayTransaction() {
    return `Transaction from ${this.sender} to ${this.recipient}
      for ${this.funds}`;
  }
}

const HashTransaction = Object.assign(
  Object.create(Transaction),
  HasHash(['sender', 'recipient', 'funds'])   ◁──┐
);
```

> Copies the properties of the mixin returned by calling HasHash. By using a function, it's simple to specify which properties of the object's state the mixin has access to as part of calculating the object's hash value.

Listing 3.13 shows the final version of `Transaction` (class + mixins). This code integrates all the mixins into the class prototype reference so that the same hashing functionality is available to all instances of `Transaction`. The `Object.assign` call with all mixins happens at the end.

Listing 3.13   `Transaction` object using mixin concatenation

```
class Transaction {
  transactionId = '';     ◁──┐
  timestamp = Date.now();
```

> The transactionId is set in the constructor by calling calculateHash, dynamically assigned to this instance's prototype and available to all instances.

```
  #feePercent = 0.6;

  constructor(sender, recipient, funds = 0.0, description = 'Generic') {
    this.sender = sender;
    this.recipient = recipient;
    this.funds = Number(funds);
    this.description = description;
    this.transactionId = this.calculateHash();
  }

  displayTransaction() {
    return `Transaction ${this.description} from ${this.sender} to
      ${this.recipient} for ${this.funds}`;
  }

  get netTotal() {
    return  Transaction.#precisionRound(
      this.funds * this.#feePercent, 2);
  }

  static #precisionRound(number, precision) {
    const factor = Math.pow(10, precision);
    return Math.round(number * factor) / factor;
  }
}

Object.assign(
  Transaction.prototype,
  HasHash(['timestamp', 'sender', 'recipient', 'funds']),
  HasSignature(['sender', 'recipient', 'funds']),
  HasValidation()
)
```

Using Object.assign to glue together (or include) the objects that make up a Transaction

The HasSignature mixin handles signature generation and verification.

HasValidation groups common validation tasks for any object (to be discussed in chapter 5).

NOTE Using a class (such as `Transaction`) as the target object for dynamic mixin extension is the scenario you'll most likely encounter in your own coding due to the popularity of classes. But you can use mixins with any of the construction patterns discussed so far.

You may find this pattern, also known as traits, in programming languages such as PHP (https://www.php.net/manual/en/language.oop5.traits.php). When you use classes, all the properties are added to the class's prototype reference. For this reason, we use `Object.assign` to extend the class's prototype dynamically and avoid having to repeat the logic of assigning mixins every time we need a new transaction.

Also, from a memory-efficient point of view, augmenting the prototype object causes all transaction objects to have the same set of properties. Instantiating a new `Transaction` looks the same as in chapter 2:

```
const tx = new Transaction('luis@tjoj.com', 'luke@tjoj.com', 10);
tx.transactionId; // 241936169696765470
```

The important thing to notice is that although this version of `Transaction` is different from the previous ones, it retains the best parts by

- Using the convenient syntax of classes to nicely group and encapsulate all the pertinent transactional details.
- Integrating reusable pieces from other mixins for maximum code reuse.
- Separating the object definition (such as `Transaction` class) and mixin configuration from instantiation, akin to OLOO.
- Integrating only the direct, public interface of a mixin object by skipping non-enumerable and not-owned properties (because it uses `Object.assign`).
- Allowing mixins to encapsulate hidden properties and methods of their own that only its public API can use, but that do not become part of the overall object and are not reachable from the class. The reverse is also true: mixins don't have access to any private (#) properties declared inside the class. Only their public interfaces communicate, which prevents a tighter form of coupling. I'll come back to this topic in section 3.5.1.
- Avoiding deep and cumbersome prototype configurations, making objects flatter and therefore simpler to use and combine with other parts of the code.

Now that you know how the mixins integrate into the bigger object, let's evaluate the structure of a mixin.

3.4.1   *Anatomy of a mixin*

In this section, we're going to discuss the shape of the mixins used in our blockchain application. `Transaction` uses two important extensions that implement the two main cryptographic concepts underpinning blockchain technology: hashing (`HasHash`) and digital signatures (`HasSignature`). Our current version of `HasHash` still does not produce cryptographically secure hashes. We need to improve that algorithm, but we'll save the nitty-gritty of the logic for chapter 4 and focus only on its shape for now. When we have the public interface and calls wired up, swapping algorithms in and out is simple.

Listings 3.14 and 3.15 show the updated structures of `HasHash` and `HasSignature`, respectively.

Listing 3.14   `HasHash` mixin

```
const DEFAULT_ALGO_SHA256 = 'SHA256';
const DEFAULT_ENCODING_HEX = 'hex';

const HasHash = (
  keys,
  options = { algorithm: DEFAULT_ALGO_SHA256,
              encoding:  DEFAULT_ENCODING_HEX }
) => ({
  calculateHash () {
    //...
  }
})
```

Default options passed to configure the hashing process. Here, we're using the SHA256 algorithm with hexadecimal encoding.

Because HasHash accepts a list of keys representing the properties involved in computing the hash, it could work with with any target object. Here's an example:

```
const hashable = Object.assign(
  { foo: 'foo', bar: 'bar' },
  HasHash(['foo', 'bar'])
);


hashable.calculateHash();  // '1610053822743955500'
```

Coming back to encapsulation, assuming that the mixins are their own modules (chapter 6), any data outside the scope of the mixin function (such as DEFAULT_ALGO_SHA256) is virtually private and self-contained, as it is part of the mixin function's closure.

With a similar structure, the next listing contains the skeleton for HasSignature. This mixin packs a bit more behavior.

Listing 3.15 HasSignature mixin

```
const DEFAULT_ENCODING_HEX = 'hex';
const DEFAULT_SIGN_ALGO = 'RSA-SHA256';

const HasSignature = (
  keys,
  options = {
    algorithm: DEFAULT_SIGN_ALGO,
    encoding: DEFAULT_ENCODING_HEX
  }
) => ({

  generateSignature(privateKey) {
    //...

  },
  verifySignature(publicKey, signature) {
    //...
  }
});
```

The body of these methods deals with using Node.js's crypto modules to sign the contents of an object, as well as read and verify public/private key pairs, which we don't cover in this book. Feel free to visit the code repo for the internals. Keep in mind, though, that in the real world of open, distributed ledgers, the public key is what identifies a user's wallet to rest of the world. From the caller's point of view, the next listing shows how you would use HasSignature.

Listing 3.16 Using HasSignature to sign the contents of an object

```
const signable = Object.assign(
  { foo: 'foo', bar: 'bar' },
  HasSignature(['foo', 'bar'])
);
```

```
const publicKey = fs.readFileSync('test-public.pem', 'utf8');
const privateKey = fs.readFileSync('test-private.pem', 'utf8');

const signature = signable.generateSignature(privateKey);

signable.verifySignature(publicKey, signature); // true
```

Signs the object's data, using the private key

You can verify that the signature is correct by using the corresponding public key.

You've seen examples of HasHash and HasSignature. I cover HasValidation (another mixin) and its internal logic in chapter 5. Note that I named these mixins with the full intention of showing that composition is happening, clearly establishing HAS-A relationships with the target objects, as shown in figure 3.4.

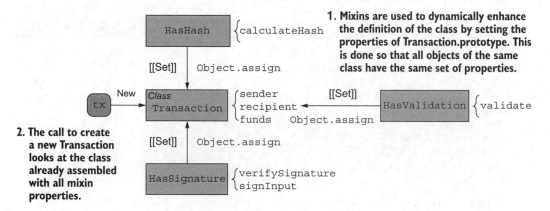

1. Mixins are used to dynamically enhance the definition of the class by setting the properties of Transaction.prototype. This is done so that all objects of the same class have the same set of properties.

2. The call to create a new Transaction looks at the class already assembled with all mixin properties.

Figure 3.4 When using composition, the mechanism by which an object is built consists of gluing together other independent objects: **HasHash**, **HasSignature**, and **HasValidation**. The properties of each one get mashed up into a single source, forming a single object from the user's point of view.

Figure 3.4 shows a theoretical or conceptual view of object composition. Practically speaking, after the target object is formed, the Transaction class looks like figure 3.5 to the caller.

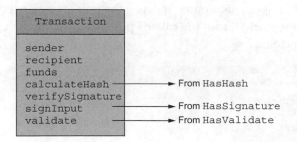

Figure 3.5 Shape of **Transaction** after object assignment

It might seem that with the composition of mixins, we can obtain something similar to multiple inheritance—a controversial software topic. If you've done some research on this topic, you've come across the "diamond of death" problem. The problem refers to the ambiguity present when a class extends multiple classes, each declaring the same method. Languages with sophisticated support for this feature, such as Scala, overcome the problem by using a technique known as linearization. In section 3.4.2, we'll see how JavaScript solves this problem.

3.4.2 *Multiple inheritance and linearization*

Generally speaking, mixins have two main benefits over traditional inheritance schemes:

- Mixins reduce some limitations of single inheritance by enabling a developer to reuse sets of methods freely from several independent objects rather than one.
- The algorithm that `Object.assign` uses removes the ambiguity caused by multiple inheritance and makes this process predictable.

The first point is a direct result of the prototype chain mechanism, as there's a 1-1 correspondence between an object and its prototype. Concatenation overcomes this limitation because you are free to mash together as many objects as needed into a single one.

The second point is more puzzling. How can mixins fix the infamous diamond problem? The premise of the problem is easy to understand: a child class C extends from two parent classes, B1 and B2, and each of these classes in turn extends from a base class A. This problem is more common in class-oriented languages, which label relationships to parent classes as IS-A. From that standpoint, how can a class *be* a template for two different things? Consider the animal taxonomies example again (figure 3.6). At the base, you may have a class `Animal`, with child classes `Terrestrial-Animal` and `AquaticAnimal`.

First, a little biology lesson: amphibians such as frogs, toads, and salamanders start as larvae, with gills to breathe underwater, and later mature to adults with lungs to

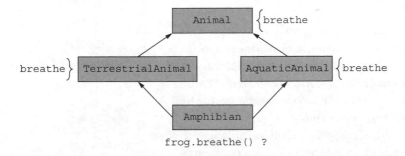

Figure 3.6   The classic diamond problem of multiple inheritance. Assuming that a class may extend form multiple other classes with a conflicting method signature, which method is dispatched at runtime?

breathe air. Some amphibians even rely on their skins as a secondary respiratory alternative. It makes perfect sense for a class `Amphibian` to extend from both of these classes. But when `frog.breathe` is called, which implementation will it pick? With software, we can't leave the answer to Mother Nature.

As you might expect, we can use mixins to model this type of object:

```
const TerrestrialAnimal = {
  walk() {
    ...
  },
  breathe() {
    return 'Using my lungs to breathe';
  }
};

const AquaticAnimal = {
  swim() {
    ...
  },
  breathe() {
    return 'Using my gills to breathe';
  }
};

const Amphibian = name => Object.assign(
  {
    name
  },
  AquaticAnimal,
  TerrestrialAnimal
);

const frog = Amphibian('Frog');

frog.walk();

frog.swim();
```

To return to the original question, if `frog` calls breathe, which implementation does it use? Seemingly, we have entered a diamond situation. But the rules of `Object.assign` remove this ambiguity because it's predictable: always favor the properties of the object that gets added last. You can picture this situation by collapsing the diamond of death to a straight line (hence, linearizing) in an orderly sequence. Linearizing the diamond problem would look like figure 3.7.

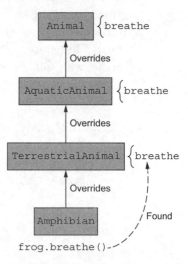

Figure 3.7 **Applying linearization to a multiple inheritance situation**

The way in which `Object.assign` is implemented allows the same behavior to occur. Behind the scenes, the implementation works like figure 3.8.

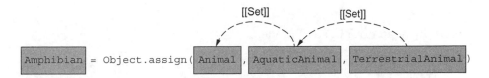

Figure 3.8 Multiple inheritance is possible with `Object.assign`'s mechanism that takes care of establishing a predictable order in which source objects are assigned to the target.

Now if you call `breathe` on the `frog` object, you always get the expected result, choosing `TerrestrialAnimal` as the implementation:

```
frog.breathe(); // 'Using my lungs to breathe'
```

3.4.3 *Composing objects using Object.assign and the spread operator*

Merging objects this way is so common that since ECMAScript 2018, we can streamline this technique even more. Instead of using the `Object.assign` API directly, we have language support to accomplish something similar, using the spread operator over objects. This operator gives you a compact, idiomatic syntax to copy the state of an object in an immutable way.

In section 3.3, I briefly mention some examples in which `Object.assign` is useful. The spread operator works equally well for each of those cases. Consider the example of performing shallow clones of some object `obj`:

```
const clone = { ...obj };
```

This example is analogous to

```
const toad = Object.assign({}, obj);
```

We can use the spread operator to create object templates:

```
const toad = { ...frog, name: 'Toad' };
```

In a single line, we copied all owned properties from `frog` and overrode the name property to yield a new object called `toad`. From a practical point of view, `Object.assign` and the spread operator have similar uses, the exception being that the spread operator yields a new object instead of assigning to an existing object. In most cases, this exception doesn't matter, but if we were to use the spread operator with the `Transaction` class where we opted to augment `prototype` directly, the code would fail with an error. So

```
Transaction.prototype = {
    ...HasHash(['timestamp', 'sender', 'recipient', 'funds']),
    ...HasSignature(['sender', 'recipient', 'funds']),
    ...HasValidation()
}
```

would throw an error in strict mode:

```
TypeError: Cannot assign to read only property 'prototype' of function 'class
    Transaction...
```

Although both patterns allow you to create objects by combining others, that subtle difference is enough for us to continue using `Object.assign` in our application. In section 3.5, we use this pattern to complete the main classes of our domain model.

3.5 Applying shared mixins to multiple objects

Now that you have a good understanding of dynamic object concatenation, to see the benefits of code reuse, we'll apply it to other parts of our application. In this section, you'll see how the mixins we've created so far apply to more than `Transaction`. To keep things a bit consistent in the domain layer, and because you're more likely to run into classes in the wild, I'll use classes to model the concepts of `Blockchain`, `Block`, and `Wallet`. In listing 3.12, I showed how to use mixins with OLOO. Both patterns use implicit linking, so you should be able to port this code to OLOO style without much effort.

First, let's define the `Blockchain` class in the next listing with a similar structure.

Listing 3.17 `Blockchain` definition with mixins

```
class Blockchain {

    #blocks = new Map();

    constructor(genesis = createGenesisBlock()) {
        this.#blocks.set(genesis.hash, genesis);
    }

    height() {
        return this.#blocks.size;
    }

    lookup(hash) {
        const h = hash;
        if (this.#blocks.has(h)) {
            return this.#blocks.get(h);
        }
        throw new Error(`Block with hash ${h} not found!`);
    }

    push(newBlock) {
        this.#blocks.set(newBlock.hash, newBlock);
```

```
      return newBlock;
    }
}

function createGenesisBlock(previousHash = '0'.repeat(64)) {
  //...
}

Object.assign(Blockchain.prototype, HasValidation());
```

As with Transaction, extends blockchain with validation functionality. (Full implementation of validation logic is covered in chapter 5.)

A blockchain stores blocks, which in turn store transactions. Listing 3.17 shows a basic class declaration of `Block`, which we'll fill in as we go along. The most important job of this class is to manage a collection of transactions and the hashing calculation by using its previous hash. What makes tampering detectable in a blockchain is that every block's hash depends on the hashes of all the previous blocks, starting with the genesis. So if a block is tampered with, all you need to do is recompute its hash and compare it with the original to detect the malfeasance. The next listing shows how `Block` also mixes `HasHash`.

Listing 3.18 `Block` definition

```
class Block {
  #blockchain;

  constructor(index, previousHash, data = []) {
    this.index = index;
    this.data = data;
    this.previousHash = previousHash;
    this.timestamp = Date.now();
    this.hash = this.calculateHash();
  }

  set blockchain(b) {
    this.#blockchain = b;
    return this;
  }

  isGenesis() {
    return this.previousHash === '0'.repeat(64);
  }
}

Object.assign(
  Block.prototype,
  HasHash(['index', 'timestamp', 'previousHash', 'data']),
  HasValidation()
);
```

A block's data field can contain a collection of pending transactions found in the blockchain at the moment a new block is mined or mined transactions found after the block is mined into the chain.

Every block always contains the hash of the block that preceded it (which establishes the chain).

HasHash augments Block with hashing functionality.

As of now, we've built the skeleton of most of the domain layer of our application. As you read on, you will learn more about JavaScript and programming a blockchain as we continue to add the finer details to this code. For additional reference, figure 3.9 shows the objects and the shared mixins we've created so far.

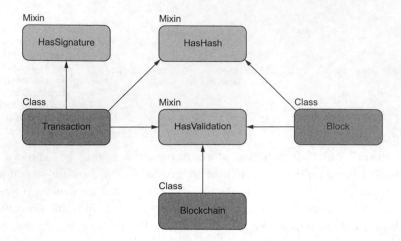

Figure 3.9   The main objects at play, with their respective mixins. As you can see, mixins are designed to be shared structures.

Furthermore, to make teaching blockchain simpler, I tried to avoid some of the cryptography topics by using email addresses to identify a transaction's sender and recipient. In the real world, emails are way too personal for a public ledger, in which user information always needs to be secure. A transaction stores `sender` and `receiver` addresses in the form of cryptographically secure public keys. When you visit the blockchain application's source code in GitHub, you'll see keys being used instead of emails. This information identifies each user's digital `Wallet`, as shown in the following listing. Think of a `Wallet` as being your personal banking mobile app.

Listing 3.19   `Wallet` object

```
class Wallet {
  constructor(publicKey, privateKey) {
    this.publicKey = publicKey
    this.privateKey = privateKey
  }
  get address() {
    return this.publicKey
  }
  balance(ledger) {
    //...            ⟵——  Details deferred
  }                        to chapter 4
}
```

Figure 3.10 shows the basic interactions among blocks, transactions, wallets, and blockchain.

In this chapter, we explored two more object construction patterns: OLOO (also known as simple object linking) and concatenative object extension (also known as

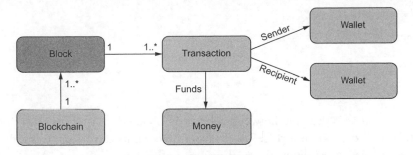

Figure 3.10 **The main objects at play in our simple blockchain application. I have not shown** `Money`**, a value object that describes an amount and currency.**

mixins). Parting from the techniques you reviewed in chapter 2, these alternatives give you more flexibility in modeling your objects.

There's always a downside, however. JavaScript engines highly optimize processes that take advantage of the [[Prototype]] mechanism. When deviating a bit by using mixins instead of object hierarchies, which prefer more state copying and are more resilient to fragile base objects or prototype pollution, we create a slightly bigger combined memory footprint because we have a lot more objects in memory. We mitigated this situation by extending a class's prototype instead of mixin into new instances directly, as the next listing shows.

Listing 3.20   Assigning mixins to a single instance of `Transaction`

```
Object.assign(
    new Transaction(...),          Creates a new object each time
    HasHash(['timestamp', 'sender', 'recipient', 'funds']),   with a copy of all methods
    HasSignature(['sender', 'recipient', 'funds']),
    HasValidation()
)
```

With this code, you would have to repeat this complex construction call every time you need a new transaction. In most or all of your cases, having to copy state is negligible, considering that most performance bottlenecks in applications occur with I/O bound calls (database, network, file system, and others). Nevertheless, it's important to pay attention to this situation in those rare cases in which you'd need hundreds of these objects.

Another issue to pay attention to is the implicit assumption that a mixin makes about the target object in which it's embedded. You might have seen this assumption when we discussed the code inside `HasHash` in section 3.5. The next listing shows that code again.

Listing 3.21   `HasHash` mixin

```
const HasHash = keys => ({                    Creates an implicit
  calculateHash() {                           dependency between the
    const data = keys.map(f => this[f]).join('');   mixin and the whole object
```

```
      let hash = 0, i = 0;
      while (i < data.length) {
        hash = ((hash << 5) - hash + data.charCodeAt(i++)) << 0;
      }
      return hash**2;
    }
});
```

As you can see, this is the glue between the whole object and its mixins. Mixins bind really tightly to the public interface of its target object and can become fragile when target objects are further extended and mixin code starts to change. Also, from an optics perspective, it's hard to see the shape of the objects being coupled here. You'd have to navigate to all objects that mix this behavior to understand whether the code will work for all of them.

There's no hard-and-fast rule about whether to use linking-based models versus inheritance-based models. As with all software, the answer depends on the types of problems you're solving, the team's expertise, and how complex your domain model is. Unlike other languages, however, JavaScript gives you options.

Now that we've examined JavaScript's object model in great depth, it's time to start talking about functions. One interesting fact about JavaScript is that functions are also objects in the language (aka first-class functions). In chapter 4, you'll learn how to exploit the benefits of first-class functions and see how they enable functional programming.

Summary

- JavaScript offers behavior delegation via implicit links and mixins for building objects in a compositional manner.
- Behavior delegation is the natural way to model objects in JavaScript. It uses the implicit delegation mechanism present in JavaScript's lookup process and the prototype chain.
- Object concatenation offers a simple approach based on structural object composition, which allows you to build objects by attaching (embedding) behavior from other independent objects.
- You can use mixins to extend objects (or classes) dynamically and favor structural composition over inheritance.
- Mixins address the issue of multiple inheritance through a mechanism known as mixin linearization.
- JavaScript offers a shortcut for Object.assign by using the spread operator, although Object.assign and the spread operator are not interchangeable.

Part 2

Functions

Part 2 takes the objects defined in the first part and brings them to life. Functions kick the gears into motion on any JavaScript application. Unfortunately, most JavaScript developers don't take full advantage of the power of JavaScript functions. By taking advantage of the fact that functions are also objects in the system, you'll begin to appreciate the joy of JavaScript. Part 2 also introduces new syntax that will change how you structure your JavaScript code: the pipeline and bind operators.

Chapter 4 starts by teaching you how to use JavaScript in a functional manner. You'll learn to decompose problems into small tasks, each represented by a function, and to compose them back together. To enable this capability, higher-order functions allow you to pass, return, and dynamically call functions. You'll learn how to use partially applied (curried) functions to prebake or configure the functions you'll assemble into compositional chains. Also in store in chapter 4 is a preview of JavaScript's proposed pipeline operator, which will bring the power of functional languages like Elixir and F# to JavaScript.

I've said that functions are objects, but chapter 5 reverses this definition, teaching you to think of objects as behaving like functions. Here, you'll learn about a pattern that's becoming pervasive on many language platforms: Algebraic Data Type (ADT). An ADT is an object with simple, specialized behavior. You can use ADTs to represent common tasks (data validation, error handling, null checks, and so on) in a compositional, fluent way. You'll be able to execute objects as easily as you call functions—a concept called a *functor*. In fact, you've been using functors all along without realizing it. Arrays and promises (discussed in part 4) are perhaps the most commonly used functors in JavaScript, and you'll learn which part of their respective APIs makes them behave like functors and even monads. What's cool is that you'll be able to extract this API and apply Java-Script's proposed bind operator syntax to any type of object.

Writing composable, pure code

This chapter covers

- Refactoring imperative coding to a declarative, functional style
- Mastering JavaScript's higher-order functions
- Introducing pure functions and immutability
- Combining pure logic with curry and composition
- Improving readability and structure of code with a point-free style
- Creating native function chains with the pipeline operator

If you want to see which features will be in mainstream programming languages tomorrow, then take a look at functional programming languages today

—Simon Peyton Jones

If objects are the fabric of JavaScript, functions represent the needles used to thread the pieces together. We can use functions in JavaScript to describe collections of objects (classes, constructor functions, and so on) and also to implement the business logic, the machinery that advances the state of our application. The reason why functions are so ubiquitous, versatile, and powerful in JavaScript is that they are objects too:

```
Function.prototype.__proto__.constructor === Object;
```

JavaScript has higher-order or first-class functions, which means you can pass them around as arguments to another function or as a return value. With higher-order functions, you can dramatically simplify complex patterns of software to a handful of functions, making JavaScript a lot more succinct than other mainstream languages such as Java and C#.

In chapter 3, we looked at how objects compose their structure to some extent using OLOO and more fully using mixins. Higher-order functions compose too—not structurally, but behaviorally, by being chained together and passed around as callbacks to represent sequences of computational logic. Higher-order functions are JavaScript's most powerful features by far, and the best way to learn about them is through the functional programming (FP) paradigm.

FP is a force to be reckoned with. These days, it's almost impossible to read about the wonders of JavaScript without seeing a shout-out to FP. I think JavaScript has continued to flourish thanks to its FP support, which is one of the things that drew me toward JavaScript many years ago. Although, theoretically, FP is an old school of thought, it's become pervasive recently in JavaScript coding and application design. Good examples are libraries such as Underscore and Lodash for processing data, React and Hooks for building modern UIs, and Redux and RxJS for managing state. In fact, if you look at 2019's State of JavaScript results for most-used utility libraries (https://2019.stateofjs .com/other-tools/#utilities), you will find Lodash, Underscore, RxJS, and Ramda ranking at the top. All these libraries enhance the functional capabilities of JavaScript.

Fundamentally speaking, FP promotes a different approach to problem solving from the more common structured or imperative way to which we're all accustomed. Wrapping your head around FP requires a mastery of JavaScript's main unit of computation, which has always been functions. Any type of object definition tries to associate the data (instance fields) with the logic (methods) that process that data. Objects compose at a coarse-grained level, as you learned about in chapter 3. Functions, on the other hand, separate data (arguments) and logic (function body) more distinctly and compose at a more fine-grained, lower level. FP programs are made up of a set of functions that receive input and produce a result with this data.

In this chapter, we'll take two important parts of our blockchain application and improve them by using FP. The goal is not a complete redesign of the application. Rather, we'll keep things simple and take a more lenient approach that combines the benefits of OO and FP paradigms together—aka a hybrid model. You'll learn that although imperative and FP disagree on fundamental principles, you can benefit from their strengths when tackling different parts of your application. To help you transition to an FP way of coding, we'll visualize how an imperative program is converted to a functional one (section 4.2).

Unless you're an expert, I recommend that you start by slowly adopting the basics of FP covered in this chapter and then finding ways to embed FP in your application. Later, how far you want to take this paradigm in your own code is up to you. Core business logic is usually a good candidate for this way of thinking. We'll go through the exercise of refactoring some imperative code into functional so that you can get a sense of how these two kinds compare.

It's been a noticeable trend for a few years now that platform teams, including JavaScript, are adding more features to their programming languages to support a functional style. ECMAScript 2019 (aka ES10), for example, added `Array.prototype`
`.{flat, and flatMap}`, which are integral to using data structures in a functional way. As of this writing, the road map for TC39 features a set of functional-inspired proposals moving up the ranks that will affect how you write JavaScript code in the years to come. So learning about this paradigm now will prepare you for what's ahead. In this book, we'll be looking at the

- Pipeline operator (https://github.com/tc39/proposal-pipeline-operator)
- Bind operator (https://github.com/tc39/proposal-bind-operator)

We still have a way to go before we understand why these features are so important. Understanding these features begins with understanding functional programming.

4.1 What is functional programming?

In this section, I'll provide a suitable definition of FP. First, I'll show you a short example and go over some of the basic qualities of functional code. Many people relate FP to the array APIs `map`, `reduce`, and `filter`. You've probably seen these APIs in action many times. Let's start with a quick example to jog your memory: determine whether all block objects in an array are valid. For this example, you can assume that you can skip validating the genesis block and that all blocks have an `isValid` method. Implementing this logic by using the array APIs would look like the next listing.

Listing 4.1 Combining `map`, `filter`, and `reduce`

```
const arr = [b1, b2, b3];

arr
    .filter(b => !b.isGenesis())        ← Skips the genesis block
                                          (which is always assumed
                                          to be valid)
    .map(b => b.isValid())              ←
    .reduce((a, b) => a && b, true);    ←
                                          Converts the array of
                                          blocks to an array of
        Performs a logical AND of all the Boolean values    Boolean values by calling
        together, parting from true, to obtain the final result    isValid on each block
```

As you know, these array APIs were designed to be higher-order functions, which means that they either accept a callback function or return one and delegate most of the logic to the callback function you provide. You've probably written similar code before but never thought about it from an FP point of view. An FP-aware programmer always prefers writing code that is heavily driven by higher-order functions this way.

Aside from the tendency to use functions for almost anything, another important quality of FP programs is immutability. In listing 4.1, even though arr is being mapped over and filtered, the original arr reference is kept intact:

```
console.log(arr); // [b1, b2, b3]
```

Code that is immutable avoids bugs that arise from inadvertently changing your application's state, especially when you deal with asynchronous functions that can run at arbitrary points in time. Did you know that methods such as reverse and sort mutate the array in place? What would happen if you passed that original array object to some other part of your program? Now the result is unpredictable.

An immutable function that always returns a predictable result, given a set of arguments, is known as *pure*, and with that definition, we arrive at the definition of FP:

> *Functional programming is the art of composing higher-order functions to advance the state of a program in a pure manner.*

So far, I've talked a little about composition and pure code. FP takes these ideas to the practical extreme. Now I'll unpack the key parts of the definition of FP:

- As you know by now, a *higher-order function* is one that can receive a function as a parameter or produce another function as a return value. With FP, you use functions for pretty much anything you do, and your program becomes one big assembly of functions glued together by composition.
- *Pure functions* compute their results based entirely on the set of input arguments received. They don't cause side effects—that is, they don't rely on accessing any outside or globally shared state, which makes programs more predictable and simple to reason about because you don't have to keep track of unintended state changes.

FP developers use functions to represent any type of data.

4.1.1 Functions as data

You can use functions to represent data in the form of expressions. Expressions can be evaluated to produce a value right away or passed to other parts of your code as callbacks to be evaluated when needed. Here are a few examples:

- Declare a constant value:

```
const fortyTwo = () => 42;
```

  As with regular constants, you can assign an expression to a variable or pass it as a function argument.
- Echo the same value, also known as the identity function:

```
const identity = a => a;
```

- Create new objects or implement arbitrary business logic:

```
const BitcoinService = ledger => { ... };
```

This function is known as a factory function, which always produces a new object.

- Encapsulated, private data (closure):

```
const add => a => b => a + b;
```

a is stored as part of the outer function's closure and referenced later in the internal function when the entire expression is evaluated:

```
add(2)(3) === 5
```

NOTE The arrow function notation used here is syntactically convenient to embed in fluent method chains, such as when you code with map, filter, reduce, and others or when you need an one-line expression. Although this chapter uses this notation often because of its terse design, regular function syntax is equally appropriate for all these examples.

All these expressions (except the first one) receive input and return output. The return value of a pure function is always a factor of the input it receives (unless it's always a constant); otherwise, the implication is that you've somehow opened the door to side effects and impure code.

Listing 4.2 shows a simple, naïve example that illustrates combining some of these expressions, which contain computation or data, as higher-order functions. The code attempts to perform some mathematical operation only if conditions allow; otherwise, it returns a default value.

Listing 4.2 Combining higher-order functions

```
const notNull = a => a !== null;        ◁──┐  Checks whether a
const square = a => a ** 2;                 │  value is not null

const safeOperation = (operation, guard, recover) =>    ◁──  Executes a safe
  input => guard(input, operation) || recover();             operation; otherwise,
                                                             calls a recovery function

const onlyIf = validator => (input, operation) =>    ◁──┐  Runs operation only if the
  validator(input) ? operation(input) : NaN;            │  validator function returns
                                                        │  true; otherwise, returns NaN

const orElse = identity;        ◁──

const safeSquare = safeOperation(    ◁──     Uses the identity function as
    square,                                  recovery, aliased under the
    onlyIf(notNull),                         name orElse
    orElse(fortyTwo)
);                                           Computes the square of a number
                                             if the input is not null; otherwise,
safeSquare(2); // 4                          recovers with the value 42
safeSquare(null); // 42
```

If you look at the structure of `safeSquare`, notice that it's made up of functions that clearly communicate the intent of the program. Some of these functions carry only data (`orElse`); other functions carry out a computation (`square`); some functions do both (`onlyIf`). This listing gives you a good first look at code done the functional way.

4.1.2 *The functional way*

As the saying goes, less is more. The functional paradigm imposes restrictions that are meant not to diminish what you can do, but to empower you. In this section, you'll look at a set of guidelines that help you code the functional way. In section 4.3.2, you'll learn how to work with these guidelines to tackle any type of problem.

An FP programmer always codes with a certain set of rules in mind. These rules can take some getting used to but become second nature with practice. Learning them will be well worth your time, however, because you'll end up with code that is more predictable and simpler to maintain.

The functional way in JavaScript involves these four simple rules:

- Functions must always return a value and (with a few exceptions) declare at least one parameter.
- The observable state of an application before and after a function runs does not change; it's immutable and side-effect-free. A new state is created each time.
- Everything a function needs to carry its work must be passed in via arguments or inherited from its surrounding outer function (closure), provided that the outer function abides by the same rules.
- A function called with the same input must always produce the same output. This rule leads to a principle known as referential transparency, which states that an expression and its corresponding value are interchangeable without altering the code's behavior.

With these simple rules, we can remove side effects and mutations from your code, which are one of the leading causes of bugs. When a function obeys all these rules, it is said to be pure. Sound simple enough? To rephrase, FP is the art of combining functions that play by these rules to advance the state of a program to its final outcome.

According to these rules, how is something like printing to the console pure? It's not. Functions that reach out of their scope, to perform I/O in this case, are *effectful*—that is, they cause a side effect. Side effects can also include functions that read/write to variables outside their own scope, accesses the filesystem, writes to a network socket, relies on random methods such as `Math.random`, and so on. Anything that makes the outcome of a function unpredictable is considered bad practice in the FP world.

But how can anything useful come out of functional coding when we can't touch all the things that mutate the state of our program? Indeed, working with immutable code requires a different mindset and, in some cases, a different approach to a problem, which is the hardest part. With FP, objects shouldn't be manipulated and changed directly. A change to an object means that a new one is always created, similar to version control, in that every change, even in the same line, results in a new commit ID. With respect to reading files, printing to the console, or any other practical real-world task, we need to learn to deal with these cases in a practical way.

So far, we've been talking about FP at a high level. To make this discussion more concrete, section 4.2 compares functional and imperative code.

4.2 *Functional versus imperative at a glance*

So that you can begin to wrap your head around this paradigm shift, it's best to tackle a couple of problems. We'll quickly go over the techniques needed to implement this shift throughout the chapter so that you get an end-to-end view of using FP in JavaScript.

The first problem we're tackling in this chapter is a functional way to implement the logic behind calculating hashes. Here, we will swap the insecure algorithm for a secure implementation of the HasHash mixin logic. This implementation will be a good warmup for our second example, which involves calculating the balance of a user's digital wallet by using only pure functions. In the latter exercise, we will see a complete refactoring of imperative code into functional. The balance calculation involves processing all the blocks from the public ledger and tallying all the transactions that refer to a specific user. If the user appears as the recipient, we add funds; otherwise, we subtract funds.

To give you a frame for comparison, the imperative version of our second problem looks something like the following:

```
function computeBalance(address) {
    let balance = Money.zero();
    for (const block of ledger) {
        if (!block.isGenesis()) {
            for (const tx of block.data) {
                if (tx.sender === address) {
                    balance = balance.minus(tx.funds);
                }
                else {
                    balance = balance.plus(tx.funds);
                }
            }
        }
    }
    return balance.round();
}
```

You'll learn how to transition this version into a more functional style, like so:

```
const computeBalance = address =>
  compose(
    Money.round,
    reduce(Money.sum, Money.zero()),
    map(balanceOf(address)),
    flatMap(prop('data')),
    filter(
      compose(
        not,
```

```
      prop('isGenesis')
    )
  ),
  Array.from
);
```

You're probably wondering whether these two programs are the same: the first version has loops and conditionals, and the second one doesn't. Shockingly, the programs are the same. You probably recognize some of the constructs in this code block, such as `map` and `filter`, but how this code works may not be clear, especially because the control and data flow is in the opposite direction of its imperative counterpart. The rounding instruction appears at the top rather than at the end, for example.

Looking at the FP style again, you may also wonder where the tallying of the total is taking place. Compare figures 4.1 and 4.2 to see the different control and data flows of the imperative and functional approaches.

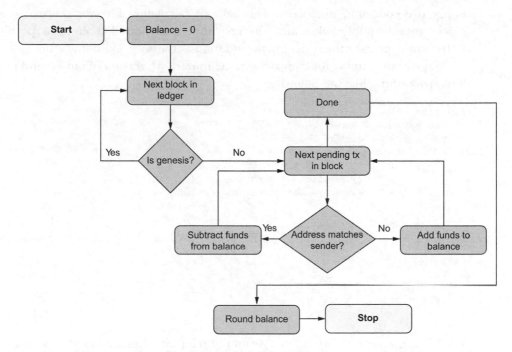

Figure 4.1   Imperative flow of control for the logic in calculating a user's total balance in a blockchain

The imperative approach (figure 4.1) describes not only the changes in state, but also how this change is produced as data flowing through all the control structures (loops, conditionals, variable assignment, and so on). The functional approach (figure 4.2), on the other hand, models a unidirectional flow of state transformations that hides the intricate control details; it shows you the steps needed to obtain the final result without all the unnecessary cruft. Also, each step is immutable, as mentioned earlier, which allows you to laser-focus on any of them without having to worry about the rest (figure 4.2).

Figure 4.2 is modeling a declarative flow. Think of this figure as being like summarizing the highlights of the imperative version in the form of a recipe. Declarative code is written to match how it will be read. Write code for your users and colleagues, not for the machine, that's what compilers are for.

A good example of a declarative language is SQL. In SQL, the beauty of declarative programming is that it focuses on what you're trying to accomplish rather than how, so mundane details such as code splitting, looping, and state management are tucked inside their respective steps. The hardest part about embracing FP is letting go of your old ways and your imperative bias. After you cross this line, you start to see how the structure, readability, and maintainability of your code improve, especially in JavaScript, which gives you the freedom to mutate data in many ways. We're fortunate that JavaScript allows us to write code this way, and we should take advantage of it.

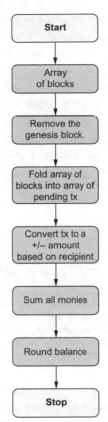

Figure 4.2   Functional flow of control for the logic in calculating a user's total balance in a blockchain

To embrace the FP mindset, you must understand function composition, discussed in the next section.

4.3   Composition: The functional way

Generally speaking, composition occurs when data combines to make like-data or data of the same type; it preserves type. Objects fuse into new objects (like the mixins from chapter 3), and functions combine to create new functions (like the functions in this chapter). When mixins create new objects, this process is known as coarse-grained, structural composition. This section teaches you how to assemble code at the function level, known as fine-grained or low-level composition.

Function composition is the backbone of functional programming, and it's the guiding principle by which you arrange and assemble your entire code. Although JavaScript doesn't enforce any restrictions, composition is most effective when your functions play by the rules of purity mentioned in section 4.1.2.

In this section, we'll implement the business logic of the `HasHash` mixin. First, you'll learn how to convert the imperative `calculateHash` method we started in chapter 2 to use a more functional style. We'll use this method to fill in the skeleton implementation we started in chapter 3. Second, you'll learn how composition can help you work around code that has side effects. This capability is important because most of the time, you will need to mix pure code with effectful code in your daily activities.

The best way to understand how functions compose is to start small, with only two functions, because then that same logic can be extended to an arbitrary number of them. So given the functions f and g, you can order them in a such a way that the output of the first becomes the input of the second, like binary plumbing, as shown in figure 4.3.

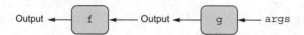

Figure 4.3   High-level diagram of composition. The directions of the arrows are important. Composition works right to left. So in f composed with g, g receives the initial input arguments. Then g's output is input to f. Finally, f's result becomes the output of the entire operation.

In code, composition can be represented concisely by `f(g(args))`. Because JavaScript executes eagerly, it will try to evaluate any variable with a set of parentheses in front of it immediately. If you want to express the composition of two functions and assign it to a variable name, you can wrap a function around that expression. Let's call this expression `compose` (see the next listing).

Listing 4.3   Composition of two functions

```
const compose = (...args) => f(g(...args));    ◁─┐  Using JavaScript's spread operator
                                                  │  to support an arbitrary number of
                                                  │  arguments
```

Listing 4.3 assumes, however, that f and g are functions that exist outside the context of `compose`. We know that this situation is a side effect. Instead, make f and g input arguments, and use the closure around the inner function so that this code works with any two functions that you provide. Closures are important features that work amazingly well with higher-order functions; I'll review them in section 4.4.

Let's wrap this expression yet again with another function around `compose` and call it `compose2`:

```
const compose2 = (f, g) => (...args) => f(g(...args))
```

This code is a lot more flexible. Because `compose2` accepts functions as arguments and returns a function, it's of higher-order, of course. Also, notice that `compose2` evaluates the functions right to left (f after g) to align with the mathematical definition of function composition. Here's a more-concrete example:

```
const count = arr => arr.length;
const split = str => str.split(/\s+/);
```

You could combine these functions directly:

```
const countWords = str => count(split(str));
```

When you use compose2, the same expression becomes

```
const countWords = str => compose2(count, split)(str);
```

Here's a little pro tip. Because you can assign functions directly to a variable, any time you have the input argument repeated to the left and the right of an expression, you can cancel it and make your code more compact:

```
const countWords = compose2(count, split);
```

```
countWords('functional programming');  // 2
```

Figure 4.4 shows the flow from figure 4.3.

Figure 4.4   Sequentially executed count after split

compose2 is superior to a direct call because it's able to separate the declaration of functions involved in the sequence from its evaluation. The concept is similar to OLOO, which allows you to instantiate a ready-to-use set of objects and initialize those objects when you need to. By capturing the functions passed in as variables (f and g), we can defer any execution until the caller supplies the input parameter. This process is called lazy evaluation. In other words, the expression

```
compose2(count, split);
```

is itself a function made from two other functions (like an object made from two mixins). Yet this function will not run until the caller evaluates it; it sits there dormant. compose2 allows you to create a complex, ready-to-use expression from a couple of simple ones and assign it a name (countWords) to use in other parts of the code, if needed. Let's embellish this example a bit more in the next section; we'll tackle something a bit more realistic that works in a side effect in the mix.

4.3.1   *Working with side effects*

Exception handling, logging to a file, and making HTTP requests are some of the tasks we work on every day. All these tasks involve side effects in one way or another, and there's no avoiding them. The way to deal with side effects in a functional-style application is to isolate and push them away from our main application logic. This way, we can keep the important business logic of our application pure and immutable, and then use composition to bring all the pieces back together.

To see how you can split pure from non-pure code, let's tackle another task: counting the words in a text file. Assume that the file contains the words "the quick brown fox jumps over the lazy dog." For simplicity, let's use the synchronous version of the filesystem API built into Node.js, as shown in the next listing.

Listing 4.4   Imperative function that counts the words in a text file

```
function countWordsInFile(file) {
   const fileBuffer = fs.readFileSync(file);
   const wordsString = fileBuffer.toString();
   const wordsInArray = wordsString.split(/\s+/);
   return wordsInArray.length;
}

countWordsInFile('sample.txt'); // 9
```

Listing 4.4 is trivial but packs in a few steps. As in `calculateHash`, you can identify four clear tasks: reading the raw file, decoding the raw binary as a string, splitting the string into words, and counting the words. Arranging these tasks with `compose` should look like figure 4.5.

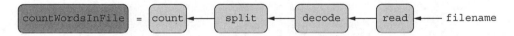

Figure 4.5   The logic of `countWordsInFile` derives from the logic of composing other single-responsibility functions such as `read`, `decode`, `split`, and `count`.

First, represent each task as its own expression. You saw `count` and `split` earlier; the next listing shows the other two tasks.

Listing 4.5   Helper functions to support `countWordsInFile`

```
   const decode = buffer => buffer.toString();

   const read = fs.readFileSync;
```
Creating an alias to shorten the filesystem API call

In listing 4.5, we gave each variable a specific name to make the program easy to follow. In imperative code, variable names are used to describe the output, if any, of executing a statement or series of statements, but these variable names don't describe the process of computing them. You have to parse through the code to see that process. When you push for a more declarative style, the function names indicate what to do at each step. Let's work our way there. A direct call would look like

```
const countWordsInFile = file => count(split(decode(read(file))));
```

You can see that all variable assignment was removed. But we can agree that this style of code can become unwieldy as complexity grows. Let's use compose2 to fix this problem:

```
const countWordsInFile = compose2(
    compose2(count, split),
    compose2(decode, read)
);
```

Each compose2 segment can be represented by its own micro module, as shown in figure 4.6.

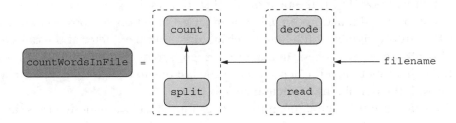

Figure 4.6 Diagram countWordsInFile improved with compose2

But wait a minute—we already have a named abstraction that handles compose2(count, split). That abstraction is called countWords. Let's plug it in:

```
const countWordsInFile = compose2(
    countWords,
    compose2(decode, read)
);
```

The reason why you can swap portions of the code in and out like Lego bricks is referential transparency. In other words, the expression is pure and doesn't rely on any global, shared state. The outcome of either expression would be the same and, therefore, does not alter the result of the program. Plugging in this abstraction is better, but we can do even better.

For more complex logic, you're probably thinking that grouping functions in pairs is a lot of typing. To simplify the code, it would be ideal to have a version of compose2 that can work on any number of functions or an array of functions. Let's repurpose compose and use Array#reduce with compose2 to extend combining two functions to any number of functions. This technique is analogous to putting together clusters of Lego bricks at a time instead of assembling individual bricks.

In `Array#reduce`, the reducer is the callback function that accumulates or folds your data into a single value. If you're not familiar with how `reduce` works, here's a simple example. Consider a function, `sum`, as a reducer for adding a list of numbers:

```
const sum = (a,b) => a + b;

[1,2,3,4,5,6].reduce(sum);  // 21
```

The reducer takes the current accumulated result in `a` and adds it to the next element, `b`, starting with the first element in the array.

By the same token, `compose2` is the reducer for `compose`:

```
const compose = (...fns) => fns.reduce(compose2);
```

In this case, the reducer takes two functions at a time and composes them (adds them), creating another function. That function is remembered for the next iteration and then composed with the next one and so on, resulting in a function that is the composition of all functions provided by the user. Function composition works right to left, with the rightmost function receiving the input parameter at the call site and kicking off the entire process. In that order, `reduce` folds all the functions in the array with the first function in the declaration as the last one to be executed, which matches nicely with the definition of function composition.

Now let's use this technique in the next listing to peel those nested calls shown in the preceding code snippets into a much more streamlined, unidirectional flow.

> **Listing 4.6** `countWordsInFile` **implemented with** `compose`

```
const countWordsInFile = compose(
    count,
    split,
    decode,
    read
);

countWordsInFile('sample.txt'); // 9
```

This code looks like pseudocode at first, doesn't it? If you compare listings 4.4 and 4.6, you can see that the latter is a basic outline of the former; it's declarative! This style of coding is also known as point-free, which we'll discuss in section 4.6.

The level of modularity used (fine-grained function level or coarse-grained modules with multiple functions) is up to you; you can compose to your heart's content (figure 4.7).

Whether you're composing simple functions or entire modules of code with a function interface, the simplicity of assembling composable code doesn't change. (We'll talk about importing and using modules in chapter 6.)

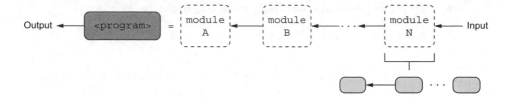

Figure 4.7 The structure of composable software. A program is implemented by composing other subprograms, which can be as small as a function or as big as another program. Each module (consider Module N) uses composition, finally arriving at assembling individual functions.

Now that you understand the composition pattern, let's use it to decompose and simplify the hashing logic of our blockchain application.

4.3.2 Decomposing complex code

In chapters 2 and 3, we began creating a hashing method for our transaction classes called calculateHash. This hashing algorithm, or the digest string that it generated, was insecure and prone to collisions. In the cryptocurrency world, this situation is a no-go, so let's improve it. You'll see how a more functional design will enable you to easily swap the insecure algorithm for a more secure one that uses Node.js's crypto module. Here's the last version of that code again for reference:

```
const HasHash = keys => ({
  calculateHash() {
    const data = keys.map(f => this[f]).join('');
    let hash = 0, i = 0;
    while (i < data.length) {
      hash = ((hash << 5) - hash + data.charCodeAt(i++)) << 0;
    }
    return hash**2;
  }
});
```

Using the four rules outlined earlier in section 4.1.2, is this function/method pure? Before answering this question, let's practice a little reverse engineering. First, let's decompose the function into its main parts; then we'll analyze each piece individually. When we split the function apart, we'll compose it back together by using a more functional approach. With lots of practice, you'll get better at this process, which will become second nature.

calculateHash performs two main tasks, split into two methods:

- Assembling the data from the set of keys:

```
function assemble(keys) {
  return keys.map(f => this[f]).join('');
}
```

- Computing the digest or cipher from this data:

```
function computeCipher(data) {
    let hash = 0, i = 0;
    while (i < data.length) {
        hash = ((hash << 5) - hash + data.charCodeAt(i++)) << 0;
    }
    return hash**2;
}
```

This thought process itself is beneficial because smaller functions are much simpler to reason about than larger ones, and you can carry this thought process as deep as you deem reasonable. Now to answer the question at hand: Are these two methods pure? Believe it or not, `computeCipher` is pure from a practical standpoint, whereas `assemble` is not. The reason is that `assemble` makes assumptions about its context when it attempts to read properties from `this`—a potential downside of mixins that we highlighted in chapter 3. With a standalone function declaration, `this` is bound to the function, not the surrounding object. To fix this problem, we can use JavaScript's dynamic binding:

```
const HasHash = keys => ({
  calculateHash() {
    return compose2(computeCipher, assemble.bind(this, keys))();
  }
});
```

The call to `bind` will correct the `this` reference and point it to the surrounding object whose properties we want to read. This code is looking better, but relying on this type of binding can make it hard to follow. Also remember that making assumptions about the environment is a side effect, which we still have in `calculateHash`. To put it another way, a function that infers state is harder to work with because its own behavior is dependent on external factors. For that reason, you'll never see references to external variables, including `this`, used in a pure FP code base. On the other hand, functions that are explicit about the data they need are self-documenting and, thus, simpler to use and maintain.

Let's change `assemble` to a function that is explicit about its contract and accepts the set of keys for the properties used in the hashing process, as well as the object to hash:

```
function assemble(keys, obj) {
  return keys.map(f => obj[f]).join('');
}
```

By not making any assumptions, this generic, standalone function is completely divorced from its surrounding class or object context. The fine line in the sand where OO departs to FP in a hybrid model is where we disassociate or extract the code under a class's methods and move it into one or more pure functions. This separation or segregation from the mutable, stateful components to immutable ones will help you avoid making assumptions about your data and use FP where it makes sense.

Let's come back to computeCipher, the heart of the hashing process. Earlier, I mentioned that in by-the-book functional programming, mutations are prohibited. In practice, though, we accept making code easier to implement as long as state changes don't ripple out or leak from the function's scope. In this case, all the mutations are kept locally, so the code is acceptable as is.

Nevertheless, computeCipher doesn't capture the true functional spirit; it still feels a bit procedural. By inspecting computeCipher as its own microenvironment, you can see that its logic still depends on setting and changing variables like the loop counter i and the accumulated hash. You have room for improvement. Working with lists and arrays is simple with APIs such as map and reduce, but when you need to keep track of and reuse state in an iterative manner, recursion is the best way to achieve your goal. The next listing shows how you can refactor the while loop as a recursive function.

Listing 4.7 Refactoring `computeCipher` as a recursive function

```
function computeCipher(data, i = 0, hash = 0) {
  if(i >= data.length) {
    return hash ** 2;
  }
  return computeCipher(          <──  Calls itself recursively with the updated hash at
    data,                              each iteration as an input argument to avoid
    i + 1,                             assigning and changing data in place
    ((hash << 5) - hash + data.charCodeAt(i)) << 0
    );
}
```

This function brings us back to our four main FP rules, without any trade-offs, and here's what we gained:

- We used JavaScript's default argument syntax to capture the initial state properly.
- We eliminated all variable reassignment.
- We created expressions in which every branch produces a return value.

Now that we have these two smaller, simpler functions, we can compose them to compute the cipher of a transaction object:

```
calculateHash() {
    return compose2(computeCipher, assemble(keys, this))();
}
```

But wait a second—we have a problem. compose2 expects a function but instead got a string when assemble ran, so this code fails to run. Let's use lazy evaluation to make a small adjustment to assemble, turning it into a higher-order function that accepts the keys and returns a function that is ready to receive the object of the call, taking advantage of closures:

```
function assemble(keys) {
  return function(obj) {
    return keys.map(f => obj[f]).join('');
  }
}
```

This small adjustment is enough to get to our more functional approach:

```
const HasHash = keys => ({
  calculateHash() {
    return compose2(computeCipher, assemble(keys))(this);
  }
});
```

In essence, what we did to `assemble` was convert a 2-arity (two-argument) function to two single-arity (single-argument) functions—the premise behind a technique called curried function evaluation.

4.4   Currying and closures

Currying is a technique that will help you compose functions when they require multiple arguments. It relies on JavaScript's amazing support for closures. In this section, we'll begin with a quick review of closures and then move on to curried function application.

You are probably familiar with closures, which are central to how JavaScript works. In fact, they're among the most compelling JavaScript features. To keep the discussion focused, I won't cover closures in depth but will provide some detail in case you're not familiar with them.

A *closure* is another form of scope or context created around functions that allows a function to reference surrounding variables. When a function is called, JavaScript retains references to variables of a function's local and global lexical environment— that is, all variables syntactically declared around this function. In the specification, the internal reference [[Scope]] links a function to its closure. In other books and online resources, you may see the term *backpack* used to describe this linkage. The reason I say *around* and not *before* is because hoisted variables and functions are also part of a function's closure. The following listing provides an example.

> **Listing 4.8   Basics of scope with closures**

```
const global = 'global';
  function outer() {
    const outer = 'outer';
    function inner() {
      const inner = 'inner'
      console.log(inner, outer, global);      ◁┐ Prints inner
    }                                            outer global
    console.log(outer, global);      ◁┐ Prints outer
    inner();                            global
  }
outer();
```

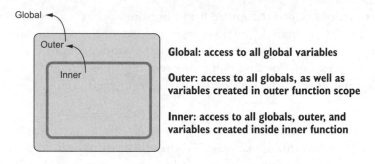

Global: access to all global variables

Outer: access to all globals, as well as variables created in outer function scope

Inner: access to all globals, outer, and variables created inside inner function

Figure 4.8 The closure mechanism in JavaScript allows any function to reference its lexical environment. The innermost function has access to all the state from its outer scopes (outer + global), and the outer scope can access everything from its surrounding global scope.

You can visualize this example in figure 4.8.

JavaScript gives you complete freedom to access a sizeable subset of application state from which a function is declared, implying the global scope as well as any outer variables that lexically appear around a function. In essence, closures make all this state implicit function arguments. Although access to these variables is certainly convenient at times, it can also lead to code that is hard to maintain. Theoretically, FP considers accessing any state surrounding a function to be a side effect; after all, we're reaching outside. In practice, however, using closures is permissible so long as they are bounded and narrow in scope and, more important, don't incur any observable changes beyond the surrounded function. Using closures is the way to code with JavaScript, and we should take advantage of them. Closures enable some powerful patterns in JavaScript, currying being one of them.

4.4.1 Curried function application

A function that has its argument list expanded as stepwise, single, nested functions of single arguments is said to be curried. The next listing shows a simple example of manual currying.

Listing 4.9 Evaluating add as separate single-argument functions

```
const add = x => y => x + y;

const addThreeTo = add(3);

addThreeTo(7); // 10
```

Addition does not take place until the last variable is bound.

Bind the expression, and the function executes.

Instead of add receiving x and y arguments in one shot, the code accepts them as singular functions that get called sequentially. More formally, currying is the process of converting a function of multiple arguments (or arity N) to be evaluated it as N unary (arity 1) functions. Until the entire list of arguments has been provided and all functions evaluated, a curried function always returns the next function. If you take a small step back, you can see that currying is another form of composition: you're taking a complex function and evaluating it as multiple simple ones. Because add takes two arguments, x and y, it's evaluated as two single-argument functions:

```
add(3)(7); // 10
```

Going back to our word-counting example, let's use this manual currying technique to buy more flexibility in decoding the binary buffer as a result of the file IO. As decode stands right now, the toString method on buffers assumes a UTF-8 encoding:

```
const decode = buffer => buffer.toString();
```

Most of the time, this method is what you'll want to use. But it'd be nice to have flexibility in case we ever need ASCII encoding as well. Instead of refactoring decode to accept another argument, let's embed another function in between to capture the encoding parameter (with its own default argument):

```
const decode = (encoding = 'utf8') => buffer => buffer.toString(encoding);
```

Now we can call decode once to partially curry/set the encoding parameter and plug the resulting (remaining) function into the compose expression as such:

```
const countWordsInFile = compose(
    count,
    split,
    decode('utf8'),
    read
);
```

The declarative quality of this code is enhanced even further because you can see not only the steps that make up your solution, but also the attributes or the configuration of these functions in each step.

Let's continue working our way toward calculating secure object hashes in a functional way. Consider a helper function called prop, again manually curried:

```
const prop = name => obj => obj[name] &&
    isFunction(obj[name]) ? obj[name].call(obj) : obj[name];
```

With the helper isFunction

```
const isFunction = f =>
        f
    && typeof f === 'function'
    && Object.prototype.toString.call(f) === '[object Function]';
```

prop can access a property from any object by name. You can partially bind the name parameter to create a function with the name in its closure and then accept the object from which to extract the named property. Consider this simple example:

```
const transaction = {
    sender: 'luis@tjoj.com',
    recipient: 'luke@tjoj.com',
    funds: 10.0
};

const getFunds = prop('funds');
getFunds(transaction); // 10.0
```

You can also create a function that extracts multiple properties into an array by mapping prop over an array of keys:

```
const props = (...names) => obj => names.map(n => prop(n)(obj));

const data = props('sender', 'recipient', 'funds');

data(transaction); // ['luis@tjoj.com', 'luke@tjoj.com', 10.0]
```

Calling prop on a single object is not as exciting as calling it on a collection of objects. Given an array of three transaction objects with funds, 10.0, 12.5, and 20.0, respectively, you can map prop over it:

```
[tx1, tx2, tx3].map(prop('funds')); // [10.0, 12.5, 20.0]

[tx1, tx2, tx3].map(prop('calculateHash'));

// [64284210552842720, 1340988549712360000, 64284226272528960]
```

In this code, the higher-order function prop('funds') did not produce a result until map used it, which is convenient. But when functions get more complex, the awkward notation used to write functions with expanded arrow syntax becomes hard to read, not to mention that multifunction evaluation—add(x)(y)—is cumbersome. You can automate the process of manually expanding into multiple functions with the curry function.

curry automates the manual currying process that we've been doing so far, converting a function of multiple arguments to several nested functions of a single argument. Thus, a function like add

```
const add = a => b => a + b;
```

can be written as

```
const add = curry((a, b) => a + b);
```

The wonderful quality of `curry` is that it dynamically changes the way the function evaluates and smooths over the syntax needed to partially pass arguments. You can call add piece-wise as `add(3)(7)` or, preferably, at the same time as `add(3,7)`.

> **NOTE**   In theory, currying is a much stricter form of partial application that requires that returned functions take a single parameter at a time. In partial application, a returned function can take one or several arguments.

As with `compose`, you can import `curry` from any FP library (Ramda, underscore.js, and so on), but studying the implementation is interesting; it uses a lot of modern JavaScript idioms (such as rest and spread operators) to manipulate function objects. It also uses a bit of reflection to dynamically figure out the function's length (a topic that I'll circle back to in chapter 7).

In keeping with the pure FP spirit of avoiding loops and reassignment of variables, you can implement `curry` as a recursive, arrow function quite elegantly. You may also find versions that take a more imperative, iterative approach:

```
const curry = fn => (...args1) =>
  args1.length === fn.length
    ? fn(...args1)
    : (...args2) => {
        const args = [...args1, ...args2]
        return args.length >= fn.length ? fn(...args) : curry(fn)(...args)
      };
```

The following listing shows how to use `curry` to enhance `prop` and `props`.

> **Listing 4.10   Curried versions of `prop` and `props`**

```
const prop = curry((name, obj) =>
  obj[name] && isFunction(obj[name]) ? obj[name].call(obj) : obj[name]
);

const props = curry((names, obj) => names.map(n => prop(n, obj)));
```

Internally, curry adds runtime support to rewrite the (name, a) pair into partially evaluated arguments name => a => ...

We no longer use the varargs ...name argument, as this is allowed only as the last (or only) argument.

Not everything can be curried, unfortunately

As wonderful and powerful as `curry` is, in JavaScript there are a few edge cases where `curry` can change the expected behavior of a function when it relies on features such as variadic parameters or parameters with default values.

In listing 4.11, to make `props` work with `curry`, we needed to change `...names` to a normal, nonvariadic parameter, `names`, that is allowed to appear as a first argument. Variadic parameters always need to appear at the end of the function signature.

Another, more subtle issue to watch out for is default parameters. Looking at the implementation of curry in this section, you can see that it relies on Function.length. This property is a bit tricky in JavaScript because it does not count functions with default values, as this snippet of code illustrates:

```
const add = (a, b) => a + b;        // add.length = 2
const add = (a = 0, b = 0) => a + b; // add.length = 0
```

To reiterate, curry mandates that you satisfy all the arguments of a function before it evaluates. Until that happens, curry keeps returning the partially applied functions with the remaining arguments waiting to be passed in. This situation also prevents running functions with unsatisfied or undefined arguments. As I said earlier, add(3) returns a function to the caller, but add(3,7) evaluates to 10 immediately. There's no way to call a function with an unsatisfied set of arguments, which is great!

With curried functions, the order of arguments is important. Normally, we don't pay a lot of attention to order in object-oriented code. But in FP, argument order is crucial because it relies so much on partial application. In all the curried functions shown in this chapter, notice that the arguments are arranged to benefit from partial evaluation. For that reason, it's best to place the most static, fixed arguments first and allow the last ones to be the more dynamic call-specific arguments, as in the definition for prop:

```
const prop = curry((name, obj) =>
  obj[name] && isFunction(obj[name]) ? obj[name].call(obj) : obj[name]
);
```

The last parameter, obj, is left unbounded (free) so that you can freely extract a particular field from any object as you're mapping over an array, for example. Given the transactions tx1 and tx2, one for $10 and the other for $12.50, respectively, you can create a new function, fundsOf, with a partially bound funds property key. Now you can apply this function to any object with that key or even map this function an array of similar objects:

```
const fundsOf = prop('funds');
fundsOf(tx1); // 10.0
fundsOf(tx2); // 12.5
```

Now that you've learned about currying and composition, you can use them together to create a functional version of the calculateHash logic inside HasHash. Alone, curry and compose offer lots of value, but together, they are even more powerful.

4.4.2   *The curry and composition dynamic duo*

One of the goals of this chapter is to generate a more secure hashing digest for calculateHash in our HasHash mixin. So far, we're at this point in using the recursive definition of computeCipher:

```
const HasHash = () => ({
  calculateHash() {
    return compose(computeCipher, assemble)(this);
  }
});

function computeCipher(data, i = 0, hash = 0) {
  if(i >= data.length) {
    return hash ** 2
  }
  return computeCipher(
      data,
      i + 1,
      ((hash << 5) - hash + data.charCodeAt(i)) << 0
    );
}

const assemble = ({ sender, recipient, funds })
      => [sender, recipient, funds].join('');
```

HasHash is aware of its surrounding context (namely, the transaction object referenced by this), but the functions are kept pure and side-effect-free. By building these small islands of pure logic, we can put all this code aside and lessen the mental burden of having to keep track of everything that's happening.

But we're not done yet. Now that each function is separate, let's improve the code a bit more to make HasHash more secure and applicable to the other blockchain domain objects. We will make two additional changes:

- *Integrate* HasHash *with any object.* This change involves refactoring assemble to take an array of the parts of an object used in hashing, giving us extra flexibility when assigning HasHash to other classes. Part of this change also involves mapping a call to JSON.stringify to ensure that any object provided (primitive or otherwise) gets converted to its string representation. JSON.stringify is a good way of ensuring that we get a string out of any type of data, and it works well, provided that the objects are not incredibly long:

  ```
  const assemble = (...pieces) => pieces.map(JSON.stringify).join('');
  ```

  This line creates the string with the necessary object data to seed to the hashing code. Here's an example:

  ```
  const keys = ['sender', 'recipient', 'funds'];
  const transaction = {
     sender: 'luis@tjoj.com',
     recipient: 'luke@tjoj.com',
  ```

```
        funds: 10
    };

    assemble(keys.map(k => transaction[k]));

    // ["luis@tjoj.com","luke@tjoj.com",10]
```

- *Implement a more secure hash.* Let's use Node.js's crypto module. This module gives you the option to generate hashes using widely adopted algorithms, such as SHA-2, as well as different output encodings, such as hexadecimal:

```
const computeCipher = (options, data) =>
    require('crypto')
        .createHash(options.algorithm)
        .update(data)
        .digest(options.encoding);
```

The next listing shows an example that creates the SHA-256 representation of a simple object.

Listing 4.11 Computing a SHA-256 value from the contents of an object

```
computeCipher(
    {
        algorithm: 'SHA256',       ◁────  SHA-2 is a set of secure cryptographic hash
        encoding:  'hex'           ◁──    functions. The longer the bit string, the more
    },                                    secure it is. In this case, I'm using SHA0256,
    JSON.stringify({                      which is widely adopted in the industry
        sender: 'luis@tjoj.com',
        recipient: 'luke@tjoj.com',       Returns a hexadecimal-encoded string
        funds: 10                         instead of a binary buffer, making the
    })                                    output more legible
); // '04a635cf3f19a6dcc30ca7b63b9a1a6a1c42a9820002788781abae9bec666902'
```

Hash computation must be reliable and predictable; given the same input, it must produce the same output. If you recall from our starting guidelines, predictability conveniently points to the principle of referential transparency. All that's left to do now is compose these two:

```
compose(computeCipher, assemble);
```

But there's an issue here. Can you spot why this code won't work? computeCipher is not a function of a single argument. Invoking this function as is will pass the output of assemble into the options part and undefined for data, which will break the entire flow. We can use currying to address this mismatch by partially configuring compute-Cipher to produce a function that gets inserted into compose. First, add curry to the function definition:

```
const computeCipher = curry((options, data) =>
    require('crypto')
        .createHash(options.algorithm)
```

```
    .update(data)
    .digest(options.encoding));
```

Then call `computeCipher` piecewise, as you did with `add` and `prop`:

```
compose(
  computeCipher({
      algorithm: 'SHA256',
      encoding:  'hex'
   }),
   assemble);
```

The next listing puts everything together.

Listing 4.12   Final implementation of `HasHash`

```
const HasHash = (
  keys,
  options = {
      algorithm: 'SHA256',
      encoding:  'hex'
  }
) => ({
  calculateHash() {
     return compose(
      computeCipher(options),
      assemble,
      props(keys)
    )(this);
  }
});
```

Passing this works well when it's your own code, but when you're using third-party libraries, it's best to send a copy of only the data needed.

Figure 4.9 shows the flow of data using a simple transaction object literal:

```
    const hashTransaction = Object.assign(
      {
        sender: 'luis@tjoj.com',
        recipient: 'luke@tjoj.com',
        funds: 10
      },
      HasHash(['sender', 'recipient', 'funds'])
    );


    hashTransaction.calculateHash();

    // '04a635cf3f19a6dcc30ca7b63b9a1a6a1c42a9820002788781abae9bec666902'
```

We used `curry` and `compose` to drive the execution of `calculateHash`, which are known as function combinators—functions that build up (combine) other functions. Combinators have no special logic of their own; they work on either the structure of the functions themselves or on coordinating their execution. `curry` manipulates the arguments so that they can be evaluated one at a time. Similarly, `compose` is in charge

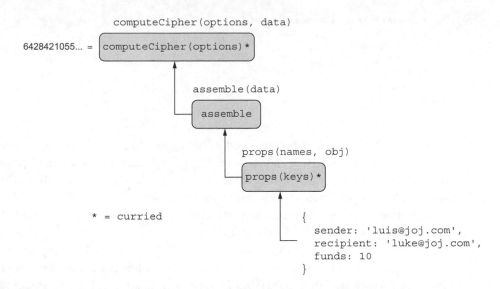

Figure 4.9 Composing with `curry` in the implementation of `calculateHash`. The label above each box shows the complete function signature. `computeCipher` and `props` are curried and have been partially applied. The far-right parameter (or the only parameter) of all functions is used to receive the input of one function in the chain.

of threading through a function's output with the next function's input. All this control flow is abstracted from you in this snippet of code:

```
compose(
    computeCipher(options),
    assemble,
    props(keys)
)(this);
```

The object referenced by `this` enters the composition chain, and on the other side, you get its hash value. Passing the original context (`this`) here is safe because all these functions are side-effect-free. But what happens when someone else changes them or when you're integrating with other functions you don't know about? In JavaScript, object values are stored by reference. When you pass an object to a function, that reference is passed by value, not the object itself (as with primitives). You can guard against any undesirable mutations and make your code more predictable by sending a copy. This situation is also a good opportunity for the input object being hashed to use only the data you need. To do so, let's use the `Object.fromEntries` API. This API allows you to turn any iterable object of key/value pairs (`Array`, `Map`, and so on) into an object. `HasHash` already has the list of keys for the data to hash, so it's easy to construct an object with only that data:

```
calculateHash() {
    const objToHash = Object.fromEntries(
```

```
      keys.map(k => [k, prop(k, this)])
  );
  return compose(
    computeCipher(options),
    assemble,
    props(keys)
  )(objToHash);
}
```

With this snippet, we've completed our HasHash mixin. As you can see, it's not an entirely pure object, because it depends on the global this to exist, which points to the prototype of the object to which HasHash is assigned. But we can call it a hybrid because it relies on pure functions to carry out its work.

We still have to tackle the other coding example: calculating a user's total balance from blockchain transactions. In the code snippets you've seen so far, we've always used a regular float to represent the funds amount. I did this to keep things simple. In the real world, funds always has two components: a numerical value and a currency denomination (such as $10.0 or ฿10.0). To represent currency, let's create an object called Money, designed to be immutable.

4.5   *Working with immutable objects*

The notion of purity extends beyond functions to objects. So far, the main entities of our blockchain application (Block, Transaction, and so on) are *mutable*, which means that you can easily change the properties of the object after instantiation. We made this design decision to allow these objects to recalculate their hashes on update, and also to allow the object to be dynamically extended via mixins or traditional class-based inheritance if need be. We could also have decided to make the objects immutable, and there are many good use cases for this design, one of which we'll explore in this section.

Consider an object called Money that represents the amount of currency being transacted. Money is an object with perpetual value: ten cents will always equate to ten cents. Its identity is given by the amount and the currency name. If you change ten cents to five cents, conceptually, that's a new Money entity. Think about what it means to change a date value. Isn't this value a different moment in time? Changing a point in a Cartesian plane is another point. Other examples widely used in industry that lend themselves to this type of design include DateTime, Point, Line, Money, and Decimal:

```
const coord2_3 = Point(2, 3);
coord2_3.x = 4; // No longer the same point!
```

Immutable objects are a well-known pattern in industry. In chapter 2, we discussed how Object.create allows you to define immutable fields by using data descriptors upon creation. Generally speaking, an immutable object is one for which you can't set any fields. Its data descriptors have writable: false for all fields. A popular pattern based on this is called the Value Object pattern. A value object is immutable upon creation and has some fields to describe identity and comparison. Similar to the guidelines imposed by pure functions, here are some guidelines to keep in mind when deciding whether to use this pattern:

- *Has no global identity*—There's no way to fetch an instance of a value object by some sort of ID. Conversely, transactions are globally identified by their hash values (`transactionId`). Similarly, a `Block` is identified by index value or position in the ledger.
- *Closed to modification*—When the object is instantiated, you may not alter any of its properties. Doing so results in the creation of a new object or an error.
- *Closed to extension*—You may not dynamically add properties to (mixins) or remove properties from this object, and you may not derive new objects from it (inheritance).
- *Defines its own equality*—With no unique ID, it's beneficial to implement an `equals` method that knows how to compare two value objects based on their properties.
- *Override `toString` and `valueOf`*—Value objects need seamless representation as either a string or primitive. Overriding methods such as `toString` and `valueOf` affects how an object behaves next to a mathematical symbol or when concatenated with a string.

For our blockchain, we're going to represent the `funds` field of `Transaction` as a `Money` object. Before we look at the internal details, let's see how it's used:

```
Money('฿', 1.0);  // represents 1 Bitcoin
Money('$', 1.0);  // represents 1 US Dollar
Money.zero('$');  // bankruptcy!
```

Let's implement `Money` by using a simple function instead of a class. Unlike class constructors, normal functions can be curried. So we can do things like

```
const USD = Money('$');

USD(3.0);        // $ 3
USD(3.0).amount;  // 3
USD(7.0).currency; // $
[USD(3.0), USD(7.0)].map(prop('amount')).reduce(add, 0); // 10
```

Also, `Money` supports a few key operations such as adding, subtracting, rounding, and (most importantly) implementing some sense of equality. Why is equality important? Without some field describing its identity, value objects are comparable only by their attributes:

```
USD(3.0).plus(USD(7.0)).equals(USD(10));  // true
```

In the case of `Money`, we're not interested in using inheritance or any of the instantiation patterns of previous chapters, which are intended to build complex objects; using a simple function to return an object literal is more than enough. This pattern also goes by the name Function Factory.

To implement the "closed for modification and extension" guarantees, we can use the `Object.freeze` and `Object.seal` JavaScript built-in methods, respectively. Both methods are easy to compose. The next listing shows the implementation details of `Money`.

Listing 4.13 Details of the `Money` value object

```
const BTC = '฿';

const Money = curry((currency, amount) =>          The new object is first
  compose(                                          frozen and then sealed.
    Object.seal,
    Object.freeze                                  Uses Object.assign with Object.create(null)
  )(Object.assign(Object.create(null),             to create a value object without any
    {                                              prototype references, making it closer
      amount,                                       to a true value in the system
      currency,
      equals: other => currency === other.currency &&
          amount === other.amount,
      round: (precision = 2) =>
          Money(currency, precisionRound(amount, precision)),
      minus: m => Money(currency, amount - m.amount),
      plus: m => Money(currency, amount + m.amount),
      times: m => Money(currency, amount * m.amount),
      compareTo: other => amount - other.amount,
      asNegative: () => Money(currency, amount * -1),   Overrides Object#valueOf
      valueOf: () => precisionRound(amount, 2),         and Object#toString to help
      toString: () => `${currency}${amount}`            JavaScript's type coercion
    }
  ))
);

// Zero
Money.zero = (currency = BTC) => Money(currency, 0);   Implemented outside the
                                                        object literal definition to
// Static helper functions                              make static methods
Money.sum = (m1, m2) => m1.add(m2);

Money.subtract = (m1, m2) => m1.minus(m2);

Money.multiply = (m1, m2) => m1.times(m2);

function precisionRound(number, precision) {
  const factor = Math.pow(10, precision);
  return Math.round(number * factor) / factor;
}
```

The code in listing 4.13 packs in a lot of functionality because we're trying to arrive at an object that behaves and feels like a primitive. Aside from making the object immutable and closed for extension, we're instantiating it from a "null object" prototype `Object.create(null)` in a single step, using `Object.assign` (chapter 3). `Money` won't automatically inherit any of Object.prototype's member fields (such as toString and valueOf), in particular one that doesn't apply in this case: Object#isPrototypeOf. The downside is that you're responsible for implementing these properties correctly.

Hence, we'll implement toString and valueOf to work as follows:

```
const five = Money('USD', 5);
console.log(five.toString()); // USD 5
```

valueOf is a bit more interesting. Unlike with toString, you don't invoke valueOf directly. JavaScript automatically calls it when the object is expected to behave as a primitive, especially in a numeric context. When the object is next to a math symbol, we can downgrade (coerce) Money to Number. Then you can wrap that result back into Money with proper a currency denomination, if needed:

```
five * 2;    // 10
five + five  // 10
Money('USD', five + five).toString() // USD 10
```

Now let's see the effects of applying Object.seal and Object.freeze to these objects. We used compose to apply each method sequentially. Object.freeze prevents you from changing any of its attributes (remember that we're assuming strict mode), as shown here:

```
const threeDollars = USD(3.0);
threeDollars.amount = 5;

// TypeError: Cannot assign to read only property 'amount' of object '[object
    Object]'

Object.isFrozen(threeDollars); // true
```

And Object.seal prevents clients from extending it:

```
threeDollars.goBankrupt = true;
// TypeError: Cannot add property goBankrupt, object is not extensible

delete threeDollars.plus;
// TypeError: Cannot delete property 'plus' of [object Object]

Object.isSealed(threeDollars); // true
```

Finally, notice that all the methods in Money (plus, minus, and so on) use copy-on-write semantics, returning new objects instead of changing the existing one and embracing the principles of purity we've discussed so far.

Pure object manipulation

In functional programming, there's an approach to manipulate data inside objects known as lenses so that you don't have to roll your own version of copy-on-write.

> *(continued)*
>
> A lens allows you to target a specific property or path inside an object so that you can perform changes to it in a composable, immutable manner. Behind the scenes, it uses copy-on-write, but everything is done for you automatically. You can learn more about this technique on your own by exploring the Ramda lens APIs (https://ramdajs .com/docs/#lens).

At this point, you've learned how to structure functional code by using composition and currying. Primitive data can be manipulated and mutated at will (because it's immutable by design), whereas custom data objects need a bit more attention. In the latter case, using value objects when appropriate or passing copies of data to code can help divert lots of nasty bugs.

With all the fundamentals behind us, let's improve the design of our code with a paradigm known as point-free coding—the last piece needed to implement the logic of calculating the balance of a user's digital wallet.

4.6   *Point-free coding*

Point-free coding is a byproduct of adopting declarative programming. You can use point-free coding without FP. But because point-free is all about improving the readability of code at a glance and making it simpler to parse, having the guarantees imposed by FP furthers this cause.

Learning the point-free style is beneficial because it allows developers to understand your code at first sight without necessarily having to dive into the internals. Point-free refers to a style in which function definitions do not explicitly identify the arguments (or the points) they receive; they are implicitly (tacitly) passed through the flow of a program, usually with the help of `curry` and `compose`. Removing this clutter usually reveals a leaner code structure that humans can parse visually with ease. By being able to see the forest for the trees, you can spot higher-level bugs that could arise from using bad logic or making bad assumptions about requirements.

Because JavaScript has curried, first-class functions, we can assign a function to a variable, use this named variable as an argument to `compose`, and effectively create an executable outline of our code. In this section, you'll learn about the benefits of using a point-free style with JavaScript, such as

- Improving the legibility of your code by reducing syntactical noise
- Making composition clearer and terser
- Avoiding introducing unnecessary parameter names
- Building a vocabulary describing the actions and tasks that make up your application

Before we begin learning about this style, it helps to see it in comparison with non-point-free coding. Let's do a quick review:

```
function countWordsInFile(file) {
    const fileBuffer = fs.readFileSync(file);
    const wordsString = fileBuffer.toString();
    const wordsInArray = wordsString.split(/\s+/);
    return wordsInArray.length;
}
```

To get a high-level idea of what this function does, you're forced to read every statement and trace the flow. Each statement in the function describes in detail how every function is called and the parameters (or points) each function receives at the call site.

On the other hand, using compose removes the unnecessary overhead and focuses on the high-level steps required to create a higher-level representation of the same logic. When we applied FP to countWordsInFile earlier, we arrived at this code:

```
const countWordsInFile = compose(
    count,
    split,
    decode('utf8'),
    read
);
```

This program is point-free. Notice that nothing in this program tells you how to invoke countWordsInFile. The only thing you see is the structure of this function or what steps are involved. Because the signature of the function (and all the embedded functions) is missing, you may feel that this style obscures the code a bit for someone who is not familiar with these functions. That point is a valid one, and I've seen how it can make using a debugger a bit more challenging. But for someone who is familiar with this style and knows their way around a debugger, point-free coding makes composition much cleaner and allows you to visualize the high-level steps as though they were plug-and-play components.

A common analogy for point-free code is Lego bricks. When you're looking at a Lego structure from a distance, you can't see the pins that hold everything together, yet you appreciate the overall structure. If you look at the imperative version of countWordsInFile once more, the "pins" in this case refer to the intermediate variable names that connect one statement to the next.

Suppose that you're working on another task, such as counting an array of serialized block data from a JSON file. At a high level, you should be able to see that the structure of this code is similar to the preceding snippet of code. The only difference is that instead of dealing with space-separated words, you will deal with parsing an array of elements. Pure functions are easy to swap in and out because they don't depend on any external data other than their own arguments. countBlocksInFile is implemented simply by swapping split with JSON.parse:

```
const countBlocksInFile = compose(
    count,
    JSON.parse,
    decode('utf8'),
```

```
    read
);
```

Again, this swap is evident because point-free coding cleans up the process of passing functions and arguments around, allowing you to focus on the task at hand, such as changing a red Lego brick for a green one. It should be obvious at this point that `countBlocksInFile` is another Lego bundle (a module) that can be composed (pinned) further. You can build entire complex applications from this fundamental idea (figure 4.10).

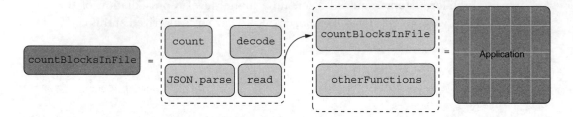

Figure 4.10   Functions composed to build entire applications

All these Lego bricks become the taxonomy, or vocabulary, if you will, of the Lego set that is your application.

Now that you understand how to structure your code by using composition and currying, let's tackle a more complex imperative-to-functional transformation that involves computing a user's digital-wallet balance.

4.7   *Imperative to functional transformation*

In chapter 3, I looked at the skeleton of the `Wallet` class (listing 3.9) but deliberately omitted the `balance` method. Here is that snippet of code again:

```
class Wallet {
  constructor(publicKey, privateKey) {
    this.publicKey = publicKey
    this.privateKey = privateKey
  }
  get address() {
    return this.publicKey
  }
  balance(ledger) {
    //...
  }
}
```

Now we're prepared to fill in the complex logic details. To compute the balance of a user, given a blockchain (`ledger`) object argument, we need to tally all the transactions from all the blocks that have been mined for that user since the beginning of the ledger. We can omit the genesis block because we know that it doesn't carry any data we're interested in.

Let's look at this problem again with an imperative mindset and compare it with a functional one. This time, we'll be using all the bells and whistles that we've learned thus far. The algorithm can look like the following listing.

Listing 4.14   Imperative algorithm for computing total balance

```
balance(ledger) {
    let balance = Money.zero();
    for (const block of ledger) {          ◄─   ledger is a Blockchain object, and iterating over
        if (!block.isGenesis()) {                it delivers each block. You'll learn how to make
            for (const tx of block.data) {       any object iterable in chapter 7. For now, you
                if (tx.sender === this.address) { can safely assume that it's an array of blocks.
                    balance = balance.minus(tx.funds);   ◄─   If the user is the sender of the
                }                                               transaction, we discount the
                else {                                          amount in the transaction;
                    balance = balance.plus(tx.funds);   ◄─     otherwise, we add it to the
                }                                               running balance.
            }
        }
    }
    return balance.round();
}
```

Comparing this algorithm with the FP guidelines, you can see that it involves looping over the blockchain data structure, which means that you need to keep a running count of the balance as you iterate through all blocks and then through each transaction of that block. Within each iteration, there's a lot of branching to accommodate different conditions—an imperative "pyramid of doom," you might say. Let's revisit that flow in figure 4.11.

All the diamond-shaped boxes represent branching logic, nested within circulating arrows that represent loops. Arguably, this figure is not trivial to parse; it represents a simple piece of code.

In addition, listing 4.14 has side effects in the way it references this to access a wallet's properties and reassigns balance at each iteration. Refactoring this code by using a hybrid (FP + OO) approach involves

- Making the data explicit function arguments instead of implicitly
- Transforming loops and nested conditionals to a fluent data transformation with map and filter
- Removing variable reassignments with an immutable reduce operation

The best course of action is to extract the logic into its own function, free from side effects, and have balance internally delegate to it with all the initial data. We can call this new method computeBalance:

```
balance(ledger) {
    return computeBalance(this.address, ledger);
}
```

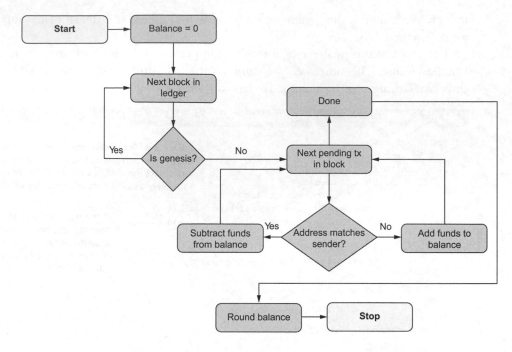

Figure 4.11   Imperative flow of control for the logic in calculating a user's total balance in a blockchain

It's reasonable to start with the handy array essentials we're familiar with: map, filter, and reduce. The following code represents the same algorithm, functionally inspired. Figure 4.12 shows what the new flow will look like.

There's a small caveat in the functional approach shown in listing 4.15, which can be a bit confusing. Because the flow of data involves processing the array of blocks and, within each one, an array of transactions, we're forced to deal with an array of arrays. To make things simple, when you encounter this issue, the best thing to do is flatten these structures. You'll learn in chapter 5 that this occurrence is common in functional code. For now, we'll use Array#flat to flatten the nested structure.

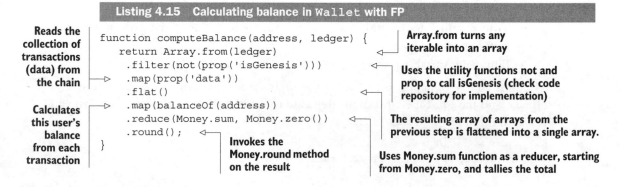

Listing 4.15   Calculating balance in Wallet with FP

Reads the collection of transactions (data) from the chain

```
function computeBalance(address, ledger) {
    return Array.from(ledger)
        .filter(not(prop('isGenesis')))
        .map(prop('data'))
        .flat()
        .map(balanceOf(address))
        .reduce(Money.sum, Money.zero())
        .round();
}
```

Calculates this user's balance from each transaction

Array.from turns any iterable into an array

Uses the utility functions not and prop to call isGenesis (check code repository for implementation)

The resulting array of arrays from the previous step is flattened into a single array.

Uses Money.sum function as a reducer, starting from Money.zero, and tallies the total

Invokes the Money.round method on the result

For the most part, you can see that this algorithm is a reincarnation of the imperative logic but takes advantage of the higher-order functions from the array that connects each piece of the transformation, radically changing the flow of data. Also, the fact that we're performing addition through code such as reduce(Money.sum, Money.zero()) speaks to the mathematical nature that functional programs tend to exhibit.

For completeness, here's the balanceOf function used in the functional version, now done as a lambda expression, which maps a user ID in a transaction to a positive or negative monetary value depending on whether said user is the sender or the recipient:

```
const balanceOf = curry((addr, tx) =>
    Money.sum(
      tx.recipient === addr ? tx.funds :
    Money.zero(),
      tx.sender === addr ? tx.funds.asNegative() :
    Money.zero()
    );
  )
```

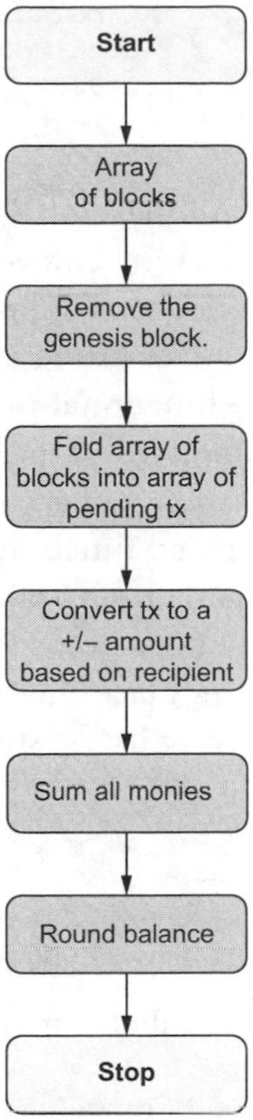

If you look back at listing 4.15 again, perhaps the most complex step you see is the call to flat on the array of arrays structure that is built during the flow of the data. Here's flat with a simple example so that you can see how it peels off the nested array:

```
[['a'], ['b'], ['c']].flat()      // ['a', 'b', 'c']
```

Figure 4.12 Functional flow of control for the logic in calculating a user's total balance in a blockchain

Because the algorithm performs a map operation beforehand, there's a shortcut: using Array#flatMap method directly. We'll revisit map and flatMap in more detail in chapter 5, but for now, we'll go over them in order to understand how computeBalance works. As you can see, flat is intuitive, but what the heck is flatMap? The combination of map followed by flat occurs frequently in functional programs, so often that it makes sense to alias the composition of these two methods as a single method. The agreed-upon name in the functional communities is flatMap. The preceding code simplifies to the next listing.

Listing 4.16 computeBalance using map, filter, and reduce

```
function computeBalance(address, ledger) {
  return Array.from(ledger)
    .filter(not(prop('isGenesis')))       Substituting flatMap
    .flatMap(prop('data'))            for map and then flat
```

```
    .map(balanceOf(address))
    .reduce(Money.sum, Money.zero())
    .round();
}
```

With these APIs, you can solve virtually any array processing task you need and probably even remove loops from your code. This capability is the future of working with collections in JavaScript.

This listing is a good stopping point, but for the joy of it, let's go one step further. In functional programs, it's not common to use dot notation to invoke sequences of functions (map(...).filter(...).reduce(...)), as this notation assumes the inner workings of an object chaining these operations together. Instead, use their extracted, curried function forms with the help of compose to thread through the entire flow of data, passing said object to each call (no assumptions), making it point-free!

Let's go over this technique slowly. When extracting a method into its own function, place the instance object as the last argument, and curry the function. The following listing shows how to extract Array#map(f).

Listing 4.17   Extracting map in curried form

```
const map = curry((f, arr) => arr.map(f));          ⟵┤ Array arr is the
                                                        last parameter.
```

To embed map in a chain, partially apply the first argument, the mapper function:

```
map(balanceOf(address));
```

The dynamic array (arr) argument isn't provided directly because compose will do it for you in a point-free way. Most third-party FP libraries carry these helper functions (map, filter, reduce, and many more) in curried form. The more functional version of this code, shown in the next listing, takes advantage of fine-grained, point-free design. The point-free design requires a fixed address parameter, whereas ledger is provided at the call site.

Listing 4.18   Point-free version of computeBalance

```
const computeBalance = address =>
  compose(                                      ⟵┤ With compose, the
    Money.round,                                    logic reads right to left.
    reduce(Money.sum, Money.zero()),
    map(balanceOf(address)),                         Uses the curried extracted
    flatMap(prop('data')),                           forms of the equivalent
    filter(                                          Array#filter method
      compose(              ⟵┐
        not,                  │  Uses nested composition
        prop('isGenesis')     │  to make the code more
      )                       │  modular
    ),
```

```
    Array.from
  );
```

```
const computeBalanceForSender123 = computeBalance('sender123');
computeBalanceForSender123(ledger);
```

> **Third-party FP libraries**
>
> Functional languages such as Haskell and F# have built-in native operators to imple-
> ment many of these techniques. In this chapter, you were introduced to the operators
> compose and curry. Normally, you would not write these operators by hand. Instead
> you'd import a third-party library such as Ramda (https://ramdajs.com), Crocks (https://
> crocks.dev), Lodash (https://lodash.com), or UnderscoreJS (https://underscorejs.org)
> to import a lot of these utility functions. You can find the ones used in this book in
> the code repo (http://mng.bz/pVy2).

FP takes a little getting used to, but thinking this way puts you on the path to writing highly modular, maintainable, cleaner, and more reliable code. In fact, it saves you from potential bugs because JavaScript gives you total freedom to mutate almost anything, making your development experience a lot more enjoyable.

Fanning out to pure functions like this one is a compelling idea that will become more and more prominent as JavaScript continues to embrace more functional features and make creating function chains a native part of the language.

4.8   *Native function chains*

Now that you understand the basic functional programming concepts, you're one step ahead in learning a new feature that could make landfall in the near future. In this chapter, you learned (among other things) how to create functional chains by using compose. One of the most noticeable qualities of this operator is that the flow of data happens in reverse, which can be quite jarring for some people. Luckily, there's a solution: the pipe operator. A close cousin of compose, pipe takes the functions in the natural left-to-right order. The buildout of pipe is exactly the same as that of compose. The only change would be to use reduceRight instead of reduce:

```
const pipe = (...fns) => fns.reduceRight(compose2);
```

This operator is inspired by the way in which UNIX-based programs pipe data forward into one another. With pipe, you could rearrange the logic to calculate a balance like this:

```
pipe(
  Array.from,
  filter(
    pipe(
      prop('isGenesis')
      not,
    )
  ),
```

```
    flatMap(prop('data')),
    map(balanceOf(address)),
    reduce(Money.sum, Money.zero()),
    Money.round
);
```

You'll also find `pipe` in most FP libraries for JavaScript, such as Ramda and Crocks. If you prefer this way of thinking, JavaScript has a nice surprise in store for you. Introducing the pipeline operator: |> (https://github.com/tc39/proposal-pipeline-operator). Inspired by functional languages such as Elixir and F#, this native operator allows you to call sequences of functions with the data flowing unidirectionally to the right without needing any special third-party libraries.

It's important to start learning about this new feature now because when it becomes official, it will radically change the way we write code. Here's an example:

```
'1 2 3' |> split |> count;  // 3
```

You can even mix it with lambda expressions:

```
'1 2 3' |> split |> count |> (x => x ** 2); // 9
```

Now imagine that you had some of the common array methods extracted in curried, function form, as provided in these functional utility libraries. You'll be able to write code like this:

```
ledger
  |> Array.from
  |> filter(b => (b |> prop('isGenesis') |> not))
  |> flatMap(prop('data'))
  |> map(balanceOf(address))
  |> reduce(Money.sum, Money.zero())
  |> Money.round;
```

This example is a terser, more idiomatic way of designing code, and it pairs extremely well with `curry` for a declarative, native point-free design. For details on experimenting with this operator now, see appendix A.

> **More about functional programming in JavaScript**
>
> JavaScript's support for the functional programming paradigm is a huge subject to cover. In this book, I'll cover only enough FP to open your eyes to how it's steering JavaScript's future, as well as helping you become proficient and do more with less. If you'd like more information about functional programming and broader topics, you can read about them in detail in my 2016 book *Functional Programming in JavaScript* (http://mng.bz/0mMN).

From now on, if anyone asks whether JavaScript is object-oriented or functional, say "Yes!" The previous chapters highlighted the object-oriented nature of JavaScript.

This chapter focused on functional programming and the art of composing pure, higher-order functions. Pure functions guarantee consistent and predictable results based on their input. Their purpose is clearly depicted by their signatures or, as Eric Evans puts it in *Domain-Driven Design* (Addison-Wesley Professional, 2013), "A pure function is an intention-revealing interface."

Although the functional paradigm has many benefits, it doesn't have to be an all-or-nothing process. I deliberately used a hybrid style for the blockchain application with OO and FP concepts intertwined. You can not only take advantage of prototypal object models, but also create highly testable and portable modules of functions that encapsulate your critical business logic. Functional programming helps you write more robust and bug-free code, especially in a language such as JavaScript, where almost everything is mutable. We'll circle back to coding with immutability in chapter 5.

Summary

- JavaScript's higher-order functions are the means by which we can achieve functional code.
- Code written in a functional style is declarative, composable, lazy, and simple to reason about.
- The composition of pure functions is the bread and butter of any functional codebase.
- Shifting to a functional mindset requires a different approach to problem-solving based on decomposing code into fine-grained behavior.
- Lazy programming allows you to defer computation, and with curry, you can create composable software by using functions of any arity (number of arguments).
- Learning about FP principles will give you the competitive edge you need to begin using the new JavaScript features that will be available in the years to come.
- Using the pipeline operator (|>) makes it incredibly easy and idiomatic to implement point-free function chains.

Higher-kinded composition

This chapter covers

- Transforming arrays and objects safely with `map` and `flatMap`
- Composable design patterns with algebraic data types
- Writing a `Validation` data type to remove complex branching logic
- Chaining ADTs using the new bind operator (`::`)

The purpose of abstraction is not to be vague, but to create a new semantic level in which one can be absolutely precise.

—Edgar Dijkstra

In chapter 4, you learned how function composition leads to fluent, compact, and declarative code when you use `compose` to chain your function's inputs and outputs as data passes through them. Composition has a lot of benefits because it uses Java-Script's strongest feature, as I've said many times: higher-order functions. With functions, you can achieve low-level composition at the lowest unit of abstraction. But a higher-kinded composition also exists in the way objects compose. Making objects compose as strongly as functions do is a key idea that we'll discuss in section 5.3.

114

The type of composable object pattern you'll learn about in this chapter is known as the Algebraic Data Type (ADT) pattern. An *ADT* is an object with a particular, well-known interface that allows a similar abstraction to compose to chain multiple ADTs together. Much like any class, ADTs can also contain or store other objects, but they are much simpler than a class in that they model a single concept, such as validation, error handling, null checking, or sequences. Because you've learned about function composition, you can see that it's simple to compose functions in a world where nothing fails and all the inputs and outputs of your functions are well-defined. It's a different story when you also need to validate data and catch exceptions while taking advantage of this pattern. Learning to use ADTs is extremely beneficial for this purpose because they provide concise APIs that allow you to build whole programs from simpler parts—composition at its core.

Take a moment to reflect on some of the problems we tackled in chapter 4. Given a user's digital wallet address, for example, we computed the total amount of Bitcoin in the blockchain. But what would happen if the provided address was null? Well, in that case, the program would fail because we didn't add any guards against this possibility.

More generally, how can we deal with invalid data (null, undefined) flowing through a composition sequence? The syntax of compose doesn't give you much room to insert imperative conditional validation statements between functions. Rather than clutter each function with common validation logic, your best bet is to extract it, as shown in the following listing.

Listing 5.1   Embedding validation checks before each composed function

```
compose(f3, validate, f2, validate, f1, validate);

function validate(data) {
   if(data !== null) {        Pass the data along
      return data;            to the next function
   }                          in the chain.
   throw new TypeError(`Received invalid data ${data}`);    Otherwise, exit
}                                                           with an error.
```

This process doesn't work, however, because

- It's repetitive.
- You lose the context in which validation takes place, which means that you can't apply specific rules or exit with a proper validation message in the event of a failure.
- Throwing an exception creates a side effect.

As far as the last point is concerned, if the first function fails to produce a useful result, chances are that the rest of the flow shouldn't be allowed to continue. The same thing happens when you're working with some third-party code that may throw exceptions. In the imperative world, you would add try/catch guards. But again, try/catch is not something you can easily plug into compose; it's an impedance mismatch between FP and OO, and you'd be fighting against FP to try to keep things linear and point-free. Take a look at the next listing.

Listing 5.2 The inconvenience of mixing `try/catch` with `compose`

```
compose(
  c => {
    try {
      return f3(c);
    }
    catch(e) {
      handleError(e);
    }
  },
  b => {
    try {
      return f2(b);
    }
    catch(e) {
      handleError(e);
    }
  },
  a => {
    try {
      return f1(a);
    }
    catch(e) {
      handleError(e);
    }
  }
)
```

Because each function is surrounded by imperative error handling code, you can't take advantage of a declarative, point-free style (chapter 4).

This poor design is a result of combining paradigms the wrong way. Instead of throwing an error abruptly, we might like to handle this task in a way that mitigates the side effect. To fix this problem, we need to add the necessary guardrails or wrappers that can control the context in which a function and its validation operation execute, yet keep things separate, compact, and declarative. Does that sound like a tall order? It is if we don't have the necessary techniques in place. This chapter teaches these techniques, all of which revolve around higher-order functions, with the help of some more FP principles.

ADTs expose a well-known, universal API that facilitates composability. You'll learn that the map interface (in the same spirit as Array#map) indicates that a particular object behaves like a functor. Similarly, the flatMap interface indicates that an object behaves like a monad. We'll unpack both of these terms soon. Both of these interfaces allow an ADT to compose with others.

NOTE The terms *functor* and *monad* originate from category theory, but you don't need to understand mathematics to learn and use them in practice.

After teaching some of the fundamentals, this chapter works its way up to creating an ADT from scratch, tackling the complexity behind validating or checking the contents of a block, transaction, and even the entire blockchain data structure. By the end, you'll understand what code like this does:

```
Validation.of(block)
    .flatMap(checkLength(64))
    .flatMap(checkTampering)
    .flatMap(checkDifficulty)
    .flatMap(checkLinkage(previousHash))
    .flatMap(checkTimestamps(previousTimestamp));
```

This code addresses all the concerns we raised earlier, although how may not be obvious yet. The code removes repetition, creates no additional side effects, and (best of all) is declarative and point-free. This type of abstraction `Validation` creates a closed context around the validation logic. Let's begin by understanding what we mean by closed context.

5.1 Closing over data types

When we write functions, it would be ideal to assume the perfect application state. That is, all the data coming in and out of our functions is always correct and valid, and none of the objects in our system have a `null` or `undefined` value. This state would allow us to reduce the boilerplate of data checks everywhere. Sadly, this situation is never the case. Alternatively, we could think about wrapping functions with some abstraction that always checks for invalid data of any nature. In this section, we'll create a simple abstraction to start getting used to the pattern presented in this book. In section 5.5, we'll build on that pattern to build an actual ADT.

Functions can become complex when we interleave their business logic with side work such as data validation, error handling, or logging. We can say that these concerns are tangential to the task at hand, yet they are important parts of the working application. Other tasks may include handling exceptions or logging to a file. We'll call these tasks effects.

> **NOTE** An effect is not to be confused with a side effect. A side effect may be a type of effect, as used in this context, but an effect is more of an arbitrary task.

Let's focus on one of these effects: data validation. Suppose that you're writing a small algorithm, using a sequence of functions. At each step, you want to make sure that the arguments each function receives are valid (not null, greater than zero, not empty, and so on). These are important to ensure that the algorithm is correct from a practical point of view but are not essential parts of the algorithm itself. Instead of cluttering each function, you remove or wrap this effect in some form of abstraction.

Suppose that this hypothetical algorithm has three steps: `f1`, `f2`, and `f3`. You already saw the interleaving happening in this code in listing 5.1:

```
compose(f3, validate, f2, validate, f1, validate);
```

The data is validated before each function runs. Let's improve this code to remove the repetition. Using the lessons of chapter 4, we'll wrap these functions (close over them), using a higher-order function that accepts the function being executed as input and the data in curried form. Higher-order functions are great at converting some body of code into callable form. This approach would allow `validate` to decide whether to apply the function based on the validity of the data provided.

To illustrate a possible solution, let's make our problem more concrete by focusing only on calling functions, with the condition that the `null` check is successful (not null). Consider a function such as `applyIfNotNull`:

```
function applyIfNotNull(fn) {
  return data => {
    if (data !== null) {
      return data;
    }
    throw new Error(`Received invalid data: ${data}`);
  }
}

compose(applyIfNotNull(f3), applyIfNotNull(f2), applyIfNotNull(f1));
```

As you can see, the null check is repeated around every function call. Because `applyIfNotNull` is curried manually, we can remove duplication by mapping it over the functions that make up your business logic, as shown in the next listing.

Listing 5.3   Applying multiple functions to `compose` with `map`

```
compose(...[f3, f2, f1].map(applyIfNotNull));    ◁──┐  Applies applyIfNotNull to every function
                                                      and then spreads the resulting array
                                                      as arguments to compose
```

This step gets us closer to a more declarative, expression-oriented code instead of imperative branching logic, but we still need to account for two items:

- A `null` check is not the only form of validation we'll need in the real world. We need to support more kinds of logic.
- We're using an exception, which is itself a side effect, to break out of the logic in a dramatic fashion.

We need to increase the level of abstraction from a function to some form of contextual data structure that can somehow keep track of the validation results along the way and apply the functions accordingly. One way is to use a wrapper object that encapsulates data and abstracts the application of an effect to this data as part of exercising its business logic, much as `applyIfNotNull` did earlier, in an immutable way without leaking side effects.

Possibly the simplest type of container data structure in JavaScript is `Array`, which among its comprehensive set of methods has a few that we can use for this type of abstraction:

- A *static function to construct new containers with a value*—For a class C, this function is usually called C.of or C.unit. The function, which is similar to Array.of, is also called a *type-lifting function* as it allows you to bring some typed variable into a context on which you will perform operations. Lifting some object and placing it in a box is a good analogy.
- A *function to transform this data*—This transformation is usually done via a map method on the object with a specific contract. map is shared by all instances, so it should be defined at prototype level (C.prototype.map).
- A *function to extract the result from the container*—This function is implementation-specific. For arrays, you can use something like Array#pop.

Anything beyond this protocol depends on what additional logic you need for the specific wrapper.

Before we start implementing our own wrappers, let's continue down the path of using an array to represent encapsulation and immutability. This practice will help us warm up on the coding patterns used by ADTs.

Wrapping a value inside some container, such as an array literal, gives you automatic fluent-coding capabilities on several values, not just one. For the sake of this discussion, let's focus on one value. Consider this example. Given a string, suppose that you want to remove duplicate characters and capitalize the final string. With input of "aabbcc", for example, the result should be "ABC".

Simple enough. As you know, the best way to apply a sequence of computations to an array of elements is through map, which is a stateless method, so you're never changing the original array that called it or its elements. This situation satisfies the immutability requirement. Also, we need methods to put a value inside the array and then a way to extract the data. For this task, we can use lifting operations Array.of and Array#pop, respectively, as shown in the next listing.

Listing 5.4 Mapping functions on an array

```
const unique = letters => Array.from(new Set(letters));
const join = arr => arr.join('');
const toUpper = str => str.toUpperCase();

const letters = ['aabbcc']
   .map(unique)   // [['a', 'b', 'c']]
   .map(join)     // ['abc']
   .map(toUpper)  // ['ABC']
   .pop();

letters; // 'ABC'
```

> Uses the capabilities of Set, which accepts an iterable object, to remove duplicates

> Could have also used Array.prototype.shift or [0]

JavaScript gives us some syntactic improvement (in the shape of a box) by using the array literal directly:

```
['aabbcc']
   .map(unique)
```

```
    .map(join)
    .map(toUpper)
    .pop();  // 'ABC'
```

If you want to be a little more precise, you can use the `Array.of` as a generic constructor function:

```
Array.of('aabbcc')
    .map(unique)
    .map(join)
    .map(toUpper)
    .pop();  // 'ABC'
```

> **NOTE**   When you construct a new array, using the `Array` constructor function with `new` is not the best way to go about it. This function has unpredictable behavior, depending on the type used. The function `new Array('aabbcc')`, for example, creates an array with the single element `['aabbcc']`, as we'd expect. But `new Array(3)` creates an empty array with three empty slots: `[ , , ]`. The `Array.of` API corrects for this situation, but in most cases, the simplest approach is to use array literal notation directly: `['aabbcc']`.

The container that results from using an array is analogous to what we call an identity context. This term comes from the simple yet popular `identity` function (`const identity = a => a`), which you learned about in chapter 4. This function is commonly used in functional programs and echoes the value it's given. In FP, *identity* means that some value is left untouched.

Similarly, an identity context would not have any computational logic of its own. It wraps a single value and doesn't do any additional processing beyond what you provide in your mapping functions; it has no effect on the data. We say that it's contextless, or side-effect-free.

Let's take the array example a bit further. One way we could easily implement an `Id` class in JavaScript is to extend from `Array`, as shown in listing 5.5. This example is meant only to illustrate how the `map` operator could apply generically over simple containers that enclose a single value. Normally, I don't recommend extending (monkeypatching) from standard types; this example is for teaching purposes, and its use will become clearer later.

Listing 5.5   Implementing a contextless container by extending from `Array`

```
class Id extends Array {
  constructor(value) {
    super(1);              ◁──┐ Initializes the underlying array
    this.fill(value);          with a size of 1 because we need
  }                            to wrap only a single value
}

Id.of('aabbcc')     ◁──┐ Inherits Array.of as the
  .map(unique)            type-lifting function
```

```
.map(join)
.map(toUpper)
.pop(); // 'ABC'
```
Inherits Array#pop to extract the value from the container

Both `Id` and `[]` (empty array) are examples of closed contexts. Although this example may not look exciting, there's more than meets the eye here. Concretely, `Id`

- Enables a fluent data transformation API in which each stage performs a predictable transformation toward the end result, as in an assembly line.
- Provides some level of data encapsulation.
- Performs all operations in an immutable fashion because every stage of the process returns a new container with a new value. The mapped function may transform the data inside `Id` to any shape, as long as it advances our logic toward the final outcome. We say that the mapping function is any function from `a -> b` (`a` and `b` are any objects) that changes the container from `Id(a)` to a new `Id(b)`.

Conceptually, programming with containers metaphorically resembles an assembly line or a railway, as shown in figure 5.1.

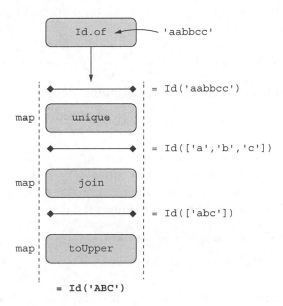

Figure 5.1 Assembly-style computing with containers. In this case, every step of the line maps a different transformation, creating a new intermediate result along the way until reaching the desired product.

NOTE In section 5.5.4, you'll see that implementing validation (which is a binary operation) with wrappers will result in two paths or railways.

This last point, which refers to creating new containers as a result of applying functions, is the most important one to guarantee that the mapped functions are pure. Remember that purity is the key ingredient to make your code simple to reason about. Take as examples Array's `sort` and `reverse`, which modify the original object in place. These APIs are harder to use because they can lead to unexpected behavior. On the other hand, immutable APIs like the ones in section 5.2 are much safer to use.

5.2   *New Array APIs: {flat, flatMap}*

Array#{flat, flatMap} are two major additions to the almighty, all-encompassing Java-Script Array object. You saw these methods used briefly toward the end of chapter 4. Both of these methods allow you to manage multidimensional arrays easily:

```
[['aa'], ['bb'], ['cc']].flat();        // ['aa', 'bb', 'cc']
[[2], [3], [4]].flatMap(x => x ** 2); // [4, 9, 16]
```

Like all the recently added Array methods, these operations are immutable; instead of changing the original, they create new ones. Let's start with flat.

5.2.1   *Array.prototype.flat*

Array#flat allows you to work with multiple array dimensions without having to break out of your lean and fluent pattern. Here are a few examples:

```
[['aa'], ['bb'], ['cc']].flat().map(toUpper);   // ['AA', 'BB', 'CC']
```

The method even has the built-in smarts to skip nested nonarray objects. Empty slots in the array are left untouched:

```
[['aa'], , ['bb'], , ['cc']].flat().map(toUpper);   // ['AA', 'BB', 'CC']
```

A fun fact about flat is that you can collapse structures of infinite depth:

```
[[[[['down here!']]]]].flat(Infinity); // ['down here!']
```

flat also allows you to work with functions that themselves return arrays. Recall from listing 5.4 that unique takes a string and returns an array with all letters minus duplicates. Mapping unique over ['aa', 'bb', 'cc'], for example, would produce a nested structure [['a'], ['b'], ['c']], which we can easily flatten at the end:

```
const unique = letters => Array.from(new Set([...letters]));
```

```
['aa', 'bb', 'cc'].map(unique).flat(); // ['a', 'b', 'c']
```

Because map and flat are often used together, JavaScript provides an API that takes care of both methods.

5.2.2   *Array.prototype.flatMap*

The map-then-flat sequence is used frequently in regular day-to-day coding. You might iterate over all blocks in the chain and then iterate over all transactions within each block, for example. Fortunately, a shortcut called flatMap calls both operations at the same time, as shown in the following listing.

Listing 5.6 Basic use of `flatMap`

```
['aa', 'bb', 'cc'].flatMap(unique);

// ['a', 'b', 'c']
```

◁─┐ **unique returns an array. Instead of producing a nested array, flatMap runs the built-in flat logic after mapping the callback function to all elements.**

We all understand `map` and `flatMap` as operations that allow you to apply callback functions to an array. Conceptually, however, these operations extend beyond arrays. If you've read chapter 4 and understand the basics of functional programming, code of this form should resemble a familiar pattern:

```
Id.of('aabbcc')
  .map(unique)
  .map(join)
  .map(toUpper);
```

Would you say that this code looks like composition? As a matter of fact, the following code produces the same result (`'ABC'`) as the previous one:

```
const uniqueUpperCaseOf = compose(toUpper, join, unique)

uniqueUpperCaseOf('aabbcc') // 'ABC'
```

How is it that `map` and `compose` lead to the same result? Except for minor syntactic differences compared with `compose`, `map` and `flatMap` represent contextual composition and are largely equivalent.

5.3 *The map/compose correspondence*

In section 5.1, I said that `map` allows objects (like `Id` and others) to apply functions. This statement applies equally to `flatMap`. In this section, you'll learn that at a fundamental level, both of these operators behave like `compose`, so in essence, using `map` is nothing more than function composition, which cements the mental model of functional programming.

This equivalence is also important technically speaking, because you get all of the benefits of using `compose` that we covered in chapter 4, but now applied to objects. Let's demonstrate this equivalence by defining `map` in terms of `compose`:

```
Function.prototype.map = function (f) {
  return compose(
      f,
      this
  );
};
```

Now all functions inherit `map` automatically. Using it reveals once again the close correspondence between the two:

```
compose(toUpper, join, unique)('aabbcc'); // 'ABC'
unique.map(join).map(toUpper) ('aabbcc'); // 'ABC'
```

What this correspondence tells us is that all the benefits that you gain with the composition of functions can easily be applied to composite types. In our simple use cases, map is an interface that allows both Array and Id to compose functions, and it will allow any ADT you use to compose functions.

Now that you've seen how these concepts intertwine, let's define a universal interface for map that allows any object that implements it to compose together.

5.4   Universal contracts

In the examples earlier in this chapter, you probably noticed that map and flatMap preserve the same caller type. For arrays, both return new arrays; for functions, both return new functions. This fact can't be taken for granted. It's a core part of the map interface, one that is universally accepted and allows your objects to work with other functional libraries, such as Ramda (https://ramdajs.com) or Crocks (https://crocks.dev). In this section, you'll learn a little bit about the theory behind patterns such as functors and monads and how they are implemented in JavaScript.

> **Fantasy-land**
>
> The protocol for how functors and monads work in JavaScript, for the most part, abides by the rules put forth in the fantasy-land specification (https://github.com/fantasyland/fantasy-land). This document is thorough, and I highly recommend that you take the time to understand it if you want to become a serious FP programmer. This chapter definitely gives you a jump start.

The full theory on ADTs is extensive and better covered in books dedicated to functional programming or abstract algebra. I'll cover enough here so that you can unlock the FP patterns that enable composable software, beginning with functors.

5.4.1   Functors

A book that focuses on the joy of programming with JavaScript and FP would not be complete without a proper dose of functors, because functors bring out the best in the language by relying on higher-order functions for data transformation.

A *functor* is anything (such as an object) that can be mapped over or that implements the map interface properly. Arrays in JavaScript are close to being functors, for example, and the map method enables a style of programming that's superior to and less error-prone than regular for loops. As you learned in section 5.3, compose makes functions functors too, so you've used them quite a bit already without realizing it.

For an object to behave like a functor, it needs to follow two simple rules, which follow from the map/compose equivalence (section 5.3). I'll use arrays again for simplicity to illustrate rules:

- *Identity*—Mapping the identity function over a container yields a new container of the same type, which is also a good indicator that map should be side-effect-free:

```
['aa','bb','cc'].map(identity);  // ['aa', 'bb', 'cc']
```

- *Composition*—Composing two or more functions, such as f after g, is equivalent to mapping first g and then f. Both statements are equivalent to ['A', 'B', 'C']:

```
['aa','bb','cc'].map(
      compose(
        toUpper,
        join,
        unique
      )
   );
```

and

```
['aa','bb','cc']
    .map(unique)
    .map(join)
    .map(toUpper);
```

Notice that I've been using the word *equivalent* loosely. The reason is to avoid eliciting the other forms of equivalence you're accustomed to, such as the double equals operator (==), which is loosely equivalent to type coercion, and triple equals (===), which is a strict quality in value and type. *Equivalent* here means referentially transparent; the meaning or result of the program doesn't change if you substitute an expression for its value.

Implementing a functor involves defining map with these simple rules and creating the contract of a closed context described in section 5.1, such as the implementing of a type-lifting function F.of, as well as a mechanism to extract the value from the container, such as a get method. As you learned in chapter 3, the best way to apply reusable interfaces to any object is to use a mixin. Let's refactor Id (shown in the next listing) to take advantage of the Functor mixin.

> **Listing 5.7 Id class with minimal context interface**

```
class Id {
   #val;
   constructor(value) {
      this.#val = value;
   }

   static of(value) {          Type-lifting
      return new Id(value);     function
   }

   get() {                     Getter to extract the
      return this.#val;         value from the container
   }
}
```

Functor is a mixin that exposes a map method, as shown in the following listing. map is a higher-order function that applies the given function f to the wrapped value and stores the result in the same container, like Array#map.

Listing 5.8   Functor mixin

```
const Functor = {
  map(f = identity) {
    return this.constructor.of(f(this.get()));
  }
}
```

> map accepts a callback function to apply, using identity as default function argument

> Applies the callback function to the value and wraps the result in a new instance of the same container, using the generic type-lifting function

Because the functor contract must preserve the enclosing structure, we can figure out the container instance calling it and invoke its static type-lifting constructor by using `this.constructor.of`. The fact that we're using classes makes this procedure simple because it configures the `constructor` property and makes it easy to discover. Now let's extend `Id` with `Functor` as we did with `Transaction` back in chapter 3:

```
Object.assign(Id.prototype, Functor);
```

Everything continues to work as before. `Array#map` resembles the same contract as a `Functor`'s map, so we can use it in the same way, as the next listing shows.

Listing 5.9   Sequential data processing with the `Id` functor

```
Id.of('aabbcc')
  .map(unique)    // Id(['a', 'b', 'c'])
  .map(join)      // Id(['abc'])
  .map(toUpper)   // Id('ABC')
  .get();         // 'ABC'
```

> Mapping from Id returns new Id objects

Let's visualize the inner workings of a functor as opening the container to expose its value to the mapped function and then rewrapping the value in a new container, as shown in figure 5.2.

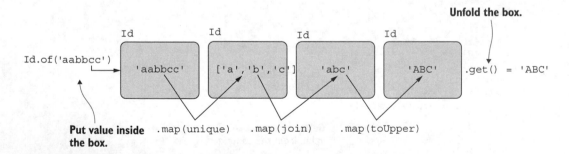

Figure 5.2   The mapping of functions over a container

If you glance once more at listing 5.9, you'll notice that it's fairly generic. Except for an implementation of a value-extracting method (`Id#get` or `Array#pop`), everything follows the generic functor contracts.

Functors let you map a simple function to transform the wrapped value and put it back in a new container of the same type. Frontend developers probably recognize that the jQuery object behaves like a functor. jQuery is a functor as well and is one of the first JavaScript libraries to popularize this style of coding (https://api.jquery.com/jquery.map).

Now let's look at a slightly different case. What would happen if you were to map a function that itself returns a container, such as mapping a function that returns an Id object? From what you've learned about arrays in this chapter, an operator like flat-Map is designed to solve this problem. To understand why, we'll study monads.

5.4.2 Monads

Monads are designed to tackle composing container-returning operations. Composing functions that return Id can result in an Id inside another Id; when composing Array, you get a multidimensional array, and so on. You get the idea.

An object becomes a monad by implementing the functor specification and the flatMap contract with its own simple protocol. The reason is that we'll need to map functions that return wrapped data. Suppose that each of the functions in this code snippet returned an Id:

```
Id.of('aabbcc')
    .map(unique)
    .map(join)
    .map(toUpper)
    .get();
```

The result would look like figure 5.3.

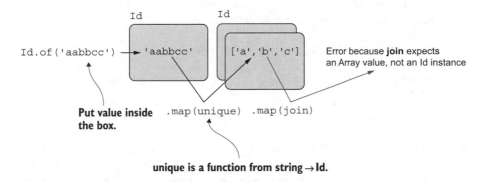

Figure 5.3 Mapping a function that returns an Id containing a wrapped value

Monads take chaining a sequence of computations to the next level so that you can compose functions that work with the same container or other containers. We're going to stick with the same container for now, because this pattern is the most common one used in practice. For reference, the fantasy-land entry is at https://github.com/fantasyland/fantasy-land#monad. Consider a monad M and equivalence as defined in section 5.4.2:

- *Left identity*—Type-lifting some value a and then calling `flatMap` with function f should yield the same result as if you simply called f with a. In code, both expressions are equivalent:

```
M.of(a).flatMap(f)  and   f(a)
```

Let's showcase left identity with simple arrays:

```
const f = x => Array.of(x**2);
Array.of(2).flatMap(f); // [4]
f(2);  //[4]
```

- *Right identity*—Given a monad instance, calling `flatMap` with the type-lift constructor function should produce an equivalent monad. Given a monad instance m, the snippets in the next listing are equivalent.

Listing 5.10   Array examples that illustrate right identity

```
m.flatMap(M.of))  and   m

Array.of(2).flatMap(x => Array.of(x));  // [2]
Array.of(2); // [2]
```
◁── Because the implementation of Array.of in JavaScript has multiple arguments, we're not able to pass the function by name into flatMap; instead, we must use a function x => Array.of(x).

- *Associativity*—As numbers are associative under addition, monads are associative under composition. The precedence instilled by the way you parenthesize an expression doesn't alter the final result. Given a monad instance m and functions f and g, the following are equivalent:

```
m.flatMap(f).flatMap(g) and m.flatMap(a => f(a).flatMap(g))

const f = x => [x ** 2];
const g = x => [x * 3];
Array.of(2).flatMap(f).flatMap(g);   // [12]
Array.of(2).flatMap(a => f(a).flatMap(g)); // [12]
```

When you work with single values, the action of a `map-then-flat` can also be understood as returning the result of the mapping function alone, thereby ignoring the outermost layer. Our `Monad` mixin in the following listing accomplishes that task.

Listing 5.11   Monad mixin

```
const Monad = {
  flatMap(f) {
    return this.map(f).get();
  },
```
◁── Ignores the extra wrapping layer and assumes that the type is a functor

```
chain(f) {
  return this.flatMap(f);
},
bind(f) {
  return this.flatMap(f);
}
};
```

You may also find this method called bind or chain.

This example teaches us that when we're dealing with JavaScript arrays specifically, `flatMap` is much more efficient than calling `map` and then `flat` manually. This procedure is more efficient in terms of CPU cycles and memory footprint. Keep in mind that every time you call `map` or `flat`, a new array is created, so combining them in one fell swoop prevents the additional overhead.

Method fusion

The fact that arrays behave monadically has many advantages. The law of composition is not only a core part of the behavior of functors and monads, but also a performance enhancement for container types called method fusion, also known as shortcut fusion. In essence, you can use `compose` to fuse or combine the execution of multiple calls to `map` into one. Take a look at the examples used for this protocol:

```
['aa','bb','cc'].map(
    compose(
      toUpper,
      join,
      unique
    )
  );
```

and

```
['aa','bb','cc']
    .map(unique)
    .map(join)
    .map(toUpper);
```

Both snippets generate the same output, but the first one uses a quarter of the space. `compose` avoids the multiple calls to `map`, each creating another copy of the array in memory. With an array this size, the performance is negligible. But if we were processing lots of data, method fusion could save us from running out of memory. Libraries such as Lodash (https://lodash.com), which uses lazy evaluation, can analyze an expression that combines calls to `map`, `filter`, and others, and then fuse them together.

For the sake of completeness, consider a similar example using `Id`:

```
const square = x => Id.of(x).map(a => a ** 2);
const times3 = x => Id.of(x).map(a => a * 3);
```

```
Id.of(2)
  .flatMap(square)
  .flatMap(times3)
  .get(); // 12

Id.of(2)
  .flatMap(a => square(a).flatMap(times3))
  .get(); // 12
```

For this code to work, we will extend `Id` once more with the monadic behavior integrating that mixin:

```
Object.assign(Id.prototype, Functor, Monad);
```

> **Emulating typeclasses**
>
> There's another reason why I think mixins are a sound implementation strategy here for these APIs: they model an equivalent concept in functional languages such as Scala and Haskell. A typeclass allows you to define a generic interface so that any object can conform to a certain behavior. `Functor` and `Monad` can make any type behave monadically with little work, for example.

We can continue to optimize this example a little bit more. Earlier, I mentioned that monads are also functors. Following that definition, it makes sense to compose the `Functor` mixin into the `Monad` mixin. Consider the `Monad` definition in the next listing.

Listing 5.12   Defining `Monad` and `Functor`

```
const Monad = Object.assign({}, Functor, {
  flatMap(f) {
    return this.map(f).get();      ◁── References map
  }                                      in Functor
  //...         ◁── Omits the other
});                   method aliases
```

This example shows how flexible and versatile composition is. Now you can make a type a `Functor` or a full `Monad` with its full contract:

```
Object.assign(Id.prototype, Monad);
```

At this point, you've learned in a basic way how functors and monads are defined. Although these sets of rules may feel contrived and limiting, they're giving you immense structure—the same structure you get from using `Array#{map, filter, reduce}` instead of straight `for` loops and `if` conditions.

Functor and monads are universal interfaces (protocols) that can plug generically into many parts of your application. Abide by them, and any third-party code or any other parts of your application that implement or support these types know exactly how to work with it. A good example of how this protocol integrates with other code is the `Promise` object, which you're probably familiar with. Promises are modeled, to some extent, after functors and monads; substitute `then` for `map` or `flatMap`, and a lot of these rules discussed in section 5.4 apply. We'll look at promises more closely in chapter 8.

Monads are not an easy pattern to grok, but it's important to start learning about them now; more of these patterns are starting to emerge in modern software development, and you don't want to get caught wrapped in a burrito (https://youtu.be/dkZFtimgAcM); you want to be ready.

In practice, you will probably never need to implement `Id` as such in your own applications. I did it to show you how the pattern works and how appending the `Functor` and `Monad` mixins endow this class with powerful composable behavior. The real bang for your buck will come from more embellished, smarter types with computational logic of their own within their `map` and `flatMap` methods. In section 5.1, I defined a closed context and showed how it models a railway-driven approach to data processing. With the basics behind us, we're going to kick things up a notch and create our own ADT to implement contextual validation.

5.5 Contextual validation with higher-order functions

An ADT is nothing more than an immutable composite data structure that contains other types. Most ADT in practice implement the monad contract, much like the `Id` container.

Before we dive in, it's worth pointing out that an ADT is a different pattern from an Abstract Data Type (which goes by the same acronym): a collection that should hold objects of the same type, such as `Array`, `Set`, `Stack`, and `Queue` (although Java-Script does not enforce this rule). An Algebraic Data Type pattern, on the other hand, can and usually does contain different types. The *Algebraic* part of the name comes from the mathematical protocol of identity, composability, and associativity (section 5.4).

In this section, we'll learn about the fundamentals of ADTs and see how to use the Functor and Monad contracts to solve contextual data validation in a composable manner.

5.5.1 Kinds of ADTs

ADTs are more prominent in the strongly typed world, where type information makes code more explicit and rigorous. (For more information on using types with Java-Script, see appendix B.) But there's still a lot we can do even without type information. This section looks at the two most common kinds of ADTs: `Record` and `Choice`. Both of these encapsulate some useful coding patterns.

RECORD

A record type is a composite that contains a fixed number of (usually primitive) types, called its operands. This is similar to a database record in which the schema describes the types it can hold and has a fixed length. Some JavaScript libraries, such as Immutable.js, provide a `Record` type that you can import and use. The most common example of a record is an immutable `Pair`:

```
const Pair = (left, right) =>
  compose(Object.seal, Object.freeze)({
    left,
    right,
    toString: () => `Pair [${left}, ${right}]`
  });
```

A `Pair` is an immutable object with a cardinality of 2 that can be used to relate two pieces of information (of any type), such as a username and password, a public and private key, a filename with an access mode, or even a key/value entry in a map data structure. `Pair` is a generic record type of which `Money`, introduced in chapter 4, or a type like `Point(x, y)` can be derived implementations.

The best use of a `Pair` is to return two related values from a function at the same time. Most often, a simple array literal or even a simple object literal is used to express a rudimentary `Pair`. Then you can take advantage of destructuring to access each field. You could have something like

```
const [id, block] = blockchain.lookUp(hash);

const {username, password} = getCredentials(user);
```

Unfortunately, these two approaches don't work well because they are mutable, and because array is generic, it doesn't communicate any relationship among its values. A record semantically communicates an AND relationship among its values, implying they must exist or make sense together (such as username AND password).

Records also go by the name of product or tuple. A pair is a 2-tuple, and a triple is a 3-tuple, all the way to an n-tuple. JavaScript has no native tuple or record concept, but an early proposal might bring it to JavaScript in the near future (https://github .com/tc39/proposal-record-tuple).

5.5.2 *Choices*

Whereas a record enforces a logical AND, a choice represents a logical OR relationship among its operands or the values it accepts. A choice is also known as a discriminated union or a sum type. Like a record, a choice type can hold multiple values, but only one of them is used at any point in time. A simple analogy involves using JavaScript's null coalesce and nullish coalesce operators, respectively. Consider the simple example in the next listing.

```
Listing 5.13  Null and nullish coalesce operators
```

```
const hash = precomputedHash || calculateHash(data);   ⟵─┤ Evaluates right side when left
                                                           side contains a falsy value

const hash = precomputedHash ?? calculateHash(data);   ⟵─┤ Evaluates right side only
                                                           when left side is null
```

In the case of the null coalesce operator, if `precomputedHash` is not a *falsy* value (null, undefined, empty string, 0, or so on), this expression evaluates the left side of the || operator; otherwise, it evaluates to the right. I recommend that you use the nullish (or nullary) coalesce operator (`??`), as it evaluates the right side only when the `precomputed-Hash` is `null` or `undefined`, which is what you intend to do most of the time.

Choice types are often used in cases that involve data checks, data validation, or error handling. The reason is that a choice models mutually exclusive branches such as success/failure, valid/invalid, and ok/error. These cases are simple binary (of cardinality 2) use cases, for which we mistakenly are tempted to abuse Booleans.

If you have experience with TypeScript, for example, an enumeration type or a utility type is a common way to represent an object that could be in one of multiple states. Consider this definition:

```
type Color = 'Red' | 'Blue';
```

With minimal tooling, you could also extend JavaScript with types (appendix B) and use enumerations the same way. Another analogy is a `switch` statement, which is often used to invoke conditional logic with multiple possible states. With two cases, the logic of a choice type would look something like this:

```
switch(value) {
  case A:
    // code block
    break;
  case B:
    // code block
    break;
  default:
    // code block
}
```

Using this structure, consider the hypothetical use case in the next listing that checks for the validity of a certain value.

> **Listing 5.14 Using a `switch` statement to perform an action based on one condition**

```
switch(isValid(value)) {
  case 'Success':
    return doWork(value);
  case 'Failure':
    logError(...);              ← return/break
  default:                        intentionally skipped to
    return getDefault();          return default value
}
```

You can think of a choice ADT as always keeping track of multiple mutually exclusive states and reacting accordingly. Validating data is no different in that you can have only one of two possible outcomes: success or failure.

5.5.3   *Modeling success and failure with the Validation monad*

Data validation is a common programming task, usually involving a lot of code split-ting (if/else/switch statements) that are often duplicated and scattered in several parts of the application. We're all well aware that code with lots of conditionals gets messy and difficult to abstract over, not to mention hard to read and expensive to maintain. This section teaches you how to implement and use monads to address this issue while keeping your code simple to read, modular, and (most important) composable.

Generally, when implementing an ADT, you must take two dimensions into account. One is the kind (record or choice), and the other is the level of composability needed (functor or monad). In this section, we will create a Validation object as a choice type with monadic behavior so that we can compose sequences of individual validated operations together. By the end, we'll finish implementing the logic behind the HasValidation mixin and use it to run validation code on every element of the block-chain in a consistent way.

Validation models two states that make up its computation context, Success and Failure, as shown in figure 5.4.

Figure 5.4   Structure of the Validation type. Validation offers a choice of Success or Failure, never both.

We'll allow the Success branch to apply functions (such as doWork) on the contained value when it's active. Indeed, this job sounds like one for map and flatMap. Other-wise, in the event of a validation failure, we'll skip calling the logic and propagate the error encountered. This pattern is useful when you need to bubble up an error that occurred during a complex sequence of operations—something that if/else and even try/catch blocks struggle with.

In addition, think about how many times you have written validation functions that return Boolean. I know I have, but this is a bad habit. By returning a Validation object from your functions, you're directly forcing users to handle Success and Fail-ure cases properly instead of testing a Boolean. Another clear benefit is that your functions become self-documenting or, in Edsger Dijkstra's words, "more precise." In JavaScript, this benefit is important because documentation is often lacking, and you need to trace through the code to see what exceptions are being thrown or any special error values, such as null or undefined. Acknowledging that some operations might fail ahead of time is much better than having your users guess that an error, if any, might occur when invoking a particular function. We can all agree that returning false conveys nothing to the caller about which operation or data in question was invalid; there's no context.

Finally, another good quality of validation procedures is that they fail-fast. Because composition chains a function's inputs and outputs, it's pointless to have functions run with invalid data when an error has already been discovered. Short-circuiting is sensible.

Let's look at a hypothetical example in blockchains that involves validating whether a block has been tampered with. This check is easily made by recomputing a block's hash and checking it against its own:

```
const checkTampering = block =>
  block.hash === block.calculateHash()
    ? Success.of(block)
    : Failure.of('Block hash is invalid');

const block = new Block(1, '123456789', ['some data'], 1);
checkTampering(block).isSuccess; // true

block.data = ['data compromised'];
checkTampering(block).isFailure; // true
```

This function checks for a certain condition and returns a Success wrapper containing the correct value or a Failure object with an error message. This function doesn't care how the error propagates forward or how it would work as part of a longer composition chain; it focuses on its own task.

Both Success and Failure branches are part of the Validation composite and are the central abstractions that drive a series of validations to a final result or to an error. Success and Failure are closed contexts, modeling the notion of an operation that passes or fails as a first-class citizen of your application. The following listing uses a class to implement this behavior.

Listing 5.15 Parent `Validation` class

```
class Validation {
  #val;
  constructor(value) {                          ◁──┐  Value is private
    this.#val = value;                               and read-only
    if (![Success.name, Failure.name].includes(new.target.name)) {   ◁──┐
      throw new TypeError(
        `Can't directly instantiate a Validation.
          Please use constructor Validation.of`
      );
    }
  }
  get() {                    ◁──┐  Reads the value
    return this.#val;              from the container
  }
```

> Value is private and read-only

> Prevents direct instantiation, effectively making Validation an abstract class and forcing its behavior to be accessed through its variant types: Success and Failure

> Reads the value from the container

```
static of(value) {
  return Validation.Success(value);
}
```
Generic type-lifting function that returns a new instance of Success

```
static Success(a) {
  return Success.of(a);
}

static Failure(error) {
  return Failure.of(error);
}

get isSuccess() {
  return false;
}
```
Queries the type of container at runtime; set to false as default to indicate that none of the branches is active

```
get isFailure() {
  return false;
}
```

Provides a generic way to recover

```
getOrElse(defaultVal) {
  return this.isSuccess ? this.#val: defaultVal;
}

toString() {
  return `${this.constructor.name} (${this.#val})`;
}
}
```

Extending from this class are the concrete variant choices: Success and Failure. The Success path is what we call the happy path, so there's not much to differentiate it from the parent. Failure overrides the behavior of some of those inherited methods, as shown in the next listing.

Listing 5.16 Success and Failure branches of Validation

```
class Success extends Validation {
  static of(a) {
    return new Success(a);;
  }

  get isSuccess() {
    return true;
  }
}
```
Overrides the type of container

```
class Failure extends Validation {
  get isFailure() {
    return true;
  }

  static of(b) {
    return new Failure(b);
  }
```

```
get() {
    throw new TypeError(`Can't extract the value of a Failure`);
}
}
```
Calling get directly on failure is considered to be a programming error.

Using classes vs. objects to model ADTs

I chose to use classes to design `Validation` because this is what the majority of JavaScript developers use. Nevertheless, any of the patterns covered in chapters 2 and 3 (constructor functions, OLOO, mixins) would work as well. For comparison, here's an OLOO version of the `Validation` ADT:

```
const Validation = {
    init: function(value) {
        this.isSuccess = false;
        this.isFailure = false;
        this.getOrElse = defaultVal => this.isSuccess ? value :
            defaultVal;
        this.toString = () => `Validation (${value})`;
        this.get = () => value;
        return this;
    }
};

const Success = Object.create(Validation);
Success.of = function of(value) {
    this.init(value);
    this.isSuccess = true;
    this.toString = () => `Success (${value})`;
    return this;
};

const Failure = Object.create(Validation);
Failure.of = function of(errorMsg) {
    this.init(errorMsg);
    this.get = () =>
        throw new TypeError(`Can't extract the value of a Failure`);
    this.toString = () => `Failure (${errorMsg})`;
    return this;
};
```

As you can see, by not shoehorning class-based design into JavaScript, OLOO greatly reduces the amount of complexity in the code by removing the need for special syntax for private variables, enforcement of abstract class behavior, and all references to class-oriented inheritance mental model (`class`, `extends`) while keeping all the same functionality.

It may not be immediately obvious, but given that `Validation` can hold only a single value at a time (valid value or an error), it's more memory-efficient than record types, which store all values in the tuple.

Now that we've implemented the basic pieces, let's see them in action.

5.5.4   *Composing with monads*

To show this type in action, let's refactor `countBlocksInFile` (started in chapter 4) to a function that also features validation:

```
const countBlocksInFile = compose(
    count,
    JSON.parse,
    decode('utf8'),
    read
);
```

This function reads from a file to a binary buffer, decodes this buffer to a UTF-8 string, parses this string to an array of blocks, and finally counts it. But this function is missing an important part: checking whether the file exists. If the file doesn't exist, `read` will throw an exception. Likewise, without a valid `Buffer` object, `decode` will throw an exception, and so on.

Because the critical point of inflexion is whether the file exists, we can use `Validation` to abstract over this split point. Let's refactor the `read` function to return a `Validation` instance instead in the next listing.

Listing 5.17   Creating a version of `read` that returns a `Validation` result

```
const read = f =>
    fs.existsSync(f)
        ? Success.of(fs.readFileSync(f))          ◁
        : Failure.of(`File ${f} does not exist!`);   ◁
```

The conditional expression here models the logical OR to decide which branch to follow.

An array is useful so that you can concatenate more than one error message.

Now this code works as follows:

```
read('chain.txt'); // Success(<Buffer>)
read('foo.txt');   // Failure('File foo.txt does not exist!')
```

Executing the rest of the code is a matter of mapping each transformation to each `Success` container, like any generic functor. The `Functor` mixin is sufficient:

```
Object.assign(Success.prototype, Functor);
```

By doing this, we get the benefit of tightly coupling the validation branches and shared data with the loosely coupled, Lego-style extension of mixins for shared behavior. With `map`, this code works as it did with `compose` due to the `map`/`compose` equivalence. Once again, you see the deep impact of this ostensibly trivial equivalence:

```
const countBlocksInFile = f =>
    read(f)
        .map(decode('utf8'))
        .map(JSON.parse)
        .map(count);

countBlocksInFile('foo.txt');   // Success(<number>)
```

Furthermore, it's a common pattern for choice ADTs to map functions on one side and skip them (no-op) on the other. Validation executes on the success branch, which we'll call the right side, also known as right-biased. In the previous example, we made Success (the right side) a functor. We also need to account for the Failure branch so that any composed operations are ignored or skipped in the event of a read error. For this purpose, we can create a NoopFunctor mixin with the same shape as the regular Functor, as the next listing shows.

Listing 5.18 Using `NoopFunctor` in failure cases to skip calling mapped functions

```
const NoopFunctor = {
  map() {
    return this;          ⟵──  Because the data is left
  }                            untouched, it's sensible to return
}                              the same object to the caller.
```

Let's assign NoopFunctor to Failure (the left side):

```
Object.assign(
  Failure.prototype,
  NoopFunctor
);
```

After we account for both case classes, the flow of execution looks like figure 5.5.

First, let's look at a simple example of a failure branch so that you can understand how this object handles errors.

Suppose that you want to use Validation to abstract over checking for null objects. First, create the function that implements the branching logic (fromNullable):

```
const fromNullable = value =>
  (value === null)
    ? Failure.of('Expected non-null value')
    : Success.of(value);
```

This abstraction helps us apply functions to data without having to worry about whether the data is defined, as shown in the following listing.

Listing 5.19 Using `fromNullable` to process valid strings

```
fromNullable('joj').map(toUpper).toString() // 'Success (JOJ)'

fromNullable(null).map(toUpper).toString()        ⟵──  Underlying implementation of map
// 'Failure (Expected non-null value)'                  is the NoopFunctor, which ignores
                                                         the operation when data is invalid
```

To showcase this type in the real world, let's use it in our blockchain application. Validating or verifying the contents of a blockchain is such an important part of this technology that companies specialize in implementing this aspect of the protocol. We're

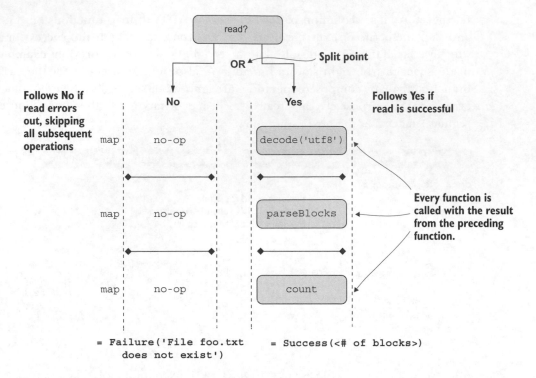

Figure 5.5   Detailed execution of the composition of functions mapped over a `Validation` type. When the operations are successful, the container allows each operation to map over the wrapped data; otherwise, it skips to a recovery alternative.

implementing a much more simplified version for this book, of course. Aside from `checkTampering` (as implemented in section 5.5.3) we must ensure that blocks are in the right position in the chain (`checkIndex`) and that their timestamps are greater than or equal to that of the previous one (`checkTimestamp`). Both simple rules look like this:

```
const checkTimestamps = curry((previousBlockTimestamp, block) =>
  block.timestamp >= previousBlockTimestamp
    ? Success.of(block)
    : Failure.of(`Block timestamps out of order`)
);

const checkIndex = curry((previousBlockIndex, block) =>
  previousBlockIndex < block.index
    ? Success.of(block)
    : Failure.of(`Block out of order`)
);
```

We're going to use currying to make applying these functions easier. Notice that we defined these functions as curried functions (see chapter 4) to facilitate composing them as a validation sequence. Because blocks are linked in a chain, to compare one block, you need to load the previous one (after the genesis block). From any block, this process is always simple because each block has a reference to the previous block's hash and a reference to the chain of which it is part, as shown in the next listing.

Listing 5.20 `isValid` method of `Block`

```
class Block {
  //... omitting for brevity

  isValid() {
    const {
      index: previousBlockIndex,              Uses destructuring with
      timestamp: previousBlockTimestamp       variable name change
    } = this.#blockchain.lookUp(this.previousHash);

    const validateTimestamps =
      checkTimestamps(previousBlockTimestamp, this);
                                                        These functions
    const validateIndex =                               return either
      checkIndex(previousBlockIndex, this);             Success or
                                                        Failure.
    const validateTampering = checkTampering(this);


    return validateTimestamps.isSuccess &&
           validateIndex.isSuccess        &&
           validateTampering.isSuccess;

  }
}

const ledger = new Blockchain();
let block = new Block(ledger.height() + 1, ledger.top.hash, ['some data']);
block = ledger.push(block);
block.isValid(); // true             Alters the
                                     block's data
block.data = ['data compromised'];         Validation check fails
block.isValid(); // false                  due to tamper check
```

This code seems perfectly fine if we want to return a Boolean result, which lacks any context of the running operation. The best approach here, however, is for `isValid` to return a `Validation` object instead of a Boolean. That way, if we want to validate the entire blockchain data structure (not one block), we can compose all the `Validation` objects together, and in the event of a failure, we could report exactly what the error is.

5.5.5 *Higher-kinded composition with Validation*

As we did with `Id` in section 5.4.2, let's bestow upon `Validation` the ability to compose with other objects of the same type and form chains. For this task, we can attach the `Monad` mixin, which includes `Functor` as well as the ability to `flatMap` other `Validation`-returning functions. For the `Success` branch, we can assign the `Monad` mixin:

```
Object.assign(Success.prototype, Monad);
```

For `Failure`, we can apply the logicless `NoopMonad`:

```
const NoopMonad = {
  flatMap(f) {
    return this;
  },
  chain(f) {
    return this.flatMap(f);
  },
  bind(f) {
    return this.flatMap(f);
  }
}
```

Then extending `Failure` is similar:

```
Object.assign(
  Failure.prototype,
  NoopMonad
);
```

The next listing shows how you can type-lift a block object into `Validation`. Then the ADT takes over, and all you need to do is chain the validation rules, like building a small rules engine.

Listing 5.21 `Block validation with flatMap`

```
class Block {
  ...

  isValid() {
    const {
      index: previousBlockIndex,
      timestamp: previousBlockTimestamp
    } = this.#blockchain.lookUp(this.previousHash);

    return Validation.of(this)
      .flatMap(checkTimestamps(previousBlockTimestamp))
      .flatMap(checkIndex(previousBlockIndex))
      .flatMap(checkTampering);
  }
}
```

> The curried form is useful so that the block object (the dynamic argument) is passed into each call to flatMap.

As you can see, this implementation looks a lot more elegant than the previous one and serves as another good example of a hybrid OOP/FP implementation using mixins. To ensure a more rigorous transition from OO to FP land, you could opt to pass a frozen version of the object:

```
return Validation.of(Object.freeze(this))
    .flatMap(checkTimestamps(previousBlockTimestamp))
    .flatMap(checkIndex(previousBlockIndex))
    .flatMap(checkTampering);
```

A happy path run of this algorithm looks like figure 5.6.

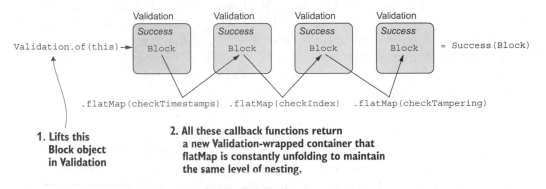

Figure 5.6   Sequential application of different `Validation`-returning check functions composed together with `flatMap`

This new version of `isValid` outputs a `Validation` result instead of a Boolean, so using in in the `Success` case looks like this:

```
block.isValid().isSuccess;  // true
```

If any of the checks fails, `Validation` will be smart about skipping the rest:

```
block.isValid().isFailure;  // true
block.isValid().toString(); // 'Failure (Block hash is invalid)'
```

Perhaps you're thinking that although this code looks more succinct, having to call `flatMap` every time is a bit verbose. Why not try something more point-free? In chapter 4, you learned how to create point-free function compositions with `compose` and `curry`. You can also achieve a point-free style with monads in JavaScript. To understand how this could work, first we need to implement a slightly different variation of `compose` called `composeM`, which uses `flatMap` to control the flow of data.

5.5.6   *Point-free coding with monads*

Point-free coding has the advantage of making complex logic much simpler to read at a high level. To allow for point-free coding using monads, we need to build up a little more plumbing. In section 5.3, you learned that composing two functions is equivalent to mapping one over the other. Parting from this idea, the following is also correct:

```
const compose2 = (f, g) => g.map(f);
```

Again, you can extend this code to work with a list of functions (instead of only two) by using `reduce`:

```
const compose = (...fns) => fns.reduce(compose2);
```

By a similar reasoning, a correspondence exists that allows `flatMap` to become the basis of composing two monad-returning functions—in our case, `Validation`-returning functions. Using code to demonstrate this correspondence follows a similar train of thought of the buildup of `compose` in chapter 4 and the `compose/map` equivalence (section 5.3). I'll spare you the details for the sake of brevity and focus on what's important. An alternative to `compose2` that works with monads, called `composeM2`, is implemented like this:

```
const composeM2 = (f, g) => (...args) => g(...args).flatMap(f);
```

As you can see, this implementation is similar to the `map`-based implementation of `compose2`. Because the functions in the pipeline are returning monad instances, `flatMap` is used to apply the function to the value and automatically flatten the container along the way. Finally, to support more than two functions, we do a similar reduction:

```
const composeM = (...Ms) => Ms.reduce(composeM2);
```

Don't be concerned about understanding all the details or having to implement this code anew every time. Functional JavaScript libraries already have support for both types of composition; one works at a higher level of abstraction than the other. The gist is that you use `compose` to sequence the execution of functions that return unwrapped (simple) values and `composeM` for functions that return wrapped values (monads). That is why the former is based on `map` and the latter is based on `flatMap`.

Now that we've defined `composeM`, let's put it to work. `composeM` orchestrates and chains the logic of each function, and `Validation` steers the overall result of the entire operation. With the right guardrails in place, you can sequence complex chains of code with automatic, built-in data validation along the way, as shown in the next listing.

Listing 5.22   Block validation with `composeM`

```
class Block {
  //...
```

```
isValid() {
   const {
      index: previousBlockIndex,
      timestamp: previousBlockTimestamp
   } = this.#blockchain.lookUp(this.previousHash);

   return composeM(
      checkTimestamps(previousBlockTimestamp),
      checkIndex(previousBlockIndex),
      checkTampering,
      Validation.of
   )(Object.freeze(this));
   }
}
```

There's no need to test this logic again; you can do this on your own, following the previous examples. If you examine the structure of the composition part, you again see that it retains its point-free nature where all function arguments (except the curried ones) are not directly specified.

At this point, you've learned enough functional programming concepts that you can start taking advantage of this paradigm in your day-to-day tasks. Monads are not a simple concept to grok, and many books and articles teach it differently, but when you understand that behind the scenes, it's all about map (which you do understand from working with arrays), things start to fall into place.

Let's continue with our blockchain validation scenario. To recap, unlike regular data structures, a blockchain can't be tampered with or altered in any way. Changing one block would involve recalculating the hashes of all subsequent blocks in the chain. This restriction also ensures that no one can dominate and re-create the entire history of the chain, which prevents the infamous 51% attack, because no single entity would be able to harness 51% of all the necessary computational power to run all these calculations:

- Are the blocks in the right order?
- Are the timestamps in proper chronological order?
- Is the integrity of the chain intact, and does each block point to the correct previous block? (To check, we see whether the previousHash of the block equals the hash property of the block that went before it.)
- Has the block's data been tampered with? (To check, we recalculate the hash of each block. If something changed inside a block, the hash of that block changes.)
- Is the length of the hash correct (using only 64-character-length hashes in this book)?

```
class Block {
   ...

   isValid() {
      const {
         index: previousBlockIndex,
```

```
      timestamp: previousBlockTimestamp
} = this.#blockchain.lookUp(this.previousHash);

return composeM(
      checkTampering,
      checkDifficulty,
      checkLinkage(previousBlockHash),
      checkLength(64),
      checkTimestamps(previousBlockTimestamp),
      checkIndex(previousBlockIndex),
      Validation.of
)(Object.freeze(this));
}
```

The code in listing 5.22 executed only three validation rules. Observe how this code snippet shines when you scale out to many more rules. You can follow the implementation of each rule in the code accompanying this book. The thing to focus on here is how well-structured and readable the algorithm is. You'll never sacrifice readability if you want to add even more rules. Point-free coding with monads truly resembles an assembly-line-style, embedded rules engine. This trade of semicolons for commas is the reason why monads are also called programmable commas.

Up until now, we've been able to validate only a single block instance. Fortunately, because our code is composable, we can validate any amount of objects needed. Blockchains store billions of objects. You can imagine the work involved in validating billions of these blocks. As you know, blocks contain transactions, which also need to be validated. For this book, it's simple to think of a blockchain as being a list of lists (blocks with transactions), but in reality it's a tree. All the elements of this tree need to be vertically traversed and validated. A single error should cause the entire process to halt (fail-fast).

5.5.7   *Reducing complex data structures*

In this section, you'll learn that having a well-defined, composable interface allows you to reduce complex data structures easily.

To validate all the objects of a blockchain (the blockchain object itself, all its blocks, and all its transactions), we'll use the HasValidation mixin and assign it to all the objects involved. The logic implemented by this mixin is used to traverse any object of a blockchain and validate its structure, as shown in figure 5.7.

HasValidation augments objects with a new API: validate. Also, HasValidation-requires that every element of the blockchain declare an isValid method (returning an object of type Validation, of course) that knows how to check itself. This interface is the minimal interface required.

isValid is in charge of implementing all the business rules pertaining to the object in question, as you saw with Block in section 5.5.6. The algorithm uses validate recursively and is designed to start verifying a blockchain from any node in the tree.

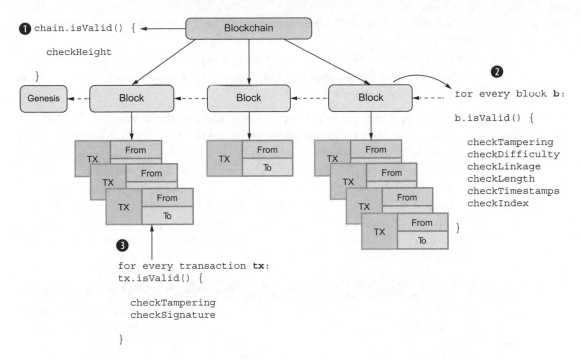

Figure 5.7 Traversing a blockchain's objects, starting with the `Blockchain` object itself and moving down to each block's transactions. You can think of the routine as forming a treelike structure, with the `Blockchain` object itself as the root, blocks as the second-level nodes, and transactions as the leaves of the tree.

Before I outline the steps, let me prepare you for the code you'll see in listing 5.23. Because we're dealing with a tree-like structure, we'll use recursion to traverse all its nodes. The first part of the algorithm involves enumerating the object by using the spread operator. Some built-ins are already iterable. We can enumerate all the values inside a map like this:

```
const map = new Map([[0, 'foo'], [1, 'bar']]);

[...map.values()]; // ['foo', 'bar'])
[...map.keys()];   // [0, 1])
```

With JavaScript, you can define how spread behaves in custom objects as well with a special property type known as `Symbol.iterator`. You may have played with or read code that uses symbols, which are quite powerful. I haven't covered symbols yet or shown how iteration works; I cover these topics in detail in chapter 7. For now, when you see this idiom `[...obj]`, think of it as returning an array representation of the object, hypothetically as `obj.toArray()`.

Here are the main steps:

1   Enumerate the object into an array. In the case of blockchain, this step returns an array with all its blocks. For block, it returns all its transactions.

2 Reduce the array of each object's `isValid` result, starting from the object's own `isValid`.

3 Call `validate` on each object, and return to step 1.

4 Return `Validation.Success` if all elements validate; otherwise, return `Validation.Failure`.

Listing 5.23 combines the techniques we've been learning about, such as `flatMap` and `reduce`, to determine whether all the elements in the chain are valid. Remember from chapter 4 that `reduce` is a way to think about composition, and by pairing it with `flatMap`, you achieve composition of objects, not functions. At each step, the algorithm spreads the object being validated (a block will return its list of transactions, for example); then it converts the list of objects to a list of `Validation` objects by using `map`. Finally, it uses `flatMap` as the reducer function to collapse the result to a single `Validation` object. Recursively, all the levels are collapsed into the final `validation-Result` accumulator variable.

Listing 5.23   `HasValidation` mixin

```
const HasValidation = () => ({
    validate() {
        return [...this]                                    Invokes the object's [Symbol.iterator]
         .reduce((validationResult, nextItem) =>            to enumerate its state through the
             validationResult.flatMap(() => nextItem.validate()),   spread operator
           this.isValid()
          );
    }
});
```

Begins with the result of checking the current object in question

Reduces the result of all validation calls into a single one

Given everything that's happening in listing 5.23, this algorithm is terse and compact. I'll explain it again from the point of view of a reduction now that you've seen the code because recursion is hard to grok sometimes. Conceptually, you can think of validating an entire data structure as somehow reducing it to a single value. That's happening here. `reduce` allows you to specify a starting value: the check of the object that starts `validate`. From that point on, you start composing a sequence of validation objects, one on top of the other. Then `flatMap` folds all the levels to a single value as it traverses down the tree.

One thing that might catch your attention is the arrow function passed to `flatMap`. Because we're not interested in knowing which object is currently passing all checks, only that it did, we throw away the input argument. `Validation` is doing the heavy lifting of keeping track of the error details for us. If it detects an error, the underlying type internally switches from `Success` to `Failure`, records the error, and sidesteps the rest of the operations (flat-mapping failures on top of failures).

The downside of listing 5.23 is that it creates an array in memory at each branch of the blockchain. This code will not scale for real-world blockchains with billions of objects, however. In chapter 9, we'll address this problem with a programming model that allows us to process infinite amounts of data.

Remember from chapter 3 that `Blockchain`, `Block`, and `Transaction` all implemented this mixin. Now you know how it works. Here's the snippet of code that attaches this mixin to each of the main classes of our domain:

```
Object.assign(
   Blockchain.prototype,
   HasValidation()
);

Object.assign(
  Block.prototype,
  HasHash(['index', 'timestamp', 'previousHash', 'data']),
  HasValidation()
);

Object.assign(
  Transaction.prototype,
  HasHash(['timestamp', 'sender', 'recipient', 'funds', 'description']),
  HasSignature(['sender', 'recipient', 'funds']),
  HasValidation()
);
```

Now that you understand how monads work, you've gained a universal vocabulary that allows you to easily integrate with any other code that understands it, including third-party code, and compose like-shaped code

5.5.8 *Third-party integration*

If all the APIs we use spoke the same protocol, our job as developers would be much easier. Luckily, the universal functor and monad interfaces are well established and known, and are already ubiquitous in functional JavaScript libraries, but this is not the case for all aspects of software. In this chapter, I briefly mentioned Ramda and Crocks as being good functional libraries to use. You may have also seen, heard about, or even used Underscore.js or Lodash. These libraries are among the most-downloaded NPM libraries.

Ramda, for example, speaks the language of functors and monads by also following the fantasy-land definitions. The following listing shows how `Validation` integrates seamlessly with Ramda.

Listing 5.24 Integrating a custom `Validation` object with FP library Ramda

```
const R = require('ramda');
const { chain: flatMap, map } = R;          ◁——  chain is an alias for
                                                  flatMap. Ramda calls
const notZero = num => (num !== 0                 it chain.
   ? Success.of(num)
   : Failure.of('Number zero not allowed')
);

const notNaN = num => (!Number.isNaN(num)
   ? Success.of(num)
```

```
      : Failure.of('NaN')
   );

const divideBy = curry((denominator, numerator) =>
   numerator / denominator
);

const safeDivideBy = denominator =>
   compose(
      map(divideBy(denominator)),
      flatMap(notZero),
      flatMap(notNaN),
      Success.of
   );
```

Ramda delegates to the functor's flatMap, if present.

```
const halve = safeDivideBy(2);
halve(16); // Success(8)
halve(0);  // 'Failure(Number zero not allowed)'
halve(0).getOrElse(0); // 0
```

Shows the default value feature of Validation

The function versions of map and flatMap imported from Ramda will delegate to the object's map and flatMap, if present. This integration is possible because we're abiding by the universal contracts that both require.

Under the hood, the version of map used here is implemented slightly differently from our implementation of map in the Functor mixin shown in listing 5.8:

```
const Functor = {
  map(f = identity) {
    return this.constructor.of(f(this.get()));
  }
}
```

General-purpose third-party libraries such as Ramda expose curried, standalone functions that order arguments to facilitate composition. Those functions have a signature like function map(fn, F), where the functor F is the object being composed and chained with compose. We decided to use a mixin object, so in our case, F is implied and becomes this.

Alternatively, we could use JavaScript's dynamic context binding capabilities to create our own extracted forms so that we can arrive at a similar experience as with a standalone implementation.

5.6   *Higher-kinded composition with method extraction and dynamic binding*

So far, we've made our objects functors and monads by assigning them the proper mixins. This isn't the only way to use the Functor pattern. In this section, you'll learn how you can extract a map method as a function that you can apply to any type of functor using dynamic binding.

You're already aware that JavaScript makes it simple to change the environment or context that a function is bound to by using prototype methods bind, call, or apply.

Given the `Functor` mixin, we can extract the `map` method with a simple destructuring assignment:

```
const { map } = Functor;
```

Using `Function#call`, we can call it on any functor like so:

```
map.call(Success.of(2), x => x * 2); // Success(4)
```

This example is close to a generalized function implementation of `map` like the one that ships with Ramda, except with reversed arguments. Calling methods this way can be a bit verbose, especially if you want to compose them together. Suppose that you want to combine `Success.of(2)` with a function that squares its value. Let's follow this simple example:

```
map.call(map.call(Success.of(2), x => x * 2), x => x ** 2); // Success(16)
```

This style of writing code won't scale, because as our logic gets more complicated, the code gets harder to parse. Let's try to smooth it with a simple abstraction:

```
const apply = curry((fn, F) => map.call(F, fn));
```

This higher-order function both solves the argument order and uses currying to make composition better, which matches closely what you'd get from an external library:

```
apply(x => x * 2)(Success.of(2)); // Success.of(4)
```

Now we can `compose` functors without needing `composeM`:

```
compose(
    apply(x => x ** 2),
    apply(x => x * 2)
)(Success.of(2)); // Success(16)
```

> **NOTE** With regard to `apply`, another extension to monads, known as *applicative monads,* builds on functors to provide an interface to apply a function directly to a container, similar to what we did here. The method name usually is `ap` or `apply`. Applicatives are beyond the scope of this book, but you can learn more about them at http://mng.bz/OE9o.

These improvements are good ones, but it would be nice to be able to process ADTs fluently directly with our extracted map function without needing anything extra. A solution to this problem is in the works, and in the spirit of having fun with JavaScript, I will introduce you to the newly proposed bind operator (https://gitub.com/tc39/proposal-bind-operator).

This proposal introduces the `::` native operator, which performs a `this` binding (as the `Function#{bind,call,apply}` API would) in combination with method extraction. It comes in two flavors: binary and unary.

In binary form (`obj :: method`), the bound object is specified before the method:

```
Success.of(2)::map(x => x * 2); // Success(4)
```

Much as we do with the pipeline operator, we can now easily call a sequence of functor/monadic transformations on an ADT:

```
Success.of(2)::map(x => x * 2)::map(x => x ** 2); // Success(16)
```

Here's a refactored version of the Ramda code snippet from section 5.5.8 that removes the dependency on this library:

```
const { flatMap } = Monad;

const safeDivideBy = denominator => numerator =>
    Success.of(numerator)
        :: flatMap(notNaN)
        :: flatMap(notZero)
        :: map(divideBy(denominator));

const halve = safeDivideBy(2);

halve(16); // Success(8)
```

You may also find the bind operator in unary form (`::obj.method`). Suppose that you want to pass a properly bound `console.log` method as a callback function. You could use `::console.log`, as in

```
Success.of(numerator)::map(::console.log);
```

or as bound to method:

```
const MyLogger = {
   defaultLogger: ::console.log
};
```

Here's another example:

```
class SafeIncrementor {
    constructor(by) {
        this.by = by;
    }
    inc(val) {
        if (val <= (Number.MAX_SAFE_INTEGER - this.by)) {
          return val + this.by;
        }
        return Number.MAX_SAFE_INTEGER;
    }
}
```

`SafeIncrementor` is used to safely add to an integer without risking overflow or misrepresentation. If you wanted to run this operation over an array of numbers, you would have to set the proper bind context so that the incrementor remembers what `this.by` refers to using `Function#bind`:

```
const incrementor = new SafeIncrementor(2);

[1, 2, 3].map(incrementor.inc.bind(incrementor)); // [3, 4, 5]
```

With the bind operator in unary form, this code reduces to

```
[1, 2, 3].map(::incrementor.inc); // [3, 4, 5]
```

Both options work in much the same way. The bind operator creates a bound function to the object on the left or the right side of the operator. See appendix A for details on enabling this feature with Babel.

In this chapter, we explored the functor and monad patterns by writing our own ADT. `Validation` is not the only ADT; many others exist. In fact, Haskell programs execute completely wrapped in the context of an I/O monad so that you can do simple things such as write to standard out in a side-effect-free way. ADTs are simple yet powerful tools. They allow you to represent everyday common tasks in a composable manner. After reading this chapter, you know to never use your data naked. When you want to apply functions in a more robust way, try wrapping them inside a container.

In this chapter, we implemented `Validation` from scratch, but many ADTs are widely used in practice. They are becoming so widespread that you can find them all as userland libraries and frameworks. Some have even evolved into new additions to a language. JavaScript will meet both of these cases with `Promise` (first a library, now a native API) and then `Observable` (chapter 9). Although `Promises` do not abide by the same universal interface, they behave like one, as you'll learn in chapter 8.

By understanding the basic concepts of ADTs, you have a stronger grasp of how these APIs work. Composable software doesn't involve code alone; it also involves the platform. JavaScript's revamped module system is the Holy Grail of composition and the subject of chapter 6.

Summary

- Wrapping bare data inside a mappable container provides good encapsulation and immutability.
- JavaScript provides an object-like façade for its primitive data types that preserves their immutability.
- `Array#{flat, flatMap}` are two new APIs that allow you to work with multidimensional arrays in a fluent, composable manner.
- `map` and `compose` have a deep semantic equivalence.
- An ADT can be classified by how many values it can support (record or choice) and by the level of composability (functor or monad).

- Functors are objects that implement the `map` interface. Monads are objects that implement the `flatMap` interface. Both support a set of mathematically inspired protocols that must be followed.

- Validation is a composite choice ADT modeling `Success` and `Failure` conditions.

- Whereas `compose` is used for regular function composition, `composeM` is used for monadic, higher-kinded composition.

- By implementing the universal protocols of Functor and Monad, you can integrate your code easily and seamlessly with third-party FP libraries.

- Use the newly proposed pipeline operator to run sequences of monadic transformations in a fluent manner.

Part 3

Code

Now that you have your objects and functions in place, how and where do you place them? Part 3 looks into how to organize the components of your applications and take advantage of separation of logic. Up until now, this task was never easy because it required you to dive into the sea of module systems for your client-side code, which were managed differently from modules in the backend. And if you're expecting any modules of shared, common logic to transition from, say, browsers to server easily, think again. This transition wasn't possible before, but everything changed with JavaScript's official, standard module system.

Chapter 6 introduces you to JavaScript's official module system: ECMAScript Modules (ESM). ESM builds on the painfully learned lessons of earlier technologies with the goal of standardizing how code is imported and exported consistently in both client and server environments.

The whole purpose of using modules is to change one part of your application without affecting another, a process also known as separation of concerns. Chapter 7 takes this principle to heart and combines it with metaprogramming techniques so that you can lift and shift common functionality (such as logging and performance counters) to separate modules and then hook them into different parts of your application dynamically—only when and where you need them. You'll learn how to use symbols to create static hooks and then how to use dynamic proxies to create dynamic, revocable (on/off) hooks.

ECMAScript Modules

This chapter covers

- Evaluating programmatic module patterns
- Reviewing Immediately Invoked Function Expressions (IIFEs)
- Introducing the ECMAScript Module syntax and the new .mjs extension
- Comparing dynamic and static module systems
- Using tree-shaking and dead-code elimination

Scope is like oxygen to a programmer. It's everywhere. You often don't even think about it. But when it gets polluted . . . you choke.

—David Herman (*Effective JavaScript*)

The world of JavaScript development is changing frantically, and the part of the language that has undergone the most change is its module system.

In modern application development, we take the notion of modular programming for granted. The practice of breaking our applications into different files and then recombining them is already second nature to us. We don't do these things to avoid getting blisters on our fingers from endless scrolling; we do them so that we can reason about and evolve different parts of our applications separately without fear of breaking others.

You may have heard the term *cognitive load* used to refer to the amount of information a person can hold at any point in time. Too much information—such as the state of all variables, the behavior of all components involved, and all the potential side effects—leads to cognitive overload. Computers can easily track millions of operations or changes of states per second, but humans can't. A scientific fact is that humans can store around seven artifacts at the same time in short-term memory. (Think of a small cache.) This is why we need to subdivide our code into subprograms, modules, or functions so that we can examine each element in isolation and reduce the amount of information we take in at the same time.

As I said back in chapter 1, the days of modern JavaScript development are upon us. Every major programming language must have good support for modules, but until recently, JavaScript did not. In chapters 4 and 5, you learned about breaking complex code into functions and reassembling them with composition. That process was function/object-level modularization. This chapter covers modularization at the file level, using native JavaScript keywords.

We start with a brief overview of today's landscape of module solutions and then move to a discussion of JavaScript's new official standard: ECMAScript Modules (ESM), also known as ECMA262 Modules, which began as ECMAScript 2015 Modules. Unlike early module systems, ESM enhances the JavaScript syntax to use static dependency definitions, which has four significant benefits:

- Improves the experience of sharing code across your applications
- Makes tools such as static code analysis, dead-code elimination, and tree-shaking much more efficient
- Unifies the module system for server as well as client, which solves the huge problem of requiring different module systems depending on the platform
- Optimizes the way in which compilers analyze code

NOTE   It's important to mention that this book does not cover how to package JavaScript code or how to deliver it with package managers such as NPM and Yarn. Also, because there are many JavaScript compilers, I don't cover any specific compiler optimizations related to ESM.

We'll start by reviewing today's JavaScript modules landscape so that you understand what problem ESM addresses and why we're fortunate to have it.

6.1   *Past state of affairs*

Modular programming has been a mainstream concept in other language communities for many years, but not for JavaScript. Even today, it's challenging to manage dependencies and build code that can run uniformly across many environments. Keep in mind that JavaScript is in the unique position of supporting both server and client (browser) environments, which are very different in nature.

If you're developing client-side applications, it's likely that you've already had to deal with some sophisticated build tool that could take all your independent scripts and merge them into a single bundle. At the end of the day, the application runs as one endless file to create the illusion of modularity. To understand the motivation behind ESM and why it's so important, it helps to spend a little time understanding the current state of affairs of JavaScript and modules and how we got here.

If you've been writing JavaScript code for some years, you probably remember that JavaScript faced a lot of pushback and criticism due to its lack of a proper module system. Without a doubt, this limitation caused the greatest amount of pain to web developers. Without modules, any decent-size codebase quickly entered a global clash of named variables and functions. This clash was magnified when multiple developers worked on the same application. You'd be surprised how many arrays named `arr`, functions named `fn`, and strings named `str` exist globally across hundreds of thousands of lines of code, all potentially colliding in unpredictable order. Something needed to be done urgently.

Opinions on modules for JavaScript are heated and diverse. In the past, any attempt at normalizing it added yet another element of variability to the madness. Over time, out of necessity, different schools of thought for a module specification emerged. The most notable ones were Asynchronous Module Definition (AMD) and CommonJS (CJS). Both concepts were stepping stones to the (long overdue) development of the formal standard ECMAScript Modules (ESM) (https://github.com/nodejs/modules). Figure 6.1 shows a brief approximate timeline of the evolution of the module system in JavaScript.

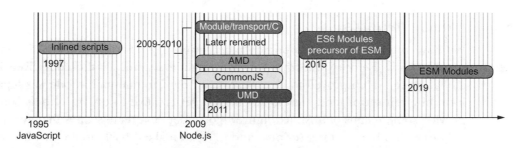

Figure 6.1   Overview of the evolution of JavaScript's module system, from simple inline scripts in the early browser days to official ESM. All dates are approximate.

AMD and CJS had different design goals. The latter is synchronous and used in the server where there's fast file I/O; the former is asynchronous and used in the browser, where access to files is slower and travels through the internet. Although the browser side was contested, AMD made the most progress by dramatically simplifying dependency management of large-scale, client-side JavaScript applications, especially when used in conjunction with the RequireJS (https://requirejs.org) script loader library.

AMD was one reason why the Single Page Apps (SPA) architecture was possible. An SPA contains not only layout, but also a good chunk of the business logic loaded into the browser. Combined with Web 2.0 technologies such as AJAX, entire apps were being put in browsers.

Still, nothing had become standard. This lack of consensus drove the creation of yet another proposal that tried to unify and standardize module systems. The Universal Module Definition (UMD) came to the rescue, along with a module loader API called SystemJS (https://github.com/systemjs/systemjs), which works on client and server. Although reading through a UMD-built module is complex and convoluted (because it involves lots of conditional logic to support any module style and environment), this standard was a blessing because it allowed plugin and library authors to target a single format that could run on both client and server.

After many years of deliberation, ESM was the be-all and end-all of module systems for JavaScript. ESM is a platform-agnostic, standardized module system for JavaScript that works on both servers and browsers, eventually replacing CJS and all other module formats. Currently, ESM is the official standard; all platform vendors are starting to adopt it and all library authors are beginning to use it. Adoption will be a slow process and one that requires all of us to help.

Before any of these formal proposals existed, JavaScript developers were hard at work creating amazing websites. So how were we modularizing applications back then, and what was considered a module? To get around making everything global scripts, developers invented clever patterns and naming schemes, and even used objects and the scope inside functions as pseudo-namespaces to avoid name collisions in the global context. We'll explore these patterns in section 6.2.

6.2   *Module patterns*

We have multiple ways to approach modularity in JavaScript even without module specifications. Before JavaScript had any module system, all the code lived in the global space, which proved to be exceptionally hard to maintain. Code was separated into different script files. Developers had to get creative to organize their code and provide some means of abstraction over global data to create scopes that avoid name clashes with other running scripts—and to try to make it back home for dinner every day. JavaScript's fundamental scoping mechanism has always been and will always be function scope, so it made complete sense to rely on functions to create isolated scopes of code where you could encapsulate data and behavior.

In this section, we'll review some of the ad hoc modular programming patterns that arose out of sheer necessity before modules became a core part of the language:

- Object namespaces
- Immediately Invoked Function Expressions (IIFEs)
- IIFE mixins
- Factory functions

These patterns are worth reviewing because they still work today and are great for small applications and scripts, especially if you're targeting any of the older browsers, such as Internet Explorer 11.

6.2.1 *Object namespaces*

Object namespaces grew in the browser out of the need to scale out simple scripts into full-fledged applications before tools such as AMD existed. Because browsers don't do any dependency management of their own, the order in which you included your files (via <script /> tags) was important.

Developers got into the habit of first loading any third-party libraries (jQuery, Prototype, and others) that they needed and then loading the application-specific code that depended on those libraries. The main issue was that with the exception of iframes and web workers, scripts ran within the same global browser realm. (I'll discuss realms briefly in chapter 7.) Without property encapsulation, a global variable, a class, or a function in one file would collide with that of the same name loaded from a different file. These issues were hard to debug, especially because browsers gave no signs or warnings of any kind when collisions happened.

> **NOTE** Now you can load asynchronously by using the async HTML 5 attribute of the script tag, which makes this problem even worse.

One way to get around this problem was to create artificial namespaces under the global object, using object literals to group your code and identify variables uniquely. In fact, the now-discontinued Yahoo! User Interface (YUI) library for building web applications used this pattern extensively. A class called Transaction, for example, could be defined in many projects and libraries because it applied to myriad domains. To avoid errors when declaring this name multiple times, you needed to define Transaction canonically. For Node.js, this definition could look something like the next listing.

> **Listing 6.1 Defining Transaction object with a global object namespace**

```
global.BlockchainApp.domain.Transaction = {};
```
⟵ In the browser, you use window instead of global.

> **NOTE** Remember that global is the implicit global object inside a Node.js file or module, analogous to the window object in browsers.

You saw the Transaction constructor function in chapter 2, and I'll repeat it in the next listing, now defined under some arbitrary object namespace, which I call BlockchainApp. The properties of this object could more or less match the static directory structure of your application.

> **Listing 6.2 Using an object namespace**

Defines the BlockchainApp object if it doesn't exist by querying global

```
let BlockchainApp = global.BlockchainApp || {};
BlockchainApp.domain = {};
```
⟵ Defines a new (nested) object namespace called domain inside BlockchainApp

The pattern of using a function that is immediately invoked is called an IIFE (discussed in section 6.2.2).

```
BlockchainApp.domain.Transaction = (function Transaction() {

    const feePercent = 0.6;

    function precisionRound(number, precision) {
        const factor = Math.pow(10, precision);
        return Math.round(number * factor) / factor;
    }

    return {
        construct: function(sender, recipient, funds = 0.0) {
            this.sender = sender;
            this.recipient = recipient;
            this.funds = Number(funds);
            return this;
        },
        netTotal: function() {
            return precisionRound(this.funds * feePercent, 2);
        }
    }
})();
```

Private variables and/or privileged functions encapsulated inside the function's scope

Public variables and/or functions exposed to the caller

Alternatively, you can use an inline class expression (see the next listing). Classes are essentially functions, so this syntax should not surprise you.

Listing 6.3   Defining a class expression in an object namespace

```
let BlockchainApp = global.BlockchainApp || {};
BlockchainApp.domain = {};
BlockchainApp.domain.Transaction = class {
    #feePercent = 0.6;
    constructor(sender, recipient, funds = 0.0) {
        this.sender = sender;
        this.recipient = recipient;
        this.funds = Number(funds);
        this.timestamp = Date.now();
    }

    static #precisionRound(number, precision) {
        const factor = Math.pow(10, precision);
        return Math.round(number * factor) / factor;
    }

    netTotal() {
        return BlockchainApp.domain.Transaction.precisionRound
            (this.funds * this.#feePercent, 2);
    }
}
```

Defines a new Transaction class within the BlockchainApp.domain namespace, using a class expression

With this alternative, you can instantiate a new transaction by always specifying the canonical path to the class expression, which is meant to lessen the possibility of any collisions from, say, some third-party banking library you decided to use:

```
const tx = new BlockchainApp.domain.Transaction(...);
```

NOTE Another common technique was to use your company's reverse URL notation. If you worked at MyCompany, the notation would look something like this:

```
const tx = new com.mycompany.BlockchainApp.domain.Transaction(...);
```

Classes offer great support for private data, but before classes, the most popular pattern for encapsulating state was the IIFE.

6.2.2 Immediately Invoked Function Expressions (IIFEs)

Immediately Invoked Function Expressions (IIFEs), which you may already know as the Module pattern, take advantage of JavaScript's function scope to house variables and functions and provide encapsulation from the outside world. As you're probably aware, the function is "immediately invoked" because the unnamed function (in parentheses) is evaluated at the end, giving you the opportunity to expose what you want and hide what you don't, as with classes.

Listing 6.4 demonstrates how you can create a `Transaction` IIFE as an object namespace without leaking any private data. In this code snippet, all variable declarations (regardless of scope modifier `var`, `const`, or `let`) and functions (such as `calculateHash`) exist and are visible only from within this surrounding function.

Listing 6.4 Using an IIFE

```
(function Transaction(namespace) {          ⟵  Private properties defined
                                                in the module's scope
    const VERSION = '1.0';              ⟵
    namespace.domain = {};              ⟵   Creates the nested
                                            domain namespace

    namespace.domain.Transaction = class {     ⟵
        #feePercent = 0.6;                          Public Transaction class

        constructor(sender, recipient, funds = 0.0) {
            this.sender = sender;
            this.recipient = recipient;
            this.funds = Number(funds);           Has access to the
            this.timestamp = Date.now();          calculateHash private
            this.transactionId = calculateHash (  method defined later
              [this.sender, this.recipient, this.funds].join()
            );
        }

    ...
        }
    function calculateHash(data) {    ⟵
      ...
    }
})(global.BlockchainApp || (global.BlockchainApp = {}));   ⟵
```

Private method. Function definitions automatically get hoisted to the top of the surrounding function scope.

Checks whether Blockchain exists globally and if necessary creates global.BlockchainApp as an empty object namespace to use

This function executes immediately upon declaration, so `Transaction` is created on the spot. You can instantiate it as before:

```
const tx = new BlockchainApp.domain.Transaction(...);
```

IIFEs were among the most popular patterns before ECMAScript 2015 classes and still continue to be used today. In fact, many developers and JavaScript purists prefer them to classes. It's worth pointing out that placing variables and objects in a local scope makes the property resolution mechanism (discussed in chapter 2) faster, because JavaScript always checks the local scope before the global. Finally, when used in conjunction with object namespaces, IIFEs allow you to organize your modules in different namespaces, which you'll need to do in a medium-sized application.

Functions are versatile, to the point where you can augment their context to securely define mixins in your domain. Because we explored mixins in chapter 3, section 6.2.3 explores how these legacy solutions integrate with them.

6.2.3   *IIFE mixins*

Remember the mixin objects we discussed and defined in chapters 3 and 4? We can also use IIFEs to implement `HasHash`. To do so, we can take advantage of JavaScript's context-aware function operators `Function#call` or `Function#apply` to dynamically set the object context to be extended (referred to via `this`) at the call site. The enhancement process is enclosed in the function, adequately walled off from the rest of the code.

Listing 6.4 shows a rehash (no pun intended) of the `HasHash` mixin you learned about in chapter 4. Similar to the previous techniques, we use a function to create a private boundary around the code we want to modularize. In listing 6.5, the use of an arrow function notation is a lot more intentional. `calculateHash` is an arrow function so that `this` refers to the augmented object, which is the context object or environment passed to `HasHash.call`.

> **NOTE**   As you know, arrow functions don't provide their own `this` binding; they borrow `this` from their surrounding lexical context.

`HasHash` accepts a set of keys that identify the properties to use during the hashing process. The last part of the next listing shows how to augment the `Transaction` and `Block` classes created under the global `BlockchainApp` namespace.

Listing 6.5   The `HasHash` mixin using an IIFE

```
const HasHash = global.HasHash || function HasHash(keys) {

   const DEFAULT_ALGO_SHA256 = 'SHA256';
   const DEFAULT_ENCODING_HEX = 'hex';

   const options = {
      algorithm: DEFAULT_ALGO_SHA256,
```

```
      encoding:  DEFAULT_ENCODING_HEX
    };

    this.calculateHash = () => {
      const objToHash = Object.fromEntries(
        new Map(keys.map(k => [k, prop(k, this)]))
      );
      return compose(
        computeCipher(options),
        assemble,
        props(keys)
      )(objToHash);
    };
}

HasHash.call(
   global.BlockchainApp.domain.Transaction.prototype,
   ['timestamp', 'sender', 'recipient', 'funds']
);

HasHash.call(
   global.BlockchainApp.domain.Block.prototype,
   ['index', 'timestamp', 'previousHash', 'data']
);
```

> **this maps to the object's prototype and adds the calculateHash method.**

> **The hash of each type of object includes a different set of keys.**

6.2.4 *Factory functions*

A *factory function* is any function that always returns a new object. You saw an example of this pattern in the implementation of Money in chapter 4. Creating objects via factories has two important benefits:

- You can skip using the new keyword during instantiation.
- You don't have to rely on this to access instance data. Instead, you can use the closure formed around the object to achieve data privacy.

As another example, let's introduce a new object to our blockchain application. BitcoinService handles the interaction of multiple pieces of the blockchain domain with tasks such as transferring funds and mining transactions. Services are typically stateless objects that bring together business logic orchestrating the job of multiple entities of your domain. Because service objects don't transport any data, being stateless, we don't need to worry about making them immutable. Listing 6.6 shows the shape of the BitcoinService with a factory function.

> **Listing 6.6 `BitcoinService` object constructed via a factory function**

```
function BitcoinService(ledger) {
  const network = new Wallet(
     Key('public.pem'),
     Key('private.pem')
  );
```

> **Both ledger and network become part of the returning object's closure and are used by all functions.**

```
async function mineNewBlockIntoChain(newBlock) {

    //... omitted for now
}
```

Mines a new block into the chain. The body of this function is shown in chapter 8.

```
async function minePendingTransactions(rewardAddress,
    proofOfWorkDifficulty = 2) {

    //... omitted for now
}
```

Mines transactions into a new block

```
function transferFunds(walletA, walletB, funds,
    description, transferFee = 0.02) {

    //... omitted for now
}
```

Transfers funds between two users (digital wallets)

```
function serializeLedger(delimeter = ';') {

    //... omitted for now
}
```

Serializes a ledger into a string buffer of JSON objects separated by the provided delimiter

```
function calculateBalanceOfWallet(address) {

    //... omitted for now
}

return {
  mineNewBlockIntoChain,
  minePendingTransactions,
  calculateBalanceOfWallet,
  transferFunds,
  serializeLedger
};
}
```

You can obtain a new service object and use it like this:

```
const service = BitcoinService(blockchain);

service.transferFunds(luke, ana, Money('฿',5),
    'Transfer 5 btc from Luke to Ana');
```

With the factory function approach, private data (such as network) exists only within the function's scope, as with an IIFE. Accessing private data is always possible from within the new object API because it closes over that data at time of definition. In addition, not having to rely on this allows us to pass service methods around as higher-order functions without having to worry about any this bindings. Consider the transferFunds API, which has the following signature:

```
function transferFunds(userA, userB, funds, description,
    transferFee = 0.02)
```

Suppose that you want to run a batch of transfers, all with the same default transfer fee:

```
const transfers = [
  [luke, ana, Money('฿',5.0), 'Transfer 5 btc from Luke to Ana'],
  [ana, luke, Money('฿',2.5), 'Transfer 2.5 btc from Ana to Luke'],
  [ana, matt, Money('฿',10.0), 'Transfer 10 btc from Ana to Matthew'],
  [matt, luke, Money('฿',20.0), 'Transfer 20 btc from Matthew to Luke']
];

function runBatchTransfers(transfers, batchOperation) {
   transfers.forEach(transferData => batchOperation(...transferData))
}
```

You can extract the method directly from the object as a function, using destructuring assignment, and use that method as the batch operation, as shown next.

Listing 6.7   Using an extracted form of `transferFunds` as a callback function

```
const { transferFunds } = service;

runBatchTransfers(transfers, transferFunds);        ⟵
```

Passing the service method as a higher-order function. All closed-over data is still available and accessible via the method's closure.

If `BitcoinService` had been defined as part of a class design, you would have been forced to set the context object explicitly, which is not straightforward, using `Function#bind`

```
runBatch(transfers, service.transferFunds.bind(service));
```

or the new binding operator (chapter 5):

```
runBatch(transfers, ::service.transferFunds);
```

Overall, the four techniques—object namespaces, IIFEs, IIFE mixins, and factory functions—have a graceful, simple elegance because they use a subset of JavaScript's minimal canonical language. Although these patterns are still predominant in industry, the downside is that we are responsible for making sure that all the modules are defined properly and have the proper level of encapsulation and exposure. A good module system should handle these tasks for us.

In section 6.3, we go from programmatic patterns to language-level module systems. At a high level, these systems can be classified as static or dynamic. It's important to understand the difference because ESM is different from all others due to its static syntax.

6.3   *Static vs. dynamic module systems*

A dynamic module system is one in which the management of dependencies and the specification of what a module exposes and consumes is done programmatically. This task involves writing the code yourself or using a third-party module loader. The techniques discussed in section 6.2 fall into this category, so the specification and definition of a module (what it exposes and what it hides) are created in memory when the code runs. You can do certain tricks with dynamic modules, such as enabling conditional access to include modules or parts of a module. Examples include the CommonJS APIs, the AMD-compatible RequireJS library, the SystemJS library, and Angular's dependency injection mechanism.

Dynamic modules are quite different from a static format such as the new ESM. A static module system, on the other hand, defines the module's contracts by using native language syntax—specifically, the keywords `import` and `export`. This difference is important to understand. For starters, JavaScript has never had static module definitions, which makes them uncharted territory for most developers. Also, static definitions have certain advantages; they allow the JavaScript runtime to prefetch or preload modules and allow you to build tools to optimize the package size of your application by removing code that will never execute.

Table 6.1 shows loading the `Transaction` class via the methods discussed in section 6.2. The most obvious difference is that dynamic module systems use the usual JavaScript functions, whereas static systems use `import` and `export`.

Table 6.1   Loading the `Transaction` class with different module systems

System	Type	Example
CommonJS	Dynamic	`const Transaction =` `    require('./domain/Transaction.js');`

RequireJS	Dynamic	`requirejs(['domain/Transaction.js'], Transaction => {`
		`    //... use Transaction`
		`});`

ESM	Static	`import Transaction from './domain/Transaction.js';`

How each loading call works is not important right now; what's important is that you see the difference in the syntax used. With ESM, instead of function calls that traverse the file system to load new code modules, you use an `import` statement that abstracts this process. The caveat is that in static systems, `import` statements must appear at the top of the file. This requirement also exists in most other languages and should not be viewed as a limitation, for good reason: making these statements static and clearly defined at the top helps compilers and tools map the structure of the application ahead of time. Also, you can run tools that perform better static-code analysis, dead-code elimination, and even tree-shaking, which I'll cover briefly in section 6.5.

Another noticeable difference in a static module system is the type of bindings used. In CJS, modules are plain object references. Importing an object via the `require` function is no different from obtaining an object from any other function call. The shape of the object is given by the properties assigned to `module.exports` inside the module file. Here's how you would import `Validation` (created in chapter 5) by using CJS:

```
const {Success, Failure} = require('./lib/fp/data/Validation.js');
```

A more common example is importing from Node.js's filesystem `fs` built-in module:

```
const { exists, readFileSync } = require('fs');
```

Conversely, ESM modules take advantage of a more native and declarative syntax. Access to the API still looks somewhat like regular objects, but only for consistency with the language's mental model and to piggyback on the success of CJS's compact approach. Here's the preceding example with ESM:

```
import { Success, Failure } from './lib/fp/data/Validation.js';

import { exists, readFileSync } from 'fs';
```

On the exterior, these approaches look and feel the same, but there's a subtle difference: ESM uses immutable, live code bindings, not a regular, mutable copy of an object. The next listing shows a simple fee calculator CJS module to illustrate this difference.

Listing 6.8 calculator.js module defined with CJS

```
let feePercent = 0.6;

exports.feePercent = feePercent;

exports.netTotal = function(funds) {
  return precisionRound(funds * feePercent, 2);
}

exports.setFeePercent = function(newPercent) {
  feePercent = newPercent;
}                                               Function
                                                is private to
function precisionRound(number, precision) {    the module
  const factor = Math.pow(10, precision);
  return Math.round(number * factor) / factor;
}
```

Pay close attention to the result of each statement in the following listing.

Listing 6.9 Using calculator.js as a CJS module

```
let { feePercent, netTotal, setFeePercent } = require('./calculator.js');

feePercent;   // 0.6          Resets the value of that variable
netTotal(10); // 6            of the locally defined variable
feePercent = 0.7;
feePercent;   // 0.7          Uses the original module's value of 0.6
netTotal(10); // 6            Sets the value inside the module to 0.7
setFeePercent(0.7);
netTotal(10); //7            New feePercent is being used
require('./calculator.js').feePercent; // 0.6      Original value
                                                   preserved
```

As you can see, reassigning `feePercent` to 0.7 changes your local exported copy of that reference, but not the reference inside the module, which is probably what you'd expect. With ESM, instead of a simple variable reference, the exported properties in ESM are connected (bound) to the properties inside the module. In the same vein, changing an exported binding within the module itself alters the binding used outside somewhere else; it's bound both ways. There are many good uses for live bindings, but they can certainly lead to confusion. My recommendation is to try to avoid reassigning to exported references at all costs. Take a look at the code sample in the next listing.

Listing 6.10   Using calculator.js as an ESM module

```
import { feePercent, netTotal, setFeePercent }  from './calculator.js';

feePercent;   // 0.6          Throws an error stating that
netTotal(10); // 6            feePercent is read-only. Value
feePercent = 0.7;             is immutable from the client.
netTotal(10); // 6
setFeePercent(0.7);           Sets the value inside the
netTotal(10); // 7            module to 0.7 via an API
feePercent;   // 0.7

feePercent reflects           New feePercent
the new live value.           is being used
```

As you can see, CJS and ESM have slightly different behavior. By design, most of the differences happen behind the scenes to make ESM adoption simpler. From a practical standpoint, ESM works similarly to CJS in that nearly every file is considered to be a module and every module has its own local scope, where you can safely store code and data (similar to the function scope created under an IIFE). If you've used CJS, ESM shouldn't be a huge paradigm shift.

The future of JavaScript lies with ESM, which will eventually supersede any other module format and interoperate with existing ones. When this will happen is uncertain because Node.js (for example) needs to support CJS for some time to provide backward compatibility and allow the transition to go smoothly.

Now, without further ado and the past behind us, let's jump into ESM.

6.4   *ESM basics*

In this section, you'll learn about the fundamentals of ESM and how it's used in code. Specifically, you'll learn how to write module path identifiers, as well as the syntax needed to expose and consume modules by using variations of the `import` and `export` keywords.

ESM was designed in TC39 as a declarative module system with the goal of unifying dependency management for client and server. You can use ESM experimentally, starting with Node.js 12, by activating an experimental flag (`--experimental-modules`) and in Node.js 14 without a flag. Node.js treats a file with the extension .js or .mjs (section 6.4.4) as a module.

ESM standardizes on a single module format that draws experience from both CJS and AMD formats. This standardization is similar to what the Universal Module Definition (https://github.com/umdjs/umd) project set out to do many years ago, with some success. The problem is that none of these aforementioned module formats was ever fully standardized. In ESM, you get the best of both worlds: synchronous live binding statements as well as dynamic, asynchronous APIs. ESM also retains the terse syntax that CJS uses, which has withstood the test of time.

Before we dive into this topic, one important thing to keep in mind is that ESM modules automatically enter in strict mode without you having to write it explicitly.

A JavaScript module is nothing more than a file or directory that's specified remotely (browser) or from the local file system (server) with some special semantics. ESM makes these specifiers compatible with both of these environments. Unfortunately, this constraint means that we will have a less-flexible module system on the server because we lose the extensionless specifiers that we've become accustomed to on the server side. On a positive note, ESM works toward a truly universal format, which helps in the long run with technologies such as Server-Side Rendering and building isomorphic applications.

First, let's go over the syntax for importing and exporting modules, starting with path specifiers.

6.4.1 Path specifiers

One important design goal of ESM is to remain compatible with the browser to truly guarantee one module format for all environments. Unlike in CJS, all module specifiers in ESM must be valid URIs, which means (sadly for Node.js) that there are no extensionless specifiers or directory modules. With the exception of bare specifiers (such as `'ramda'`), if a JavaScript module file has an extension, that extension must be explicitly added to the import specifier for it to resolve properly. (We were allowed to omit it before.) The following listing is more in line with how regular browser `<script>` includes work.

Listing 6.11 Path specifiers using ESM

```
import Transaction from './Transaction.js';
import Transaction from '../Transaction.js';
import { curry } from '/lib/fp/combinators.js';
import { curry } from 'https://my.example.com/lib/fp/combinators.js';   <-
```

Valid only in browser environments; not supported in Node.js

NOTE It's worth mentioning that in browsers, unlike Node.js, the file extension does not tell the browser how to parse a module as JavaScript code. It's done with the proper MIME type (`text/javascript`) and shows whether the file was included with `<script type='module'>`, as in

```
<script type="module"
    src=" https://my.example.com/lib/fp/combinators.js">
</script>
```

If you're using a relative path, you must start with `./` or `../`. The following code generates a module-not-found error (compatible with CJS). Neither of these snippets would pass as a valid URI:

```
import Transaction from 'Transaction.js';
import Transaction from 'lib/fp/combinators.js';
```

Another drawback is that you won't be able to perform directory imports in Node.js as with CJS. In CJS, having an index.js or a proper package.json file in a folder lets you perform an import of the folder implicitly without appending the index.js part of the specifier. Because CJS was made for the server, it had smarts built in to detect and autocomplete the index.js bit, much as web servers serve index.html from a folder by default. Sadly, because the same rules need to apply to both client and server, this behavior did not carry over to ESM.

   In sections 6.4.2 and 6.4.3, we jump into the two main features of ESM: exporting and importing.

6.4.2 *Exporting*

The `export` statement is used to expose a module's interface or API and is analogous to `module.exports` in CJS. A module is defined as a single file and may contain one or many classes and functions. By default, everything within a file is private. (Thinking of a module file as an empty IIFE may help.) You need to declare what to expose via the `export` keyword. For brevity, I won't cover all the possible `export` combinations. For a full list of possible combinations, visit http://mng.bz/YqeK. The combinations described in the following sections are used in the sample application.

SINGLE-VALUED (DEFAULT)

So far in the book, when showing parts of the domain classes, I've deliberately left out how they map to the filesystem—in other words, the `import` statement that was used to obtain the class. The general convention in exporting is for classes to become modules of their own. You have options. You can export a single class in a single step

```
export default class Transaction {
    // ...
}
```

or in two steps:

```
class Transaction {
    // ...
}

export default Transaction;
```

Single-valued export is usually the preferred way of exporting code for others to consume. Before Node.js had native support for classes, a class was transpiled into its own

IIFE function. Think about how data that lives outside the `export` declaration inside the module file is completely hidden from the callers. The semantics are similar to that of an IIFE, which is nice and consistent. You can imagine one big IIFE function in which the body is your entire module code, giving you the opportunity to declare variables, functions, or other classes accessible only to the module code itself. We used this technique in `HasHash` to declare top-level constants, for example:

```
const DEFAULT_ALGO_SHA256 = 'SHA256';
const DEFAULT_ENCODING_HEX = 'hex';

const HasHash = (
  keys,
  options = { algorithm: DEFAULT_ALGO_SHA256,
              encoding: DEFAULT_ENCODING_HEX
            }
) => ({
  // ...
});

export default HasHash;
```

Using the `default` keyword allows you to export one piece of data. You could also export multiple values from a single module.

MULTIVALUE

A multivalue `export` is an elegant way to create utility modules. This is used for the validation functions in `Block` and `Transaction`. Because you've already seen these functions, I'll show you the `export` syntax and omit the body of each method:

```
export const checkDifficulty = block => //...

export const checkLinkage = curry((previousBlockHash, block) =>
  // ...
);

export const checkGenesis = block => // ...

export const checkIndex = curry((previousBlockIndex, block) =>
  // ...
);
```

API modules based on multivalue exports of standalone functions have another great benefit: they push you into writing with purity in mind. Because you never know the context under which a function will execute, you can't assume or rely on any shared or closed-over state. Moreover, instead of using a factory function, another way to create the `BitcoinService` object is to expose individual, pure functions that declare all the data they need up front as function arguments. Instead of inheriting `ledger` and `network` from the function's closure, you need to make them actual arguments:

```
export async function mineNewBlockIntoChain(ledger, newBlock) {
   //...
},

export async function minePendingTransactions(ledger, network,
      rewardAddress, proofOfWorkDifficulty = 2) {
   //...
},

export function transferFunds(ledger, network,
      walletA, walletB, funds, description) {
   //...
}
```

PROXYING

A module can export and bypass the bindings of another module, acting as a proxy. You can accomplish this task by using the export ... from statement. In our case, we can use this statement to group all the individual domain modules (including Block and Transaction) in a single module file, called domain.js:

```
export { default as Block } from './domain/Block.js'
export { default as Transaction } from './domain/Transaction.js'
export { default as Blockchain } from './domain/Blockchain.js'
```

Unlike with import, you can export at any line of your module. No rules force the placement.

On the flip side, exported code is consumed by clients or other modules through the import statement.

6.4.3   *Importing*

To consume an API, you must import the desired functionality, which you can do as a whole or in pieces. You have many ways to import from a module and can find a complete reference guide at http://mn.bz/Gx4R. The following sections describe some of the most common techniques.

SINGLE-VALUE IMPORT

To import a single object from a default export, you can use

```
import Block from './Block.js';
```

This is the simplest case, but you can also request components of a module.

MULTIVALUE IMPORT

You can break out pieces of a single module. The next listing shows how to do a multivalue import.

Listing 6.12 Multivalue import of validation.js

```
import { checkIndex, checkLinkage } from './block/validations.js';
```

The curly braces indicate that we're reaching into the module.

Notice that although the code snippet in listing 6.12 suggests that destructuring is occurring, as used with CJS, it's not. Following are the main differences:

- Imports are always connected with their exports (live bindings), whereas destructuring creates a local copy of the object. Because CJS imports a copy of the object, a destructure is a copy of a copy.
- You can't perform a nested destructure within an `import` statement. The following code won't work:

```
import {foo: {bar}} from './foo.js';
```

- The syntax for property renaming (*aliasing*) is different, as shown in the next listing.

Listing 6.13 Property renaming in CJS and ESM

```
// CJS
const { foo: newFoo } = require('./foo.js');
```

CJS: Renames foo to newFoo

```
// ESM
import {foo as newFoo} from './foo.js';
```

ESM: Does not rename but creates an alias called newFoo pointing to the bound foo property

You can also compose a multivalued exported API into a single object namespace by using a wildcard (alias) import:

```
import * as ValidationsUtil from './shared/validations.js';

ValidationsUtil.checkTampering(...);
```

USING A PACKAGE MANAGER (NPM)

As with native modules, importing third-party modules with ESM is done via a bare path, with no path separators or extensions. As expected, the package name needs to match the directory name inside node_modules. Then the entry point or module to load is determined by the main property in its accompanying package.json. Here's an example:

```
import { map } from 'rxjs/operators';
```

DYNAMIC IMPORTING

If you've been coding in Node.js for a while, you're probably used to loading modules conditionally with CJS. Unlike ESM, which requires dependencies to be declared at the beginning of the file, CJS allows you to `require` modules from anywhere. One use case where this happens a lot in the wild is the notion of using a module containing global settings or feature flags to roll out new code to your customers slowly. The following listing shows an example.

Listing 6.14   Loading modules dynamically with CJS

```
const useNewAlgorithm = FeatureFlags.check('USE_NEW_ALGORITHM', false);

let { computeBalance } = require('./wallet/compute_balance.js');

if (useNewAlgorithm) {
    computeBalance =
        require('./wallet/compute_balance2.js').computeBalance;
}

return computeBalance(...);
```

Depending on the status of the global USE_NEW_ALGORITHM setting, the application may decide to use the traditional compute_balance module or begin using a new one. This technique looks handy, but the first time a library or file is required, the JavaScript runtime needs to interrupt its process to access the filesystem. Because modules are singleton, this situation would happen only the first time a library is loaded. Afterward, the modules are cached locally (a behavior that both ESM and CJS support). Similarly, the second require statement blocks the main thread to access the filesystem before caching the module.

In the spirit of nonblocking code, filesystem access should be done asynchronously. The ESM specification corrects for this problem and offers a callable version of import that is asynchronous, based on promises, and aligned with loading code inside the browser. The import function fetches, instantiates, and evaluates all the requested module's dependencies and returns a namespace object whose default property references the requested module's (export) default API, as well as properties that match the module's other exports. We'll get back to asynchronous features of JavaScript in chapter 8, but I'll show you how import works now as it pertains to the module system. Refactoring the code in listing 6.14 looks like this:

```
const useNewAlgorithm = FeatureFlags.check('USE_NEW_ALGORITHM', false);

let computeBalanceModule = await import(
    './ domain/wallet/compute_balance.js'
);

if (useNewAlgorithm) {
    computeBalanceModule = await
        import('./domain/wallet/compute_balance2.js');
}

const {computeBalance} = computeBalanceModule;

return computeBalance(...);
```

By the way, this code snippet uses a feature known as top-level-await, which is supported only in ESM. You'll learn more about this feature in chapter 8. The basic premise is that you can use `await` directly to trigger an asynchronous action (loading a script in this case) without having to write an `async` function explicitly.

Another important part of the ESM specification is the introduction of a new extension: .mjs.

6.4.4 A new extension in town

To instruct Node.js to load modules by using ESM, you have two options:

- You can set the `type` field of package.json to `"module"`. This option works by dynamically looking up the package.json nearest to your given .js file, starting with the current directory, followed by its parent, and so on. If JavaScript is unable to determine the type, CJS is used.
- Use the new file extension (.mjs) to identify JavaScript module files. This extension will be helpful during the transitional period of moving to ESM. By the same token, .cjs files will force the use of CommonJS.

Package and library authors are encouraged to provide a type field in their package.json files to make their code clearer and better documented. Also, modern browsers support `<script type='module'>` to match this new behavior.

Although many people have deemed the .mjs extension to be unattractive, it has precedent. React uses .jsx to declare HTML components, for example, and we've all used .json as a convention to store plain-text JSON data. Browsers don't pay much attention to the file extension; they care mostly about the MIME type (`text/javascript` for executable scripts or `application/json` for data imports). I view .mjs as being a transitional route before JavaScript applications catch up to ESM; then .js will prevail.

Nevertheless, here are some of the concrete benefits of using .mjs:

- There are no problems with backward compatibility. Because the extension is new, enforcing certain properties from the start (such as mandatory strict mode on all modules) is simple.
- The extension helps with deprecating non-browser-friendly module environment variables such as `__dirname`, `__filename`, `module`, and `exports`. Also, you will not be able to use `require` on files with an .mjs extension, or vice versa. (Use `import` on .cjs files.)
- The new extension communicates purpose, which is a clear departure from the existing module formats (AMD, CJS, and UMD).
- No additional instructions or parsing (so no performance penalty) are needed for the compiler to treat and prepare/optimize a JavaScript file for modules.
- There is special processing of module files. You can now use module-scoped metaproperties such as `import.meta`, for example. Currently, this object contains only the URL or full path of the module, but more functionality can be

added later. The `url` property will supersede the global `__dirname` and `__file-name` globals. The example in the next listing uses `import.meta`.

> **Listing 6.15   Printing the contents of `import.meta`**
>
> ```
> console.log(import.meta);          <——| Inside Transaction.js
>
> // { url: "file:///home/user/../src/blockchain/domain/Transaction.js" }
> ```

- Tooling experience is improved. IDEs can be more intuitive when it comes to things like refactoring, syntax highlighting, code completion, and visualization. Static code analyzers and linters can give you better heuristics and guidance.

Supporting this new extension and phasing out the existing module systems won't happen overnight. Millions of packages and lots of tools need to start this process. When ESM begins to trickle in with new packages and old packages get updated, we'll be able to reap the benefits of ESM. These benefits extend to much more than code. Section 6.5 describes how tools can take advantage of the static nature of this module format.

6.5   *Benefits of ESM for tooling*

ESM's static, declarative structure has many benefits. The one obvious benefit is good IDE support for static code checking. Other important benefits include dead-code elimination and tree-shaking, faster property lookups, and type-friendliness, all discussed in the following sections.

6.5.1   *Dead-code elimination and tree-shaking*

In simple terms, *dead code* is code that could never run through any paths of your code. Tools can identify dead code by closely examining the static structure of the code and tracing through the possible execution paths. The most obvious form is code that's commented out. Naturally, it's pointless to send that code across the network to the browser or to a remote Node.js server, so transpilers and build tools typically strip it out. You may also find dead code in the unreachable lines that appear after a function's `return` statement. This situation sometimes happens in code that relies on automatic semicolon insertion (http://mng.bz/QmDj). Other, less obvious cases include unused local variables and function calls whose results are never used elsewhere.

On the server, the module system is a reflection of the filesystem. On the browser, the situation is not quite the same, but ESM aims to close this gap. For large SPAs, you need a bundling/build strategy. Instead of requesting thousands of small files (each file a module) over the wire, it makes sense to bundle them at build time (and while you're at it, compress them) into a single payload.

I don't cover build tools such as Browserify, Webpack, and Rollup in this book, but I highly recommend that you research them all and pick the best tool for your project. Build tools are essential parts of coding with JavaScript. The central job of these tools is to map the entire dependency tree to one or two entry points (index.js, main.js, app.js, and so on). Build tools are smart at detecting whole modules or parts of a module that are never used and then ignoring them. Hence, unused modules down the dependency tree are virtually considered to be dead and dropped by shaking the tree. Aside from reducing cognitive load, modularizing your code as much as possible instead of packing everything into a single file is good practice.

ESM's static structure imposes restrictions that simplify tree-shaking:

- You can import modules only at the top level, never inside a conditional.
- You can't use variables or functions in import statements.

A build tool can rely on the matching sets of export and import statements to map out all unused modules and remove them as shown in figure 6.2.

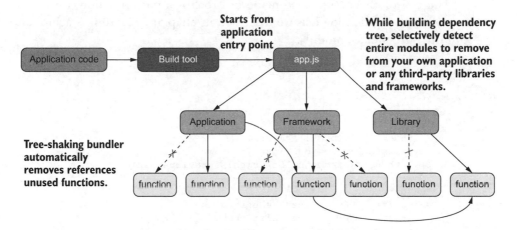

Figure 6.2 Bundler tools can use the static structure of your application to achieve tree-shaking by identifying any unused modules of code and removing them from the packaged application file.

Without these guarantees, eliminating unused parts would be complex. Going back to CJS, for example, you can require modules dynamically and sprinkle these calls anywhere in the code, making it harder to figure out what to remove and what to keep.

Furthermore, with ESM, when you're looking at the bundled code generated, depending on the tool, you might see a comment like this when removing the foo module:

```
// unused export foo
```

A good tip is to design your modules as loosely coupled and internally cohesive as possible to facilitate analyzing your code. Some build tools even have additional support to identify when a function is pure and its result is not used and then can safely remove that call, which is a nice benefit of coding with a functional style. Recall from chapter 4 that pure functions have no side effects or use of shared state, so a pure function whose result is not used does not contribute anything to your application. Detecting whether a function is pure and free of side effects is not an easy problem to solve, so you can help the tooling by writing a bit of metadata in front of pure calls:

```
/*#__PURE__*/checkTampering(...)
```

You can run certain plugins that support this notation as part of your build process. One example is the library Terser (https://github.com/terser-js/terser), which looks for these PURE pragmas and determines whether to classify them as dead code based on whether the result of the function is used.

The call to checkTampering made in Block is a pure function, for example. It's part of the validation logic as we discussed in chapter 5. Here it is again, annotated with the pure metacomments:

```
class Block {
  ...

  isValid() {
    const {
      index: previousBlockIndex,
      timestamp: previousBlockTimestamp
    } = this.#blockchain.lookUp(this.previousHash);

    return composeM(
        /*#__PURE__*/checkTampering,
        /*#__PURE__*/checkDifficulty,
        /*#__PURE__*/checkLinkage(previousBlockHash),
        /*#__PURE__*/checkLength(64),
        /*#__PURE__*/checkTimestamps(previousBlockTimestamp),
        /*#__PURE__*/checkIndex(previousBlockIndex),
        Validation.of
    )(Object.freeze(this));
  }
}
```

If we move checkTampering out of the composition, Terser can easily find it and mark it for elimination—this is possible because of the guarantees that a pure function gives you.

ESM also has faster property lookups from imported code.

6.5.2   *Faster property lookups*

Another advantage of using a static structure involves calling properties on the imported module. In CJS, the require API returns a regular JavaScript object in which every function call goes through the standard JavaScript property resolution process (described in chapter 2):

```
const lib = require('fs');

fs.readFile(...);
```

Although this technique keeps the mental model consistent, it's slower than ESM. ESM's static structure allows the JavaScript runtime to look ahead and statically resolve a named property lookup. This process happens internally, and the code looks much the same:

```
import * as fs from 'fs';

fs.readFile(...);
```

In addition, knowing the static structure of a module allows IDEs to provide useful hints that can check whether a named property exists or is misspelled. This benefit has always been present in statically typed languages.

6.5.3 *Type-friendliness*

JavaScript could be ready for a possible optional type system down the (long) road. ESM is paving the way, because static type checking can be done only when type definitions are known statically ahead of time. We already have reference implementations in TypeScript or even an extension library such as Flow. Some proposals include types for number, string, and symbol, different-size int and floats, and new concepts such as enum and any. Although typing information is light years away, there's some consensus about what it could look like. For more information, see appendix B.

So far, I've covered enough of the ESM syntax to get you started. But because ESM is a big addition to the language, I skipped many syntactical and technical details that you should become familiar with before making the leap. The ESM specification also supports a programmatic loader API that you can use to configure how modules are resolved and loaded, for example. For more information, visit https://nodejs.org/api/esm.html.

In JavaScript, imported modules behave like objects, and you can pass them around like variables. You can refer to this notion as "module as data." This congruence is important because in chapter 7, we enter the realm of metaprogramming.

Summary

- You can use patterns such as object and function namespaces, as well as IIFEs, to enable modularity in JavaScript without the need for any module system.
- A dynamic module system uses third-party or native libraries to manage dependencies at runtime. A static module system takes advantage of new language syntax and can be used to optimize dependency management at compile time.

- ESM is a static module system worked on by the TC39 task group with the aim of unifying the module needs of both client and server JavaScript environments, as well as replacing all existing module formats.
- ESM offers many benefits, such as dead-code elimination, tree-shaking, faster property lookup, variable checking, and compatibility with a (possible) future type system.
- A distinctive part of ESM is the introduction of a new file extension, .mjs, so that compilers can enhance JavaScript files behaving as modules.

Hooked on metaprogramming

This chapter covers

- Applying cross-functional behavior with metaprogramming and reflection
- Using symbols to create interoperability between different realms in your application
- Augmenting JavaScript's internals with symbols
- Understanding the basics of the Proxy/Reflect APIs
- Enhancing the execution of methods with decorators
- Performing leaner error handling with the throw expressions proposal

A program's text is just one representation of the program. Programs are not text. . . .
We need a different way to store and work with our programs.

—Sergey Dmitriev, president and co-founder of JetBrains

Imagine a company like Intel that builds CPU chips. To automate a lot of the repetitive tasks, the company programs robots to build chips—a task that we call *programming*. Then, to scale to higher industry demands, it programs factories that build robots that build chips—a task that we call *metaprogramming*.

I hope that by now, you're hooked on JavaScript. I know I am. As a byproduct of all the topics we've covered throughout our journey, we've uncovered some interesting dualities. One of these dualities is "functions as data" (chapter 4): the idea of expressing an eventual value as an execution of some function. We took that concept to another level in chapter 6 with "modules as data," referring to JavaScript's nature of reifying a module as a bound object that you can pass around as data to other parts of your application.

In this chapter, I'm introducing another duality: "code as data." This duality refers to the idea of metaprogramming: using code to automate code or in some way modify or alter the behavior of code. As it does for companies like Intel, metaprogramming has many applications, such as automating repetitive tasks or dynamically inserting code to handle orthogonal design issues such as logging, tracing, and tracking performance metrics, to name a few.

This chapter starts with the Symbol primitive data type, showing how you can use it to guide the flow of execution and influence low-level system operations such as how an object gets spread or iterated over, or what happens when an object appears next to some mathematical symbol. JavaScript gives you a few controls to tweak the way that this data type works. You'll learn that you can use JavaScript symbols in many ways to define special object properties, as well as inject static hooks.

Metaprogramming is also deeply related to dynamic concepts such as reflection and introspection, which happen when a computer program treats/observes its own instruction set as raw runtime data. In this regard, you'll use the `Proxy` and `Reflect` JavaScript APIs to change the runtime behavior of your code by hooking into the dynamic structure of objects and functions. Think about a time when you needed to add performance timers or trace logs around your functions to measure or trace their execution, but then had to live with that code forever. Proxies are great for enhancing and augmenting objects with pluggable behavior in a modular way without cluttering the source code. The `Proxy` and `Reflect` APIs are more frequently used in framework or library development, but you'll learn how to take advantage of them in your own code.

Before you get hooked on these features, let's begin with some simple examples of metaprogramming that occur in day-to-day coding.

7.1 Common uses of metaprogramming in JavaScript

When talking about code as data in the context of JavaScript, people might immediately relate it to writing code inside code or using variables to concatenate and/or replace code statements. The next listing shows the types of things you could do with `eval`.

Listing 7.1 Simple example that uses `eval`

```
eval(
    `
    const add = (x, y) => x + y;
    const r = add(3, 4);
```

```
      console.log(r);          <⎯⎤  Prints 7 to
                                    │  the console
);
```

In strict mode, `eval` expects code in the form of a raw string literal (data as code) and executes it in its own environment. Alarms should be going off in your head at this moment. You can imagine that `eval` can be an extremely dangerous and insecure operation, arguably considered to be unnecessary these days.

Another example of data as code is JavaScript Object Notation (JSON) text, which is a string representation of code that can be directly understood as an object in the language. In fact, with ECMAScript Modules (ESM), you can directly import a JSON file as code without needing to do any special parsing, as follows:

```
import libConfig from './mylib/package.json';
```

Also consider computed property names, which allow you to create a key from any expression that evaluates to a string. We used this concept to support the `prop` and `props` methods back in chapter 4. Here's a simple example:

```
const propName = 'foo';
const identity = x => x;

const obj = {
  bar: 10,
  [identity(propName)]: 20
};

obj.foo; // 20
```

Metaprogramming also occurs when introspecting the structure of an object. The most important use case is JavaScript's own duck typing, in which the "type" of an object is determined solely by its shape with methods such as `Object.getOwnProperty-Names`, `Object.getPrototypeOf`, `Object.getOwnPropertyDescriptors`, and `Object.getOwnPropertySymbols`. Here's a simple example:

```
const proto = {
  foo: 'bar',
  baz: function() {
    return 'baz';
  },
  [Symbol('private')]: 'privateData'
};

const obj = Object.create(proto);
obj.qux = 'qux';

Object.getOwnPropertyNames(obj); // [ 'qux' ]

Object.getPrototypeOf(obj);
// { foo: 'bar', baz: [Function: baz], [Symbol(private)]: 'privateData' }
```

```
Object.getOwnPropertyDescriptors(obj);
// {
//   qux: {
//     value: 'qux',
//     writable: true,
//     enumerable: true,
//     configurable: true
//   }
//}
```

```
Object.getOwnPropertySymbols(proto); // [ Symbol(private) ]
```

Even functions, as other objects, have some limited awareness of their own shape and contents. You can see this awareness when you use `Function#toString` to print the string representing the function's signature and body:

```
add.toString(); // '(x, y) => x + y'
```

You could potentially pass this text representation to a parser that can understand what the function does and act accordingly, or even inject more instructions into it if need be.

A more useful property of functions is `Function#length`. Consider the way that we implemented the `curry` function combinator in chapter 4, using `length` to figure out the number of arguments with which the curried function is declared and determine how many inner functions to evaluate partially.

> **NOTE**   Because JavaScript makes it simple to use data as code, JavaScript has some qualities of a *homoiconic* language. This topic is interesting to research on your own, if you like. A homoiconic language mirrors the syntax of code as the syntax of data. Lisp (*List P*rogramming) programs, for example, are written as lists, which could be fed back into another (or the same) Lisp program. All JSON text is considered to be valid JavaScript (https://github.com/tc39/proposal-json-superset), but not all JavaScript code could be understood as JSON, so it's not a full mirror. Interestingly enough, JavaScript was inspired by the language Scheme, which is a homoiconic Lisp dialect.

These tasks are examples of basic tasks in which some form of metacoding is present. But with JavaScript, there is much more than meets the eye, especially when you start to take advantage of special symbols to annotate the static structure of your code.

7.2   *JavaScript symbols*

Symbols are a subtle and powerful feature of the language, used mostly in library and framework development. Define them in the correct places, and with little effort, objects light up and take on new roles and new behavior. You can use symbols to establish behavioral contracts among objects, to keep data private and secret, and to enhance the way that the JavaScript runtime treats objects. Before we dive into all those topics, let's spend some time understanding what they are and how to create them.

The first thing to know is that unlike any new API, a `Symbol` is a true built-in primitive data type (like number, string, or Boolean).

```
typeof Symbol('My Symbol'); // 'symbol'
```

A `Symbol` represents a dynamic, anonymous, unique value. Unlike number or string, symbols have no literal syntax, and you can never serialize them into a string. They follow the function factory pattern (like `Money`), which means that you don't use `new` to create a new one. Instead, you create a symbol by calling the `Symbol` function, which generates a unique value behind the scenes. The next listing shows a snippet.

Listing 7.2 Basic use of symbols

```
const symA = Symbol('My Symbol');
const symB = Symbol('My Symbol');

symA == symB;        // false
symB.toString();     // Symbol('My Symbol')
symB.description;    // 'My Symbol'
```

Because symbols hide their unique value, you can provide an optional description, which is used only for debugging and logging purposes. This string doesn't factor into the underlying unique value or into the lookup process.

Because a symbol represents a unique value, it is used primarily as a collision-free object property, like a dynamic string key using the computed property-name syntax `obj[symbol]`. Under the hood, JavaScript maps the unique value of a symbol to a unique object key, which you can retrieve only if you possess the symbol reference. The following listing shows some simple use cases.

Listing 7.3 Using symbols as property keys

```
const obj = {};
const symFoo = Symbol('foo');          Adds property foo

obj['foo']  = 'bar';                   Adds a property with a
obj[symFoo] = 'baz';                   symbol described as foo

obj.foo;       // 'bar'                foo and Symbol('foo')
obj[symFoo];   // 'baz'                map to different keys.
obj[Symbol('foo')] !== 'baz'; // true  You can't refer to Symbol('foo'),
                                       which would create a new symbol.
```

By design, symbols are not discoverable by conventional means. So iterating over an object with `for..in`, `for..of`, `Object.keys`, or `Object.getOwnPropertyNames` won't work, mostly for backward-compatibility reasons. The only way is through introspection by explicitly calling `Object.getOwnPropertySymbols`:

```
for(const s of Object.getOwnPropertySymbols(obj)) {
  console.log(s.toString());
}
```

Even then, this technique offers a "view" of each symbol. Without the actual symbol reference, you still can't access the property value. By contrast, symbol references are copied over when you spread an object and use `Object.assign`. The difference is subtle but important. Unlike how other primitives are copied by value, the clone of `obj` copies not the value, but the symbol reference itself—the *same* symbol, not a copy. Take a look:

```
const clone = {...obj};

obj[symFoo] === clone[symFoo]; // true
```

As discussed in chapter 3, these operations rely on the `enumerable` data descriptor to be set to `true`. If you want more privacy, you could set this descriptor to `false` by using `Object.defineProperty`.

At this point, we have not dealt with specific uses of symbols—only the basics. Before we look at some interesting examples, it is important to understand how and where symbols are created.

7.3   *Symbol registries*

Understanding registries will help you understand how and where symbols are created and used. When a symbol is created, it generates a new, unique, and opaque value inside the JavaScript runtime. These values are automatically added to different registries—local or global, depending on how the symbol is created. With the `Symbol` constructor, you target the local registry, and with static methods like `Symbol.for`, you target the global registry, which is accessible across realms.

It helps to think of a registry as being a map data structure in memory that allows you to retrieve objects by means of a key, much like JavaScript's own `Map`. Let's begin with the local registry.

7.3.1   *Local registry*

To target the local registry, you call the factory function:

```
const symFoo = Symbol('foo');
```

This function adds the value generated from `Symbol('foo')` to the local registry, whether you create this symbol from a global variable scope or from within a module. Remember that you can access and use a symbol only when you possess the variable to reference it. If you declare `symFoo` inside a module (or a function), the variable is visible only within that module's (or function's) scope, and callers can access it only if you export `symFoo` from your module (or return it from your function). Nevertheless, in all these cases, the local registry is being used.

The next listing shows an example of creating a local symbol and exporting the binding from a module.

Listing 7.4   Exporting/importing a reference to a `Symbol` object

```
export const sym = Symbol('Local registry - module scope');   ⟵─┐  In someModule.js

...

import { sym } from './someModule.js';                            sym and global.sym
                                                                   point to two different
global.sym = Symbol('Local registry - global scope');   ⟵──      variables.
global.sym.toString(); // 'Symbol(Local registry - global scope)'
sym.toString();        // 'Symbol(Local registry - module scope)'
```

Section 7.3.2 shows how the global registry comes into play.

7.3.2   *Global registry*

The global registry is an internal structure available across the entire runtime. The `Symbol` API exposes static methods that interact with this registry, such as looking up symbols with `Symbol.keyFor`. Any symbols created in the local registry will not be accessible with this API. Check out the code in the following listing.

Listing 7.5   Local symbols not accessible with the global registry

```
const symFoo = Symbol('foo');
global.symFoo = Symbol('foo');          Uses local registry
Symbol.keyFor(symFoo);         // undefined
Symbol.keyFor(global.symFoo);  // undefined   Can't find either one
```

This code may seem to be rather unintuitive at first. Accessing the local registry didn't require special APIs. You treated the symbol variables as you would any other. But when you want to use the runtime-wide registry to share symbols across many parts of your application, you need the special APIs.

The static methods `Symbol.keyFor` and `Symbol.for` are designed to interact with the global symbol registry that lives inside the JavaScript runtime. The next listing shows how we can tweak the snippet of code in listing 7.5 to target this registry.

Listing 7.6   Interacting with the global registry

```
export const globalSym = Symbol.for('GlobalSymbol');   ⟵─┐  A globally
                                                            registered symbol
...                                                         in someModule.js

import { globalSym } from './someModule.js';           A globally registered
                                                       symbol in current scope
const symFoo = Symbol.for('foo');                   ⟵─┘
Symbol.keyFor(symFoo);  // 'foo'
Symbol.keyFor(globalSym); // 'GlobalSymbol'            Both keys found
```

Global symbols have the additional quality of transcending code realms. You may not be familiar with this term. Here's how the ECMAScript specification describes a realm:

> *Before it is evaluated, all ECMAScript code must be associated with a realm. Conceptually, a realm consists of a set of intrinsic objects, an ECMAScript global environment, all of the ECMAScript code that is loaded within the scope of that global environment, and other associated state and resources.*

In other words, a *realm* is the environment (set of variables and resources) associated with a script running in the browser, a module, an iframe, or even a worker script. Each module runs in its own realm; each iframe has its own window and its own realm; and unlike local symbols, global symbols are accessible across these realms, as depicted in figure 7.1.

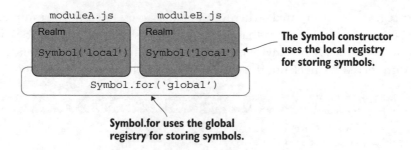

Figure 7.1   Scope of the local and global registries

As shown in listing 7.6, you can create these symbols by using `Symbol.for(key)`. If key isn't in the registry yet, JavaScript creates a new symbol and files it globally under that key. Then you can look it up with `Symbol.keyFor(key)` anywhere else in your application. If the symbol has not yet been defined in the global registry, the API returns `undefined`.

Now that you understand how symbols work, section 7.4 shows some practical applications for them.

7.4   *Practical application of symbols*

Symbols have many practical applications. In the following sections, we'll discuss using them to implement hidden properties and make objects interoperate with other parts of your application.

7.4.1   *Hidden properties*

Symbols provide a different way to attach properties to an object (data or functions) because these property keys are guaranteed to be conflict-free, collision-free, and unique in the runtime. This doesn't mean you should use them to key all your properties, however, because the access rules for symbols, as discussed in section 7.3, make it inconvenient to pull them out.

For this reason, it was thought that symbols could be used to emulate private properties because users would need access to the symbol reference itself, which you can control (hide) inside the module or class in question, as the next listing shows.

Listing 7.7   Using symbols to implement private, hidden properties

```
const _count = Symbol('count');          ◁──┐  This value would never be
                                             │  exported and, thus, is kept
class Counter {                              │  private within the module.
  constructor(count) {
    Object.defineProperty(this, _count, {    ◁──┐  Uses Object.defineProperty
        enumerable: false,                      │  to make internal property
        writable: true                          │  nonenumerable
    });
    this[_count] = count;
  }
  inc(by = 1) {                          ◁──┐
    return this[_count] += by;              │  Increases/decreases the object's
  }                                          │  internal count property by a
  dec(by = 1) {                          ◁──┘  specified amount
      return this[_count] -= by;
  }
}
```

Outside this class, there's no way to access the internal count property:

```
const counter = new Counter(1);
counter._count;                 // undefined
counter.count;                  // undefined
counter[Symbol('count')];       // undefined
counter[Symbol.for('count')]; // undefined
```

Unfortunately, this solution has a drawback: symbols are easily discovered via reflective APIs such as `Reflect.ownKeys` and `Object.getOwnPropertySymbols`. Hence, they are not truly private. Instead of using symbols for private access, why not use them to expose access and aid the interoperability among different realms of your code (aka different modules)? This use is much better for them.

Having a way to establish some cross-realm set of properties is analogous to what interfaces do for statically typed, class-based language (appendix B). In other words, symbols can be used to create contracts of interoperability among other parts of the code.

7.4.2   Interoperability

As an example, a third-party library could use a symbol to which objects could refer and adhere to a certain convention imposed by the library. Symbols are ideal for interoperable metadata values. Back in chapter 2, you learned that setting up your own prototype logic is an error-prone process. Here's one of the issues again:

```
function HashTransaction(name, sender, recipient) {
    Transaction.call(this, sender, recipient);
    this.name = name;
}

HashTransaction.prototype = Object.create(Transaction);
```

Remember that the issue was forgetting to use the prototype property of Transaction. It should have been Object.create(Transaction.prototype). Otherwise, creating a new instance resulted in a weird and confusing error:

```
TypeError: Cannot assign to read only property 'name' of object
'[object Object]'
```

This error occurred because the code was attempting to alter the nonwritable Function .name property. Before symbols existed, you had to use normal properties to represent all metadata, such as the name of the function in this case. A much better alternative would have been to use a non-writable symbol so that adding a name property to your functions would have never caused a collision. With a symbol, a function's name could be set as follows:

```
HashTransaction[Symbol('name')] = 'HashTransaction';
```

Symbols can make objects more extensible by preventing the code from accidentally breaking API contracts or the internal workings of an object. If every object in Java-Script had a Symbol('name') property, for example, any object's toString could easily use it in a consistent manner to enhance its own string representation, especially in stack traces of obfuscated code. (In section 7.5, you'll learn about a well-known symbol that performs this task.)

Furthermore, library authors could use symbols to force their users to adhere to conventions imposed by the library. The following sections present a couple of practical examples extracted from the blockchain application.

CONTROL PROTOCOLS

Let's look at an example that uses symbols to define a control protocol. As you know, a *protocol* is a convention (contract) that defines some behavior in the language. This behavior needs to be unique and must never clash with any other language feature. Symbols fit in nicely for this kind of task.

The example that we're about to discuss comes directly from our blockchain application. This concept is known as proof-of-work.

The "mining" or proof-of-work process of Bitcoin for obtaining a new block could be rather expensive in terms of energy use. Although the algorithm is simple to understand, it's time-consuming to run even with today's computing capabilities. The puzzle involves finding a block's cryptographic hash value that fulfils certain conditions. The hash value should be hard to find but easy to verify. The only condition we'll implement is that the computed hash string must start with an arbitrary number of leading zeroes, given by the block.difficulty property.

> ### Why is proof of work important?
>
> For some asset to acquire value, it needs to be both scarce and hard to extract or obtain. The value of a resource also follows the rules of supply and demand. Oil and petroleum acquire value, for example, because they're nonrenewable resources and expensive to extract. The process is the same for gold, silver, and diamonds, which require expensive mining processes. Similarly, bitcoin is capped at around 21 million as of this writing, which looks like a large amount but is rather scarce compared with other forms of currency.

The next listing shows the proof-of-work function and also introduces a new proposal, throw expressions (https://github.com/tc39/proposal-throw-expressions), that will make error handling code leaner.

Listing 7.8   Proof-of work-algorithm (proof_of_work.js)

padStart is used to fill or pad the current string with another string and was added to JavaScript as part of the ECMAScript 2017 update. If difficulty is set to null or missing, it defaults to using a difficulty value of 2.

Uses a throw expression as a default parameter to throw an exception if the provided block is undefined

Increments the nonce at every iteration

Rehashes the block

Tests whether the new hash contains the string of leading zeroes

```js
function proofOfWork(block =
        throw new Error('Provide a non-null block object!')) {
    const hashPrefix = ''.padStart(block ?.difficulty ?? 2, '0');
    do {
        block.nonce += 1;
        block.hash = block.calculateHash();
    } while (!block.hash.toString().startsWith(hashPrefix));
    return block;
}
```

Before we discuss the algorithm, let's spend a little bit of time talking about throw expressions as used in listing 7.8. A throw expression can be assigned like a value or an expression (function). Without it, the only way to throw exceptions in place of a default argument would be to wrap the exception inside a function. In other words, you would need to create a block context ({}) somewhere else in which throw is allowed. With this new feature, throwing an exception works like a first-class artifact, like any other object, and significantly cuts the amount of typing required. You will be able to throw exceptions in many ways, including parameter initializing (as used here); one-line arrow functions, conditionals, and switch statements; and even evaluation of logical operators, all without requiring a block scope. See appendix A for details on enabling this feature.

Listing 7.8 is a brute-force algorithm, as most proof-of-work functions are. `proofOfWork` will loop and compute the block's hash until it starts with the given hashPrefix, created from a string of zeroes of size block.difficulty. Naturally, the higher the difficulty value, the harder it is to find that hash. In the real world, the miner that solves this puzzle first cashes in the mining reward, which is how miners are incentivized to invest and spend energy in dedicated mining infrastructure. Because a block's data is constant at every iteration, the hash value is always the same, so you compute a nonce for it. (*Nonce* is jargon for a "*n*umber you use only *once*.") You change the nonce in a certain way to differentiate the block's data between hash calculations. If you recall the definition of `Block`, nonce is one the properties we provided to `HasHash`:

```
Object.assign(
  Block.prototype,
  HasHash(['index', 'timestamp', 'previousHash', 'nonce', 'data']),
  HasValidation()
);
```

What does this have to do with symbols? Remember that a blockchain is a large, distributed protocol. At any point in time, miners can be running any version of the software, so changes need to be made with caution and rolled out in a timely manner. To make enhancements or even bug fixes easier to apply to large Bitcoin networks, you must keep track of versions, and code must fork accordingly. In the real world, blocks contain metadata that keeps track of the version of the software. The following listing shows another part of the `Block` class that I omitted earlier for brevity.

Listing 7.9   Version property inside the `Block` class implemented as a symbol

```
const VERSION = '1.0';

class Block {
  ...

  get [Symbol.for('version')]() {        ◁──  Registers the
    return VERSION;                             software version
  }                                             as a global symbol
}
```

Having each block tagged with a global version symbol allows you to preserve backward compatibility with blocks persisted with a previous version of your blockchain software. Symbols let you control this compatibility in a seamless and interoperable way.

Suppose that we want to push a new release of our software that enhances `proof-OfWork` to make it a bit more challenging and harder to compute. Listing 7.10 shows the `mineNewBlockIntoChain` method of `BitcoinService`, which uses the global symbol registry to read the version of the software implementing a `Block` to decide how to route the logic behind proof-of-work. We can use dynamic `import` to load the right `proofOfWork` function to use.

Although I haven't covered all the details of `async/await` yet, you should be able to follow the next listing because I covered dynamic `import` in chapter 6 when handling a similar use case.

Listing 7.10 Mining a new block

```
async function mineNewBlockIntoChain(newBlock) {
    let proofOfWorkModule;
    switch (newBlock[Symbol.for('version')]) {
      case '2.0': {
        proofOfWorkModule =
            await import('./bitcoinservice/proof_of_work2.js');
        break;
      }
      default: case '1.0':
        proofOfWorkModule =
            await import('./bitcoinservice/proof_of_work.js');
        break;
    }
    const { proofOfWork } = proofOfWorkModule;

    return ledger.push(
      await proofOfWork(newBlock)
    );
}
```

Using a symbol here is much better than adding a regular version property to every block, which is what you would have had to do pre-ECMAScript 2015. This technique protects users of your API from accidentally breaking the contract by adding their own or modifying version at runtime. The following listing shows an enhanced proof-of-work implementation that uses a pseudorandom nonce value instead of incrementing it at every iteration.

Listing 7.11 Enhanced proof-of-work algorithm (proof_of_work2.js)

```
function proofOfWork(block) {
  const hashPrefix = ''.padStart(block.difficulty, '0');
  do {
    block.nonce += nextNonce();          ◁──  Instead of
    block.hash = block.calculateHash();        incrementing by 1,
  } while (!block.hash.toString().startsWith(hashPrefix));   increments by a
  return block;                                              random number
}

function nextNonce() {
  return randomInt(1, 10) + Date.now();
}

function randomInt(min, max) {
  return Math.floor(Math.random() * (max - min)) + min
}
```

In the real world, as blocks become more scarce and the difficulty parameter algorithm increases, it gets harder to compute the hash. Proof-of-work is one step required in transferring Bitcoin. In chapter 8, we'll see the entire process involved in mining a new block into the chain and the reward that comes with it.

Section 7.4.3 looks at another practical example of symbols, this time involving functions.

7.4.3   *Serialization*

Serialization is the process of converting an object from one representation to another. One of the most common examples is going from an object in memory to a file (serialization), and from a file into memory (deserialization or hydration). Because different objects may need to control how they're serialized, it's a good idea to implement a serialization function that gives them this control.

Years ago, Node.js tried to do a similar thing in its implementation of `console.log`, checking for the `inspect` method on the provided object and using it if it was available. This feature was clunky because it could easily clash with your own `inspect` method that you accidentally implemented to do something else, causing `console.log` to behave unexpectedly. As a result, the feature was deprecated. Had symbols been around back then, the story might have been different.

The next listing does things the right way, adding another global symbol property to the `Block` class in charge of returning its own JSON representation.

> **Listing 7.12   `Symbol(toJson)` that creates a JSON representation of the object**

```
class Block {

  ...

  [Symbol.for('toJson')]() {          ◁── Uses a global symbol so
    return JSON.stringify({                that it can be read out
        index: this.index,                from other modules
        previousHash: this.previousHash,
        hash: this.hash,
        timestamp: this.timestamp,
        dataCount: this.data?.length ?? 0,   ◁── Uses optional chaining
        data: this.data.map(toJson),    ◁──     operator with the nullish
        version: VERSION                        coalesce operators, both added
      }                                         as part of the ECMAScript 2020
    );                                          specification
  }
}
```

Uses optional chaining operator with the nullish coalesce operators, both added as part of the ECMAScript 2020 specification

Converts data contents by using a toJson helper function (shown in listing 7.14)

This JSON representation is a tailored, summarized version of the block's data. With this function, any time you need JSON, you can consult this symbol from anywhere in your application—even across realms. Serializing a blockchain to JSON uses a helper called `toJson` that inspects this symbol. The following listing shows the code to serialize in `BitcoinService.serializeLedger`.

> **Listing 7.13   Serializing a ledger as a list of JSON strings**

```
import { buffer, join, toArray, toJson } from '~util/helpers.js';

...
```

```
function serializeLedger(delimeter = ';') {
    return ledger |> toArray |> join(toJson, delimeter) |> buffer;    <
}
```

Uses the pipeline operator to run a sequence of functions, assuming that the pipes feature is enabled (appendix A)

I've taken the liberty of combining many of the concepts you've learned in previous chapters. The most noticeable of these concepts is breaking logic into functions and currying those functions to make them easier to compose (or pipe). As you can see, I used the pipeline operator to combine this logic and return the data as a raw buffer that can be written to a file or sent over the network, effectively keeping side effects away from the main logic. The next listing shows the code for those helper functions.

Listing 7.14 Helper functions used in serializing an entire blockchain object to a buffer

```
import { curry, isFunction } from './fp/combinators.js';
```

Converts any object to a JSON string. If the object implements Symbol('toJson'), the code uses that as its JSON string representation; otherwise, it defaults to JSON.stringify.

Spreads any object to an array

```
export const toArray = a => [...a];

export const toJson = obj => {                                       <
    return isFunction(obj[Symbol.for('toJson')])
        ? obj[Symbol.for('toJson')]()
        : JSON.stringify(obj);
}

export const join = curry((serializer, delimeter, arr)
        => arr.map(serializer).join(delimeter));                    <

export const buffer = str => Buffer.from(str, 'utf8');
```

Helper function that applies a serializer function to elements of an array and joins the array using the provided delimiter

Converts any string to a UTF-8 Buffer object

As you can see, toJson checks the object's metaproperties first for any global JSON transformation symbol; otherwise, it falls back to JSON.stringify on all fields. The rest of the helper functions are ones that you've seen at some point and are simple to follow.

Recall from chapter 4 that pipe is the reverse of compose. Alternatively, you could have written the logic in listing 7.13 this way, provided that you implemented or imported the compose combinator function:

```
return compose(
        buffer,
        join(toJson),
        toArray)(ledger);
```

Custom symbols such as Symbol.for('toJson') and Symbol.for('version') are known to the entire application. This use of symbols is so far-reaching and compelling that JavaScript ships with a set of well-known system symbols of its own, which you can use to bend JavaScript's runtime behavior to your desires. Section 7.5 explores these symbols.

7.5   *Well-known symbols*

As you can use symbols to augment some key processes in your application, you can also use JavaScript's well-known symbols as an introspection mechanism to hook into core JavaScript features and create some powerful behavior. These symbols are special and are meant to target the JavaScript runtime's own behavior, whereas any custom symbols you declare can only augment userland code.

The well-known symbols are available as static properties of the `Symbol` API. In this section, we'll briefly explore

- `@@toStringTag`
- `@@isConcatSpreadable`
- `@@species`
- `@@toPrimitive`
- `@@iterator`

NOTE   For simplicity and ease of documentation, a well-known `Symbol.<name>` is often abbreviated as `@@<name>`. `Symbol.iterator`, for example, is `@@iterator`, and `Symbol.toPrimitive` is `@@toPrimitive`.

7.5.1   *@@toStringTag*

Soon, you'll try to log an object to the console by calling `toString`, only to get the infamous (and meaningless) message `'[object Object]'`. Fortunately, we now have a symbol that hooks into this behavior. JavaScript checks whether you have `toString` overridden in your own object, and if you don't, it uses Object's `toString` method, which internally hooks into a symbol called `Symbol.toStringTag`. I recommend adding this symbol to classes or objects for which you don't have or need `toString` defined, because it will help you during debugging and troubleshooting.

Here are a couple of variations, the first using a computed-property syntax, used mostly in object literals, and the second using computed-getter syntax, used mostly inside classes:

```
function BitcoinService(ledger) {
  //...
  return {
    [Symbol.toStringTag]: 'BitcoinService',
    mineNewBlockIntoChain,
    calculateBalanceOfWallet,
    minePendingTransactions,
    transferFunds,
    serializeLedger
  };
}

class Block {
  //...
    get [Symbol.toStringTag]() {
      return 'Block';
```

```
  }
}
```

Now `toString` has a bit more information:

```
const service = BitcoinService();
service.toString(); // '[object BitcoinService]')
```

For objects built with classes and pseudoclassical constructors (chapter 2), to avoid hardcoding, you could use the more general

```
get [Symbol.toStringTag]() {
  return this.constructor.name;
}
```

`@@toStringTag` is also used for error handling. As an example, consider adding it to `Money`:

```
const Money = curry((currency, amount) =>
  compose(
    Object.seal,
    Object.freeze
  )({
    amount,
    currency,
    //...

    [Symbol.toStringTag]: `Money(${currency} ${amount})`
  })
)
```

If you try to mutate `Money('USD', 5)`, JavaScript throws the following error, using `toStringTag` to enhance the error message:

```
TypeError: Cannot assign to read only property 'amount' of object '[object
    Money(USD 5)]'
```

7.5.2 @@isConcatSpreadable

This symbol is used to control the internal behavior of `Array#concat`. What outcome would you expect from this expression?

```
[a].concat([b])
```

Do you expect `[['a'], ['b']]` or `['a', 'b']`? Most of the time, you'd want the latter. And that is exactly what happens. When concatenating objects, `concat` determines whether any of its arguments are "spreadable." In other words, it tries to unpack and flatten all the elements of the target object over another, using semantics similar to those of the spread operator. Here's a simple example that shows the effect of this operator:

```
const letters = ['a', 'b'];
const numbers = [1, 2];
letters.concat(numbers);  // ["a", "b", 1, 2]
```

```
letters[Symbol.isConcatSpreadable] = false;
letters.concat(numbers); // Array ["a", "b", Array [1, 2]]
```

In some cases, however, you don't want the default behavior. Consider implementing record types, such as a Pair, as a simple array:

```
class Pair extends Array {
    constructor(left, right) {
      super()
      this.push(left);
      this.push(right);
    }
}
```

For Pair, you would not want to spread its elements by default when concatenating with another Pair, because then you'll lose the proper two-element grouping:

```
const numbers = new Pair(1, 2);
const letters = new Pair('a', 'b');

numbers.concat(letters) // Array [1, 2, 'a', 'b']
```

What you want in this case is a collection of pairs. If you turn off the Symbol.isConcat-Spreadable knob, everything works as expected:

```
class Pair extends Array {
    constructor(left, right) {
      super();
      this.push(left);
      this.push(right);
    }

    get [Symbol.isConcatSpreadable]() {
      return false;
    }
}
```

```
numbers.concat(letters); // Array [Array [1, 2], Array ['a', 'b']]
```

The symbols described so far hook into some superficial behavior; others go even deeper into the nooks and crannies of the JavaScript APIs. Section 7.5.3 looks at Symbol.species.

7.5.3   *@@species*

Symbol.species is a nice, clever artifact used to control what the constructor should be on a resultant or derived object after operations are used on some original object. The following sections look at two use cases for this symbol: information hiding and documenting closure of operations.

INFORMATION HIDING

You can use `Symbol.species` to avoid exposing unnecessary implementation details by downgrading derived types to base types. Consider the simple use case in the next listing.

Listing 7.15   Using `@@species` so that `EvenNumbers` becomes `Array`

```
class EvenNumbers extends Array {            Excludes odd numbers from
  constructor(...nums) {                     being pushed into this array
    super();
    nums.filter(n => n % 2 === 0).forEach(n => this.push(n));   ◄
  }
  static get [Symbol.species]() {      ◄    Hides the derived class
    return Array;                            after any mapping
  }                                          operations
}

new EvenNumbers(1, 2, 3, 4, 5, 6); // [2, 4, 6]
```

At this point, this object created an instance of both `EvenNumber` and `Array`, as you'd expect. But the fact that this data structure was constructed from `EvenNumber` is not important to users of this API after it's been initialized, because `Array` would be more than adequate. With the `@@species` metasymbol added, after mapping over this array, you see that the type is downgraded to `Array` and used thereafter for all operations (`some`, `every`, `filter`), effectively hiding the original object. Here's an example:

```
const result = evens.map(x => x ** 2);
result instanceof Array;        // true
result instanceof EvenNumbers;  // false
```

Aside from `Array`, types such as `Promise` support this feature, as do data structures such as `Map` and `Set`. By default, `@@species` points to their default constructors:

```
Array[Symbol.species] === Array
Map[Symbol.species] === Map
RegExp[Symbol.species] === RegExp
Promise[Symbol.species] === Promise
Set[Symbol.species] === Set
```

Here's another example, this one using promises. Suppose that after some user action, you'd like to fire a task that starts after some period of time has elapsed. (Normally, you should not extend from built-in types, but I'll make an exception here for teaching purposes.) After the first deferred action runs, every subsequent action should behave like a standard promise. Consider the `DelayedPromise` class shown in the following listing.

Listing 7.16   Deriving `DelayedPromise` as a subclass of `Promise`

```
class DelayedPromise extends Promise {       Creates a promise that delays its initial
  constructor(executor, seconds = 0) {   ◄   execution by the provided seconds
```

```
        super((resolve, reject) => {
          setTimeout(() => {
            executor(resolve, reject);
          }, seconds * 1_000);
        })
      }

      static get [Symbol.species]() {        ⟵      Hides the derived class so
        return Promise;                             that subsequent calls to
      }                                             then are not delayed
    }
```

You can wrap any asynchronous task as you would any other promise, as shown next.

Listing 7.17   Using `DelayedPromise`

```
const p = new DelayedPromise((resolve) => {        Returns the number 10
      resolve(10);                      ⟵          after three seconds
}, 3);
                                  Squares the eventual
                                  number returned
p.then(num => num ** 2)          ⟵
 .then(console.log);              ⟵
//Prints 100 after 3 seconds              Uses the bind operator to pass in a
                                          reference to the log function of a
                                          properly bound console object
```

DOCUMENTING CLOSURE OF OPERATIONS

Here's another example in which `@@species` can be useful in an application, particularly in the area of functional programming. Let's circle back to the `Functor` mixin in chapter 5 that implements a generic `map` contract:

```
const Functor = {
  map(f = identity) {
    return this.constructor.of(f(this.get()));
  }
}
```

Remember that functors have a special requirement for `map`: it must preserve the structure of the type being mapped over. `Array#map` should return a new `Array`, `Validation#map` should return a new `Validation`, and so on. You can use `@@species` to guarantee and document the fact that functors close over the type that you expect—helping preserve the species, you might say. It's the responsibility of the implementer to respect this symbol when it exists. Arrays use this symbol, and we can add it to `Validation` as well, as shown in the following listing.

Listing 7.18   `@@species` as implemented in the `Validation` class

```
static get [Symbol.species]() {
  return this;                    ⟵      In a static context, refers to
}                                        the surrounding class
```

Then we can enhance `Functor` to hook into `@@species` before defaulting to the object's constructor, as shown in the next listing.

Listing 7.19 Inspecting the contents of `@@species` when mapping functions on functors

```
const Functor = {
  map(f = identity) {
    const C = getSpeciesConstructor(this);     ⟵┐ Looks into the species
    return C.of(f(this.get()));                   │ function-valued symbol
  }                                                │ first to decide the derived
}                                                  │ object type

function getSpeciesConstructor(original) {
  if (original[Symbol.species]) {
    return original[Symbol.species]();
  }
  if (original.constructor[Symbol.species]) {      ⟵┐ Falls back to using
    return original.constructor[Symbol.species]();    │ constructor if no
  }                                                     │ @@species symbol
  return original.constructor;                    ⟵    │ is defined
}
```

This code results in

```
Validation.Success.of(2).map(x => x ** 2); // Success(4)
```

7.5.4 @@toPrimitive

This symbol gets queried by JavaScript when it converts (or coerces) some object into a primitive value such as a string or a number—when you place an object next to a plus sign (+) or concatenate it to a string, for example. JavaScript already has a well-defined rule for its internal coercion algorithm (called an *abstract operation*) that goes by the name ToPrimitive.

`Symbol.toPrimitive` customizes this behavior. This function-valued property accepts one parameter, `hint`, which could have a string value of `number`, `string`, or `default`. This operation is in many ways equivalent to overriding `Object#valueOf` and `Object#toString` (discussed in chapter 4), except for the additional hinting capability, which allows you to be smarter about the process. In fact, both of these methods are checked when `@@toPrimitive` is not defined and JavaScript needs to coerce an object into a value that makes sense. For strings and numbers, the general rule is as follows:

- When `hint` is a number, JavaScript attempts to use `valueOf`.
- When `hint` is a string, JavaScript attempts to use `toString`.

When implementing `@@toPrimitive`, we should try to stay consistent with these rules. A classic example is the `Date` object. When a `Date` object is hinted to act as a string, its `toString` representation is used. If the object is hinted as a number, its numerical representation (seconds from the epoch) is used:

```
const today = new Date();

'Today is: ' + today;
// Today is: Thu Oct 31 2019 14:02:29 GMT+0000 (Coordinated Universal Time)

+today; // 1572530549275
```

Let's go back to our `EvenNumbers` example, adding this symbol to that class with an implementation that sums all the numbers in the array when a number is requested or creates a comma-separated-values (CSV) string representation of the array in a string context, as shown in the next listing.

Listing 7.20   Defining `@@toPrimitive` in class `EvenNumbers`

```
class EvenNumbers extends Array {
  constructor(...nums) {
    super();
    nums.filter(n => n % 2 === 0).forEach(n => this.push(n));
  }

  static get [Symbol.species]() {
    return Array;
  }

  [Symbol.toPrimitive](hint) {
    switch (hint) {
      case 'string':
        return `[${this.join(', ')}]`;       ◄── Returns a string
      case 'number':                              representation of
      default:                                     this array (showing
        return this.reduce(add);   ◄──            only even numbers)
    }                                  Returns a single number
  }                                    representation of this array by
}                                      adding up all even numbers
```

You can also think of `@@toPrimitive` as a means of unboxing or unfolding some container into its primitive value. The next listing adds this metasymbol to `Validation`.

Listing 7.21   Adding `@@toPrimitive` to the `Validation` class to extract its value

```
class Validation {
  #val;

  //...

  get() {
    return this.#val;
  }                                  When a Validation instance is
                                      in a primitive position, the
  [Symbol.toPrimitive](hint) {   ◄──  JavaScript runtime folds the
    return this.get();                container automatically.
  }
}
```

Now you can use these containers with less friction in the code because JavaScript takes care of the unboxing for you, as shown in the following listing.

Listing 7.22 Taking advantage of `@@toPrimitive` used with `Validation` objects

```
'The Joy of ' + Success.of('JavaScript'); // 'The Joy of JavaScript'

function validate(input) {
    return input
        ? Success.of(input)
        : Failure.of(`Expected valid result, got: ${input}`);
}

validate(10) + 5;    // 15
validate(null) + 5;  // "Error: Can't extract the value of a Failure"
```

The plus operator causes the Validation.Succes object to be in primitive position. It automatically unwraps the container with its value, 10.

The plus operator causes a Validation.Failure to wrongfully unbox and throw an error.

Value objects are also good opportunities to use this symbol. In `Money`, for example, we can use this symbol to return the numerical portion directly and make math operations easier and more transparent, as the next listing shows.

Listing 7.23 Using `@@toPrimitive` in `Money` to return its numerical portion

```
const Money = curry((currency, amount) =>
  compose(
    Object.seal,
    Object.freeze
  )({
    amount,
    currency,

    ...

    [Symbol.toPrimitive]: () => precisionRound(amount, 2);
  })
)

const five = Money('USD', 5);
five * 2;    // 10
five + five; // 10
```

Both arithmetic operators unwrap Money objects to perform the numerical operation.

The last well-known symbol covered in this book, and by far the most useful, is `@@iterator`.

7.5.5 @@iterator

Most class-based languages have standard libraries that support some form of an `Iterable` or `Enumerable` interface. Classes that implement this interface must abide by a contract that communicates how to deliver data when some collection is looped over. JavaScript's response is `Symbol.iterator`, which acts like one of these interfaces and is used to hook into the mechanics of how an object behaves when it's the subject of a `for...of` loop, consumed by the spread operator, or even destructured.

As you can expect, all of JavaScript's abstract data types already implement `@@iterator`, starting with arrays:

```
Array.prototype[Symbol.iterator](); // Object [Array Iterator] {}
```

Arrays are an obvious choice. What about strings? You can think of a string as being a character array. Spread it, destructure it, or iterate over it, as the next listing shows.

Listing 7.24 Enumerating a string as a character array

```
[...'JoJS']; // [ 'J', 'o', 'J', 'S' ]          ◁——— Spread operator

const [first, ...rest] = 'JoJS';          ◁——  Destructuring
first;   // 'J'                                  the array
rest;    // ['o', 'J', 'S' ]


const str = 'JoJS'[Symbol.iterator]();          ◁——  Manual
str.next(); // { value: 'J', done: false }             iteration
str.next(); // { value: 'o', done: false }
str.next(); // { value: 'J', done: false }
str.next(); // { value: 'S', done: false }
str.next(); // { value: undefined, done: true }
```

Similarly, it makes sense that `Blockchain` could seamlessly deliver all blocks when it's put through a `for` loop or spread over. After all, a blockchain is a collection of blocks. `Blockchain` delegates all of its block storage needs to a private instance field of `Map` (chapter 3). The following listing shows the pertinent details.

Listing 7.25 Using `@@iterator` for blockchain

```
class Blockchain {

  #blocks = new Map();

  constructor(genesis = createGenesisBlock()) {
    this.#blocks.set(genesis.hash, genesis);          ◁—┐
  }

  push(newBlock) {
    this.#blocks.set(newBlock.hash, newBlock);             Delegates to the
    return newBlock;                                       iterator object
  }                                                        returned from
                                                           Map#values
  //...

  [Symbol.iterator]() {
    return this.blocks.values()[Symbol.iterator]();   ◁—┘
  }
}
```

Map is also iterable, so calling `values` on a Map object delivers the values (without keys) as an array, which is iterable by design, meaning we can easily have Blockchain's `@@iterator` symbol delegate to it, as listing 7.25 shows. The same is true for Block to deliver the items contained in `data`, which in this case is each Transaction object, as shown in the next listing.

Listing 7.26 Implementing `@@iterator` in Block to enumerate all transactions

```
class Block {

  //...
  constructor(index, previousHash, data = []) {
    this.index = index;
    this.data  = data;
    this.previousHash = previousHash;
    this.timestamp = Date.now();
    this.hash = this.calculateHash();
  }

  //...

  [Symbol.iterator]() {
    return this.data[Symbol.iterator]();
  }
}
```

> **Automatically delivers transactions when a Block object is spread or looped over**

To read out all the transactions in a block, loop over it:

```
for (const transaction of block) {
  console.log(transaction.hash);
}
```

You have nothing to gain from iterating over a Transaction, which is a terminal/leaf object in our design. So you can let JavaScript error out abruptly if a user of your API tries to iterate over it, or you can manipulate the iterator yourself to handle this situation gracefully and silently by sending back the object `{done: true}`:

```
class Transaction {
  // ...

  [Symbol.iterator]() {
    return {
      next: () => ({ done: true })
    }
  }
}
```

Furthermore, `@@iterator` is a central part of the validation algorithm in `HasValidation` that we implemented in chapter 5, which relies on traversing the entire blockchain structure. Here's that code again (listing 7.27).

Iterator protocol

JavaScript has a well-defined iterator protocol that communicates to the runtime what the next value is and when iteration has reached its conclusion. The shape of that object looks like this:

```
{value: <nextValue>, done: <isFinished?>}
```

Both iterators (and generators) in JavaScript work the same way. We'll study generators in more depth in chapter 8 and async generators in chapter 9.

Listing 7.27 `HasValidation` mixin

```
const HasValidation = () => ({
    validate() {
        return [...this]                                    ◁── Invokes the Symbol.iterator
        .reduce((validationResult, nextItem) =>                   property of the object
            validationResult.flatMap(() => nextItem.validate()),  being validated
          this.isValid()
        );
    }
})
```

Now that you know that `@@iterator` plugs into the behavior of `for..of` as well as the spread operator, you can design a more memory-friendly solution than the algorithm in listing 7.27. As it stands, `validate` is creating new arrays in memory when executing: `[...this]`. This code won't scale to large data structures. Instead, you can loop over the objects inline with a more traditional `for` loop, as shown in the next listing.

Listing 7.28 Refactoring `validate` to use `for` loops to benefit from `@@iterator`

```
const HasValidation = () => ({                      ◁──┐ Calls the internal @@iterator
    validate() {                                          property of Blockchain, Block,
        let result = model.isValid();                     and Transaction
        for (const element of model) {
            result = validateModel(element);
            if (result.isFailure) {
                break;
            }
        }
        return result;
    }
})
```

You can do many things with `@@iterator`. Data structures that extend from or depend on arrays are natural candidates, but you can do much more, especially when you combine these structures with generators. A `Generator` is an object that is returned from a generator function and abides by the same iterator protocol. `@@iterator` is a function-valued property, and generators can implement it elegantly. The next listing shows a variation on a `Pair` object that uses a generator to `yield` the `left` and `right` properties during a destructuring assignment.

Listing 7.29 Using a generator to return `left` and `right` elements of a `Pair`

```
const Pair = (left, right) => ({
    left,
    right,
    equals: otherPair => left === otherPair.left &&
                         right === otherPair.right,
    [Symbol.iterator]: function* () {
       yield left;
       yield right;
    }
});
```

> The function* notation identifies a generator function.

> The yield keyword is equivalent to a return in a regular function.

```
const p = Pair(20, 30);
const [left, right] = p;
left;  // 20
right; // 30
[...p]; // [20, 30]
```

Again, don't worry too much now about how generators work behind the scenes. All you need to understand is that calls to `yield` within the function are analogous to calling the returned iterator object's next method. Behind the scenes, JavaScript is taking care of this task for you. I'll cover this topic in more detail in chapter 8.

To sum up the well known symbols, here's `Pair` implementing all of the symbols at the same time, as well as our custom `[Symbol.for('toJson')]`:

```
const Pair = (left, right) => ({
    left,
    right,
    equals: otherPair => left === otherPair.left &&
                         right === otherPair.right,
    [Symbol.toStringTag]: 'Pair',
    [Symbol.species]: () => Pair,
    [Symbol.iterator]: function* () {
       yield left;
       yield right;
    },
    [Symbol.toPrimitive]: hint => {
       switch (hint) {
         case 'number':
           return left + right;
         case 'string':
           return `Pair [${left}, ${right}]`;
         default:
           return [left, right];
       }
    },
```

```
      [Symbol.for('toJson')]: () => ({
        type: 'Pair',
        left,
        right
      })
    });

const p = Pair(20, 30);
+p;             // 50
p.toString(); // '[object Pair]'
`${p}`;        // 'Pair [20, 30]'

const p2 = p[Symbol.species]()(20, 30);
p.equals(p2);  // true
```

Normally, you wouldn't load objects with all possible symbols; their true power comes from using the ones that truly affect your code globally to remove sources of duplication. These examples are for teaching purposes only.

You can hook into many symbols other than the ones discussed in this chapter. The following code

```
Object.getOwnPropertyNames(Symbol)
  .filter(p => typeof Symbol[p] === 'symbol')
  .filter(s =>
    ![
        'toStringTag',
        'isConcatSpreadable',
        'species',
        'toPrimitive',
        'iterator'
    ]
      .includes(s));
```

returns

```
  [
     'asyncIterator',
     'hasInstance',
     'match',
     'replace',
     'search',
     'split',
     'unscopables'
  ]
```

I'll cover @@asyncIterator in chapter 8.

As you can see, symbols allow you to create static hooks that you can use to apply a fixed enhancement to the behavior of your code. But what if you need to turn things on or off at runtime? In section 7.6, we turn our attention to other JavaScript APIs that dynamically hook into running code.

7.6 *Dynamic introspection and weaving*

The techniques discussed so far fall under the umbrella of static introspection. You created tokens (aka symbols) that you or the JavaScript runtime can use to change how running code behaves. This technique, however, requires that you add symbols directly as properties of objects. For the extended functionality that well-known symbols give you, this is the only option. But when you're considering any custom symbols, modifying the shape of objects syntactically may seem a bit invasive. Let's consider another option.

In this section, you'll learn about a technique that involves changing the behavior of your code externally via dynamic introspection. Along the way, you'll learn how to use this technique to consolidate cross-cutting logic such as logging/tracing and performance, and even the implementation of smart objects.

JavaScript makes it easy to manipulate and change the shape and structure of objects at runtime. But special APIs allow you to hook into the event of calling a method or accessing a property. To understand the motivation here, it helps to think about the popular, widely used Proxy design pattern (figure 7.2).

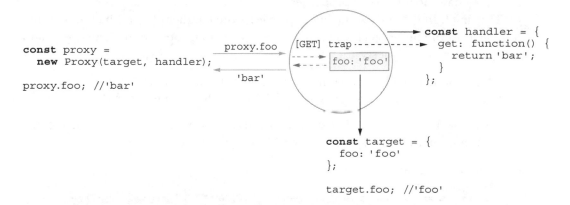

Figure 7.2 **The Proxy pattern uses an object (proxy) to act on behalf of a target. When fetching for a property, if it finds the property in the proxy, the code uses that property; otherwise, it consults the target object. Proxies have lots of uses, including logging, caching, and masking.**

As shown in figure 7.2, a proxy is a wrapper to another object that is being called by a client to access the real internal object. The proxy object usurps an object's interface and takes full control of how it's accessed and used. Proxies are used quite a bit to interface network communications and filesystems, for example. Most notably, proxies are used in application code to implement a caching layer or perhaps a centralized logging system.

Instead of requiring you to roll your own proxy code scaffolding every time, JavaScript takes this pattern to heart and makes it first-class APIs: `Proxy` and `Reflect`. Together, these APIs allow you to implement dynamic introspection so that you can weave or inject code at runtime in a non-invasive manner. This solution is optimal because it keeps your application separate from your injectable code. In some ways, this solution is similar to dynamic extension via mixins (chapter 3), except that dynamic extension occurs during object construction, whereas dynamic weaving occurs during object use.

In section 7.6.1, we use dynamic introspection to weave performance counters and logging statements into important parts of the code without touching their implementation, beginning with the `Proxy` API.

7.6.1 *Proxy objects*

Proxies have many practical uses, such as interception, tracing, and profiling. A `Proxy` object is one that can intercept or trap access to a target object's properties. When an object is being used with a `get`, `set`, or method call, JavaScript's internal [[Get]] and [[Set]] mechanisms are executed, respectively. You can use proxies to plant traps in your objects that hook into these internal operations.

Proxies enable the creation of objects with the full range of behaviors available to host objects. In other words, they look and behave like regular objects, so unlike symbols, they have no additional properties.

The first thing to understand about proxies is the handler object, which sets up the traps against the host object. You can intercept nearly any operation on an object and even inherited properties.

> **NOTE** You can apply many traps to an object. I don't cover all traps in this book—only the most useful ones. For a full list, visit http://mng.bz/zxlX.

Let's start with an example that showcases a tracer proxy object to trace or log any property and method access, beginning with the get ([[Get]]) trap:

```
const traceLogHandler = {
  get(target, key) {
    console.log(`${dateFormat(new Date())} [TRACE] Calling: ${key}`);
    return target[key];
  }
}

function dateFormat(date) {
  return ((date.getMonth() > 8)
    ? (date.getMonth() + 1)
    : ('0' + (date.getMonth() + 1))) + '/' +
      ((date.getDate() > 9)
          ? date.getDate()
          : ('0' + date.getDate())) + '/' + date.getFullYear();
}
```

As you can see, after creating the log entry, the handler allows the default behavior to happen by returning a reference to the original property accessed by `target[key]`. To see this behavior in action, consider this object:

```
const credentials = {
  username: '@luijar',
  password: 'Som3thingR@ndom',
  login: () => {
    console.log('Logging in...');
  }
};
```

Creating a proxied version of this object is simple:

```
const credentials$Proxy = new Proxy(credentials, traceLogHandler);
```

The statements

```
credentials$Proxy.login();    // Prints 'Logging in...'
credentials$Proxy.username;   // '@luijar'
credentials$Proxy.password;   // 'Som3thingR@ndom'
```

print the following logs:

```
11/06/2019 [TRACE] Calling:  login
11/06/2019 [TRACE] Calling:  username
11/06/2019 [TRACE] Calling:  password
```

I said before that proxies allow you to intercept anything, and I mean *anything*, even symbols. So trying to log the object itself (not by calling `toString`) invokes certain symbols behind the scenes. This code

```
console.log(credentials$Proxy);
```

prints

```
11/06/2019 [TRACE] Calling:  Symbol(Symbol.toStringTag)
11/06/2019 [TRACE] Calling:  Symbol(Symbol.iterator)
```

The dynamic weaving happens without the API objects having any knowledge of it, which is an ideal separation of concerns. We can get a bit more creative. Suppose that we'd like to obfuscate and hide any sensitive information (such as a password) from being read as plain text. Consider the handler in the next listing, which traps `get` and `has`.

Listing 7.30 `passwordObfuscatorHandler` proxy handler

```
const passwordObfuscatorHandler = {
  get(target, key) {
    if(key === 'password' || key === 'pwd') {
      return '\u2022'.repeat(randomInt(5, 10));    ⟵  U+2022 is
    }                                                   Unicode for a bullet
    return target[key];                                 character (•).
  },
  has(target, key) {
    if(key === 'password' || key === 'pwd') {
```

```
        return false;
    }
    return true;
  }
}
```

Now reading out a password from credentials returns the obfuscated value:

```
credentials$Proxy.password;  // '●●●●●'
```

And checking for the password field with the in operator invokes the has trap:

```
'password' in credentials$Proxy; // false
```

Unfortunately, you seem to have lost the tracing behavior you had earlier. Because proxies wrap an object (and are themselves plain objects), you can apply proxies on top of proxies. In other words, proxies compose. Composing proxies allows you to implement progressive enhancement or decoration techniques:

```
const credentials$Proxy =
    new Proxy(
      new Proxy(credentials, passwordObfuscatorHandler),
      traceLogHandler);
```

```
credentials$Proxy.password; // '●●●●●'
                            // 11/06/2019 [TRACE] Calling:  password
```

The FP principles that you learned in chapter 4 apply here. You can turn those nested proxy objects into an elegant right-to-left compose pipeline. Consider this helper function:

```
const weave = curry((handler, target) => new Proxy(target, handler));
```

weave takes a handler and waits for you to supply the host object, which can be credentials or a credential proxy. Let's partially apply two handler functions, one for log tracing and the other for automatic password obfuscation:

```
const tracer = weave(traceLogHandler);
const obfuscator = weave(passwordObfuscatorHandler);
```

Compose the functions in the right order to obfuscate before printing:

```
const credentials$Proxy = compose(tracer, obfuscator)(credentials);
```

```
credentials$Proxy.password; // '●●●●●'
                            // 11/06/2019 [TRACE] Calling:  password
```

You can also use the more natural left-to-right pipe operator (provided that pipes are enabled). See how clean and terse the code becomes?

```
const credentials$Proxy = credentials |> obfuscator |> tracer;
```

It's great to see how core principles apply to all sorts of scenarios. In this case, by combining metaprogramming with functional and object-oriented paradigms, we get a best-of-breed implementation.

In section 7.6.2, we look at the mirror API to a proxy handler: `Reflect`.

7.6.2 *The Reflect API*

`Reflect` is a complementary API to `Proxy` that you can use to invoke any interceptable property of an object dynamically. You could invoke a function by using `Reflect` `.apply`, for example. Arguably, you could also use the legacy parts of the language, such as `Function#{call,apply}`. `Reflect` has a similar shape to `Proxy`, but it provides a less verbose, more contextual, easier-to-understand API for these cases, which makes `Reflect` a more natural and reasonable way to forward actions on behalf of `Proxy` objects.

`Reflect` packs the most useful internal object methods into a simple-to-use API. In other words, all the methods provided by proxy handlers—get, set, has, and others— are available here. You can also use `Reflect` to uncover other internal behavior about objects, such as whether a property was defined or a setter operation succeeded. You can't get this information with regular reflective inquiries such as `Object.{get-PrototypeOf`, `getOwnPropertyDescriptors`, and `getOwnPropertySymbols}`.

One example of some internal behavior exposed by `Reflect` is `Reflect.define-Property`, which returns a Boolean stating whether a property was created successfully. By contrast, `Object.defineProperty` merely returns the object that was passed to the function. `Reflect.defineProperty` is more useful for this reason.

The sample code in the following listing takes advantage of the Boolean result to define a new property on an object.

Listing 7.31 Using `Reflect.defineProperty` to create a property

```
const obj = {};

if(Reflect.defineProperty(obj, Symbol.for('version'), {      ◁──┐  Returning true means
  value: '1.0',                                                   that the property was
  enumerable: true                                                added successfully.
})){
    console.log(obj);  // { [Symbol(version)]: '1.0' }
}
```

Again, because `Reflect`'s API matches that of the proxy handler for all traps, it's naturally suitable to be the default behavior inside proxy traps. The [[Get]] trap for `passwordObfuscatorHandler`, for example, can be refactored as such, as shown next.

Listing 7.32 [[Get]] trap of `passwordObfuscatorHandler`

```
const passwordObfuscatorHandler = {
  get(target, key) {
    if(key === 'password' || key === 'pwd') {
```

```
        return '\u2022'.repeat(randomInt(5, 10));
      }
      return Reflect.get(target, key);        ◄─── Uses Reflect.get(target, key)
    }                                              instead of target[key]
}
```

Furthermore, this API parity means that you don't have to declare all parameters explicitly every time if you don't need to use them. Let's clean up `traceLogHandler` a bit:

```
const traceLogHandler = {
  get(...args) {
    console.log(`${dateFormat(new Date())} [TRACE] Calling: ${args[1]}`);
    return Reflect.get(...args);
  }
}
```

Section 7.6.3 discusses some interesting and practical uses for this feature.

7.6.3 *Additional use cases*

In this section, you'll learn about some interesting use cases for dynamic proxies in our blockchain application, starting with a smart block that knows to rehash itself on the fly when any of its hashed properties change. Then you'll use proxies to measure the performance of the blockchain `validate` function.

AUTOHASHED BLOCKS

Recall that a block computes its own hash upon instantiation:

```
const block = new Block(1, '123', []);

block.hash;
// '0632572a23d22e7e963ab4fe643af1a3a77cf11a242346352a1ad0ebc3fb0b73'
```

A hash value uniquely identifies a block, but it can get out of sync if some malicious actor changes or tampers with the block data, which is why validation algorithms for blockchain are so important. Ideally, if a block's property value changes (a new transaction is added or its nonce gets incremented, for example), we should rehash it. To implement this behavior without proxies, you would need to define setters explicitly for all your mutable, hashed properties and call `this.calculateHash` when each one changes. The properties of interest are `index`, `timestamp`, `previousHash`, `nonce`, and `data`. You can imagine how much duplicated code that process would require.

Consolidating this dynamic behavior is what proxies are all about. The ability to implement this on/off behavior from a single place is a plus too. Let's start by creating the proxy handler, as the following listing shows.

Listing 7.33 **Implementing the `autoHashHandler` proxy handler**

```
const autoHashHandler = (...props) => ({
    set(hashable, key) {
        if (props.includes(key) && !isFunction(hashable[key])) {
```

```
                    Reflect.set(...arguments);
Reflect.apply calls       const newHash = Reflect.apply(                   Executing the default set
calculateHash on              hashable['calculateHash'], hashable, []      behavior. Normally, it's best
the target object         );                                              to stay away from using
being proxied.            Reflect.set(hashable, 'hash', newHash);          arguments, but in this case,
                          return true;                                    arguments make the code
                      }                                                   shorter.
                  }
              })
```

In this case, we used a function to return a handler that monitors the properties we want, as shown in the next listing.

Listing 7.34   Using `autoHashHandler` to automatically rehash an object that changes

```
const smartBlock = new Proxy(block,
    autoHashHandler('index', 'timestamp', 'previousHash', 'nonce', 'data')
);

smartBlock.data = ['foo'];          This [[Set]] operation calls
smartBlock.hash;                    calculateHash and updates
                                    the block's hash value.
// e78720807565004265b2e90ae097d856dad7ad34ae1edd94a1edd839d54fa839
```

Making blocks autohashable is a nice property when you're building your block objects, but you want to make sure that you revoke this behavior as soon as a block gets mined into the chain. (Checking the hash is part of validating the tamperproof nature of a blockchain.)

MEASURING PERFORMANCE WITH REVOCABLE PROXIES

In the world of blockchains, one of the most important, time-consuming operations is validating the entire chain data structure from genesis to the last mined block. You can imagine the complexity of validating a ledger with millions of blocks, each with hundreds or thousands of transactions. Capturing and monitoring the performance of the chain's `validate` method can be crucial, but you don't want that code to litter the application code. Also, remember that `validate` is an extension through the `HasValidate` mixin, so adding the code there would mean measuring the validation time not only of blockchain, but also of each block, which we don't need. To collect these metrics, we'll use Node.js' `process.hrtime` API. We'll start by defining the proxy handler in the next listing.

Listing 7.35   Defining the `perfCountHandler` proxy handler object

```
const perfCountHandler = (...names) => {
  return {
    get(target, key) {                       Uses BigInt to
      if (names.includes(key)) {             represent integers of
        const start = process.hrtime().bigint();   arbitrary precision
        const result = Reflect.get(target, key);
        const end = process.hrtime(start).bigint();
```

```
            console.info(`Execution time took ${end - start} nanoseconds`);
            return result;
        }
        return Reflect.get(target, key);
    }
  }
}
```

`process.hrtime` is a high-resolution API that captures time in nanoseconds, using a new ECMAScript2020 primitive type called `BigInt`, which can perform arbitrary precision arithmetic and prevent any issues when operating with integer values that exceed $2^{53} - 1$ (the largest value that `Number` can represent in JavaScript).

We use this handler to instantiate our ledger object proxy. But because performance counters should be switchable (on/off) at runtime, instead of a plain proxy, we're going to use a revocable proxy. A *revocable proxy* is nothing more than an object that has a `revoke` method, aside from the actual proxy object:

```
const chain$RevocableProxy = Proxy.revocable(new Blockchain(),
    perfCountHandler('validate'));

const ledger = chain$RevocableProxy.proxy;
```

After a few blocks and transactions are added, at the end of calling `ledger.validate`, something like this prints to the console:

```
Execution time took 2460802 nanoseconds
```

Instead of printing to the console, you can send this value to a special logger to monitor your blockchain's performance. When you're done, call `chain$RevocableProxy.revoke` to switch off and remove all traps from your target blockchain object. Let me remind you that the wonderful thing about this feature is the fact that whether it's switched on or off, objects never have knowledge that any traps were installed in the first place.

A technique known as method decorators centers on the same idea. In section 7.7, we'll see how to use JavaScript's Proxy API to emulate this technique.

7.7   *Implementing method decorators*

Method decorators help you separate and modularize cross-cutting (orthogonal) code from your business logic. Similar to proxies, a method decorator can intercept a method call and apply (decorate) code that runs before and after the method call and is useful for verifying pre- and postconditions or for enhancing a method's return value.

For illustration purposes, let's circle back to our simple `Counter` example:

```
class Counter {
    constructor(count) {
        this[_count] = count;
    }
```

```
inc(by = 0) {
    return this[_count] += by;
}
dec(by = 0) {
    return this[_count] -= by;
}
}
```

We'll write a decorator specification as an object literal that describes the actions or the functions to execute before and after a decorated method runs, as well as the names of the methods to decorate. Here's the shape of this object:

```
const decorator = {
    actions: {
        before: [function],
        after: [function]
    },
    methods: [],
}
```

The before action preprocesses the method arguments, and the after action postprocesses the return value. In case you want to bypass or pass through any before or after action, the identity function (discussed in chapter 4) serves as a good placeholder.

The next listing creates a custom decorator called validation that captures the following use case: "Validate the function arguments passed to the function calls inc and dec on Counter objects."

Listing 7.36 Defining a custom decorator object with before and after behavior

```
const validation = {
    actions: {
        before: checkLimit,          ← Applies checkLimit to enforce preconditions
        after: identity              ← Leaves the method's return value untouched after it runs
    },
    methods: ['inc', 'dec']          ← Decorates both inc and dec methods
}
```

Here, we're going to apply custom behavior before the method runs and use a pass-through function (identity) as the after action. checkLimit ensures that the number passed in is a valid, positive integer; otherwise, it throws an exception. Again, we'll use the throw expression syntax to write the function as a single arrow function:

```
const { isFinite, isInteger } = Number;

const checkLimit = (value = 1) =>
    (isFinite(value) && isInteger(value) && value >= 0)
        ? value
        : throw new RangeError('Expected a positive number');
```

To wire all this code up, we use the Proxy/Reflect APIs to create our action bindings, using the get trap. The challenge is that get doesn't let you gain access to the method call's actual arguments; as you know, it gives the method reference in `target[key]`. Hence, we'll have to use a higher-order function to return a wrapped function call instead. This trick was inspired by http://mng.bz/0m7l. Let's define our action binding in the next listing.

Listing 7.37 Main logic that applies a decorator to a proxy object

```
const decorate = (decorator, obj) => new Proxy(obj, {
    get(target, key) {
        if (!decorator.methods.includes(key)) {
            return Reflect.get(...arguments);
        }
        const methodRef = target[key];
        return (...capturedArgs) => {
            const newArgs =
                decorator.actions?.before.call(target, ...capturedArgs);
            const result = methodRef.call(target, ...[newArgs]);
            return decorator.actions?.after.call(target, result) ;
        };
    }
})
```

Saves a reference to the method property for later use

Returns a wrapped method reference that we can use to capture the arguments

Applies the before action

Applies the after action

Executes the original method

Now you can see how the object behaves with the decorator applied:

```
const counter$Proxy = decorate(validation, new Counter(3));
counter$Proxy.inc();    // 4
counter$Proxy.inc(3);   // 7
counter$Proxy.inc(-3);  // RangeError
```

You can see in this example how `checkLimit` abruptly aborts the `inc` operation when it sees a negative value being passed to it. Figure 7.3 reinforces the interaction between the client API augmented with a decorator.

Decorators are extremely useful for removing tangential code and keeping your business logic clean. It's simple to see how you could also refactor use cases such as logging, password obfuscation, and performance counters as `before` or `after` advice.

In fact, a proposal for static decorators (https://github.com/tc39/proposal-decorators) uses native syntax to automate a lot of what we did here. These decorators would have the look and feel of TypeScript decorators, Java annotations, or C# attributes. You could annotate a method with `@trace`, `@perf`, `@before`, and `@after`, for example, and have all the wrapping code modularized and moved away from the function code itself. Static decorators are a feature to keep your eye on; they will significantly change the game of application and framework development. This feature is used extensively in the TypeScript Angular framework.

> **NOTE** Although you can do endless things by using reflection, whether via symbols or proxies, practice due diligence. There's such a thing as too much reflection, and you don't want your teammates who are debugging your code

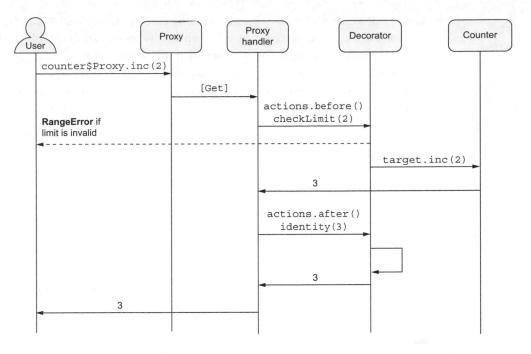

Figure 7.3   The call to `counter$Proxy.inc` **gets intercepted and wrapped with** `before` **and** `after` **actions. The method** `argument (2)` **is validated by** `checkLimit` **and allowed to pass through to the target object of** `Counter`. **Its result (** `identity(3)` **) is echoed on the way out by the** `identity` **function and is available to the caller. In the event that** `checkLimit` **detects an invalid value, however, a** `RangeError` **is returned to the caller.**

to spend hours figuring out why their code is not behaving as they expect it to, syntactically speaking. A good heuristic is duplication. When you find yourself writing the same or similar code over and over across your entire codebase, that's a good indication that you can reach into introspection and/or code weaving to refactor and modularize it.

Summary

- Metaprogramming is the art of using the programming language itself to influence new behavior or to automate code. It can be implemented statically via symbols or dynamically via code weaving.
- The `Symbol` primitive data type is used to create unique, collision-free object properties.
- Symbols make objects extensible by preventing code from accidentally breaking API contracts or the internal workings of an object.
- You can use symbols to create static hooks that you can use to alter your code's behavior with regard to fundamental operations such as looping, primitive conversion, and printing.

- JavaScript ships with native reflection APIs such as `Proxy` and `Reflect`. These APIs allow you to weave code into the runtime representation of objects dynamically without polluting their interface with other concerns.
- JavaScript's reflection APIs make it easy to develop method decorators, which allow you to implement cross-cutting behavior and modularize sources of duplication in your code.

Part 4

Data

At this point, you have an architecture with objects and functions connected to one another. All that's left is to turn the hose on and let the data flow in. As with your system of conventional PVC pipes connected to bring water to your house, your application needs to be connected to transform the input into the desired output. The complexity of connecting everything arises when you need to prepare for data that can arrive at any point in time, not only when you expect it. In other words, you don't know when someone will turn on the water, but you need to be ready for when they do.

Chapter 8 teaches you how to tame asynchronous logic with promises and direct language syntax (`async`/`await`). Promises have the advantage of being compositional objects; you can chain two or three consecutive asynchronous calls without having to worry about falling into callback hell. As the language of the web, asynchronous execution is so common that we have built-in language syntax to create `async`-aware functions with similar semantics as promises.

But the best way to emulate a connected application is to assemble the PVC pipes—virtually, that is. Chapter 9 removes the complexity of asynchronous logic to level the playing field. In this last chapter, we explore the streams paradigm to assemble functional, declarative, compositional, and fluent data flows to handle both asynchronous and synchronous data. This topic is not easy to grok by itself; you need to draw on the lessons of the previous eight chapters. For this purpose, JavaScript is introducing a proposal featuring the `Observable` object, which will allow you to treat streams of data in a consistent way. You may have had a chance to use libraries such as RxJS in the past, perhaps directly or through frameworks such as Angular. This API brings the basic component of this library directly to JavaScript.

Linear async flows 8

This chapter covers

- Reviewing a basic Node.js architecture
- Working with the JavaScript `Promise` API
- Assembling promise chains to model complex asynchronous flows
- Using `async/await` and asynchronous iterators

For over a decade prophets have voiced the contention that the organization of a single computer has reached its limits and that truly significant advances can be made only by interconnection of a multiplicity of computers.

—Gene Amdahl

As Amdhal predicted, the web is a gigantic, distributed, interconnected network, and the language we use must rise to the challenge by providing appropriate abstractions that facilitate programming this ever-evolving and ever-changing web. Programming the web is different from programming local servers, because you can't make assumptions about where the data is located. Is it in local storage, a cache, on the intranet, or a million miles away? Hence, one of the main design goals of JavaScript is that it needs to have strong abstractions for asynchronous data operations.

JavaScript developers had become accustomed to the *callback pattern*: "Here's some piece of code. Go and do something else (time) and then call it back when you're done." Although this pattern kept us going for a while (and still does), it also presented difficult and unique challenges, especially when programming on a large scale and with added complexity. One common example was when we needed to orchestrate events (such as button clicks and mouse movement) with asynchronous actions (such as writing an object to a database). It was immediately obvious that callbacks don't scale for executing more than two or three asynchronous calls. Perhaps you've heard the term *pyramid of doom* or *callback hell*.

For this book, it's expected that you are familiar with the callback pattern, so we will not get into its pros and cons. What's most important is the solution. Do we have a way to create an abstraction over callbacks that all JavaScript developers can use in a consistent manner—perhaps something with a well-defined API, such as an algebraic data type (ADT; chapter 5)? From the search for this solution, the Promise API was born, and it has become quite popular for representing most asynchronous programming tasks. In fact, new APIs, libraries, and frameworks that have any asynchronous logic are almost always represented as promises nowadays.

This chapter begins with a brief review of the architecture of a common JavaScript engine, which features, at a high-level, a task queue and an event loop. Understanding this architecture at a glance is important for understanding how asynchronous code works to provide concurrent processing. Then we move on to the Promise API to lay the foundation for JavaScript's async/await feature. With this API, you can represent asynchronous processes in a linear, synchronous way, similar to programming in a procedural style. Promises let you think about the problem at hand without having to worry about when a task completes or where data resides. Next, you'll learn how to take advantage of the composability of promises and powerful combinators to chain together complex asynchronous logic. Last, you will review the dynamic import statement (mentioned briefly in chapter 6), and look at features including top-level await and asynchronous iteration.

It's hard to talk about asynchronous programming in most programming languages without mentioning threads. That's not the case with JavaScript. What makes asynchronous programming so simple is the fact that JavaScript gives you a single-threaded model while exploiting the multithreaded capabilities of the underlying platform (the browser or Node.js). A single-threaded model is not a disadvantage, but a blessing. We'll start by taking a peek at this architecture.

8.1 *Architecture at a glance*

You may be somewhat familiar with how Node.js and most JavaScript engines work behind the scenes. Without getting into the weeds of any particular runtime implementation (V8, Chakra, or Spidermonkey), it's important to give you a high-level idea of how a typical JavaScript engine works under the hood. A typical JavaScript architecture is

- *Event-driven*—The JavaScript engine uses an event loop to constantly monitor a task queue, also known as a *callback queue*. When a task is detected, the event loop dequeues the task and runs it to completion.
- *Single-threaded*—JavaScript provides a single-threaded model to developers. There are no standard, language-level threading APIs to spawn new threads.
- *Asynchronous*—All modern JavaScript engines use multiple threads (managed by an internal worker pool) so that you can perform nonblocking I/O actions without blocking the main thread.

Figure 8.1 shows that the event loop is at the heart of this architecture. Every heartbeat or tick of the event loop picks and runs a new task or slices of a task.

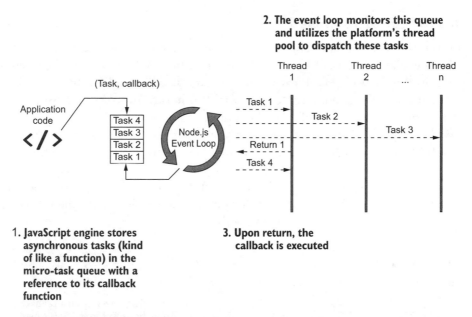

2. The event loop monitors this queue and utilizes the platform's thread pool to dispatch these tasks

1. JavaScript engine stores asynchronous tasks (kind of like a function) in the micro-task queue with a reference to its callback function

3. Upon return, the callback is executed

Figure 8.1   JavaScript's event-driven, asynchronous architecture. At the heart is the event loop (a semi-infinite loop), which is the abstraction used to handle concurrent behavior in JavaScript. The event loop takes care of scheduling new asynchronous tasks and allocating them to any threads available in the pool. When the task completes, the engine triggers the action's callback function to return control to the user.

Node.js's engine does a fine job of abstracting the execution of multiple asynchronous actions so that they appear to run simultaneously. Behind the scenes, the event loop performs fast scheduling and swapping, using its own thread to interact natively with the operating system's kernel APIs or browser thread architecture and to perform all the necessary bookkeeping of managing threads (called *workers*) in the pool. The polling loop is infinite, but it's not always spinning; otherwise, it would be resource-intensive. It starts ticking when there are events or actions of interest such as button clicks, file reads, and network sockets. When a task appears, the event loop dequeues it from the task queue and schedules it to run. Each task runs to completion and invokes the provided callback to return control to the user, along with the result (if any). This process works like a clock (literally), yet the user has no idea that any of it is happening. On the surface, JavaScript does not leak or expose any threading-related code.

Furthermore, threads can be created internally by server-side or client-side native APIs (DOM, AJAX, sockets, timers, and others) or by any third-party libraries that implement native extensions. As JavaScript developers, we are privileged to have this technology remove this complexity for us. To top it off, we have at our fingertips simple APIs that put even more layers of abstraction between us and the engine. Promise is the first line of defense against callback hell and the stepping stone to simplifying asynchronous flows.

8.2   *JavaScript as promised*

Promises were created to address the increasing complexity of having to nest callback within callback functions in favor of flattening these calls into a single, fluent expression. In this section, you'll learn how the `Promise` API simplifies the mental model of asynchronous programming. It's important to master this API, because it's the foundation of `async/await` and related features.

Simply put, a Promise object encapsulates some eventual (to-be-computed) value, much like a regular function. It is capable of delivering a single object, whether that object is a simple primitive or a complex array. Promises are similar to callbacks in that they clearly communicate "Go do something; then (time) go do something else," which makes them good candidates for one-to-one replacement. The following listing shows how you'd instantiate a new promise.

Listing 8.1   Instantiating a new `Promise` object

```
const someFutureValue = new Promise((resolve, reject) => {        ◄───
    const value = // do work...                         Promises also rely on a callback
    if(value === null) {                                function. This function is called
        reject(new Error('Ooops!'));                           the executor.
    }
    resolve(value);
});                                                  The then method allows
                                                     you to sequence multiple
someFutureValue.then(doSomethingElseWithThatValue);  ◄──┘  promises together.
```

Like callbacks, promises take advantage of the full capabilities of the JavaScript architecture. In fact, to the engine, there shouldn't be any difference. Generally, any event for which some form of callback function is provided (mouse event, HTTP request, promises, and so on) may use JavaScript's event loop. (Sometimes, for simple operations such as a `setTimeout`, a direct nonblocking system call may be used, but it is an engine-specific optimization.) The function passed to the `Promise` constructor is called the executor *function*. The executor runs without blocking the main code, and the event loop decides how to schedule the work by nicely weaving timed slices of asynchronous blocks together with the main code. Figure 8.2 depicts this process.

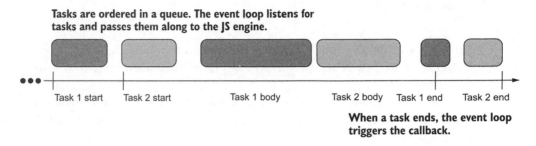

Tasks are ordered in a queue. The event loop listens for tasks and passes them along to the JS engine.

Task 1 start   Task 2 start   Task 1 body   Task 2 body   Task 1 end   Task 2 end

When a task ends, the event loop triggers the callback.

Figure 8.2   A simplified view of how the Node.js architecture handles asynchronous tasks. The event loop time slices these tasks so that code never blocks, providing the illusion of concurrency.

Every programming language nowadays supports a similar API, sometimes called a Task or a Future. The general idea is the following:

```
doSomething().then(doSomethingElse);
```

These tasks will run to completion and may take an arbitrary amount of time to run. The Promise#then method clearly communicates that promises are abstracting over time (or latency). Promises allow you to work with time in a simple manner (in plain English, if you will) so that you can focus on solving the real business issues. It helps to think of them as being the time-bound instruction separator for asynchronous calls, much like what a semicolon does with synchronous statements:

```
doSomething(); doSomethingElse();
```

Promises are ideal return wrappers for operations that may involve waiting or blocking, such as I/O or HTTP requests. In fact, the Node.js fs library has slowly evolved from using synchronous APIs to using callbacks and finally to returning promises—a good example of the adoption of this pattern over time. You can find both synchronous and asynchronous APIs to access the file system.

Let's walk through a simple example that shows this evolution, starting with the synchronous approach:

```
fs.readFileSync('blocks.txt');
```

This approach should be your least-preferred option (and the Node.js team intended it as such by explicitly labeling it Sync), as it pauses the main thread. Blocking is the opposite of scaling and goes against the event-driven, single-threaded qualities of

JavaScript. Use it with caution or only for simple one-off scripts. Second in line is the default callback version:

```
fs.readFile('blocks.txt', (err, data) => {
  if (err) throw err;
  console.log(data);
});
```

This API uses JavaScript's internal scheduler so that code never halts on the read-File call. When the data is ready, the supplied callback is triggered with the actual file contents.

An intermediate step between callbacks and a fully promise-based filesystem library is a utility called util.promisify, which adapts callback-based functions to use Promise:

```
import util from 'util';

const read = util.promisify(fs.readFile);

read('blocks.txt').then(fileBuffer => console.log(fileBuffer.length));
```

The caveat is that this utility works with *error-first callbacks*, a pattern prevalent in many JavaScript APIs, stating that callbacks should be right-biased, with the error state mapped to the left argument and the success state mapped to the right. (You learned about biased APIs in chapter 5.) Like Validation and other monads, the continuation branch (the branch to which Functor.map applies) is always on the right. This resemblance is coincidental, however. As you'll see in section 8.2.2, there's a strong connection between promises and ADTs.

Finally, there's the best approach, which is to use a built-in promisified alternative library to access the filesystem, available in Node.js as a separate namespace fs.promises:

```
import fs from 'fs';

const fsp = fs.promises;

fsp.readFile('blocks.txt').then(
    fileBuffer => console.log(fileBuffer.length));
```

Arguably, this version is a lot more fluent than the callback-based approach because code no longer appears to be nested. With a single asynchronous operation, the improvement might not be obvious, but think about the more intensive tasks that involve three or four asynchronous calls.

Now that you've seen how an API improves with the use of promises, let's dive deeper into why this API was so earth-shaking in the JavaScript world. Earlier, I said that promises wrap over values to be computed at some arbitrary time. The beauty of this abstraction, though, is that it blurs where the data resides.

8.2.1　Principle of data locality

Generally speaking, the principle of *data locality* is the idea of moving the data closer to where some computation is taking place, or vice versa. The closer the data, the faster it moves to the desired destination, through a system bus or through the internet. The varying distances between data and a computing unit, for example, are why you have different levels of caching in your CPU architecture or even in your JavaScript applications. Promises allow us to use the same programming model no matter where the data resides (local or remote) or how long a computation takes (two seconds, two minutes, or two hours). This snippet of code can read a file whether it lives locally on the server or in some remote location around the world:

```
fsp.readFile('blocks.txt').then(
    fileBuffer => console.log(fileBuffer.length));
```

We can say that promises are façades over latency and that data locality will not affect your programming model. We'll circle back to this idea when we discuss observables in chapter 9. Moreover, the idea of modeling a successful or error state is not coincidental. Remember Success and Failure for the Validation ADT in chapter 5?

8.2.2　Are promises algebraic?

In chapter 5, we studied ADTs and their importance in programming as tools to make certain types of problems composable. They're also effective at modeling an asynchronous task when we consider time to be an *effect*. In this section, you'll see that the design of ADTs helps you wrap your head around promises by automatically porting all the benefits of composability from ADTs to asynchronous code.

First, let's talk about how promises work. When a Promise object is declared, it immediately begins its work (the executor function) and sets its status internally to pending:

```
const p = new Promise(resolve => {
    setTimeout(() => {
      resolve('Done');
    }, 3000);
});

console.log(p); // Promise { <pending> }
```

When a promise settles (in this case, after three seconds), there will be only two possible states: fulfilled (resolve with a value) or rejected (reject with an error). Figure 8.3 captures all the possible states of a Promise object.

If you think about what you learned in chapter 5, Promise isn't much different from Validation. In fact, you can almost stack their diagrams, as shown in figure 8.4.

Validation also models a binary state. It assumes Success when initialized with a value and then switches depending on the outcome of the operations that are mapped

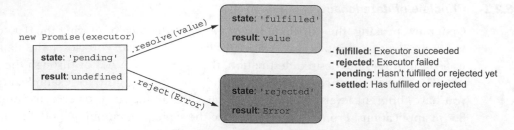

Figure 8.3   The states in which a single `Promise` object may be its life cycle

Figure 8.4   Structure of the `Validation` type. `Validation` offers a choice of `Success` or `Failure`—never both. As with promises, computations continue on the `Success` branch.

to it. You can sort of assume that the same thing happens with promises: they start as pending or fulfilled and then switch depending on what happens with each reaction or executor function passed to `Promise#then`. By the same token, if `Validation` reaches a `Failure` state, the error is recorded and the chain of operations falls through, as with `Promise#catch`.

Looking at the example from an ADT perspective, we can reason that a `Promise` is a closed context with enough internal plumbing to abstract over the effects of time. Promises follow the Promise/A+ specification (https://promisesaplus.com), with the goal of standardizing them and making them interoperable across all JavaScript engines.

Given any ADT `C`, if you think about `Promise#then` as `C.map` and `Promise.resolve` as `C.of`, many of the universal properties of ADTs continue to hold, even composability! The one small caveat is that `Promise#then` is left-biased, so it defines the fulfilled (success) callback as the left argument and the error callback as the right. The reason is usability, as most people code with fulfilled callbacks only when chaining multiple promises, using a single `Promise#catch` function at the end to handle any errors that occur at any point in the chain.

I'll briefly illustrate some of the properties that make promises ADT-like. The next listing shows some supporting helper functions used in the examples.

Listing 8.2   Helper functions used in subsequent code samples and figures

> **Takes a string of letters and removes duplicates, such as "aabb" -> "ab"**

```
const unique = letters => Array.from(new Set([...letters]));
const join = arr => arr.join('');
const toUpper = str => str.toUpperCase();
```

> **Joins an array into a string**

> **Uppercases all characters of the given string**

To prove that promises can work and be reasoned about like any ADT, here are a couple of the universal properties we discussed in chapter 5, this time using `Promise`:

- *Identity*—Executing the identity function on a `Promise` yields another `Promise` with the same value. The expressions

```
Promise.resolve('aa').then(identity);
```

and

```
Promise.resolve('aa');
```

are equivalent. Both yield

```
Promise { 'aa' }
```

- *Composition*—The composition of two or more functions, such as f after g, is equivalent to applying g first and then f. The statements

```
Promise.resolve('aabbcc')
       .then(unique)
       .then(join)
       .then(toUpper);
```

and

```
Promise.resolve('aabbcc')
       .then(compose(toUpper, join, unique));
```

are equivalent. Both yield

```
Promise { 'ABC' }
```

So if `Promise#then` is analogous to `Functor.map`, which method is analogous to `Monad.flatMap`? As you've probably noticed, `Promise#then` allows you to return unwrapped values as well as `Promise`-wrapped values; it handles both. Therefore, `Promise#then` is `Functor.map` and `Monad.flatMap` combined, with the flattening logic handled behind the scenes. The use case in the following listing showcases both scenarios.

Listing 8.3   `Promise#then` flattening a nested `Promise` automatically

```
Promise.resolve('aa')
    .then(value => {
        return `${value}bb`          ⟵──┤  Handles
    })                                      simple values
    .then(value => {
      return Promise.resolve(`${value}cc`)  ⟵──┤  Handles
    }); // Promise { 'aabbcc' }                  wrapped values
```

Can we conclude that promises are algebraic or monadic? From a theoretical perspective, they are not, because promises don't have all mathematical properties. In fact, promises don't follow the fantasy-land specification (chapter 5) that we'd expect from an ADT. But we're fortunate that on the surface, promises work the same way and that we can take advantage of this sound model of programming, which has a low barrier of entry that allows us to assemble (compose) chains of promises.

8.2.3   *Fluent chaining*

A promise chain works like any ADT and is created by subsequently calling `Promise#then` or `Promise#catch` on returned `Promise` objects. This process is shown in figure 8.5.

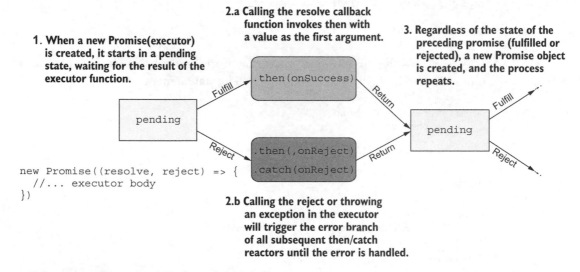

1. When a new **Promise(executor)** is created, it starts in a pending state, waiting for the result of the executor function.

2.a Calling the resolve callback function invokes then with a value as the first argument.

3. Regardless of the state of the preceding promise (fulfilled or rejected), a new Promise object is created, and the process repeats.

2.b Calling the reject or throwing an exception in the executor will trigger the error branch of all subsequent then/catch reactors until the error is handled.

```
new Promise((resolve, reject) => {
  //... executor body
})
```

Figure 8.5   A detailed view of the execution of a promise chain. Every `Promise` object starts as pending and changes states depending on the outcome of the executor callback. The result is wrapped in a new pending `Promise`. (Diagram was inspired by http://mng.bz/Xdx6.)

Each executor returns a new pending promise that changes states depending on the result of its own executor. If successful, the fulfilled values are passed to the next promise in the chain, and so on until a non-`Promise` object is returned. This process sounds a lot like composition, if you think about it.

Let's look at different scenarios of how success and error operations execute, starting with a simple scenario of a fully linked chain.

FULLY LINKED CHAIN

The following listing shows an example of passing three reaction functions that are executed only after the preceding promise succeeds. At each step, new `Promise` objects are implicitly created.

Listing 8.4 Fully linked chain of promises

```
Promise.resolve('aabbcc')
    .then(unique)
    .then(join)
    .then(toUpper);
```
Executors are called only when the preceding promise is fulfilled.

Like ADTs, promises model the conveyor-belt or railway approach to data manipulation. Every operation performs a new data transformation step and returns a new pending promise that awaits the result of its handler function. If the function is applied successfully, it settles as fulfilled. You saw a detailed flow in figure 8.5. To keep things simple for the next use case, I'll illustrate the final state of the promise at each step. Figure 8.6 describes this flow.

Listing 8.4 represents a chain with a single result, whereas listing 8.5 does not.

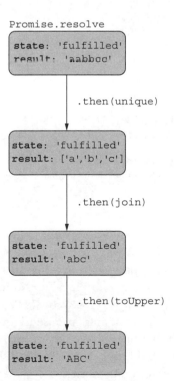

```
Promise.resolve
```
```
state: 'fulfilled'
result: 'aabbcc'
```
.then(unique)
```
state: 'fulfilled'
result: ['a','b','c']
```
.then(join)
```
state: 'fulfilled'
result: 'abc'
```
.then(toUpper)
```
state: 'fulfilled'
result: 'ABC'
```

Figure 8.6 Promise chains allow you to manipulate data as a unidirectional, forward conveyor belt where every step applies a different transformation of the data.

BROKEN CHAIN

The next listing shows a `Promise` object that never links to any other.

Listing 8.5   Broken chain of promises

```
const p = Promise.resolve('aabbcc');

p.then(unique);   // ['a','b','c']
p.then(join);     // Error
p.then(toUpper);  // 'AABBCC'
```

All executors are called when p fulfills in that order and receive the same input. This code produces three promises: two fulfilled and one rejected.

In this case, three different, disjointed `Promise` objects were created, none of them linked to the others. This code leads to a runtime error, which most likely was unintended. Figure 8.7 shows the bug and the values that would be stored inside each resulting promise.

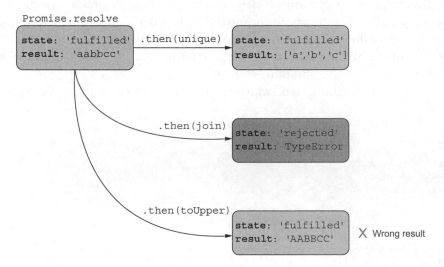

Figure 8.7   This approach does not form a chain: It's a bug. The code adds multiple handlers to the same `Promise` object, each applying one transformation to the original data, and obtains three different and unexpected results.

The example shown in listing 8.5 is a common mistake. In this approach, `unique`, `join`, and `toUpper` all receive `'aabbcc'` as input, which is not what the programmer likely intended. What happens is that the `Promise` object is passed three different reaction functions and then executes them in order against the same input value. Not only are the results incorrect, but one of the promises errors out with a `TypeError`. Let's see what would happen if we were to attach an error handler to the failing promise (figure 8.8).

As you'd expect, the `Promise#catch` handler function would apply only to the isolated `Promise` object and recover, but another one could easily fail. When tasks involve multiple asynchronous actions, it's common to see nested promises.

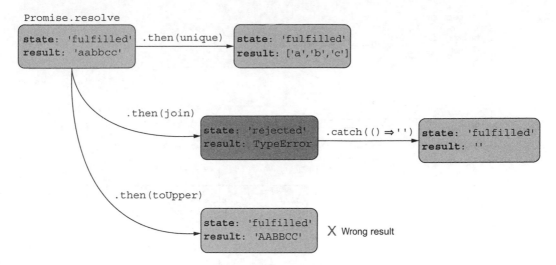

Figure 8.8 Recovering the failing promise and returning a default, empty value. This approach returns another pending promise that fulfills immediately with an empty value.

NESTED CHAINS

Suppose that you are working with some remote data store, and you want to pull data for a specific user together with their shopping-cart items and return the response as a single object. To do so, you'd need to merge data from two endpoints and combine both responses. The best option would be to use a promise combinator, which we'll look at in section 5.3. Another way would be to nest promises.

It's true that promises were designed to avoid having to write nested callbacks in favor of a flat chain. The reason why promises are much better than callbacks, though, is that a properly nested promise is still a single chained promise, indentation aside. This mental model is much easier to reason about, as the next listing illustrates.

Listing 8.6 Nested promise

```
const concat = arr1 => arr2 => arr1.concat(arr2);

Promise.resolve('aabbcc')
  .then(unique)
  .then(abc =>                                    Links with a
    Promise.resolve('ddeeff')          ◁┘        nested chain
        .then(unique)
        .then(def => abc.concat(def))
  )
  .then(join)
  .then(toUpper); // 'ABCDEF'
```

As you can see, even returning a nested promise joins back to the main chain, as shown in figure 8.9.

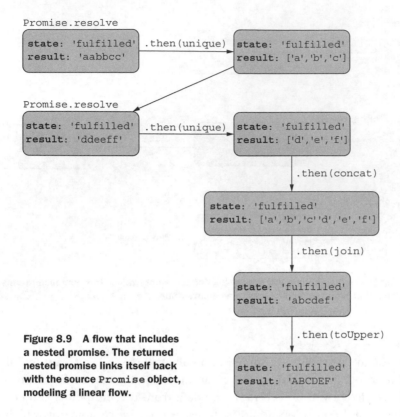

Figure 8.9   A flow that includes a nested promise. The returned nested promise links itself back with the source `Promise` object, modeling a linear flow.

The real challenge in nesting is handling errors. How you decide to structure your code depends on how you're planning your data and/or errors to propagate. Data propagates by using `Promise#then`. Errors propagate by using `Promise#then(, onRejected)` or `Promise#catch`.

Which is better: `catch` or `then`?

Each approach has pros and cons, and both work slightly differently. Generally, though, `Promise#catch` seems to be the more popular approach and also more familiar to developers from a different background, such as Java. Unless you add `Promise#catch` after every `Promise#then`, however, any errors in the chain will be handled by a downstream `Promise#catch` block, and you won't know which handler caused it. Using `Promise#then` does give you a bit more control of where the error occurred (the preceding one) at the expense of being a little less fluent, syntactically speaking. Nevertheless, both approaches follow the same chaining rules, as both return new pending promises.

JavaScript is the language of choice, after all, so use whichever approach works best for you and your coding preference. In this book, however, we'll be sticking with `Promise#catch`, because it's also in line with the downstream pattern of error handling present in observables (chapter 9).

The tricky part is determining the root promise object to which you're attaching your reaction functions. To return to our simple use case, let's cause some function in the chain to fail on purpose in the next listing.

Listing 8.7   Fully linked chain with error

```
Promise.resolve('aabbcc')
   .then(unique)
   .then(() => throw new Error('Ooops!'))
   .then(join)                                    Skipped
   .then(toUpper)
   .catch(({message}) => console.error(message));       Catch handler receives the
                                                        error object and prints Ooops!
```

The error in the third line triggers the rejection handlers downstream to the `Promise#catch` call, effectively skipping the `join` and `toUpper` steps.

The next listing shows an example of using nested promises with errors.

Listing 8.8   Nested promise chain with error

```
Promise.resolve('aabbcc')
  .then(unique)
  .then(data => {
    Promise.resolve(data)                          Nested promise fails
       .then(join)                                 with an error but
       .then(() => throw new Error('Nested Ooops!'))   goes unhandled
  })
  .then(toUpper)
  .catch(({message}) => console.error(message));       Throws property access
                                                       on undefined error
```

In this case, you'd expect the nested chain to join the main chain and print *"Nested Ooops!"* at the end. Can you spot the bug that prevents this from happening? That's right: the developer forgot to return the nested promise to be embedded properly in the chain. Now that nested promise is essentially a new rogue pending promise (figure 8.10).

This result usually happens when the author forgets to return the nested promise object or wants to use an arrow function but uses curly braces incorrectly. The following listing fixes the problem.

Listing 8.9   Rejoining the nested chain to handle the error properly

```
Promise.resolve('aabbcc')
  .then(unique)                 Removed parenthesis to
  .then(data =>                 make an arrow function
    Promise.resolve(data)
       .then(join)
       .then(() => throw new Error('Nested Ooops!'))
  )
  .then(toUpper)                              Prints "Nested Ooops!"
  .catch(({message}) => console.error(message))   to the console
```

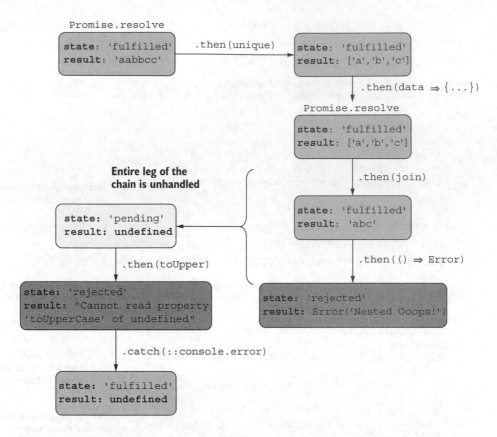

Figure 8.10   Because the developer forgot to return the Promise object, the nested promise went off on its own, and its result or error (as the case may be) would never join the main promise chain.

Now the nested promise is properly embedded in the chain, and the data (or error in this case) propagates as intended to print *"Nested Ooops!"* (figure 8.11).

The design of promises is also fluent on the Promise#catch call. This technique is useful for recovering from errors with default values. Consider the trivial fix in the following listing.

Listing 8.10   Recovering from an error with a default value

```
Promise.resolve('aabbcc')
  .then(unique)
  .then(data =>                    When you use the arrow
    Promise.resolve(data)          function, the return
      .then(join)                  statement is implicit.
      .then(() => throw new Error('Inside Ooops!'))
      .catch(error => {
        console.error(`Catch inside: ${error.message}`)
        return 'ERROR'
      })
  )
```

```
.then(toUpper)
.then(::console.log)
.catch(({message}) => console.error(message));
```

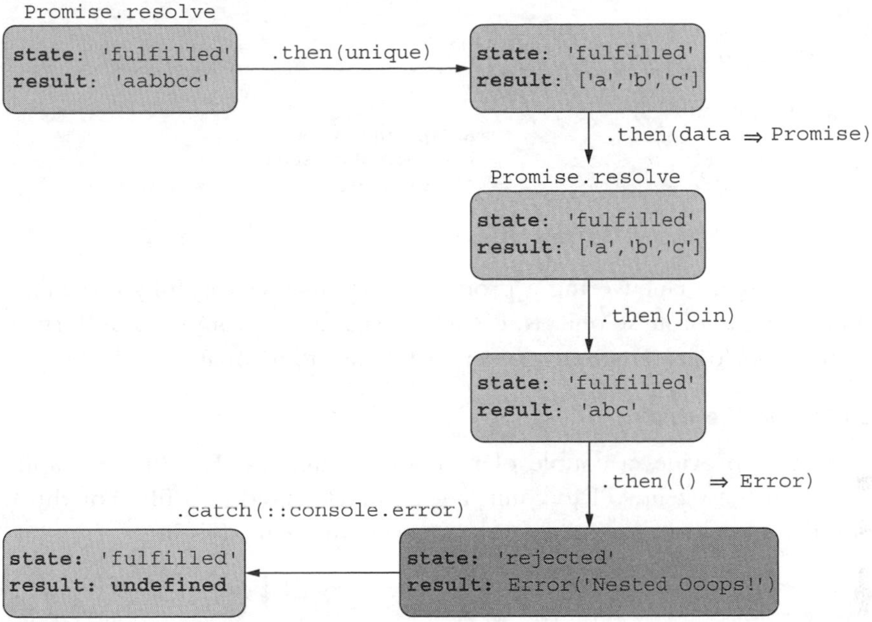

Figure 8.11 Fixing the bug effectively flattens the chain. Now each result/error is handled and accounted for.

It's important to mention that your promise chains must be able to handle error cases. If they fail to do so, JavaScript engines emit a warning (at the time of this writing). You may have seen this message in your console:

```
UnhandledPromiseRejectionWarning: Unhandled promise rejection. This error
originated either by throwing inside of an async function without a catch
block, or by rejecting a promise which was not handled with .catch().
```

```
DeprecationWarning: Unhandled promise rejections are deprecated. In the
future, promise rejections that are not handled will terminate the Node.js
process with a non-zero exit code.
```

What this message tells you is that, internally, the JavaScript engine is handling the error for you and failing gracefully. As you might expect, you wouldn't want this situation to continue forever, so if you are seeing this warning now, you're probably missing some error-handling code, and your best bet is to fix the problem right away.

Finally (no pun intended), you can end promise chains with the `Promise#finally` method. As you'd expect, the `this` callback has the same semantic structure as the finally block after a try block. The callback executed after the promises settles regardless of whether it fulfilled, as the next listing shows.

```
Promise.resolve('aabbcc')
  .then(unique)
  .then(join)
  .then(toUpper)
  .then(console.log)      ◄──┐
  .finally(() => {
    console.log('Done')   ◄──┘
  });
```

Prints 'ABC'

Always prints 'Done' regardless of the state of the promise

As you can see, maneuvering a promise chain involves carefully threading through and connecting promise objects. If you need to nest a promise to perform additional asynchronous logic, remember to connect it back to the main line.

8.2.4   *Promises in the wild*

This section provides a couple of real-world examples. The first example uses the promisified filesystem API to count all the blocks saved to a file. For this task, we'll program a function called countBlocksInFile in the next listing.

```
function countBlocksInFile(file) {
  return fsp.access(file, fs.constants.F_OK | fs.constants.R_OK)
    .then(() => {                        ◄
      return fsp.readFile(file)
    })
    .then(decode('utf-8'))
    .then(tokenize(';'))
    .then(count)
    .catch(error => {
      throw new Error(`File ${file} does not exist or you have
        no read permissions. Details: ${error.message}`)
    });
}

countBlocksInFile('blocks.txt')
  .then(result => {
    result // 3
  });
```

fsp.access does not produce a value. If access is granted, it resolves; otherwise, it rejects.

Here's another real-world example that implements the complicated logic of mining a new block into the chain. This code is complex because it mixes synchronous and asynchronous code that involves a couple of nested asynchronous operations: a long-running operation to mine a block and a dynamic import to read the mining reward setting. This service function is implemented in BitcoinService.

The code in listing 8.13 shows a crucial part of the blockchain protocol—an over-simplification, of course. It highlights the extensive work that miners need to do to gain any reward. In essence, a miner mines the new block into the chain. This mining process also runs the proof-of-work algorithm. After a successful mining, the miner would collect any rewards that were previously stored as pending transactions. After the block is inserted, a miner validates the entire blockchain structure from beginning to end. All these tasks would have run on a single miner node, which has its own copy of the entire blockchain tree. In our example, the blockchain service takes care of creating a new reward transaction and puts that transaction back into the chain as a pending transaction for the next miner to come in. All these operations can take varying amounts of time, so using promises to smooth over all of them and keep a flat, simple-to-reason-about structure is beneficial.

Listing 8.13 Mining a block in the chain

```
function minePendingTransactions(rewardAddress,
    proofOfWorkDifficulty = 2) {

  const newBlock = new Block(ledger.height() + 1, ledger.top.hash,
    ledger.pendingTransactions, proofOfWorkDifficulty);

  return mineNewBlockIntoChain(newBlock)
    .then(:: ledger.validate)
    .then(validation => {
      if (validation.isSuccess) {
        return import('../../common/settings.js')
          .then(({ MINING_REWARD }) => {
            const fee =
              Math.abs(
                ledger.pendingTransactions
                  .filter(tx => tx.amount() < 0)
                  .map(tx => tx.amount())
                  .reduce((a, b) => a + b, 0)
              ) *
              ledger.pendingTransactions.length *
              0.02;

            const reward = new Transaction(
              network.address, rewardAddress,
              Money.sum(Money('฿', fee), MINING_REWARD),
              'Mining Reward');
            reward.signTransaction(network.privateKey);

            ledger.pendingTransactions = [reward];

            return ledger;
          })
      }
      else {
        new Error(`Chain validation failed ${validation.toString()}`);
```

Mines a new block into the chain: our first async operation.

Validates the entire chain. As with fs.access, the promise resolves on a successful validation. A failed validation translates into a rejection downstream. The catch block receives the error and logs it. For more information on the bind operator, see appendix A.

Dynamically imports the settings. Dynamic import uses promises. This new nested async operation is chained back into the existing bigger chain.

Destructures the **MINING_REWARD** setting. This value is used by the blockchain system to insert a transaction that rewards the miner. This reward becomes effective when the next block is added to the chain.

More transactions mean more rewards.

Service creates a new reward transaction.

Clears all pending transactions and places reward in chain to incentivize next miners

```
      }
    })
    .catch(({ message }) => console.error(message));
}
```

Despite the complexity, at this point the chained approach should look familiar to you because we've been talking about ADTs since chapter 5 and have been building sequences of operations. Everything makes more sense when you can relate `Promise#then` as `Functor.map` and `Monad.flatMap`. Applying the right abstractions to the problem at hand makes your code leaner and more robust, which is why promises win over callbacks.

So far, I've covered single-file promise chains. Often, you'll need to handle more than one task at a time. Perhaps you're mashing up data from multiple HTTP calls or reading from multiple files. This situation leads to promise chains that introduce forks in the road.

8.3   *API review: Promise combinators*

As function combinators (`compose` and `curry`) accept functions and return a function, promise combinators take one or more promises and return a single promise. As you know, ECMAScript 2015 shipped with two incredibly useful static operations: `Promise.all` and `Promise.race`. In this section, I'll review those two APIs and introduce two new combinators that help fill in additional use cases: `Promise.allSettled` and `Promise.any`. These combinators are extremely useful for reducing complicated asynchronous flows to simple linear chains, especially when the task requires you to combine data from multiple remote sources. To illustrate these techniques better, we need to find some long-running operation we can use to put these APIs to the test.

Let me pause here to set up the code sample. In chapter 7 (listing 7.8), I showed a simple proof-of-work function. Here it is again:

```
function proofOfWork (block =
    throw new Error('Provide a non-null block object!')) {
  const hashPrefix = ''.padStart(block ?.difficulty ?? 2, '0');
  do {
    block.nonce += 1;
    block.hash = block.calculateHash();
  } while (!block.hash.toString().startsWith(hashPrefix));
  return block;
}
```

This function uses brute force to recalculate the given block's hash until its value starts with the provided prefix. At every iteration, the block's `nonce` property is updated and factored into the hashing process. This operation may occur immediately or may take a few seconds to complete, depending on how long `hashPrefix` is and on the nature of the data being hashed. Again, using promises means we don't have to worry about this operation.

The examples that we're about to see call the proof-of-work function asynchronously, using a new function called `proofOfWorkAsync`. To simulate true concurrency, we can use special Node.js libraries that implement the Worker Threads API (https://nodejs.org/api/worker_threads.html). These libraries are not part of the JavaScript language, of course. JavaScript's memory model is single-threaded, as discussed at the beginning of this chapter. Rather, these libraries use low-level OS threading processes with an abstraction called a `Worker` (a thread) to execute JavaScript in parallel.

The `worker_threads` module can help you get around this situation on the server and is similar to the Web Workers API in the browser. This function looks like the following listing.

Listing 8.14 Proof-of-work wrapper using the Worker Threads API

```
import { Worker } from 'worker_threads';
...
function proofOfWorkAsync(block) {
  return new Promise((resolve, reject) => {          ◄  Wraps the worker execution with a promise
    const worker = new Worker(<path-to-proof-of-work-script>.js, {
      workerData: toJson(block)                      ◄┐
    });
    worker.on('message', resolve);                    │  Passes serialized JSON block data to
    worker.on('error', reject);                       │  the proof-of-work script by using the
    worker.on('exit', code => {                       │  toJson helper function, which hooks
      if (code !== 0)                                 │  into the object's Symbol.for('toJson')
        reject(new Error(`Worker stopped with exit code ${code}`));  │  (see chapter 7)
    });
  });
}
```

Handles message posted back from script as a resolve

Handles error with reject

Now let's look at the code for the worker script. This script loads, calls the proof-of-work function, and posts its result back to the calling script. From the caller's point of view, the time from when the worker begins and the "message" or "error/exit" events eventually fire is hidden inside the promise, effectively removing the notion of time from the equation.

The worker code is simple; it deserializes the JSON block string message passed to it and then uses it to create a new `Block` object that `proofOfWork` requires. Finally, the result is posted back to the main thread, as shown in the next listing.

Listing 8.15 Web worker logic

```
import {
    parentPort, workerData
} from 'worker_threads';
import Block from '../../Block.js';
import proofOfWork from './proof_of_work.js';      ┐ Deserializes
                                                    │ the JSON
const blockData = JSON.parse(workerData);         ◄┘ representation

const block = new Block(blockData.index, blockData.previousHash,
    blockData.data, blockData.difficulty);
```

```
proofOfWork(block);
```
← Runs proof-of-work algorithm

```
parentPort.postMessage(block);
```
← Posts the hashed block data back to the main thread

Parallelism is beyond the scope of this book, but the main idea is that you instantiate a `Worker` with a handle to a script that performs some task in parallel. Then you use message-passing to post data (in this case, the hashed block object) back to the main thread.

The examples that you're about to see rely on running `proofOfWokAsync` passing blocks with different difficulty settings. Because we're not interested in forming a blockchain to track transactions and all the works, we can use the `Block` API directly. Also, we'll use a couple of more helper functions, one to generate random hashes to fill in the `previousHash` constructor argument for new blocks and one to simulate a rejection after some scheduled amount of time, as shown in the following listing.

Listing 8.16   Helper functions used in the next `async` examples

```
function randomId() {
  return crypto.randomBytes(16).toString('hex');
}

function rejectAfter(seconds) {
  return new Promise((_, reject) => {
    setTimeout(() => {
      reject(new Error(`Operation rejected after ${seconds} seconds`))
    }, seconds * 1_000);     ←
  });
}
```
This code uses numeric separators that make long numbers more readable, using a visual separation between groups of digits.

Because we're using a promise to encapsulate this ordeal, the caller has no idea how or where the operation is taking place; it's location-agnostic.

Let's begin reviewing promise combinators, starting with `Promise.all`.

8.3.1   *Promise.all*

You can use `Promise.all` to schedule multiple independent operations in a concurrent manner and then collect a single result when all the operations are complete. This technique is useful when you need to mash together data from different APIs as a single object, taking advantage of the internal multithreading mechanism of Node.js (discussed in section 8.1). The next listing shows an example.

Listing 8.17   Combining promises with `Promise.all`

```
Promise.all([
  proofOfWorkAsync(new Block(1, randomId(), ['a', 'b', 'c'], 1), 500),
  proofOfWorkAsync(new Block(2, randomId(), [1, 2, 3], 2), 1000)
])
  .then(([blockDiff2, blockDiff3]) => {          ←
    blockDiff2.hash?.startsWith('0');  // true
```
Returns an array of all results in the same order as the input array

```
    blockDiff3.hash?.startsWith('00'); // true
});
```

At a high level, this code looks much like the fork-join model: it starts all tasks "simultaneously," waits for them to fulfill, and then joins them into a single aggregated result. In the event of a rejection, it rejects with the first promise that rejects.

Instead of waiting for all promises to complete, suppose that you're only interested in the first operation that succeeds. In this case, you can use `Promise.race`.

8.3.2 Promise.race

This method returns a promise with the outcome of the first promise that either fulfils or rejects, with the value or reason from said promise. `Promise.race` solves interesting problems. Suppose that you're implementing a web frontend with a highly available API backend or distributed caches—a common occurrence in modern cloud deployments. You have an API backend in the US East region and one in the US West region. You can use `Promise.race` to fetch data from both regions at the same time. The region with the lowest latency wins. This situation could guarantee consistent performance of your backend as your users roam about the country.

Let's use this API to race the hashing of two blocks in the next listing.

Listing 8.18   Combining promises with `Promise.race`

```
Promise.race([
    proofOfWorkAsync(new Block(1, randomId(), ['a', 'b', 'c'], 1)),
    proofOfWorkAsync(new Block(2, randomId(), [1, 2, 3], 3))
])
.then(blockWinner => {                          ◁─────┐ Returns a
    blockWinner.hash?.startsWith('0');  // true        │ single result
    blockWinner.index;                  // 1
});
```

As you would expect, the block with the smaller difficulty value wins the race. `Promise.all` short-circuits when any promise is rejected, and `Promise.race` short-circuits when any promise is settled. By contrast, `Promise.allSettled` and `Promise.any` are less sensitive to errors, allowing you to provide better error handling. You see these combinators in action in section 8.3.3.

8.3.3 Promise.allSettled

The downside to using `Promise.all` is that the promise will reject if any of the provided promises rejects. If you're trying to load data to render multiple sections of an application, one failure means that you'll have to show error messages in all sections. If that's not what you want, perhaps you want to show an error only for the sections in which the data fetch operation failed.

As part of ECMAScript 2020, `Promise.allSettled` returns a `Promise` that resolves after all the given promises have fulfilled or rejected (settled). The result is an array of special objects that describes the outcome of each promise. Each outcome object features a `status` property (fulfilled or rejected) and a `value` property with the array of the fulfilled results, if applicable.

Let's use this API in the next listing with a promise that fulfils and one that rejects to show you how it differs from `Promise.all`.

> **Listing 8.19   Combining promises with `Promise.allSettled`**

```
Promise.allSettled([
  proofOfWorkAsync(block),            Uses setTimeout to call
  rejectAfter(2)              ◁────   reject after two seconds
]);
.then(results => {
  results.length; // 2
  results[0].status; // 'fulfilled'      First result includes
  results[0].value.index; // 1           the hashed block.

  results[1].status; // 'rejected'
  results[1].reason.message;// 'Operation rejected after 2 seconds'
});
```

Second result object includes the rejected outcome.

Up until now, you've probably used `Promise.all` to load multiple pieces of data at the same time. `Promise.allSettled` is a much better alternative because a failure won't compromise the entire promise result; it does not short-circuit. Finally, there's `Promise.any`.

8.3.4   *Promise.any*

This method is the opposite of `Promise.all`. If any promise passed in is fulfilled, regardless of any rejections, the resulting promise fulfils with the value of said promise. This API is beneficial when you care only whether a promise resolves from the collection and want to ignore any failures. `Promise.any` returns a rejected promise when all promises reject, as the next listing shows.

> **Listing 8.20   Combining promises with `Promise.any`**

```
return Promise.any([
  Promise.reject(new Error('Error 1')),
  Promise.reject(new Error('Error 2'))
])
.catch(aggregateError => {
  aggregateError.errors.length; // 2
})
```

You may think that this API behaves a lot like `Promise.race`. The small subtlety is that it returns the first resolved value (if present), whereas `Promise.race` returns the first settled (resolve/rejected) value. The one caveat is the return value. If any promise is successful, you should expect `then` to execute with the result. If all promises reject, however, `Promise#then` returns a new `Error` type called `AggregatedError` on the `Promise#catch` block, which contains an array of all failures.

At this point, you've learned how to instantiate promises, form chains, and combine the results of multiple promises. Mastering these techniques is key to designing applications that are performant and, better yet, responsive. But if promises make asynchronous programming so much easier, why not elevate them from APIs to programming-language syntax?

Section 8.4 shifts the discussion to the async/await syntax, which is a language feature that allows you to accomplish the same things you've learned about up to now.

8.4 *async made easy*

The async/await feature is designed to blur the lines between synchronous and asynchronous programming at the language level. This feature appeals to developers who prefer the imperative coding style, which uses separate statements to solve a problem, instead of one long sequence of then expressions. async/await also borrows the mental model of try/catch/finally to smooth over the then(...).catch(...) .finally(...) logic. Here's an example:

```
async function fetchData() {
  const a = await callEndpointA();
  const b = await callEndpointB();
  return {
    a, b
  };
}
```

Promises are among the building blocks of JavaScript's async/await feature. From a usability standpoint, you can think of both features as working the same way. Like promises, async functions operate in a separate order from the rest of the code via the event loop, returning an implicit Promise as its result, which you can Promise#then or await.

To understand this way of coding, refactor countBlocksInFile. As it stands now, this function returns a Promise object, and the caller is expected to process the result through the then method. Here is that function:

```
function countBlocksInFile(file) {
  return fsp.access(file, fs.constants.F_OK | fs.constants.R_OK)
    .then(() => {
      return fsp.readFile(file);
    })
    .then(decode('utf-8'))
    .then(tokenize(';'))
    .then(count)
    .catch(error => {
      throw new Error(`File ${file} does not exist or you have
        no read permissions. Details: ${error.message}`);
    });
}
```

You can refactor the function to take advantage of async/await systematically. Here are the steps:

1 Add async to the function signature. This steps communicates a Promise object's return value to the caller and makes the function self-documenting (always a good thing).

2 Move Promise#catch to its own try/catch block that wraps over the entire asynchronous logic.

3 Convert every Promise#then step to an await statement and make the input to the success function an explicit local variable. In essence, you unlink the promise chain into separate imperative statements.

The next listing shows how this function looks after the transformation.

Listing 8.21   Using `async/await` to count blocks in blocks.txt

All the await calls use promises behind the scenes, so although the code reads as though it's blocking for I/O, everything is asynchronous under the hood.

```
const fsp = fs.promises;

async function countBlocksInFile(file) {
    try {
        await fsp.access(file, fs.constants.F_OK | fs.constants.R_OK);
        const data = await fsp.readFile(file);
        const decodedData = decode('utf8', data);
        const blocks = tokenize(';', decodedData);
        return count(blocks);
    }
    catch(e) {
        throw new Error(`File ${file} does not exist or you have
            no read permissions. Details: ${e.message}`);
    }
}

const result = await countBlocksInFile('blocks.txt');
result; // 3
```

Denotes an async function that returns a Promise under the covers (required to use await in the function body)

Tests user's permissions for the specified path. Underneath, the promise will fail if the user is unable to access the file or the file does not exist.

The rejection of any await call (promise) jumps into the catch block.

Figure 8.12 shows that when the output of an awaited expression is connected to the next as input, the data flows like a promise chain.

Technically speaking, countBlocksInFile works the same as before. You can even mix the new syntax with the Promise API, and everything would work the same way:

```
countBlocksInFile('blocks.txt')
    .then(::console.log); // Prints 3
```

To clarify, the async keyword in the function signature is acting as a type definition. It's a cue to the caller and the compiler that this function needs special handling and

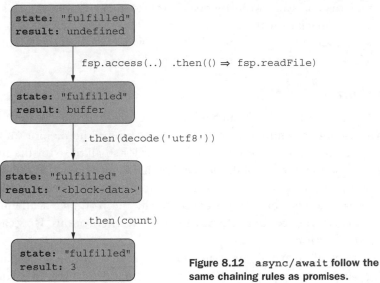

Figure 8.12 `async/await` **follow the same chaining rules as promises.**

will return a Promise. Also, the keyword `await` may be deceiving. This keyword has been standardized across many languages and makes sense from a semantics point of view. But from a technical standpoint, nothing is "waiting" or "blocking."

As mentioned earlier, `async/await` turns asynchronous code synchronous, making it more verbose and easier to read for people who prefer the imperative style. But this syntax has the same caveats as promises in that after you introduce an `async` call, every call site that leads to it needs to be `await`-ed. This drawback is easy to miss, because the code looks like a synchronous function. The same is true of errors. Rejections are easy to miss if you forget to wrap `awaited` calls inside `try/catch`. If you forget to write `await`, you'll see the underlying Promise-wrapped return value instead of the free value.

Although `async/await` promotes a more imperative style of coding, JavaScript remains flexible enough that you can use it functionally. You can use the pipeline operator to compose asynchronous calls like this one, for example:

```
const blocks = path.join(process.cwd(), 'resources', 'blocks.txt')
   |> (await countBlocksInFile)
```

In this case, the resulting path string is input into `countBlocksInFile` and awaited. The result, as expected, is an `async` value that we can unwrap with another `await` to extract its value:

```
await blocks; // 3
```

In our trivial examples so far, we've worked with small files that can be easily loaded in memory. If you need to find a particular block object, it's simple to read the file entirely into memory and work with the objects there. In the real world, this solution won't always scale, especially with larger files or in devices with much lower available memory. A better method is to stream and iterate over the file in small chunks. Section 8.5 shows how async/await can solve this problem.

8.5   *async iteration*

As simple and convenient as an API such as fsp.readFile is, these APIs don't scale to larger files because they attempt to load all the file's content into memory at the same time. You can get away with this situation on a server for small files, for the most part. But in browsers, especially on mobile devices (with reduced memory capacity), this practice is an antipattern. In these cases, you need to traverse or iterate over a file as a moving window so that you load only a chunk of the file. You face a dilemma, however: reading a file is asynchronous, whereas iteration is synchronous. How can we reconcile these two operations?

In this section, you'll learn about async iterators, which provide an elegant way to work with large amounts of data, regardless of where that data is located. The mental model is as simple as iterating through a local array.

Chapter 7 left off with simple iterators. Recall that you make any object iterable by implementing the well-known @@iterator symbol. This method returns an Iterator object with values that have the following shape:

```
{value: <nextValue>, done: <isFinished?>}
```

The JavaScript runtime hooks into this symbol and consumes these objects until done returns true. In the synchronous world, the CPU controls the flow of data in an expected, sequential way, so the value of the {value, done} pair is known at the correct times. Unfortunately, iterators and loops were not designed to work asynchronously, so we will need a little bit of extra help, as the following example shows:

```
function delay(value, time) {
    return new Promise(resolve => {
        setTimeout(resolve, time, value);
    });
}

for (const p of [delay('a', 500), delay('b', 100), delay('c', 200)]) {
    p.then(::console.log);
}
```

Following the normal loop protocol, the output should be 'a', 'b', and then 'c'. Instead, it's 'b', 'c', and then 'a'. We must communicate to the JavaScript runtime that it needs to wait to synchronize on the latency of the values being iterated over. One way is to treat the sequence of promises as a composition. Remember that composing is analogous to reducing. You can reduce the array of Promise objects into a single promise chain. reduce will aggregate a collection of elements into a single one, starting from an arbitrary initial object. In this case, we can start with an empty, fulfilled Promise object and use it to attach the reduced set of promises, forming a single chain. This approach effectively enforces execution in the expected order.

The next listing shows how to execute this task in a single expression.

Listing 8.22 Reducing an array of promises

```
[delay('a', 500), delay('b', 100), delay('c', 200)]
   .reduce(
      (chain, next) => chain.then(() => next).then(:: console.log),   ⟵
      Promise.resolve()   ⟵
   );
```
Initial object, which
becomes the first object in
the reducer chain

Reducer function concatenates the
chained promise object to the next
and prints the value.

Now the code prints the expected 'a', 'b', and then 'c', in the correct order. The way reduce is used here is incredibly elegant and terse, but it can look obtuse if you don't understand promise chaining or how reduce works (both of which are covered in this book). Let's sugar-coat this logic with async iteration as a traditional for...of loop in the following listing.

Listing 8.23 Processing an array of promises with async iteration

```
for await (const value of
      [delay('a', 500), delay('b', 100), delay('c', 200)]) {   ⟵
   console.log(value);
}
```
Note the use of
await in front of
the loop condition.

reduce helped us create the mental model for how an asynchronous loop works, which is depicted in figure 8.13.

This figure looks familiar. The await keyword in front of the loop resolves each promise so that the loop variable points to the value wrapped inside it. This syntax computes the same result as the one with reduce because it takes care of unwrapping and executing the asynchronous operation in order as part of the iteration behavior. Async iteration significantly cleans up solving complicated problems that involve working with input streams, ordering a sequence of asynchronous tasks and others.

As an example, let's rework our countBlocksInFile use case, which reads the entire file in memory, to use async iteration so that it scales to files of any size. Listing 8.24 is a bit more complex than listing 8.21, but it's well worth examining because this function can handle much larger files. Most of the complexity inside the body of the loop stems from having to deal with the integrity of the individual block objects read in chunks and figure out where one ends and the other begins.

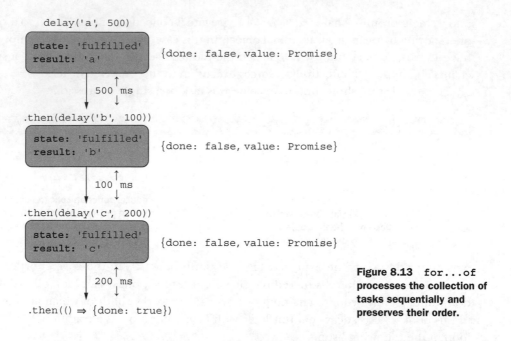

delay('a', 500)

{done: false, value: Promise}

500 ms

.then(delay('b', 100))

{done: false, value: Promise}

100 ms

.then(delay('c', 200))

{done: false, value: Promise}

200 ms

.then(() ⇒ {done: true})

Figure 8.13 `for...of`
**processes the collection of
tasks sequentially and
preserves their order.**

Listing 8.24   Counting blocks in files of any size

```
import fs from 'fs';

async function countBlocksInFile(file) {
   try {
       await fsp.access(file, fs.constants.F_OK | fs.constants.R_OK);

       const dataStream = fs.createReadStream(file,
           { encoding: 'utf8', highWaterMark: 64 });

       let previousDecodedData = '';
       let totalBlocks = 0;

       for await (const chunk of dataStream) {
          previousDecodedData += chunk;
          let separatorIndex;
          while ((separatorIndex = previousDecodedData.indexOf(';')) >= 0) {
             const decodedData =
                   previousDecodedData.slice(0, separatorIndex + 1);

             const blocks = tokenize(';', decodedData)
                   .filter(str => str.length > 0);

             totalBlocks += count(blocks);

             previousDecodedData =
                   previousDecodedData.slice(separatorIndex + 1);
          }
       }
```

**Instead of reading the entire file,
create a stream so that you can read
chunks of "highWaterMark" size.**

**For this example,
highWaterMark is set to
64 bytes so that data is
delivered in small chunks.**

**Iterates over the stream, reading
the next block of raw text**

**Handles the
block delimiter
(if present) to
obtain a clean
row of blocks**

**Starts the next row
after the last delimiter
is read to avoid reading
incomplete block data**

```
      if (previousDecodedData.length > 0) {
        totalBlocks += 1;
      }
      return totalBlocks;
    }
    catch (e) {
      console.error(`Error processing file: ${e.message}`);
      return 0;
    }
  }
```

async/await gives you the freedom to double down on the logic of the problem at hand and forget about the intricacies of asynchronous programming.

Although promises certainly are the more functional, fluent approach, async/await returns us to an imperative paradigm through the automatic wrapping and unwrapping of data. Compared with an ADT such as Validation, async is equivalent to a Success.of, await is analogous to a Validation.map (or Promise#then), and Promise#catch models the Failure state.

In listing 8.24, you saw that the object dataStream was asynchronously iterated over. You may wonder how to make your own objects async-iterable. In chapter 7, we discussed how the @@iterator symbol allows you to spread and enumerate elements of a custom object. Likewise, the @@asyncIterator symbol is executed when you use for...of with await, as before, as shown in the next listing.

> **Listing 8.25 Using async iteration with a Node.js stream object**

```
for await (const chunk of dataStream) {      ◁───┐   Invokes the asyncIterator
  //...                                            │   function-valued property
}                                                  │   of dataStream
```

dataStream has a function-valued symbol property called Symbol.asyncIterator. As of this writing, no native JavaScript APIs use this symbol, but Node.js ships with a few libraries of its own for filesystem streams and HTTP handling. As you might expect, the await on the loop call site must be matched with an async value (a promise) returned by the iterator itself. Everything you learned about the Iterator applies, with the small caveat that calls to next must return objects of {value, done} wrapped in a Promise. The next listing shows a trivial example.

> **Listing 8.26 Iterator object that emits values with a provided delay**

```
function delayedIterator(tasks) {
  return {
    next: function () {
      if (tasks.length) {
        const [value, time] = tasks.shift();      ◁───
        return new Promise(resolve => {
          setTimeout(resolve, time, { value, done: false });
        });
```

Removes the first task from the list. A task is nothing more than a value with a timeout value in the future.

Returns a promise that wraps an Iterator tuple of {value, done}

```
            } else {
              return Promise.resolve({
                done: true                    ◁──  Signals that the iterator
              });                                  should stop, as there are
            }                                      no more tasks to perform
          }
        };
      }
```

It helps to see this iterator used directly first:

```
const tasks = [
   ['a', 500],
   ['b', 100],
   ['c', 200]
];

const it = delayedIterator(tasks);

await it.next().then(({ value, done }) => {
   value; // 'a'
   done;  // false
});
```

Run it.next() two more times for tasks 'b', and 'c' to print, in that order. Finally, the last call emits the done value:

```
await it.next().then(({ value, done }) => {
   value; // undefined
   done;  // true
});
```

With Symbol.asyncIterator, we obtain the same result, shown in the following code.

Listing 8.27   Hooking into async iteration using @@asyncIterator

```
const delayedIterable = {
   [Symbol.asyncIterator]: delayedIterator
};
                                              Internally invokes
                                              @@asyncIterator
for await (const value of asyncIterable) {  ◁──
   console.log(value);
}
```

You can also take things up a notch by making next an async function:

```
function delayedIterator(tasks) {
    return {
      next: async function () {
          if (tasks.length) {
              const [value, time] = tasks.shift();
              return await delay(value, time);
          } else {
```

```
        return Promise.resolve({
          done: true
        });
      }
    }
  };
}
```

The sky's the limit in terms of what you can do when you have full control (and understanding) of the iteration behavior of your objects, especially when you have physical limitations such as bandwidth and amount of memory, which occur on slow networks and mobile devices, respectively. Chapter 9 goes one step further so that you can see how generators (and their async counterpart) blend with the iterator protocol. You can not only model a finite amount of data, but also model potentially infinite streams of data.

So far, we've discussed how to handle asynchronous tasks directly through the Promise APIs and through async/await. Most of the discussion centered on how data propagates forward through a promise chain. In this chapter, I didn't talk much about error handling, mainly because the rules are nearly the same as those for typical imperative code, and a lot of what we discussed about Promise#then applies uniformly to Promise#catch, which is a nice design trait of promises.

8.6   *Top-level await*

Generally, every await must be matched with async, but there's an exception. Some scenarios require you to initiate a call to load (await) something asynchronous as the first thing you do. Examples are dynamically loading modules and dependencies up front, such as internationalization/language bundles or a database connection handle.

Through regular async/await syntax, if you wanted to begin asynchronous tasks on script launch, you'd have to create an async context with a function and then immediately invoke it. Here's an example:

```
const main = async () => {
  await import(...);
}

main();
```

In chapter 6, we discussed Immediately Invoked Function Expressions (IIFEs), a pattern that performs function declaration and execution directly at the same time. In the same vein, we can shorten the preceding code by using an Immediately Invoked Async Function Expression (IIAFE):

```
(async () => {
  await import(...);
})();
```

Top-level `await` cleans up this code so that you can use `await` on a task without having to create an `async` function explicitly. Behind the scenes, you have one big `async` function for the entire module:

```
await import(...);
```

In chapter 6, you saw an example of a dependency fallback from a module that loads code dynamically:

```
const useNewAlgorithm = FeatureFlags.check('USE_NEW_ALGORITHM', false);

let { default: computeBalance } = await import(
    '@joj/blockchain/domain/wallet/compute_balance.js'
);

if (useNewAlgorithm) {
   computeBalance = (await
      import('@joj/blockchain/domain/wallet/compute_balance2.js')).default;
}

return computeBalance(...);
```

Top-level `await` is meant to work with ECMAScript Modules out of the box, so here's another good reason to start adopting that module format. This is understandable, because top-level `await` would require special support to create an asynchronous context for you automatically. (It helps to think of one big `async` function surrounding the entire module.) If module A imports module B, and B contains one or multiple `await` calls, A needs to wait until B finishes executing before executing its own code. Naturally, there are concerns about blocking and waiting at a critical stage of the evaluation process. (If you want to know the intricate details of this process you can read more about them at http://mng.bz/9Mwo.) As you'd expect, however, there are optimizations, so the blocking that occurs only with a dependent module does not affect loading other sibling dependencies. The event loop architecture schedules these tasks properly and yields control to the main thread to continue loading other code, as it would do with any asynchronous task. Nevertheless, developer education is key. As with dynamic `import`, use these features only when absolutely necessary.

As you can see, we've come a long way toward removing the issue of latency or time from our code. We started with the incumbent callbacks, moved on to an API-driven solution (promises), and finally saw an improvement of the language-level model via `async`/`await`. Overall, these techniques are behaviorally equivalent, and are all in line with JavaScript's nonblocking, event-driven philosophy. Remember that programming is three-dimensional: data, behavior, and time. Applications excel when data is local to the behavior or the logic that we write. But in this modern, distributed world, this problem is hardly the one you need to solve. Without the proper support of the host language, programming can quickly become unwieldy. Promises (or `async`/`await`) collapse these dimensions (data, behavior, and time) so that we can reason about our code as being two-dimensional, removing time from the equation.

Promises have some downsides, however. For starters, you can't cancel the execution of a promise in a standard way. Or should you? After all, a promise is meant to be kept. Perhaps `Future` or `Task` would have been a better name. Nevertheless, third-party libraries employ some form of internal cancellation token, but nothing has been made standard. The TC39 committee seeks a general cancellation mechanism that could apply to more than promises. You can find more information at https://github .com/tc39/proposal-cancellation.

To me, the biggest issue is that promises (async/await) are not lazy. In other words, a promise executor will run regardless of whether there's a handler function down the chain. The other issue is that promises were designed to provide single results; they can succeed or fail only once. After a promise settles, you'd need to create a new one to request or poll for more data. There are many use cases for an API that can deliver or push values to your handling code without you having to request more explicitly. This pattern is called a *stream*, which is a convenient and elegant paradigm for working with things like WebSockets, file I/O, HTTP, and user-interface events (clicks, mouse moves, and so on). Chapter 9 takes asynchronous state management to the next level.

Summary

- JavaScript is based on a single-threaded, event-driven architecture designed for scale.
- A `Promise` is a standard, nearly algebraic data type used as an abstraction or wrapper over some asynchronous task to provide a consistent programming model that is location-agnostic. Promises free you from worrying about latency and data-locality so that you can focus on the task at hand.
- Promises reuse the mechanics of callbacks and the event loop, but with much better readability.
- ECMAScript 2020 proposes enhancements to the `Promise` API's surface with the addition of `Promise.allSettled` and `Promise.any`. Both composable operators allow you to handle multiple tasks at the same time.
- `async`/`await` offers a more familiar, imperative approach to promises that convert promise chains to a sequence of statements.
- Async iterator introduces a new symbol called `@@asyncIterator`. You can use this symbol to endow any object with the capability of looping, emitting its data asynchronously. Node.js uses this symbol in its HTTP and filesystem modules, among others.
- Top-level `await` takes advantage of the ESM system to automatically create an encompassing `async` context over a module script, under which you can spawn any number of `await` calls without having to create `async` functions explicitly.

Streams programming

An Observable *is a function that takes an observer and returns a function. Nothing more, nothing less. If you write a function that takes an observer and returns a function, is it async or sync? Neither. It's a function.*

—Ben Lesh

This last chapter brings together the most important techniques covered in this book, including composable software as a whole, functional programming, mixin extensions, and reflective and asynchronous programming. Here, you'll learn how they can all come together to support a computing model known as streams programming. Streams provide an abstraction that allows us to reuse a single computing model to process any type of data source regardless of its size. Think about

260

building a real-time data application, such as a chat widget. You could set up long polling to pull messages from a server periodically, perhaps using a `Promise`-based API that you develop. Unfortunately, promises can deliver only a single value at a time, so you may receive one or two message objects (or potentially thousands if you have a chatty group), causing errors because you've exceeded the amount of data that can be transmitted in a single request. The best strategy is to set up a push solution; your application is notified when a new message is present and receives messages one at a time or in small batches. Programming with streams gives you the right level of abstraction to handle these use cases with a consistent API.

We've all been coding with streams in one way or another without realizing it. The flow of data between any piece of hardware, such as from memory to a processor or a disk drive, can be considered to be a stream. In fact, these input and output streams are used to read and write, respectively. Although this has been familiar for many years, we've never truly considered the state among the components that connect our applications—or that connect multiple applications—to be a stream.

Think about the JavaScript code you write from day to day. For the most part, the typical way to deal with state is to use a pull model. Pull occurs when a client originates a request for some piece of data it needs. This process happens asynchronously when reading from a database or a file, or querying an API. It can also happen synchronously when calling a function or looping over some data structures in memory.

The other side of the coin is the push model. With push, the client code isn't requesting data anymore; the server sends data to you. A push exchange may start with an initial pull, but after the client and server interfaces are in agreement, data can flow to clients as it becomes available—like new messages in your chat application. You may have heard of the publish/subscribe model, which is an architecture for these types of problems. A simple, useful analogy is to think of a callback function that gets called multiple times during a single request.

Push technology can make your application much more snappy and reactive. I'll come back to this notion of reactivity in section 9.3, because it's an important one. Some push examples that come to mind are server-sent events (SSE), WebSockets, and the DOM's event listeners. Imagine that instead of registering event handlers, you have to set up a timer to see when the state of a button changes to clicked. Or suppose that instead of getting notified when new message comes in, you need to explicitly click the refresh button to download new messages. We're not in the '90s anymore. When you know that data is available somewhere, you can issue a command to read it, but what happens when you don't know? It's awkward to set up polling for data that you don't know will become available (if it ever does), not to mention inefficient.

In chapters 7 and 8, I covered the concept of iterators. Here, I'll continue talking about this subject from a new angle: how it's used to represent streams of data combined with generator functions. Generators allow you to control the synchronous flow of data coming out of an iterable object (array, map, object, and so on). Also, you can emulate iterable data that can be computed on the fly.

We'll continue building on these lessons and switch gears to asynchronous itera-bles (async iterables, for short) and async generators used to compute sequences of values over time. Async iterables represent push streams and are an efficient, optimal, and memory-friendly way to read large amounts of asynchronous data (database, filesystem, or HTTP) piece by piece.

Although a push paradigm can sometimes be hard to understand, you'll see that using the same JavaScript constructs you've been learning about so far will make push more approachable. I think you'll find the stream pattern to be quite interesting and enjoyable to code with, so I'll end this chapter by looking at a new API that brings data-agnostic, reactive programming to JavaScript: `Observable`. Observables provide a single API surface to manage data flows independent of how data is generated and of its size.

First, let's talk about the Iterable and Iterator protocols in JavaScript.

9.1   *Iterables and Iterators*

Simply put, an *iterable* is an object whose elements (or properties) can be enumer-ated or looped over. As you learned in chapters 7 and 8, an iterable object defines its own `Symbol.iterator`, used to control how these elements are delivered to the caller. An iterator is the pattern or protocol that describes the structure of the itera-tion mechanism. Languages are free to define their own mechanisms for this pur-pose. In JavaScript, iteration is standardized. The following sections examine these protocols in detail.

9.1.1   *Iterable protocol*

The iterable protocol allows you to customize the iteration behavior of your objects when they appear inside a `for...of` construct or are used with the spread operator. JavaScript has built-in iterable objects such as `Array`, `Map`, and `Set`. Strings are also iter-able as an individual array of characters.

> **NOTE** Despite having similar names, `WeakSet` and `WeakMap` are not iterable (although they accept iterables in their constructors). In fact, neither extends from its non-weak counterpart (`Set` and `Map`, respectively). These APIs solve some interesting problems, but I don't cover them in this book.

An iterable object (or any object from its prototype) must implement the function-valued `Symbol.iterator`. Inside this function, `this` refers to the object being iterated over, so that you have full access to its internal state and can decide what to send during the iteration process. An interesting fact about iterables is that `Symbol.iterator` can be a simple function or a generator function. (For more information on this topic, see section 9.2.)

An iterable by itself doesn't do much without its iterator.

9.1.2 *Iterator protocol*

The *iterator* is the contract that's presented to the language runtime when iteration behavior is required. JavaScript expects you to provide a next method to an object. This method returns objects with at least two properties:

- done (Boolean)—Indicates whether there are more elements. A value of false tells the JavaScript runtime to continue looping.
- value (any)—Contains the value bound to the loop variable. This value is ignored when done is equal to true, and the sequence terminates.

If an object returned by Symbol.iterator does not abide by this contract, it's considered to be malformed, and a TypeError occurs—JavaScript's way of enforcing this particular protocol.

9.1.3 *Examples*

This section shows some examples of iterables, starting with our own Block class. As you know, this class accepts an array of data objects, which could be Transaction objects or any other type of object stored in the chain:

```
class Block {

  index = 0;
  constructor(index, previousHash, data = [], difficulty = 0) {
    this.index = index;
    this.previousHash - previousHash;
    this.data - data;
    this.nonce = 0;
    this.difficulty = difficulty;
    this.timestamp = Date.now();
    this.hash = this.calculateHash();
  }

  //...

  [Symbol.iterator]() {
    return this.data[Symbol.iterator]();
  }
}
```

If we created a block with a list of transactions, enumerating with for...of hooks into the special symbol to deliver each transaction:

```
for (const transaction of block) {
   // do something with transaction
}
```

All the main model objects of our application (Blockchain, Block, and Transaction) are iterable. This fact made it simple to create a generic validation method in the HasValidation mixin, which extends all these objects with the same interface. In chapter 5, the algorithm used APIs such as flatMap and reduce, but it created additional arrays as the validation logic flowed through the elements of the blockchain. Iterators loop over structure that's already in memory. Also, we don't have to reduce over all the elements to find out whether a failure occurred. When we find the first failure, we can break out of the algorithm early. Look at this snippet of code once more:

```
const HasValidation = () => ({
  validate() {
    return validateModel(this);
  }
});

function validateModel(model) {
  let result = model.isValid();
  for (const element of model) {
    result = validateModel(element);
    if (result.isFailure) {
      break;
    }
  }
  return result;
}
```

This implementation relies on model objects implementing Symbol.iterator. In our case, the logic was simple, as the objects delegated to their internal data structure's iterator. To see how the protocols work, let's implement a random-number generator by using the iterator schema, as shown in the next listing.

Listing 9.1   Random-number generator using an iterator

```
function randomNumberIterator(size = 1) {       ⊲─── Internal helper function
                                                     to compute the next
  function nextRandomInteger(min) {             ⊲─── random integer
    return function(max) {
      return Math.floor(Math.random() * (max - min)) + min;
    };
  }
                                                Creates a sized array
                                                and fills it with
  const numbers = Array(size)        ⊲───       random numbers
    .fill(1)
    .map(min => nextRandomInteger(min)(Number.MAX_SAFE_INTEGER));

  return {
    next() {                         Signals the
      if(numbers.length === 0) {     end of the
        return {done: true};    ⊲─── sequence
      }                                                Signals that there
      return {value: numbers.shift(), done: false};  ⊲─── are more numbers
    }                                                     to enumerate
  };
}

let it = randomNumberIterator(3);
```

```
console.log(it.next().value);    // 1334873261721158
console.log(it.next().value);    // 6969972402572387
console.log(it.next().value);    // 3915714888608040
console.log(it.next().done);     // true
```

Produces different numbers each time

Notice that the object returned by `randomNumberIterator` is an object that conforms to the iterator schema (as you can tell by the declaration of `next`), but it's not itself an iterable. To make it one, we can add `Symbol.iterator` in the next listing.

Listing 9.2   Making an object iterable with `@@iterator`

```
...
return {
  [Symbol.iterator]() {
    return this;
  },
  next() {
    if(numbers.length == 0) {
      return {done: true};
    }
    return {value: numbers.shift(), done: false};
  }
}
```

Because the object already implements next, it's enough to return itself, making it both an iterator and an iterable.

Now you can benefit from the seamless integration with `for...of`:

```
for(const num of randomNumberIterator(3)) {
  console.log(num)
}
```

This technique is powerful because the iterator protocol is data-agnostic; you can use it to implement any kind of iteration. You can represent directory traversals, graph/tree data structures, dictionaries, or any custom collection object with the simplicity of a `for...of`.

The iterable/iterator duo is ubiquitous in JavaScript, controlling how objects behave with the spread operator:

```
[...randomNumberIterator(3)];

// [ 6035653145325066, 7827953689861025, 1325390150299500 ]
```

Native, built-in types are also iterables. The following listing shows that strings behave the same way for arrays, maps, and sets. (You get the idea.)

Listing 9.3   Strings implementing `@@iterator`

```
"Joy of JavaScript"[Symbol.iterator]; // [Function: [Symbol.iterator]]

for(const letter of "Joy of JavaScript") {
  console.log(letter);
}
```

Logs all 17 characters to the console

Now, let's be honest: you've probably never heard of a random-number iterator, but you have heard of a random-number generator. Is there a difference? You will find out in section 9.2, which covers generators.

9.2   Generators

A *generator* is a special type of function. Normally, when a function returns, the language runtime pops that function off the current stack frame, freeing any storage allocated for its local context. Generator functions work the same way but have a slight twist: it seems as though its context sticks and resumes to return more values. In this section, we'll review what generator functions are, how to use them to create iterables that can send new values from thin air, and how to use them to create async iterables.

9.2.1   *To return or to yield*

A generator is a factory function of iterators. First, you can define a generator function by placing an asterisk (*) after the `function` keyword

```
function* sayIt() {
  return 'The Joy of JavaScript!';
}
```

or before a method name:

```
class SomeClass {
  * sayIt() {
    return 'The Joy of JavaScript!';
  }
}
```

These functions aren't too useful, but are useful enough to show that generators look like any regular functions. So what's with the special syntax? There's a twist in the return value. Run this function to see what you get:

```
sayIt(); // Object [Generator] {}
```

As you can see, that special syntax augments the return value with an object called `Generator`, not a string, as the normal function would have. Syntactically, this process is similar to how an `async` function augments (or wraps) the value in a `Promise`.

Like the simple `randomNumberIterator` example, `Generator` is itself an iterable and an iterator; it implements both protocols. Therefore, to extract its value, we need to call `next`:

```
sayIt().next(); // { value: 'The Joy of JavaScript!', done: true }
```

Now you can recognize the shape of the iterator protocol. Simply using an iterator of one value (done: true) is not that interesting, however. The `function*` syntax is there so that you can produce many values, via a process called *yielding*. Consider this variation:

```
function* sayIt() {
  yield 'The';
  yield 'Joy';
  yield 'of';
  yield 'JavaScript!';
}

const it = sayIt();
it.next(); // { value: 'The', done: false }
it.next(); // { value: 'Joy', done: false }
    ...
```

> **NOTE** Currently, there's no support for generator functions using lambda syntax. This lack of support may seem to be a flaw in the design, but it's not: lambda expressions are really meant to be simple expressions, and most are one-liners. It's rare to have generator functions be that simple. There is, however, a proposal to include support for generator arrow functions: http://mng.bz/yYWq.

And, of course, because `Generator` implements `Symbol.iterator`, you can stick it inside a `for...of` expression:

```
for(const message of sayIt()) {
  console.log(message);
}
```

In sum, a generator is nothing more than a simple way to create an iterator. Generators and iterators work seamlessly. The code looks like it's invoking the same function many times and somehow resuming where it left off, but it's only a function. Behind the scenes, you're consuming the iterable object that the function returns, and `yield` pushes new values into the iterator.

9.2.2 Creating iterable objects

In this section, you'll see how to integrate iterables to enhance the domain model of the blockchain application. You can add a generator helper function to `Blockchain` that can emit as many fully configured empty blocks as you want, for example. You can use this function to create chains of any size and perhaps use them for testing and running simulations.

The next listing defines a simple `newBlock` generator. The `Blockchain` class is a bit complex at this point, so I'll show only the pertinent bits.

Listing 9.4 Custom generator function

```
class Blockchain {
  #blocks = new Map();
```

```
...
    * newBlock() {          ◄─┐ Uses the generator syntax
        while (true) {          on a function method
            const block = new Block(    ◄── Looks like an infinite loop but is not. The
              this.height(),                 generator function is able to "pause"
              this.top.hash,                 its execution on yield, so the runtime
              this.pendingTransactions       doesn't keep executing infinitely.
            );
            yield this.push(block);    ◄── Pushes a new block to
        }                                  the chain and returns it
    }
}
```

The caller code calls `newBlock` 20 times to produce 20 new blocks, making the total
height of the chain 21 (remember to count the first-ever genesis block), as shown in
the following listing.

Listing 9.5 Using generators to create an arbitrary amount of new blocks

```
const chain = new Blockchain();
let i = 0;
for (const block of chain.newBlock()) {
    if (i >= 19) {
        break;                ◄── Stops after creating
    }                             20 blocks
    i++;
}
chain.height(); // 21    ◄──┐ 20 new blocks plus
                            genesis = 21
```

Furthermore, the frictionless integration between generators and iterators makes
using the spread operator and its counterpart destructuring assignment a terse, idiomatic way to read properties from any custom object. We can implement naive
pattern-matching expressions on algebraic data types (ADTs) such as `Validation`,
implemented in chapter 5. First, let's make `Validation` iterable and use generators to
return its `Failure` and `Success` branches, respectively. This ADT is biased to the right,
so the `Success` branch results from the second call to `yield`; otherwise, you can
reverse this order. `Symbol.iterator` is implemented like this:

```
class Validation {
  #val;

  ...

  *[Symbol.iterator]() {
    yield this.isFailure ? Failure.of(this.#val) : undefined;
    yield this.isSuccess ? Success.of(this.#val) : undefined;
  }
}
```

Choice ADTs, such as `Validation`, can activate only one branch at a time and omit the other. Those destructuring assignment statements look like the next listing.

Listing 9.6 Using destructuring assignment to extract success and error states

```
const [, right] = Success.of(2);          ◄─┐ Destructuring
                                              assignment that
right.isSuccess;  // true                     ignores the left      Destructuring
right.get();      // 2                         result               assignment
                                                                    that ignores
const [left,] = Failure.of(new Error('Error occurred!'));  ◄─┘      the right result

left.isFailure;    // true
left.getOrElse(5); // 5
```

Consider some simple use cases for both branches. Suppose that you're calling some validation function. For the `Failure` case, you could use destructuring with default values as an alternative to calling `left.getOrElse(5)`:

```
const isNotEmpty = val => val !== null && val !== undefined ?
    Success.of(val) : Failure.of('Value is empty');

const [left, right = Success.of('default')] = isNotEmpty(null);

left.isFailure; // true
right.get();    // 'default'
```

As you can see, iterators and generators (together with symbols) unlock idiomatic coding patterns. When you need to control how an object emits its own properties, these features make your code much more expressive and simpler to read.

As JavaScript supports async iterables by making `next` return promises, it also supports async generators, as we'll discuss in the next section.

9.2.3 *Async generators*

An *async generator* is like a normal generator, except that instead of yielding values, it yields promises that resolve asynchronously. Hence, an async generator is useful for working with `Promise`-based APIs that allow you to read data asynchronously in chunks, such as the `fetch` API in browser (which is a mixin, by the way) or the Node.js built-in "stream" library. In the next example, you'll see the difference between working with a normal async function and an async generator function.

To obtain an async generator, combine all the keywords we've covered in this chapter into a single function signature:

```
async function* someAsyncGen() {

}
```

The results returned from the generator are promises, so you need to use `for await` `...of` syntax to consume it. The next listing shows a function that uses async iteration.

Listing 9.7   Using async iteration to count the blocks in a file

```
async function countBlocksInFile(file) {
  try {
    await fsp.access(file, fs.constants.F_OK | fs.constants.R_OK);

    const dataStream = fs.createReadStream(file,
      { encoding: 'utf8', highWaterMark: 64 });

    let previousDecodedData = '';
    let totalBlocks = 0;

    for await (const chunk of dataStream) {
      previousDecodedData += chunk;
      let separatorIndex;
      while ((separatorIndex = previousDecodedData.indexOf(';')) >= 0) {
        const decodedData =
            previousDecodedData.slice(0, separatorIndex + 1);

        const blocks = tokenize(';', decodedData)
            .filter(str => str.length > 0);

        totalBlocks += count(blocks);

        previousDecodedData =
            previousDecodedData.slice(separatorIndex + 1);
      }
    }
    if (previousDecodedData.length > 0) {
      totalBlocks += 1;
    }
    return totalBlocks;
  }
  catch (e) {
    console.error(`Error processing file: ${e.message}`);
    return 0;
  }
}
```

> dataStream is an async iterable object, which means that every chunk of data is a value in the shape of the iterator protocol, wrapped by a promise.

This function returns a count of the blocks read from a file. A more helpful, useful function would return the block objects themselves so that you could do much more than count. Maybe you could validate the entire collection of blocks.

The following listing shows a slightly refactored version that removes the counting bits. Also, it uses a generator that yields each JSON object describing each block. Let's call this function generateBlocksFromFile.

Listing 9.8   Async generator that sends blocks read from a file

```
async function* generateBlocksFromFile(file) {
  try {
    await fsp.access(file, fs.constants.F_OK | fs.constants.R_OK);
```

> async function* creates an async iterator.

```
            const dataStream = fs.createReadStream(file,
                { encoding: 'utf8', highWaterMark: 64 });

            let previousDecodedData = '';

            for await (const chunk of dataStream) {
                previousDecodedData += chunk;
                let separatorIndex;
                while ((separatorIndex = previousDecodedData.indexOf(';')) >= 0) {

                    const decodedData = previousDecodedData.slice(0,
                        separatorIndex + 1);

                    const blocks = tokenize(';', decodedData)
                        .filter(str => str.length > 0)
                        .map(str => str.replace(';', ''));

                    for (const block of blocks) {
                        yield JSON.parse(block);
                    }
                    previousDecodedData = previousDecodedData.slice(
                        separatorIndex + 1);
                }
            }
            if (previousDecodedData.length > 0) {
                yield JSON.parse(previousDecodedData);
            }
        }
        catch (e) {
            console.error(`Error processing file: ${e.message}`);
            throw e;
        }
    }
}
```

Yields all parsed blocks as objects

Now the counting logic becomes extremely trivial, as the next listing shows.

Listing 9.9 Using `generateBlocksFromFile` as an async iterator

```
let result = 0;
for await (const block of generateBlocksFromFile('blocks.txt')) {
    console.log('Counting block', block.hash);
    result++;
}
result; // 3
```

Each call to the generator pulls out a new block object from the file stream.

Again, the beauty of this change is that we can do much more than count; we can also validate each block as it's being generated. This process is efficient because we don't have to read the entire file at the same time, but process it as a moving window of data. Working with data this way is known as a stream.

Suppose now that we want to use this function to validate all the blocks in the chain. `Blockchain` creates its own genesis block upon construction, so the first thing we'll do is skip the first block that comes in. Next, we'll convert the JSON object representation of a block to a `Block` object that's added to a chain; this process is called *hydration*. The validation logic checks whether a block is positioned properly in a chain. Finally, it calls `validate` mixed from `HasValidation`. The test file I use in the repository (blocks.txt) has three blocks, so we'll be validating only the remaining two. All the logic in the next listing is shown in figure 9.1.

Listing 9.10 Validating a stream of blocks generated from a file

```
let validBlocks = 0;
const chain = new Blockchain();          ◁——  Validation of each block assumes
let skippedGenesis = false                     that the blocks are part of a chain.
for await (const blockData of generateBlocksFromFile('blocks.txt')) {
    if (!skippedGenesis) {
        skippedGenesis = true;                 Skips the first block in the test file
        continue;              ◁——            because it's a genesis block from a
    }                                          different chain instance
    const block =
        new Block(blockData.index, chain.top.hash, blockData.data,
            blockData.difficulty);

    chain.push(block);          ◁——  Blocks need to be pushed
                                     into a chain for validation.

    if (block.validate().isFailure) {   ◁⌐  Validates each block by using
        continue;                             HasValidation#validate
    }
    validBlocks++
}

console.log(validBlocks) // 2
```

The diagram in figure 9.1 captures this flow at a high level. As you can see, two generator functions are at work. The first function calls `fs.createReadStream`, and the second function calls `generateBlocksFromFile`, which uses the first function to deliver its own data.

In this section, we continued to build on the lessons of chapter 8 with more asynchronous capabilities. We discussed how to use the (async) iterator protocol, symbols, and generator functions to create iterable objects. These objects can enumerate their state upon request when they become the subject of a simple `for` loop.

> **NOTE** It's worth mentioning that we haven't discussed other use cases involving generators, such as pushing values into generators and linking generator functions. Generators are functions, so you could return a generator from another or accept a generator as an argument. These techniques can be used to solve a complex class of problems that are beyond the scope of this book. Check this link to find out about these other use cases: http://mng.bz/j45p.

Async generator functions can yield values asynchronously, like emitting events. When an event source sends lots of values in a sequence, this sequence is also called a stream.

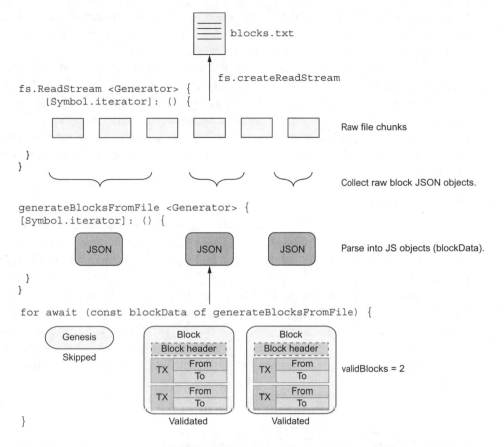

Figure 9.1 The two generator functions. One reads a file and yields binary chunks of data. The other processes each raw block, creates `Block` objects from them, validates each one, and tallies the result.

9.3 *Working with data streams*

What do objects of `String`, `Array`, `Map`, and a sequence of WebSockets events have in common? In a typical programming task, not much. When we're talking about a stream of data, at a fundamental level, however, these types of objects can be treated the same way. In fact, this consistent programming model that allows you to work across data sources makes streams necessary. Some real-world examples in which streams are compelling include

- Interacting with multiple asynchronous data sources (REST APIs, WebSockets, storage, DOM events, and others) as a single flow
- Creating a pipeline that applies different transformations to the data passing through it
- Creating a broadcast channel in which multiple components can be notified of a particular event

In situations like these, in which every single interaction is asynchronous and part of the same flow, using async generators to wrap every action is a daunting task, and the callback pattern won't scale well to this level of complexity.

In this section, we'll learn the basics of streams and the APIs needed to represent them. JavaScript's `Observable` API provides the necessary interfaces to build great reactive abstractions to process data from any push-based data sources. By the end of this section, you'll know how to transform an object into a stream so that you can manage its data through chains of `Observable` objects. You'll understand how any complex data source can be abstracted and processed as though it were a simple collection of events.

9.3.1 *What is a stream?*

To understand this concept, you must first understand how data arrives or is consumed by an application. Generally speaking, data is push or pull. In both cases, you have a producer (that creates the data) and a consumer (that subscribes to that data).

In a pull system, the producer, which could be as simple as a function, doesn't know how or when data is needed. So the consumer must pull from (or call) the producer. On the other hand, in a push system, the producer is the one in control of when an event is sent (a button was clicked, for example), and the consumer (subscriber) has no idea when it will receive said event. We say that the consumer *reacts* to the event (figure 9.2).

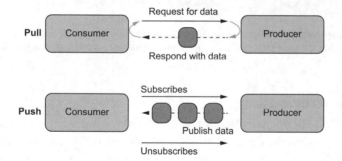

Figure 9.2 **The difference between pull and push. With pull, the consumer must always initiate a request for data. With push, when the consumer subscribes, the producer sends data as it becomes available, stopping when the consumer unsubscribes or when there's no more data to send.**

Table 9.1 summarizes pull, push, and the JavaScript features typically used in those cases.

Table 9.1   **JavaScript features to handle push and pull data**

	Single	**Multiple**
Pull	Function	`Symbol.iterator`
Push	`Promise`	`Symbol.asyncIterator` | stream

The pull techniques in table 9.1 are simple to understand. Pull happens when a function is invoked or an iterator's `next` is called many times. A simple push scenario, by contrast, occurs when asynchronous values are represented with a `Promise` object. Here, the promise (the producer) controls when the event will be emitted, abstracting this logic from a consumer. The consumer becomes the handler function passed to `next`. We can say that the function subscribes to the promise. If a promise sets a time-out function to three seconds to resolve, for example, its value is emitted three seconds from the last event handled by the event loop. The producer knows and is in control of emitting this value.

In table 9.1, a promise represents a single push, whereas an async generator can emit multiple values with different time functions. Promises and async generators are in full control of the rate at which these events will be emitted. The `for await...of` loop acts as a permanent subscription to both of these data sources behind the scenes. You can imagine the async generator as being the producer, which will emit its values at its own convenience, and the async iterator as being the consumer. Recall how listing 9.8 sets up a data stream:

```
const dataStream = fs.createReadStream(file,
    { encoding: 'utf8', highWaterMark: 64 });
```

Later, the code consumes that data stream, using `for await...of`.

Now let's raise the level of abstraction with streams. Streams solve the same problem, but in a way that makes it easier to reason about. A stream is a sequence of one or infinitely many pieces of data, called events. In this context, the word *event* does not refer only to a mouse drag or button click; it's used in the general sense to mean any piece of data. An event is some value (synchronous or asynchronous) that gets emitted over time by some source (event emitter, generator, list, and so on) and handled by a subscriber or observer.

As streams are sequences of values over time, they can nicely wrap over any producer, manifesting as a single string or even a complex async generator. On the consuming end, we can abstract over them by using `for await...of` via an object known as a `Subscription`. Subscriptions are like iterators in that you can call them as many times as you want to notify them when data becomes available, such as a call to `next`. With a stream, we talk about subscribers, not consumers. To facilitate building up this abstraction, let's warm up by creating a streamable object using arrays in the next section.

9.3.2 Implementing a streamable array

Now that you understand the basics of a stream, let's come back to the part of listing 9.8 that declares the data stream and study it more closely:

```
const dataStream = fs.createReadStream(file,
    { encoding: 'utf8', highWaterMark: 64 });
```

The Node.js API `fs.createReadStream` returns an object of `fs.ReadStream`, which in turn extends from `stream.Readable`.

> ### Node.js streams
> The stream module is a relatively new, built-in Node.js library for working with read/write streams of data. Stream objects come equipped with `Symbol.asyncIterator` properties to make consuming its data easy. You can find more information about this library at https://nodejs.org/api/stream.html.

If you peek at this API documentation, two properties stand out for the purposes of this chapter: an `on` method that emits the `'data'` event and the `Symbol.asyncIterator` method. Here's an example:

```
dataStream.on('data', chunk => {
  console.log(`Received ${chunk.length} bytes of data.`);
});
```

This interface suggests that this object is both an async iterable and an `EventEmitter`. I haven't covered event emitters in this book, but I'll review the basics quickly to support the examples in this chapter. An `EventEmitter` is an API that allows you to separate the creation of some object from its use—a rudimentary form of publish/subscribe. The following listing shows an example.

Listing 9.11 Basic use of an `EventEmitter`

```
const myEmitter = new EventEmitter();

myEmitter.on('some_event', () => {          ◄── Consumer of the data (subscriber).
  console.log('An event occurred!');            This process is similar to handling,
});                                              say, an onClick event.

myEmitter.emit('event');          ◄──  Producer of
                                       the data
```

By combining `EventEmitter` and `Symbol.asyncIterator`, we can implement a real push solution. The emitter in this case is a nice technique for separating the method that handles pushing new data (such as `push`) from the method that handles a subscriber to this data (such as `subscribe`). Arrays, for example, are pull data structures because they have functions and properties to pull its data (`indexOf` and indexing, respectively) as well as to implement `Symbol.iterator` for pulling multiple values (refer to table 9.1). If you want to run some code in response to a new value (a process called reacting), you must set up some kind of long polling solution that peeks at the status of the array at a time interval, which is not the most optimal solution. For efficiency, let's invert this flow. Instead of picking at the data, we'll subscribe to it so that it lets us know when it has a new value (a process called notifying).

  Let's extend from `Array` with push semantics by configuring an internal `EventEmitter` that fires an event every time a new value is added. Consider a class called `PushArray` that exposes two new methods to enable subscription: `subscribe` and unsubscribe. The subscribe method accepts an object that implements a next(value) method, shown in the next listing.

Listing 9.12 Subclass of `Array` that fires events when a new elements is pushed

```
class PushArray extends Array {

    static EVENT_NAME = 'new_value';

    #eventEmitter = new EventEmitter();

    constructor(...values) {
        super(...values);
    }

    push(value) {
        this.#eventEmitter.emit(PushArray.EVENT_NAME, value);     ⟵┘   Emits the
        return super.push(value);                                        new value
    }                                                                    pushed

                                                        Uses destructuring to
                                                        extract the next method
    subscribe({ next }) {                          ⟵───  from the object passed in
        this.#eventEmitter.on(PushArray.EVENT_NAME, value => {
            next(value)           ⟵┐
        });                         When the emitter fires a
    }                               new value, it's pushed
                                    to the subscriber.
    unsubscribe() {
        this.#eventEmitter.removeAllListeners(PushArray.EVENT_NAME);
    }
}

const pushArray = new PushArray(1, 2, 3);

pushArray.subscribe({
    next(value) {
        console.log('New value:', value)
        // do something with value
    }
});
pushArray.push(4);
pushArray.push(5);

pushArray.unsubscribe();

pushArray.push(6);
```

Removes all subscribers. Any further push events will not be emitted. → `unsubscribe()`

Prints 'New value: 4' and 'New value: 4' to the console. Array now has 1,2,3,4, 5.

Unsubscribes from the push array object

Subscriber does not get notified of the event. Array now has 1,2,3,4,5, 6.

Let's closely examine the call to subscribe in this example. The idea of a subscriber is central to the stream paradigm, which always requires two actors: a producer and a subscriber. When the number 4 is pushed to the array, the event emitter fires and immediately notifies the subscriber (figure 9.3).

The call to subscribe accepts an object with the shape shown in listing 9.13.

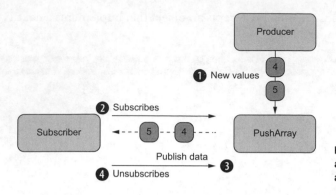

Figure 9.3   The basic flow of a push object with producer and subscriber

Listing 9.13   Subscribers accepting objects with a `next` method

```
{
    next: function (value) {            ⟵──┐  Using property syntax instead
        // do something with value          │  of shorthand, because it's
    }                                        │  more descriptive
}
```

This object is called an observer, and it's no coincidence that the name of the method is `next`. Observers align not only with the Iterable/Iterator protocols, but also with the protocol behind a push generator, which I'm omitting in this book to keep the discussions brief. If you follow this topic more closely, you'll learn that generators can not only yield values, but also allow you to push values back. Here's a link if you want to read more about the topic: http://mng.bz/WdOw.

Hence, the shape of the observer with the `next(value)` method has the sole purpose of keeping this protocol and makes the transition to stream-based programming fluid. The JavaScript API for representing a stream is known as `Observable`.

9.4   *Welcoming a new native: Observable*

At the time of this writing, a proposal slowly moving through the ranks may dramatically change the way we code on a day-to-day basis (https://github.com/tc39/proposal -observable). Some people say it has already changed the way we use third-party, stream-oriented libraries, RxJS being my favorite. This project has deeply penetrated the Angular, Vue, React, Redux, and other web communities.

In this section, we'll discuss the current status of the `Observable` API. This API supports the reactive streams paradigm, which creates a layer of abstraction over any data type and size, regardless of whether the mechanism is push or pull or whether data arrives synchronous or asynchronously.

You may have used reactive programming through RxJS if you've worked with frameworks such as Angular and React or state management libraries such as Redux. If you haven't, at a high level, observables have these two qualities, which I'll build on in the following examples:

- *Data propagation*—Data propagation naturally follows the pub/sub model. You identify a publisher (known as the source), which can be a generator or a simple array. The data stream propagates or flows in a single direction all the way to a subscriber. Along the way, you can apply business logic that transforms data according to your needs.
- *Declarative, lazy pipeline*—You can statically represent the execution of a stream regardless of publisher and subscriber, and pass it around like any other object in your application. Unlike promises, an observable object is lazy, so until a subscriber subscribes, nothing runs.

Observable streams can be hard to understand; they require strong JavaScript skills and a solid understanding of the value of composable code. Fortunately, I've covered all these topics (and more) in this book, and I'll reuse a lot of what you've already learned as I discuss how to use this API.

The following list summarizes these concepts (and if you skipped any of them, I highly recommend that you go back to the chapters that covered them to read about them):

- Observables are compositional objects, so you can combine them or create new observables from existing ones. You'll create a mixin that extends the base functionality of `Observable`'s prototype. Object composition and mixin extension are covered in chapter 3.
- Observable operators are pure, composable, curried functions. Any side effects should be carried out by subscribers. Pure functions, composition and currying are explained in chapter 4.
- The design of the `Observable` API draws on the design of ADTs, particularly in its use of `map`. Chapter 5 shows how to design your own ADT and how to implement universal protocols such as `Functor.map` and `Monad.flatMap`.
- Part of the specification defines a new function-valued built-in symbol called `Symbol.observable`. Objects that implement this special symbol can be passed to the `Observable.from` constructor. Implementing custom symbols and using built-in symbols are covered in chapter 7.
- An observable models a unidirectional, linear stream of data. Chapter 8 discusses how to create chains with promises to streamline and flatten asynchronous flows and to make them easier to reason about.

With all the foundational concepts behind us, let's dive into an observable stream in the next section.

9.4.1 What is an Observable?

In this section, we'll learn what an `Observable` is and unpack its main components. As a simple example, consider the snippet of code in the next listing.

Listing 9.14   Creating and subscribing to an `Observable`

```
const obs$ = Observable.of('The', 'Joy', 'of', 'JavaScript');

const subs = obs$.subscribe({
  next: ::console.log
});

subs.unsubscribe();
```

> Logs every word to the console and uses the unary form of the bind operator to pass a properly bound console.log function

Can you guess what will happen? This listing is the simplest possible example that uses observables. Notice the resemblance between this code and the `PushArray` class. If you guessed that it prints each individual word to the console, you nailed it! But how did you arrive at this conclusion? What assumptions did you make?

An `Observable` object is designed to model a lazy, unidirectional, push-based data source (such as streams).

> **NOTE**   It's worth pointing out that observables are different from the technology known as Web Streams (https://streams.spec.whatwg.org). Although the technologies have some of the same goals, observables offer an API to wrap over any data source, which could be a Web Stream but doesn't have to be.

You can think of data as being a river that flows downstream from some source to a destination. The conduit or the context in which this flow happens is the `Observable`. Along the way, the flow changes course, speed, and temperature until it arrives at its destination. These points of inflexion are known as operators, which I haven't shown yet.

There's no point in transmitting any data if there's nobody on the other side to receive it, however, which is why observables are lazy and wait for the call to `subscribe` to set things in motion.

The `Observable` constructor `Observable.of` lifts an iterable object and returns a `Subscription` object with the shape shown in the next listing.

Listing 9.15   `Subscription` declaring a method to `unsubscribe` from the stream

```
const Subscription = {
  unsubscribe () {
  //...
    }
}
```

> Used to cancel the subscription (the stream) at any time

> The body of this function is supplied by the producer of the data.

This simple interface declares a single `unsubscribe` method. The logic of this method is specific to how the data is being generated. If the data is sent intermittently by `setInterval`, for example, `unsubscribe` takes care of clearing the interval.

On the other side of the river, the `Observer` object is a bit more complex than a regular iterator but behaves in much the same way. The next listing shows the contract.

Listing 9.16   Shape of the `Observer` object

```
const Observer = {
  next(event) {
  //...
  },
  error(e) {
  //...
  },
  complete() {
  //...
  }
}
```

> Receives each event
> in the stream

> Triggered when an exception occurs
> somewhere along the observable

> Called when there are no more
> values to emit; not called on error

Together, `Observable`, `Observer`, and `Subscription` make up the skeleton framework being standardized by TC39. Libraries such as RxJS extend this framework to provide a programming tool belt to handle the types of tasks at which streams excel. In the next section, we'll use this interface to implement more examples with observables.

9.4.2   Creating custom observables

The static constructor functions `Observable.{of, from}` can be used to wrap or lift most JavaScript built-in data types (such as strings and arrays) or even another `Observable`. This interface is a basic one. From here, you can instantiate a new, empty `Observable` directly to define your own custom streams. This technique is used in case you want to wrap over, say, a DOM event listener and emit events through the `Observable` API. Perhaps you have created some `EventListener` objects that you want to combine. The next listing shows an `Observable` that emits random numbers every second and the subscriber that handles each event.

Listing 9.17   Using observables to emit random numbers

```
function newRandom(min, max) {
    return Math.floor(Math.random() * (max - min)) + min;
}

const randomNum$ = new Observable(observer => {
    const _id = setInterval(() => {
      observer.next(newRandom(1, 10));
    }, 1_000);

    return() => {
      clearInterval(_id);
    };
})

const subs = randomNum$
    .subscribe({
      next(number) {
          console.log('New random number:', number);
      },
```

> Returns a random
> number between
> min and max

> Uses the new keyword to
> instantiate an Observable
> with a custom observer

> A SubscriptionFunction.
> The body of this function
> is executed when calling
> subs.unsubscribe.

```
        complete() {
            console.log('Stream ended');
        }
    });

  // some time later...

  subs.unsubscribe();
```

In this snippet of code, `randomNum$` initially holds an inert `Observable` object waiting for a subscriber. The `Observable` constructor has not yet begun executing. Also, you may have noticed the dollar sign ($) used at the end of the variable name. No `jQuery` is being used here; $ is a convention indicating that this variable holds a stream. Later, the call to `subscribe` kicks off the stream so that new random numbers print to the console. This process happens infinitely until clients call `unsubscribe`. So-called marble diagrams have become a popular way of illustrating how events are emitted through an observable, as shown in figure 9.4.

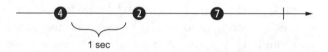

Figure 9.4   The unidirectional flow of an observable is depicted as an arrow. You can think of the producer and subscribers (not shown but implied) as being on the left and right sides, respectively. Events (marbles) move across the observable.

Each marble indicates an event that happens over time—in this case, a new random number emitted every second. In place of a random number every second, you could have events such as mouse coordinates, enumerations of the elements of an array, chunks of an HTTP response, filenames in a directory traversal, keystrokes, and so on.

At this writing, the observable specification defines rules and a skeleton only for `Observable` and `Subscriber`. In the real world, you'll need much more. Without a library like RxJS, you can't do much. You need functions that can operate on the data. These functions are called operators.

9.4.3   *Building your own reactive toolkit*

When data starts flowing through a stream, an operator allows you to process that stream before the data reaches a subscriber. An operator represents the twists and turns. The current proposal doesn't define any built-in set of operators, but it does define two important rules about observables that we must follow: laziness and composition. Operators extend observables and capture the business logic of your application. In this section, we'll create our own mini RxJS library and learn how to implement our own custom operators that extend the `Observable` prototype. If you follow the code in GitHub, all operators will be defined in a module called `rx.js`.

The way we're going to design these operators is in line with the patterns and principles of ADTs. Comparing `Observable` with `Validation`, you can see a static lifting operator called `Observable.of` (like `Validation.of`). And although `Observable` doesn't declare any methods other than `subscribe`, the proposal makes it clear that observables are composable objects. Do you recall the `map`/`compose` correspondence discussed in chapter 4? What's more compositional than a `map` operator? By design, this higher-order function gives us the ability to transform the data flowing through the observable pipeline. You can use this function to add a timestamp to each event emitted, remove fields from the event object, compute new fields on the fly, and so on.

MAP OPERATOR

The `map` operator applies a given function, `fn`, to each value emitted by an observable source. This behavior matches the behavior of any ADT and even simple arrays. I've discussed `map` at length in this book, so I'm not going to review the laws that oversee it. Let's cut straight to the chase and implement `Observable`'s version of `map`.

Remember from chapter 5 that `map` always returns a new copy of the derived constructor. For `Observable`, you need to make sure that the source's (the calling observable's) observer and the new observer are linked so that one's `next` feeds into the other's `next`. Think about this concept for a moment: it's function composition all over again, whereby one function's return value is connected to the input of the next. This linkage creates data propagation, and the goal of every operator is to allow data to continue flowing from a producer downstream to a consumer.

Let's define `map` as a standalone operator and then bind it to `Observable.prototype` to enable the fluent pattern of ADTsin the next listing.

Listing 9.18 Custom `map` operator

```
const map = curry(
    (fn, stream) =>
        new Observable(observer => {
            const subs = stream.subscribe({
                next(value) {
                    try {
                        observer.next(fn(value));
                    }
                    catch (err) {
                        observer.error(err);
                    }
                },
                error(e) {
                    observer.error(e);
                },
                complete() {
                    observer.complete();
                }
            });
```

map is structure-preserving and immutable, so it returns a new Observable whose subscription is tied to the source.

Subscribes to the source stream

Per the definition of map, applies the given function to each value emitted by the source observable and notifies observers of any errors

Propagates any errors that occurred from the source observable downstream

Currying is used to partially bind the mapping function to any stream. Currying will simplify the design of the operators to allow for standalone use as well as instance methods.

Emits the complete event from the source observable

```
        return () => subs.unsubscribe();
    });
);
```

> **Returns this subscription's SubscriptionFunction so that a call to unsubscribe downstream cancels all the midstream observables**

From the point of view of an operator function, the producer is the stream object that came before it, and the subscriber the observer object that's passed in (with a `next` method). Every operator is like `map` in that it creates a new `Observable` that subscribes to the previous one with an `Observer`, building a downstream chain. Every event is propagated downstream by calling the observer's `next` method along the way until it reaches the final observer: the subscriber. The same thing happens for `error` and the final `complete` event. By contrast, calls to `unsubscribe` bubble upstream, canceling every observable object in the chain.

The point of making `map` a standalone function is merely a design decision that resembles what you would see in a project such as RxJS. This decision gives you the flexibility to use `map` as a standalone function or as a method, which is how the latest versions of RxJS export it.

The next listing shows a simple use case that applies a `square` function over each number emitted by a stream by using the standalone version of `map`.

> **Listing 9.19   Using observables to map a function over a number sequence**

```
import { map } from './rx.js';

const square = num => num ** 2;

map(square, Observable.of(1, 2, 3))
    .subscribe({
        next(number) {
            console.log(number);
        },
        complete() {
            console.log('Stream ended');
        }
});
```

> **Prints 1, 4, and 9, followed by "Stream ended"**

The marble diagram in figure 9.5 illustrates this concept.

> **Reading marble diagrams**
>
> A marble diagram is closely tied to the Reactive Extension (Rx) community to explain how an operator works. We're going to be using a small subset of this notation. The only component of a marble diagram to understand for the purposes of this book is that a marble represents an event or a piece of data. The horizontal arrow represents time, and the space between marbles is the time between emissions, which can be synchronous (immediate) or asynchronous. The operator function (large rectangles)

acts on a specific marble and produces a new one if needed, placed on a new timeline arrow. If the operation is synchronous, it maps to the same point in time; otherwise, it shifts forward in time, depending on the operator. The `map` operator here is instant, for example, whereas an operator like `delay` (not covered) can shift the event by some provided time period. If you want to read more about this tool, you can find good resources at https://rxmarbles.com and http://mng.bz/8NzB.

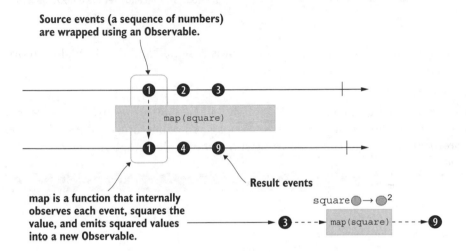

Figure 9.5   This example shows creating an observable with numbers 1, 2, and 3. As is, this code emits these numbers synchronously. The space between the marbles is added for visualization purposes.

Building on this example, the next listing and figure 9.6 showcase the composability of streams.

Listing 9.20   Composing observables

```
const add = curry((x, y) => x + y);

const subs = map(square, map(add(1), Observable.of(1, 2, 3)))    ← Composes two calls to map
    .subscribe({
        next(number) {
            console.log(number);    ← Prints 4, 9, and 16, followed by "Stream ended"
        },
        complete() {
            console.log('Stream ended');
        }
    });
```

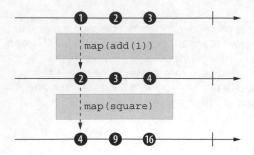

Figure 9.6   **The composition of two operators. Three instances of an observable (arrow) are shown: the source observable and two operators. Each operator subscribes to the previous stream and creates a new observable.**

Now that you understand how an operator is designed and visualized, let's move on to another operator: `filter`.

FILTER OPERATOR

After you've been through `map`, `filter` should be straightforward. Like `Array#filter`, this operator selects which values get propagated depending on the Boolean result of a predicate function. The next listing shows the implementation.

Listing 9.21   Custom `filter` operator

```
const filter = curry(
    (predicate, stream) =>
        new Observable(observer => {
            const subs = stream.subscribe({
                next(value) {
                    if (predicate(value)) {
                        observer.next(value);        ◁── If the predicate returns a
                    }                                     truthy result, the value is
                },                                        kept; otherwise, the event
                error(e) {                                is not emitted.
                    observer.error(e);
                },
                complete() {
                    observer.complete();
                }
            })
            return () => subs.unsubscribe();
        });
);
```

As you can see, most of the domain-specific logic resides in the observer's `next` method, propagating the result to the next operator in the chain, and so on. The next section jumps ahead to complete the triad with `reduce`.

REDUCE OPERATOR

The `reduce` operator reduces or folds all the values emitted by a source observable to a single value that's emitted when the source completes. The result is an observable of a single value, as shown in the following listing.

Listing 9.22 Custom `reduce` operator

```
const reduce = curry(
    (accumulator, initialValue, stream) => {
        let result = initialValue ?? {};              ◁──  Creates a new object
        return new Observable(observer => {                 when initialValue is
            const subs = stream.subscribe({                 null or undefined
                next(value) {
                    result = accumulator(result, value);
                },
                error(e) {
                    observer.error(e);
                },
                complete() {
                    observer.next(result);
                    observer.complete();
                }
            })
            return () => subs.unsubscribe();
        });
    };
);
```

Applies the accumulator callback, like Array#reduce (annotation for `result = accumulator(result, value);`)

Emits the accumulated result and sends the complete signal to end the stream (annotation for `observer.next(result);` and `observer.complete();`)

SKIP OPERATOR

The `skip` operator allows you to ignore the first *X* number of events from a source observable. The next listing shows the implementation of that operator.

Listing 9.23 Custom `skip` operator

```
const skip = curry(
    (count, stream) => {
        let skipped = 0;
        return new Observable(observer => {
            const subs = stream.subscribe({
                next(value) {
                    if (skipped++ >= count) {
                        observer.next(value);
                    }
                },
                error(e) {
                    observer.error(e);
                },
                complete() {
                    observer.complete();
                }
            })
            return () => subs.unsubscribe();
        });
    }
);
```

At this point, we've added `map`, `filter`, `reduce`, and `skip` operators. Believe it or not, with these operators we can tackle a wide range of programming tasks. Here's an example that shows them used together:

```
import { filter, map, reduce, skip } from './rx.js';
const obs = Observable.of(1, 2, 3, 4);

reduce(add, 0,
    map(square,
        filter(isEven,
            skip(1, obs)
        )
    )
)
.subscribe({
    next(value) {
        assert.equal(value, 20);
    },
    complete() {
        done();
    }
});
```

You can see the composable nature of these operators. When you're building complex chains, this type of layout is hard to parse. Normally, full-featured reactive libraries like RxJS feature a `pipe` operator that makes writing all operators straightforward. An alternative is to use dot notation to write these chains fluently, similarly to how we chained `then` methods on promise chains. To do so, we'll need to extend the built-in `Observable` object.

9.4.4   *Observable mixin extension*

Let's again use the technique of concatenative mixin extension we talked about in chapter 3, which allows us to extend any object with new functionality. First, we'll create a small toolkit module from these operators as an object mixin, calling it `Reactive-Extensions`, as shown in the next listing.

> Listing 9.24   Defining the shape of our mini-rxjs toolkit

```
export const ReactiveExtensions = {
    filter(predicate) {
        return filter(predicate, this);
    },
    map(fn) {
        return map(fn, this);
    },
    skip(count) {
        return skip(count, this);
    },
    reduce(accumulator, initialValue = {}) {
        return reduce(accumulator, initialValue, this);
```

Exported as a member of the rx.js module

Refers to the standalone versions created within the same module

```
    }
}
```

Now the extension is a simple prototype extension, like `Blockchain` and other model objects. `Object.assign` comes to the rescue once again:

```
Object.assign(Observable.prototype, ReactiveExtensions);
```

> **WARNING** Again, use caution when monkey-patching JavaScript built-in types, because doing so makes your code harder to port, upgrade, or reuse. If you're still keen on doing it for any reason, please write the required property existence checks so that you don't break upgrades.

For the joy of it, let's use the reactive extensions to create an observable chain. Listing 9.25 creates a simple stream out of a finite set of numbers; each number is an event.

As you can see, events flow downstream through the pipeline one at a time. Along the way, these chained, composable operators manipulate the data and form a chain in which one operator subscribes to the preceding operator's observable.

Listing 9.25 Using observable operators to manipulate a number sequence

```
Observable.of(1, 2, 3, 4)              Skips the first
    .skip(1)                           element, which is 1
    .filter(isEven)
    .map(square)                       Tests whether the number is
    .reduce(add, 0)                    even, if it is let it through. In
    .subscribe({                       this case, 2 and 4 make it
        next: :: console.log           through.
    })
                                       Computes the square of
                        Prints 20 to   each number (4 and 16,
                        the console    respectively)
```

Adds all of the events together (20)

Figure 9.7 illustrates how events flow through the pipeline.

The use of composition is an existential quality of streams, which allows you to chain the multiple internal subscriptions that are happening inside each operator and manage them as a single subscription object.

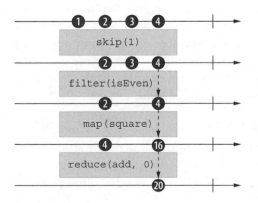

Figure 9.7 The composition of four operators, with the data (marbles) changing in response to the application of those operators. Every step of the way, a new Observable is created, and observers are connected.

Now that you've seen how to join multiple operators (figure 9.7), let's review how data flows unidirectionally downstream. If you were to visualize each operator as a black box, you'd see that although the data flows downstream, subscription objects flow upstream, starting from the last call to subscribe all the way up to the source (the initial Observable object). This last call to subscribe kick-starts everything and notifies the source to begin emitting events. Figure 9.8 explains the order of events.

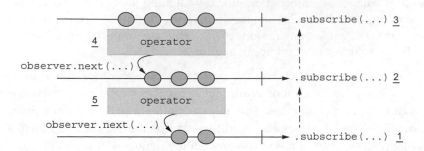

Figure 9.8   A chain of observables. Data flows downstream as observers call the next one's next(…), while subscriptions flow upstream starting with the last call to subscribe(). Steps are numbered to show how the last call to subscribe() causes all operators to subscribe internally to one another upstream, notifying the source observable to begin sending events down.

So far, we've been dealing with arrays, which are relatively simple event sources. But the rubber meets the road when we start to deal with asynchronous, potentially infinite data sources such as async generators. In place of Observable.of(1,2,3), which acts like the stream source for the operations we showed previously, we can have a generator that, after the subscribe is called on the composed observable, starts feeding values down the chain. The infinite nature of streams is in principle similar to that of generators in that until a generator returns, the function will continue to yield items indefinitely. Each call to yield in turn calls the observer's next; finally, return (implicit or explicit) calls complete.

Hence, the generator produces events over time and decides how much data to push, the observable represents your business logic, and the subscriber consumes the resulting event value flowing through the observable. Using generators is a good way to experience how to subscribe to a potentially infinite data source like a DOM event listener or receiving messages from a WebSocket. With observables, processing events from any of these data sources will look exactly the same.

9.4.5   *Representing push streams with generators*

Generators create an interesting opportunity to use streams programming, because you can generate arbitrary amounts of data and feed it to the observables all at the same time or in chunks. Previously, we dealt with examples that lifted an array of values into an observable. Now we need to be able to lift a generator function into the observable. To onboard a generator function, we'll create a simple, homegrown constructor function.

Listing 9.26 defines a new static function, `Observable.fromGenerator`. This function takes a normal generator or an async generator. We're going to use Node.js's `stream.Readable` API to abstract over the generator function with consistent behavior. This API is ideal because it uses an event emitter internally to fire events when new data is available. When the generator yields new values, `Readable` fires an event that is pushed to any subscribers that are listening. We'll create a one-to-one mapping between the data and end events and the `next` and `complete` observer methods, respectively. The use of the bind operator syntax (introduced in chapter 5) makes this mapping elegant and terse, because you can pass the bound methods directly as named functions as callbacks to those events.

Listing 9.26 Constructing `Observables` from a generator

```
Object.defineProperty(Observable, 'fromGenerator', {
   value(generator) {
      return new Observable(observer => {
         Readable
            .from(generator)
            .on('data', :: observer.next)
            .on('end',  :: observer.complete);
      });
   },
   enumerable: false,
   writable: false,
   configurable: false
});
```

- Instantiates a Readable stream from a generator object
- Passes the event value directly to the bound observer's next method
- When the stream has ended (generator returns), notifies the observer that the stream has completed

Let's put this new constructor into action with the example shown in the next listing.

Listing 9.27 Initialzing an observable with a generator function

```
function* words() {
   yield 'The';
   yield 'Joy';
   yield 'of';
   yield 'JavaScript';
}

Observable.fromGenerator(words())
   .subscribe({
      next: :: console.log,
});
```

This code would work exactly the same way if `words()` were an async generator (`async function* words`). Time is the undercurrent of a stream, and if the events are separated by seconds or nanoseconds, the programming model is the same.

Now we have a static constructor operator that lifts any generator function and a few operators to process events. Let's tackle a more complex example with these tools. Back in listing 9.8, we wrote code that validated a stream of blocks read from a file. Here's that code again:

```
let validBlocks = 0;
const chain = new Blockchain() ;
let skippedGenesis = false;
for await (const blockData of generateBlocksFromFile('blocks.txt')) {
   if (!skippedGenesis) {
      skippedGenesis = true;
      continue;
   }
   const block = new Block(
      blockData.index,
      chain.top.hash,
      blockData.data,
      blockData.difficulty
   );
   chain.push(block);

   if (block.validate().isFailure) {
      continue;
   }
   validBlocks++;
}
```

Using the small reactive extensions toolkit we've built so far, we can tackle this rather complex imperative logic and take advantage of the declarative, functional API that observables promote. When you compare the two listings, you'll see the dramatic improvement in code readability. Listing 9.28 makes the following key changes:

- Refactors the skip logic at the beginning of the loop using skip
- Moves block creation logic into a different function and calls it by using map
- Uses filter to emit only the valid blocks

Listing 9.28 Validating a stream of blocks using observables

```
const chain = new Blockchain();

// helper functions
const validateBlock = block => block.validate();
const isSuccess = validation => validation.isSuccess;
const boolToInt = bool => bool ? 1 : 0;

const addBlockToChain = curry((chain, blockData) => {
   const block = new Block(
      blockData.index,
      chain.top.hash,
      blockData.data,
      blockData.difficulty
   )
```

```
        return chain.push(block);
    });

    // main logic
```

Skips the first block (genesis)

Validates block

Keeps only valid blocks

```
const validBlocks$ =
    Observable.fromGenerator(generateBlocksFromFile('blocks.txt'))
        .skip(1)
        .map(addBlockToChain(chain))
        .map(validateBlock)
        .filter(prop('isSuccess'))
        .map(compose(boolToInt, isSuccess))
        .reduce(add, 0);

validBlocks$.subscribe({
        next(validBlocks) {
            if (validBlocks === chain.height() - 1) {
                console.log('All blocks are valid!');
            }
            else {
                console.log('Detected validation error in blocks.txt');
            }
        },
        error(error) {
            console.error(error.message);
        },
        complete() {
            console.log('Done validating all blocks!');
        }
    });
```

Adds block to chain (needed for validation algorithm)

Adds total valid blocks

The successful validation result is mapped to a number (Success = 1 | Failure = 0), so it can be added up in the next step.

Listing 9.28 instantiates a source observable validBlocks$ from a generator. This variable holds a specification of your program. I use the word *specification* because the observable captures your intent declaratively into an object whose logic hasn't yet executed. It starts by skipping the genesis block; then it maps a couple of business logic functions needed to validate; finally, it counts only blocks for which Validation returned successfully. This logic is simpler to parse, declarative, and point-free, and your code is much more modular than before. Also, you get error handling for free through the Observer's error method.

We can optimize this code even more. Can you spot where? If you recall the map/compose equivalence, you'll remember that you can fuse multiple calls to map into a single call by using compose. I'm going to show only the Observable declaration, for brevity:

```
Observable.fromGenerator(generateBlocksFromFile('blocks.txt'))
    .skip(1)
    .map(compose(validateBlock, addBlockToChain(chain)))
    .filter(prop('isSuccess'))
    .map(compose(boolToInt, isSuccess))
    .reduce(add, 0)
    .subscribe({...})
```

This version is simpler to visualize. Figure 9.9 shows how a complex algorithm can be converted to a stepwise application of functions.

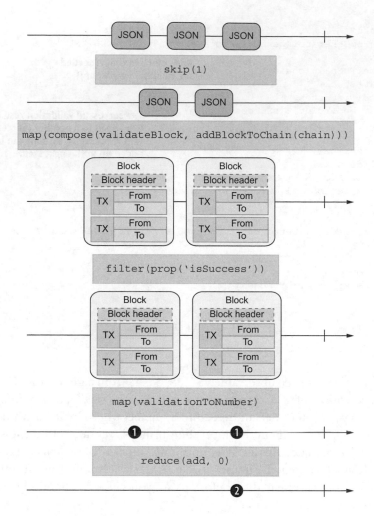

Figure 9.9   Validating blocks by using streams

Furthermore, I mentioned that observables have built-in error handling. For the sake of completeness, here's a simple example of how errors are handled. When an exception occurs anywhere in your pipeline, the error object propagates downstream to the last observer and triggers the `error` method:

```
const toUpper = word => word.toUpperCase()

function* words() {
    yield 'The'
```

```
      yield 'Joy';
      yield 'of';
      yield 42;
}

Observable.fromGenerator(words())
    .map(toUpper)
    .subscribe({
      next: :: console.log,
      error: ({ message }) => { assert.equal('word.toUpperCase is not a
        function', message) }
    })
```

As you'll recall from chapter 5, ADTs also skip business logic when validation fails so that you can handle the error from a single location, as the next listing shows.

Listing 9.29 Skipping mapped functions on `Validation.Failure`

```
const fromNullable = value =>
    (typeof value === 'undefined' || value === null)
        ? Failure.of('Expected non-null value')
        : Success.of(value);                        Returns 'Success (J)'

fromNullable('j').map(toUpper).toString();  ◁────   Skips toUpper function and
                                                    returns 'Failure (Expected
fromNullable(null).map(toUpper).toString();  ◁──    non-null value)'
```

Once again, the comparison of observables and ADTs is uncanny, which is why it was so important to understand ADTs before observables.

Let's talk a bit more about operators. A library like RxJS will provide an arsenal of operators for most of your needs, if not all of them. In the years I've worked with it, I've rarely needed to add my own operator, but it's good to know that the library is extensible in this way. These operators are designed to accept observables as input and return new observables, which is why they are called pipeable operators.

9.4.6 Pipeable operators

Observable operators are also known as pipeable functions—functions that take an observable as input and return another observable. You've seen how these functions are executed through composition and fluent chaining. In the near future, you will be able to synthesize observables with the pipeline syntax (|>) natively in pure, idiomatic, vanilla JavaScript without the help of any combinator functions, as shown in the next listing.

Listing 9.30 Combining observables with the new pipeline operator

```
import { filter, map, reduce, skip } from './rx.js';

Observable.of(1, 2, 3, 4)
    |> skip(1)
    |> filter(isEven)
```

```
|> map(square)
|> reduce(add, 0)
|> ($ => $.subscribe({ next: :: console.log }));
```

Prints the value
20 to the console

Now we're really kicking into hyperstream! But wait. Instead of a simple number sequence, what would happen if the data were asynchronous? Would the model break? Absolutely not. This code

```
async function* words() {
    yield 'Start';
    yield 'The';
    yield 'Joy';
    yield 'of';
    yield 'JavaScript';
}

Observable.fromGenerator(words())
    |> skip(1)
    |> map(toUpper)
    |> ($ => $.subscribe({ next: :: console.log, complete: done }));
```

prints

```
THE
JOY
OF
JAVASCRIPT
```

In this case, the observable and promises provide the right level of abstraction so that you can deal with time or latency as though it didn't exist. This code prints the right result and in the right order.

Alternatively, you can use bind (::) syntax to perform method extraction from our catalog of reactive extension methods. Here's that object again with map:

```
const ReactiveExtensions = {
    ...
    map(fn) {
        return map(fn, this);
    }
    ...
}
```

With the bind operator, we can control the binding of this, much as we would a virtual method. The next listing shows the same program as listing 9.30.

Listing 9.31 **Combining observables with the new bind operator**

```
const { skip, map, filter, reduce } = ReactiveExtensions;

const subs = Observable.of(1, 2, 3, 4)
    :: skip(1)
    :: filter(isEven)
    :: map(square)
    :: reduce(add, 0);
```

this points to the source observable
Observable.of(1, 2, 3, 4).

Each function's this will be set to
the preceding observable source.

```
subs.subscribe({
    next(value) {                          Prints 20 to
        console.log(value);    ◁──┘        the console
    }
});
```

In this snippet of code, `Observable.of(...)` becomes the `this` reference in `skip`, creating a new `this` reference in `filter`, and so on. It's simple to see how a collection of elements or a generation function can be converted to a stream, but what about custom objects?

9.4.7 *Streamifying objects*

In chapter 8, you learned that you can create iterable objects or async iterable objects by implementing the built-in `Symbol.iterator` or `Symbol.asyncIterator`, respectively. These symbols allow objects to be enumerated by a `for...of` loop. It would be nice if you could do something similar so that you can treat an object like an `Observable`. This capability would allow us to treat any custom object in our program as an observable and enjoy all the nice capabilities I have been describing, such as composition, powerful operators, declarative API, and built-in error handling.

It turns out that we can. The TC39 observable specification proposes the addition of another well-known function-valued symbol: `Symbol.observable` (`@@observable` for short). The semantics are consistent with those of other symbols. This new symbol works in conjunction with `Observable.from` to lift any custom objects that need to be interpreted as observables. The symbol follows a couple of rules:

- If the object defines `Symbol.observable`, `Observable.from` returns the result of invoking that method. If the return value is not an instance of `Observable`, it's wrapped as one.
- If `Observable.from` can't find the special symbol, the argument is interpreted as an iterable, and the iteration values are delivered synchronously when `subscribe` is called—a sensible fallback.

I'll show a couple of examples now, beginning with adding `Symbol.observable` to our custom `Pair` object in the next listing. I'll omit the other symbols and properties.

Listing 9.32   Adding `@@observable` to `Pair`

```
const Pair = (left, right) => ({
    left,
    right,
    [Symbol.observable]() {
        return new Observable(observer => {
            observer.next(left);
            observer.next(right);
            observer.complete();
        });
    }
});
```

```
Observable.from(Pair(20, 30))                    ◄──────
  .subscribe({
     next(value) {
        console.log('Pair element: ', value);
     }
  });
```

> Because Pair's @@observable property returns an Observable object, the source becomes the result of invoking it. It prints Pair element: 20 and Pair element: 30

A `Blockchain` can also become a stream of blocks. Any time a new block is added to the chain, it pushes into the stream, and any subscribers are notified. The next listing shows a similar configuration to the `PushArray` example in section 9.3.2.

Listing 9.33   Streaming blocks in a blockchain

```
class Blockchain {
  blocks = new Map();
  blockPushEmitter = new EventEmitter();
  constructor(genesis = createGenesisBlock()) {
    this.top = genesis;
    this.blocks.set(genesis.hash, genesis);
    this.timestamp = Date.now();
    this.pendingTransactions = [];
  }


  push(newBlock) {
    newBlock.blockchain = this;
    this.blocks.set(newBlock.hash, newBlock);
    this.blockPushEmitter.emit(EVENT_NAME, newBlock);    ◄──    Notifies listeners
    this.top = newBlock;                                        of a new block
    return this.top;
  }

  //...

  [Symbol.observable]() {                             Invokes Blockchain's
    return new Observable(observer => {               @@iterator to enumerate
      for (const block of this) {                     the current list of blocks
        observer.next(block);            ◄──
      }
      this.blockPushEmitter.on(EVENT_NAME, block => {
        console.log('Emitting a new block: ', block.hash);
        observer.next(block);               ◄──
      });                                        Upon receiving new
    });                                          block, pushes it into
  }                                              the stream
}
```

One thing to note about this logic is that it never calls `observer.complete`. It's infinite. Subscribers need to `unsubscribe` when they no longer want to receive new data, as shown in the next listing.

Listing 9.34 Subscribing to and unsubscribing from a reactive `Blockchain` object

```
const chain = new Blockchain();
chain.push(new Block(chain.height() + 1, chain.top.hash, []));
chain.push(new Block(chain.height() + 1, chain.top.hash, []));

const subs = Observable.from(chain)          ◁——  Passes the blockchain object
   .subscribe({                                    directly to the constructor
       next(block) {
           console.log('Received block: ', block.hash);
           if (block.validate().isSuccess) {
             console.log('Block is valid');
           }
           else {
             console.log('Block is invalid');
           }
       }
   });
                                                Later pushes a third
                                                block, which will print
// ... later in time                            its hash to the console

chain.push(new Block(chain.height() + 1, chain.top.hash, []));   ◁——
subs.unsubscribe();          ◁——   Need to unsubscribe to
chain.height(); // 4                finalize the stream
```

If you run this code, the printout should look like the following:

```
Received block b81e08daa89a92cc4edd995fe704fe2c5e16205eff2fc470d7ace8a1372e7de4
Block is valid
Received block 352f29c2d159437621ab37658c0624e6a7b1aed30ca3e17848bc9be1de036cfd
Block is valid
Received block 93ff8219d77be5110fa61978c0b5f77c6c8ece96dd3bba2dc6c3c4b731a724e7
Block is valid
Emitting a new block:
      07a68467a3a5652f387c1be5b63159e7d1a068517070e3f4b66e5311e44796e4
Received block 07a68467a3a5652f387c1be5b63159e7d1a068517070e3f4b66e5311e44796e4
Block is valid
```

Suppose that you push a fourth block into the chain with an invalid index this time:

```
chain.push(new Block(-1, chain.top.hash, []));
```

Then you'll see

```
Emitting a new block:
      c3cc935840c71aa533c46ed7c3bfc5fc81e55519c7e52e0849afe091423bf5e0
Received block c3cc935840c71aa533c46ed7c3bfc5fc81e55519c7e52e0849afe091423bf5e0
Block is invalid
```

Allowing `Blockchain` to be treated as a stream gives you automatic reactive capabilities, which means you can connect other parts of your application that subscribe to receive notifications when new blocks are added to the chain. This example is a simple implementation, but it's not far from a real-world scenario in which other servers (nodes) in the blockchain network can subscribe to receive push notifications when a new block is mined in any of the peer nodes.

We added quite a bit of code to make the `Blockchain` class reactive. The good news is that most of this behavior relied on symbols, allowing us to extract this code into a separate module and use metaprogramming techniques (chapter 7) to augment objects by hooking into these symbols. This module can be implemented as a proxy to make any iterable object reactive.

9.4.8 *Dynamic streamification*

In chapter 7, we used a `Proxy` to implement a smart block—a block that automatically recomputes its own hash when any of its fields changes. In this section, we'll use a similar technique to make `Blockchain` a reactive data structure without adding a single line of code. The code is complex so I've divided it into a couple of functions. The following listing shows the overall layout.

> **Listing 9.35   High-level structure of the `reactive` function**

```
const reactivize = obj => {

    implementsPush (obj)
        || throw new TypeError('Object does
             not implement a push protocol');

    const emitter = new EventEmitter();

    const pushProxy = //... defined next

    const observable = //... defined next

    return Object.assign(pushProxy, observable);
}
```

Instead of adding all that observable scaffolding to `Blockchain`, we can define our own `Push` proxy to inject this behavior at runtime and keep things nicely separated. The proxy handler object requires objects to declare a `push` method, which `Blockchain` does. This code can make any pushable data structure reactive:

```
function implementsPush(obj) {
    return obj
        && Symbol.iterator in Object(obj)
        && typeof obj['push'] === 'function'
        && typeof obj[Symbol.iterator] === 'function';
}
```

Next, let's implement `pushProxy` in the next listing. This proxy will trap any calls to push and automatically augment its behavior to emit the value passed in.

Listing 9.36 Using a proxy object to trap calls to `push`

```
const ON_EVENT = 'on';
const END_EVENT = 'end';

const pushProxy = new Proxy(obj, {
    get(...args) {
        const [target, key] = args;
        if (key === 'push') {
            const methodRef = target[key];
            return (...capturedArgs) => {
                const result = methodRef.call(target, ...[capturedArgs]);
                emitter.emit(ON_EVENT, ...capturedArgs);
                return result;
            }
        }
        return Reflect.get(...args);
    }
});
```

Spread operator to capture all the arguments. The first element is the target object, and the second is the property key.

Emits the pushed object

Executes push normally and captures its result

With the `push` behavior defined, the last task is implementing the observable logic. This logic listens for push events and notifies its subscribers. Also, every time you instantiate this observable, it emits (replays) any objects the data structure currently has. In listing 9.37, I've taken the liberty of adding some logging, using the new console APIs `console.group` and `console.groupEnd`, which I think will make tracing the data flow easier. I've struggled with this task myself, especially in complicated and intertwined pipelines, so the additional logging helps.

Listing 9.37 Implementing `@@observable` to make any object behave like a stream

```
const LOG_LABEL = `IN-STREAM`;
const LOG_LABEL_INNER = `${LOG_LABEL}:push`;

const observable = {
    [Symbol.observable]() {
        return new Observable(observer => {
            console.group(LOG_LABEL);
            emitter.on(ON_EVENT, newValue => {
                console.group(LOG_LABEL_INNER);
                console.log('Emitting new value: ', newValue);
                observer.next(newValue);
                console.groupEnd(LOG_LABEL_INNER);
            })
            emitter.on(END_EVENT, () => {
                observer.complete();
            })
            for (const value of obj) {
                observer.next(value);
            }
            return () => {
                console.groupEnd(LOG_LABEL);
                emitter.removeAllListeners(ON_EVENT, END_EVENT);
```

Declares the Symbol.observable so you can pass this object works with Observable.from

Creates an outer logging group label for the entire duration of the stream. Any logs within this group are intended for better visibility.

Creates an inner level of indentation to handle every push sequence in a different level

Creates an outer logging group label for the entire duration of the stream. Any logs within this group are intended for better visibility.

```
                };
            });
        }
    }
```

Now that we have the components we need, let's compose them. The result is a proxied object decorated with `Symbol.observable` so that the `Observable` API can interoperate with it. Because `Object.assign` copies symbols as well, let's use it:

```
return Object.assign(pushProxy, observable);
```

The easy part is streamifying objects that have push/iterator behavior. Example are `Array` and `Blockchain`. To keep things simple, let's use an array:

```
const arr$ = reactivize([1, 2, 3, 4, 5]);

const subs = Observable.from(arr$)
    .filter(isEven)
    .map(square)
    .subscribe({
        next(value) {
            console.log('Received new value', value);
            count += value;
        }
    });

//... later in time

arr$.push(6);

subs.unsubscribe();
```

This code flow is easy to follow. If you were to add logging statements to `isEven` and `square`, the output of this program would look something like this (the logging enhancements help us read the output):

```
IN-STREAM
  Is even: 1
  Is even: 2
  Squaring: 2
  Received new value 4
  Is even: 3
  Is even: 4
  Squaring: 4
  Received new value 16
  Is even: 5

//... later in time

IN-STREAM:push
  Emitting new value:  6
  Is even: 6
```

```
Squaring: 6
Received new value 36
```

With this function, we can write the same code as before with a much leaner `Block-chain` class:

```
const chain$ = reactivize(chain);

Observable.from(chain$)
   .subscribe({
      next(block) {
         console.log('Received block: ', block.hash);
         if (block.validate().isSuccess) {
           console.log('Block is valid');
         }
         else {
           console.log('Block is invalid');
         }
      }
   });
```

This chapter is the extent of this book's coverage of observables. The goal was to give you a taste of this programming model, which without a doubt will change the way you write JavaScript applications. The way that JavaScript's event loop operates allows us to raise the level of abstraction seamlessly from an array to iterators to generators to async generators and now to observables, creating the perfect architecture for the language.

Want to dive deep into streams and observables?

The behavior implemented in the preceding snippet is known as a *cold observable*. Observables are said to be cold when elements are produced inside the observable itself. In this case, the observable will replay all the events to new subscribers. By contrast, *hot observables* occur when the data is produced outside the observable itself, such as from a WebSocket. In such a case, it would be impossible to replay packets that have already been transmitted without additional infrastructure and code.

If you'd like to dive deeper this topic, check out *RxJS in* Action (http://mng.bz/E21j), by Paul P. Daniels and Luis Atencio (Manning, 2017). This book discusses streams and observables from theoretical and practical standpoints, using RxJS 5 to showcase these concepts.

In this chapter, the techniques I have shown you throughout this book come together, from functional style currying and composition to ADTs to iterables and generators and to the abstraction of time. All those techniques lead us to a model of programming that could not be better suited to observables. Making observables part of ECMAScript will allow platforms, frameworks, and applications to share a push-based stream protocol.

9.5   *Closing thoughts*

This book presented a whirlwind of JavaScript topics but only scratched the surface of what you can do with the language now, as well as what lies ahead. I hope that the topics you learned here will guide and inspire you to explore different ways of problem solving, but always consistently within the framework of the paradigms you use. Employ these techniques wisely, and use the right tool for the job. For teaching purposes, I presented lots of techniques, patterns, and paradigms in the same application. This approach was purely didactical. I expect you to cherry-pick the techniques that make sense for the type of application you are building and what's best for the problem you are solving.

Strolling down memory lane, we began by inspecting JavaScript's object and prototyped inheritance model. You can take advantage of this object-oriented system to create the objects that capture the state of your application. Then you learned how functional programming can help you implement the business logic in a pure and composable way. By reducing mutation and side effects, and by harnessing the power of closures and higher-order functions, you can get rid of nasty bugs that can afflict even the best-tested business logic.

With these two foundations in place, you learned how to organize your code into fine-grained, reusable modules by using a functional and orthogonal architecture. You also set clear boundaries that separate cross-cutting logic (logging, tracing, policies, and so on) with metaprogramming.

Finally, after looking at data and functions, you tackled another dimension: time. Data can arrive in many form factors and from different locations. Asynchronous programming with promises and observables can erase data locality and simplify how you handle different types of data, using a consistent set of APIs and programming models.

It's important to realize that JavaScript has a unique challenge as the language of the web. It needs to not only remain relevant with modern programming idioms that developers want, but also continue to be the standardizing body for programming the web as a whole. These two forces are often at odds, and it's not sensible to add every possible API natively to the language. As exciting as it is to use new and shiny features, we need to balance this novelty with the need to not bloat the core modules that are downloaded over the network. There's still a strong preference for a canonical, bare JavaScript language, one with a small kernel into which you can plug APIs such as `Promise`, `Proxy`, `Reflect`, and even `Observable`. We'll have to wait to see whether the JavaScript standard libraries continue to grow and whether a modular kernel is in the works so that you can download or import only the pieces of JavaScript that you need.

Our journey ends here. In closing, I'd like to urge each of you to fund your favorite NPM library or contribute to it. We rely on open source now more than ever, and open source is the main avenue for innovation. JavaScript itself is evolving in the open. Open source is where tried and tested new ideas come to fruition. ECMAScript Modules, promises, and observables all originated from open source libraries before becoming official standards, for example.

At age 25, JavaScript continues to be reimagined each year and reequipped to tackle the challenges of modern application development. What started as a typical object-oriented language is now being classified as a lambda language, according to experts like Douglas Crockford. The cloud is the limit. If all bets are on the table, I'd continue to bet on JavaScript and its future. I hope that reading this book gave you the same joy that writing it gave me!

Summary

- An Iterator object has the method `next`, which returns an object with properties `value` and `done`. `value` contains the next element in the iteration, and `done` is the control switch that stops the iteration process.
- An async iterator follows the same behavior as a normal iterator except that `next` returns a `Promise` with a result of the same shape `{value, done}`.
- To build custom enumerable objects, you can implement `Symbol.iterator`. You can also define `Symbol.asyncIterator` to enumerate the pieces of your objects asynchronously.
- Generators are a special type of function that can produce a sequence of values instead of a single value—a factory for iterables. A generator function is identified by an asterisk (`*`).
- A generator function returns a `Generator` object that implements the iterator protocol, which means you can consume it by using the `for...of` loop.
- The difference between a normal generator and an async generator is that generated values are wrapped by a `Promise`. To consume an async generator, you can use the `for await...of` loop.
- Streams are sequences of values emitted over time. Anything can become a stream, such as a single value, an array, or a generator function. Anything that is iterable can be modeled as a stream.
- The new `Observable` API proposes to make stream-based, reactive programming easier.
- Observables are push-based, declarative streams. Their programming model is based on publish/subscribe. Observables are agnostic to the type of data in the sequence and to whether the data is synchronous or asynchronous; the programming model is the same.
- You can create and augment your own observable objects by implementing a function-valued `Symbol.observable` property.

appendix A
Configuring Babel

Babel is a JavaScript-to-JavaScript transpiler in charge of converting next-level JavaScript or future JavaScript to a version of JavaScript that runs standard on your platform, whether it's a browser or Node.js. This book introduced a few proposals that are still in their beginning stages. For this new syntax to work, we first have to use Babel to convert it to standard JavaScript for the version running inside the Docker container (Node.js 14). You can also transpile to your own platform versions. The bigger the gap between the standard that the code follows (such as ECMAScript 2020) and the standard supported by your browser or server, the more work Babel must do to transpile the code.

To configure Babel in your project, you must install the necessary dependencies. This book uses Babel 7. Here's a slice of the project's package.json:

```
"devDependencies": {
  "@babel/cli": "^7.10.1",
  "@babel/core": "^7.10.2",
  "@babel/node": "^7.10.1",
  "@babel/plugin-proposal-class-properties": "^7.10.1",
  "@babel/plugin-proposal-function-bind": "^7.10.1",
  "@babel/plugin-proposal-numeric-separator": "^7.10.1",
  "@babel/plugin-proposal-pipeline-operator": "^7.10.1",
  "@babel/plugin-proposal-throw-expressions": "^7.10.1",
  "@babel/preset-env": "^7.10.2",
  "@babel/preset-flow": "^7.10.1",
  "@babel/register": "^7.10.1",
}
```

After you install the necessary dependencies, the easiest way to configure Babel is through a .babelrc file at project level:

```
{
  "presets": [
```

```
    [
      "@babel/preset-env",
      {
        "modules": false,
        "targets": {
          "node": "current"
        },
        "debug": true
      }
    ]
  ],
  "plugins": [
    "@babel/plugin-proposal-class-properties",
    "@babel/plugin-proposal-numeric-separator",
    "@babel/plugin-proposal-function-bind",
    "@babel/plugin-proposal-throw-expressions",
    ["@babel/plugin-proposal-pipeline-operator", { "proposal": "minimal" }]
  ],
  "sourceMaps": "both",
  "comments": true,
  "highlightCode": true
}
```

When Babel is configured, you can run it by using `babel-cli`. To transpile all files into a dist directory, for example, you can run

```
babel src --out-dir dist --keep-file-extension --copy-files
```

appendix B
Typed JavaScript<T>

As we reflect on everything that we've covered about JavaScript in this book, it's hard to think that anything could be missing. But the web is a living, breathing creature, and we can count on JavaScript to continue evolving in the years to come. Believe it or not, I skipped many important topics so that this book could fit in your hands (or on your mobile device). But I felt that one of these topics was important to discuss, at least in a small appendix: types for JavaScript.

In the programming world, there's always been the epic struggle of choosing between typed and untyped languages. If you've read this far, you've already made that decision. Type systems come in many flavors. The spectrum includes strongly typed, statically typed, weakly typed, optionally typed, dynamically typed, and many more variations. What's the reason for picking one over the other? You can ask ten people and get ten different answers. Although JavaScript is and always will be dynamically typed, this topic has received more attention as languages such as TypeScript, Elm, PureScript, and Reason continue to gain momentum. Where does this leave JavaScript?

Fortunately, you don't have to switch to another language; you can use pluggable type extensions, which are widely used in industry, particularly with React's PropTypes feature.

Having a type system is valuable because it helps prevent certain classes of errors. Computers are more effective than humans at parsing structured data, and types are restrictions or boundaries that provide the necessary structure to your code. By removing the freedom of being able to assign a variable to anything you can imagine, the computer can do its job much more effectively before you even type `npm start`. Think of types as placing the virtual walls you use to close off a section of the house with your smart vacuum cleaner; the device cleans much better that way.

This appendix teaches you some features of the third-party, pluggable Flow type system for JavaScript (https://flow.org), which is an alternative to TypeScript if you want to continue using JavaScript. You'll learn about the benefits that a type checker can bring to a JavaScript project and the ways to annotate a variety of objects in your code. Even though I'm using Flow as a reference implementation for types, the library itself is not what's important; the concepts are. The specific type annotations provided by Flow look similar to the ones provided by TypeScript, as well as ones you can find in some early TC39 strawman proposals. It's likely that what you'll learn here will be compatible with any upcoming proposal that JavaScript decides to adopt.

It's a bit uncommon for a book on JavaScript to talk about static types, but this book isn't your conventional JavaScript book, after all.

B.1   *First, what?*

A bit of history is in order. JavaScript is considered to be the poster child for dynamically typed languages. So you'd be surprised to find out that a type system almost landed in JavaScript many years ago. The ECMAScript 4 proposal (http://mng.bz/NYe7) defined a type system for ECMAScript-based languages that JavaScript could adopt naturally. If you skim the document, you'll find many similarities with the contents of this appendix. The type system was never officially released, however, due to (among other things) a lack of consensus among the big players of the time, including Macromedia, Netscape, and Microsoft.

But the conversation didn't stop there. For some time now, other big web companies have tried to take a stab at this feature outside the standardization committees by creating new languages that compile to JavaScript or by pushing open source libraries that extend JavaScript syntax with annotations (such as metaprogramming) that a type checker tool can verify.

As you know, JavaScript is a weak, dynamically typed language. Now let's add a third dimension: optionally typed (also known as pluggable types). Let's unpack the following:

- *Weak*—refers to the programming language's ability to convert data types implicitly depending on use. It's an optimistic approach to figuring out what the developer is trying to do. Here are a few examples (and see whether you can guess the last one):

```
!!'false' + 0      // 1
2 * true + false   // 2
!null + 1 + !!true // ?
```

- *Dynamic*—Variable types are enforced at runtime instead of at compile time. The same variable can hold values of different types. Here's an example:

```
let foo = 4
foo = function() {}
foo = [4]
```

- *Optionally (pluggable) typed*—A pluggable type system is a collection of meta-annotations that you can bind to an optional type checker. In basic terms, the type system should not get in your way if you opt out; it's purely optional. Also, you should be able to add type information progressively in places where you need it. Optional types are not an all-or-nothing deal. Section B.3 talks about some of the type annotations that you can use.

JavaScript's type system is dynamic and weak, accompanied by a set of primitives you know well: `string`, `boolean`, `number`, `symbol`, `null`, `function`, and `undefined`. Don't forget the quirky handling of `null`, which resolves to `object`. These primitive types don't define any properties. So you might ask how this operation is possible: `3.14159.toFixed(2)`. Invoking a method is possible because you can use their corresponding object wrappers—`String`, `Number`, and so on—to work with these types directly or indirectly. By *indirectly*, I mean that code written as `'0'.repeat(64)` gets automatically wrapped (boxed) and converted to `new String('0').repeat(64)`, which does let you call methods.

With this basic set of types, we've been able to build an infinite amount of applications. These types are provided by the system; in JavaScript, you have no way to define your own custom data types. You can fix that situation by overlaying a type system, however.

In this appendix, you'll be using the Flow library from Facebook. Like Babel, Flow plugs into your development tool belt. This library is simple to install and run, so I won't bore you with the details. Rather, I'll focus on the concepts, beginning by describing the benefits that types add to your JavaScript code.

B.2   *Benefits and drawbacks of statically typed JavaScript*

In this section, I briefly go over some of the general benefits of programming with types. The goal is not to go in depth into this subject; tons of other books do a much more thorough job. The goal, rather, is to give you an idea of the benefits of using types to write enterprise-scale applications and how types fit under the modern JavaScript development umbrella.

I'm sure we've all asked ourselves at some point whether static wins over dynamic typing. The debate is probably evenly split. It's important to mention that good coding practices can go a long way; by following best practices and using the language properly, you can write JavaScript code that is easy to read and reason about despite not having type hints of any kind.

Without a doubt, type information is incredibly valuable because it gives you code correctness—a measure of how your code adheres to the protocols and interfaces that you designed. (Are all your input and output types compatible, for example, and do your objects have the correct shape?) The importance of types stems from their ability to restrict and make your code more rigid and structured. These features are good, especially in JavaScript, in which you're free to do anything and everything. As Reginald

Braithwaite eloquently put it, "The strength of JavaScript is that you can do anything. The weakness is that you will."

To set the tone, the next listing shows our proof-of-work algorithm with type information.

> **Listing B.1   Proof-of-work code with type information**

```
const proofOfWork = (block: Block): Block => {
    const hashPrefix: string = ''.padStart(block.difficulty, '0');
    do {
        block.nonce += nextNonce();
        block.hash = block.calculateHash();
    } while (!block.hash.toString().startsWith(hashPrefix));
    return block;
}

function nextNonce(): number {
    return randomInt(1, 10) + Date.now();
}

function randomInt(min: number, max: number): number {
    return Math.floor(Math.random() * (max - min)) + min;
}
```

proofOfWork is a function of type Block => Block.

hashPrefix is a variable of type string.

Notice the ": <type>" labels in front of all variables and function signatures in listing B.1. Functions and their return values should be typed as the input parameters. In this case, proofOfWork is a function that takes a Block object and returns a Block object—in short, a function from Block to Block or Block => Block. By having a clear contract, you can build correct expectations for how your APIs are meant to be used. Technically speaking, you can catch a lot of potential errors in the flow of your code at an early stage. Although this example may seem to be overkill for simple scripts or rapid prototype code, the benefits of a type system are obvious as the size of your code increases and refactoring becomes more complex. Also, IDEs can provide smart suggestions and checks that can make you more confident and productive.

Another benefit of types is that a compiler can trace through and look for inconsistencies in the inputs and outputs of your functions. So if you change the contract of some function from a major refactoring, you can be notified right away of any errors without having to run the function. Compilers help you catch hidden bugs that can occur as a result of type coercion. Your code might behave as though it works locally due to some hacky coercion rules (such as converting a string to a number or a truthy Boolean result), but most likely, it will fail with production-level use patterns. By that time, it's too late to fix any problems.

Multiple studies and surveys suggest that type information reduces the number of bugs by at least 15%. In fact, the statically typed programming language Elm claims to have no runtime execution errors, ever. (By the way, Elms compiles to JavaScript.)

The fact that you code with JavaScript doesn't mean you don't care about types, however. You always need to know the type of the variable you're working with to determine how to use it, which causes unnecessary burden on your already-overloaded brain. We JavaScript developers are forced to write lots of tests that cover as many paths of the code as possible to free us from carrying the entire structure of our applications in our heads.

NOTE   To clarify, a type system is not a replacement for well-written tests.

Types shine beyond quick prototype scripts. For large enterprise development, the perceived additional typing time they add is probably much less than what you'd spend writing comments to explain how a function is used. Like tests, types help you document your code.

Here's a list of some of the benefits you gain from type checking, in no particular order:

- *Self-documentation*—Types guide development and can even make you more productive by allowing IDEs to infer more information about your code. If you see a variable named `str`, for example, does it refer to a string or to an observable stream? You'll never know unless you have full context or crack open the code. You can use JSDoc to add documentation, which helps the IDE achieve some guidance, but it's limited, and no check is being done.

- *Structured, rigid code*—Types are your application's blueprint. JavaScript's object system is notorious for being flexible and malleable, allowing you to add properties to and remove properties from an object at runtime. This feature makes code hard to reason about, as you have to keep track of when objects might change state. Ease the cognitive load by defining the object's shape ahead of time. This practice will make you think twice about mishandling object properties, and if you do, the type checker might warn you.

- *No API misuse*—Because you can check inputs and outputs, you can avoid misusing or abusing APIs. Flow comes with type definitions for JavaScript core APIs out of the box. Without it, a subtle error occurs where `new Array("2")` is accepted when you meant to create an array of size 2, as in `new Array(2)`.

  Also, the type system can prevent you from calling functions with fewer arguments than it's declared to accept. The check for `Math.pow(2)` fails because you're missing the second exponent parameter, for example.

- *Autocheck of invariants*—An *invariant* is an assertion that must always hold true during the life cycle of an object. An example is "A block's difficulty value must not exceed 4." You'd have to write code to check this invariant at the constructor each time or use the type system to check it for you.

- *Refactoring with greater confidence*—Types can ensure that contracts are not violated by moving or changing the structure of your code.

- *Improved performance*—Types help you write code that is easier to optimize in some JavaScript engines, such as V8. As you know, JavaScript allows you to call functions with as many arguments as you want. That's not the case if you use types. The reason is that the restrictions imposed by the type checker ensure that functions remain monomorphic (guaranteed to have one input type) or at least polymorphic (two to four input types). The fewer input type variations a compiler has to account for on a given function, the better you can use the fast inline caches present inside the JavaScript engine to generate the most optimal performance. It's easier to optimize storage on an array of equally typed values (all strings, for example) than it is for an array of two or three types.

- *Reduced potential for runtime execution errors*—Types can free you from a whole class of errors that usually manifest as `TypeError` and `ReferenceError`. These errors can slip into production systems undetected and are hard to debug. Table B.1 summarizes some of these issues.

Table B.1 Errors preventable by type checking. All these errors can be caught during development instead of at runtime.

Description	Code	Runtime error	Type check
Calling an undefined property	`let foo = undefined;` `foo();`	`TypeError: foo is` not a function	Cannot call `foo` because `undefined` is not a function

Using an invalid LHS value	`function foo() {}`
	
	`if(foo() = 'bar') {`
	
	`}`
		`ReferenceError:` Invalid left side in assignment	Invalid left side in assignment

Reading properties from `null`	`let someVal = null;`
	`console.log(someVal`
	`.foo);`
		`TypeError: Cannot` read property `'foo'` of `null`	Cannot get `someVal.foo` because property `foo` is missing in `null`

Setting properties on `null`	`let someVal = null;` `someVal.foo = 1;`	`TypeError: Cannot` set property `'foo'` of `null`	`TypeError: Cannot` set property `'foo'` of `null`

As mentioned earlier, the language Elm claims that static typing is one of the reasons why it has no runtime execution errors. This won't be the case for JavaScript, but at least you can see that a large chunk of errors are preventable.

For the sake of argument, here are some drawbacks of using types:

- *Steep learning curve*—In a dynamic language, some concepts can be expressed with simple code. Adding type information to functions can be daunting because to make this information useful, you need to capture the variations of input and outputs that a function, such as `curry`, can handle. This task requires advanced understanding of the type system. Also, types for a function that relies mostly on data present in its lexical scope (closure) are not terribly useful.
- *Not portable*—At the moment, JavaScript does not define any formal proposal for a type system. Such a proposal may be a reality in the distant future, but

we're quite far from one. Although there is some general consensus about the look and feel, as demonstrated by some of the leading tools, the type system is still vendor-specific.

- *Poor error reporting*—Some type errors can be opaque and hard to trace, especially when implementing advanced type signatures.

Now that you understand the benefits and drawbacks of adding types, let's look at some of Flow's type annotations.

B.3   Type annotations

Types are compile time metadata that can describe runtime values. Although Flow has the capability to infer the types of your variables by analyzing your code, it's still helpful to annotate it at key places to enable a much deeper analysis.

Flow is complete and extensive, and it offers a wide variety of type annotations, of which I'll discuss a few. The Flow compiler analyzes files that have the `//@flow` pragma comment at the top. After Flow checks your files, and if everything looks good, you need to remove these annotations (because they are not valid JavaScript at the moment) by using another library or any transpiler, such as Babel.

I can't cover the myriad type annotations available in Flow, but these six are used frequently in daily coding:

- Class types
- Interface types
- Object types
- Function types
- Generic types
- Union types

B.3.1   Class types

As in other statically typed, object-oriented languages, classes operate both as values and as types. Here's an cxample:

```
class Block {

  //...
}

let block: Block = new Block(...);
```

This form of typing is known as nominal typing. You can also type the methods and fields inside the class, which is where you get the most benefit. The next listing shows an example with the `Block` class. I've omitted some parts for demonstration purposes.

Listing B.2   `Block` **class with type information**

```
class Block {
   index: number = 0;
```

```
previousHash: string;
timestamp: number;
difficulty: Difficulty;          Uses my own custom
                                 type called "Difficulty"
data: Array<mixed>;
nonce: number;                   "mixed" can be used as a placeholder for
                                 an array that can hold any type of object.

constructor(index: number, previousHash: string,
        data: Array<mixed> = [], difficulty: Difficulty = 0) {

    // ...
}


isGenesis(): boolean {
    //...
}


//...
}
```

The type system will ensure that the properties of this class are used properly and assigned to the correct values. The line

```
const block: Block = new Block(1, '0'.repeat(64), ['a', 'b', 'c'], 2);
```

is valid, whereas this one issues a type warning:

```
const block: Block = new Block('1', '0'.repeat(64), ['a', 'b', 'c'], 2);
```

```
Cannot call Block with '1' bound to index because string is incompatible with
    number.
```

As you can see, the type checker prevents me from using string in place of number in the constructor. Classes like Block naturally become types and are processed by Flow accordingly. In section B.3.2, we take a look at interface types.

B.3.2 Interface types

An interface is like a class, but it applies more broadly and has no implementation. Interfaces capture a set of reusable properties that multiple classes can implement. Remember from chapter 7 that our main model objects (Block, Transaction, and Blockchain) implemented a custom [Symbol('toJson')] property as a hook for a custom JSON serialization. This check happens at runtime, however, and nothing verifies whether an object implements this contract until you run the algorithm. Interfaces are a much better solution to this problem. Let's model the same solution for which we used symbols in chapter 7, this time using interfaces, as shown in the next listing.

Listing B.3   Using interfaces instead of symbols

```
interface Serializable {
    toJson(): string
}

class Block implements Serializable
    toJson() {                          ◁──  Block is required to provide
        // ...                                implementation of the interface
    }                                        methods from which it inherits.
}
```

Failing to provide the implementation results in the following type error:

```
Cannot implement Serializable with Block because property toJson is missing
    in Block but exists in Serializable.
```

Aside from classes and interfaces, object literals can also be typed.

B.3.3   *Object types*

As you saw earlier, you can assign an object the type of the class of which it's an instance. Another option is to describe the structure or shape annotated when the object is created. This form of typing applies to object literals. Recall from chapter 4 that Money is a constructor function that returns an object with properties such as currency, amount, equals, toString, plus, and minus. We can define that data structure in the following way:

```
type MoneyObj = {
    currency: string,
    amount: number,
    equals: boolean,
    round: MoneyData,
    minus: MoneyData,
    plus: MoneyData
}

const money: MoneyObj = Money('?', 0.1);
money.amount;  // 0.1

money.locale;

Cannot get money.locale because property locale is missing in MoneyObj
```

MoneyObj describes the shape of the object resulting from calling the Money function constructor. Also, if you were to mistype the name of a property, the type checker will let you know right away:

```
money.equls();
```

You won't mind this helpful hint either:

```
Cannot call money.equls because property equls (did you mean equals?) is
    missing in MoneyObj.
```

As you know, `Money` is a function object, which means that you need to describe both the input as well as the output. This type is known as a function type.

B.3.4 Function types

The basic structure of a function type declaration is similar to that of an arrow function. It describes input types, followed by fat-arrow (=>), followed by the return type:

```
(...input) => output
```

In the case of `Money`, the constructor accepts `currency` and `amount`. If you were to inspect its type signature, it would look like this:

```
type Money = (currency: string, amount: number) => MoneyObj
```

Here's a more interesting example from our functional programming topics in chapter 5. Recall that `Validation.Success` integrates the `Functor` mixin, which means that it has the ability to `map` functions to it. This trivial example may jog your memory:

```
const two: Success<number> = Success.of(2);
success.map(squared).get(); // 4
```

The next listing shows a simplified type definition for `Success`, which includes `Functor.map`.

Listing B.4 Static-typing a `Success` functor

```
class Success<T> {
    static of: (T) => Success<T>;        ◁─┐  Unary type
                                             constructor
    isSuccess: true;
    isFailure: false;
                                        ┌─  map is structure-preserving. It accepts
                                        │   a function and returns an instance of
    get: (void) => T;                   │   the same type (Success in this case).
    map: <Z>(T => Z) => Success<Z>;   ◁─┘
}
```

> **NOTE** In this appendix, I'm using a simple and concrete type definition of `map`. Theoretically, `map` should be defined generically for all types, also known as a Higher-Kinded Type (HKT), used in functional languages such as Haskell. HKTs require a powerful type system and are beyond what you can do with Flow and similar JavaScript libraries.

You may notice some weird annotations enclosed in comparison operators, such as <T>. These *generic* or *polymorphic types* occur often in software, especially when dealing with data structures and the Algebraic Data Type (ADT) pattern. Notice that `map` accepts a function (T => Z) and returns `Success`.

   If you were to provide anything other than a function to `map`, the type checker would bark at you:

```
const fn = 'foo';
success.map(fn).get();
```

Cannot call success.map with fn bound to the first parameter because **string**
       is incompatible with **function** type.

The type system infers from its right-side value that fn is a string. This code caught
that I was trying to use that value as a function.

B.3.5   *Generic types*

Generic programming is incredibly powerful and enables any unknown type (usually
known as T) to be used as a parameter to some algorithm. The algorithms you write
might involve using different types of data structures, such as collections or ADTs, to
be used as containers for the type of data you're dealing with. A data structure that
accepts a type parameter is known as a parameterized type.

   Normally, when you code JavaScript (or any language, for that matter), you should
stick to best practices to guide your coding effort. One example is creating arrays. An
array, by definition, should be an indexed collection of like-typed items. But nothing
prevents you from inserting elements of different types (other than the dreadful effort
of writing the code to process this array). An array like this one is valid JavaScript:

```
['foo', null, block, {}, 2, Symbol('bar')]
```

I hate to see the function mapped to this array, as it probably will contain lots of
if/else conditions trying to handle every type known in JavaScript. A type signature
for this type of array would be Array<mixed>, which is unbounded and accepts any
mix of types available in the language. Types are about restrictions, and in this case,
restrictions are good.

   Good JavaScript developers rarely mix types in the same array object, unless perhaps to create pairs of objects. Most of the time, we stick to the same type. How can
you enforce this practice? You can set boundaries on the types of objects you accept.
You could define an array of strings

```
const strs: Array<string> = ['foo', 'bar', 'baz'];
```

or an array of Block objects:

```
const strs: Array<Block> = [genesis, block1, block2];
```

At times, however, you don't know the type of the items you'll receive, but you want to
benefit from type safety. Suppose that we call this type T. Let's discuss an example with
an ADT. A Validation container that can lift any type can be defined as Validation<T>,
and the success branch would inherit this type as well (Success<T>):

```
class Success<T> {
    static of: (T) => Success<T>;
```

```
    isSuccess: true;
    isFailure: false;

    get: (void) => T;
    map: <Z>(T => Z) => Success<Z>;
}
```

Notice that I am passing the type parameter to key APIs such as `of`, `get`, and `map`. This technique adds type checking to every aspect of this API. Here's an example:

```
const two: Success<number> = Success.of('foo');
```

```
Cannot assign Success.of(...) to two because string is incompatible with
    number
```

Unfolding the container is checked as well:

```
const two: Success<string> = Success.of('2');
Math.pow(two.get(), 2);
```

```
Cannot call Math.pow with two.get() bound to x because string is incompatible
    with number.
```

Here's an example that shows you a type violation on a mapped function:

```
const success: Success<number> = Success.of(2);
success.map(x => x.toUpperCase()).get();
```

```
Cannot call x.toUpperCase because property toUpperCase is missing in Number.
```

> **NOTE** You may have noticed that the type checker sometimes uses the primitive name of a type (`number`) or the wrapped version (`Number`). This situation happens when the violation involves accessing a property. Because primitives don't have properties, JavaScript would attempt to wrap the primitive automatically before invoking a method such as `toUpperCase()`. In this case, the `Number` wrapper type doesn't declare that function.

Furthermore, the type checker can perform deep checks by capturing type information in those parameters and applying it to the flow of your code. In the case of `map`

```
map: <Z>(T => Z) => Success<Z>
```

two type parameters are bound in this signature: `T` and `Z`. `T` is the type of the container's value—number, in this case. `Z` stores the result and is inferred from the structure of your code. In this case, the type checker sees that `toUpperCase()` is a method that does not appear in the shape of type `Number` and alerts you accordingly.

To show you the reach of the type checker, suppose that you were to `map` a second time. The environment you had on the first `map` call would transfer to the second call.

Z would send its type into T, and the result would be captured once more by Z. Here's an example:

```
success.map(x => x.toString()).map(x => x ** 2);
```

Cannot perform arithmetic operation because **string** is not a **number**.

Figure B.1 traces the inference process.

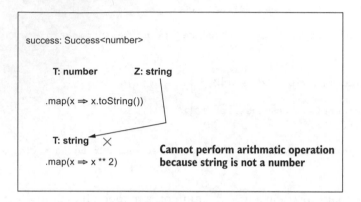

Figure B.1   The sequence of map calls, tracing the flow of types to find an invalid operation (exponentiation) being performed on a string

As you can see in figure B.1, after the value is converted to a string on the first call to map, the second call fails because x gets bound to string before the code attempts to perform arithmetic.

Another compelling use case for generic programming is streams. Providing type semantics to stream-based code gives you the chaining power of observables as well as code correctness applied to your business logic. Before we look at an example, as a fun little exercise, let's use the annotations we've learned so far to describe the main interfaces of a stream. Because the Observable class is already loaded, we'll use the convention of prefixing interfaces with I. So we get IObservable, Observer, and ISubscription, using a mix of generic interfaces, object, and function types:

```
type Observer<T> = {
    next: (value: T) => void,
    error?: (error: Error) => void,
    complete?: () => void
}

interface IObservable<T> {
    skip(count: number): IObservable<T>;
    filter(predicate: T => boolean): IObservable<T>;
    map<Z>(fn: T => Z): IObservable<Z>;
```

```
    reduce<Z>(acc: (
        accumulator: Z,
        value: T,
        index?: number,
        array?: Array<T>
      ) => Z, startwith?: T): IObservable<T>;
      subscribe(observer: Observer<T>): ISubscription;
}

interface ISubscription {
    unsubscribe(): void;
}
```

With the variable having the type information IObservable, there's no need to follow the $ suffix convention any longer. There's no doubt that you're working with an observable. In this example, the type T bound to number flows through the entire Observable declaration, and the type checker can test it at every step of the pipeline:

```
const numbers: IObservable<number> = Observable.of(1, 2, 3, 4);

numbers.skip(1)
    .filter(isEven)
    .map(square)
    .reduce(add, 0)
    .subscribe({
        next: :: console.log
    });
```

The type system analyzes the sequence of calls and checks for compatibility between the observable operators and your business logic. Suppose that you inadvertently pass an incompatible function to one of the operators:

```
const toUpper = x => x.toUpperCase();

//...

numbers.skip(1)
        .filter(isEven)
        .map(toUpper);
```

```
Cannot call x.toUpperCase because property toUpperCase is missing in Number
```

You can create another flow diagram like figure B.2. The final type annotation I'll discuss is related to what we learned about in chapter 5.

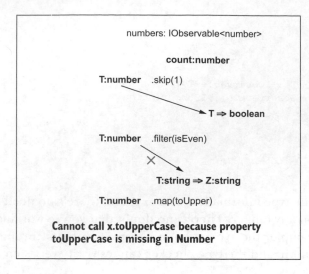

Figure B.2   Tracing the flow of types through the observable stream. Mapping `toUpper` causes a violation, as the expected event type is `number`.

B.3.6   Union types

A union type or choice type (such as `Validation`) signature defines a type that can be in one of a finite set of states at a time. You may know this type as an *enumeration* or *enum*. The `Block` class declares a parameter of type `Difficulty`. This type is a number that controls the amount of effort that the proof-of-work algorithm is required to spend. With a difficulty value of 5, for example, completing the proof of work could take hours, if not days. You'd definitely want to control the range of possible values.

To describe the possible values that this type can take, use a logical OR (|)operator, symbolizing union:

```
type Difficulty = 0 | 1 | 2 | 3;
```

A value of 0 turns off proof of work and completes instantly. As you turn the knob higher, `proofOfWork` takes a lot more effort to run.

Another common use case represents log levels like this:

```
type LogLevel = 'DEBUG' | 'INFO' | 'WARN' | 'ERROR';
```

Enumerations work seamlessly with `switch` statements, as the next listing shows.

Listing B.5   Using different log levels with an enum and a `switch` statement

```
const level: LogLevel = getLogLevel()

switch (level) {
  case 'DEBUG':
    //...
    break
```

```
case 'INFO':
  //...
  break
case 'WARN':
  //...
  break
case 'ERROR':
  //...
  break;
}
```

There's no need for a default clause because you're guaranteed that this variable can be in no other state.

We can also use union types on custom objects. In chapter 5, we implemented the Validation ADT, which is a disjoint union with two branches: Success and Failure. Like Difficulty, the Validation object can be in only one of these two states. We can symbolize that condition in the same way. Here's Validation with both of its branches:

```
class Success<T>  {
    static of: (T) => Success<T>;

    isSuccess: true;
    isFailure: false;

    get: (void) => T;

    map: <Z>(T => Z) => Success<Z>;
}

class Failure {
    isSuccess: false;
    isFailure: true;

    get: (void) => Error;

    map: (any => any) => Failure;
}

type Validation<T> = Success<T> | Failure;
```

As you can see, the Failure case is a much simpler type because it's not meant to carry a value, which is why I used the keyword <any> to represent no type information needed.

The union operator is modeling two disjointed branches of code (figure B.3).

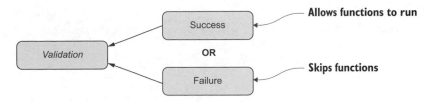

Figure B.3 Union type annotations model a logical OR describing two disjointed control flows.

You can use this type directly or indirectly in our `Block` class:

```
class Block {

  // ...


  isValid(): Validation<Block> {

    //...
  }
}
```

This variation is equivalent and works the same way:

```
class Block {

  // ...


  isValid(): Success<Block> | Failure {

    //...
  }
}
```

In my experience, types with classes, interfaces, objects, functions, generics, and unions are the ones that occur most often in day-to-day code and are likely to be the first included in any future proposal. But you can use many other type annotations. I encourage you to read about this technology on your own if you find it interesting. A good article to start with is at http://code.sgo.to/proposal-optional-types. Knowing what signatures are and what they mean will still be important for communicating efficiently about how functions are used and composed with the rest of your code. The good news is that type information is not an all-or-nothing route. You can start to add types progressively as you become more comfortable with them.

The JavaScript community has been active in this regard, developing everything from third-party extension libraries such as Flow to alt-JS languages such as Elm and PureScript. If you're intrigued, some early proposals sitting in stage 0 revive the types conversation that left off in the days of ECMAScript 4:

- http://mng.bz/MXDn
- http://mng.bz/aovB

Feel free to dig into these proposals if you're interested in learning more.

index

RELATED MANNING TITLES

Grokking Simplicity
by Eric Normand

ISBN 9781617296208
550 pages, $39.99
April 2021

Functional Programming in JavaScript
How to improve your JavaScript programs using
functional techniques
by Luis Atencio

ISBN 9781617292828
272 pages, $35.99
June 2016

Secrets of the JavaScript Ninja, Second Edition
by John Resig, Bear Bibeault, and Josip Maras

ISBN 9781617292859
464 pages, $35.99
August 2016

For ordering information go to www.manning.com

 MANNING

The Manning Early Access Program

Don't wait to start learning! In MEAP, the Manning Early Access Program, you can read books as they're being created and long before they're available in stores.

Here's how MEAP works.

- **Start now.** Buy a MEAP and you'll get all available chapters in PDF, ePub, Kindle, and liveBook formats.

- **Regular updates.** New chapters are released as soon as they're written. We'll let you know when fresh content is available.

- **Finish faster.** MEAP customers are the first to get final versions of all books! Pre-order the print book, and it'll ship as soon as it's off the press.

- **Contribute to the process.** The feedback you share with authors makes the end product better.

- **No risk.** You get a full refund or exchange if we ever have to cancel a MEAP.

Explore dozens of titles in MEAP at www.manning.com.

A new online reading experience

liveBook, our online reading platform, adds a new dimension to your Manning books, with features that make reading, learning, and sharing easier than ever. A liveBook version of your book is included FREE with every Manning book.

This next generation book platform is more than an online reader. It's packed with unique features to upgrade and enhance your learning experience.

- Add your own notes and bookmarks
- One-click code copy
- Learn from other readers in the discussion forum
- Audio recordings and interactive exercises
- Read all your purchased Manning content in any browser, anytime, anywhere

As an added bonus, you can search every Manning book and video in liveBook—even ones you don't yet own. Open any liveBook, and you'll be able to browse the content and read anything you like.*

Find out more at www.manning.com/livebook-program.

*Open reading is limited to 10 minutes per book daily